TRANSITIONAL JUSTICE AND DISPLACEMENT

This volume is the fifth in the *Advancing Transitional Justice Series*, a joint project of the International Center for Transitional Justice and the Social Science Research Council. Other volumes include:

Alexander Mayer-Rieckh and Pablo de Greiff, eds., *Justice as Prevention: Vetting Public Employees in Transitional Societies*

Ruth Rubio-Marín, ed., *What Happened to the Women? Gender and Reparations for Human Rights Violations*

Pablo de Greiff and Roger Duthie, eds., *Transitional Justice and Development: Making Connections*

Ana Cutter Patel, Pablo de Greiff, Lars Waldorf, eds., *Disarming the Past: Transitional Justice and Ex-combatants*

ADVANCING TRANSITIONAL JUSTICE SERIES

TRANSITIONAL JUSTICE
AND DISPLACEMENT

EDITED BY ROGER DUTHIE
INTERNATIONAL CENTER FOR TRANSITIONAL JUSTICE
BROOKINGS-LSE PROJECT ON INTERNAL DISPLACEMENT

SOCIAL SCIENCE RESEARCH COUNCIL • NEW YORK • 2012

INTERNATIONAL CENTER FOR TRANSITIONAL JUSTICE

ICTJ helps societies confronting massive human rights abuses to promote accountability, pursue truth, provide reparations, and build trustworthy institutions. Committed to the vindication of victims' rights and the promotion of gender justice, the center provides expert technical advice, policy analysis, and comparative research on transitional justice measures, including criminal prosecutions, reparations initiatives, truth seeking, memorialization efforts, and institutional reform.

BROOKINGS–LSE PROJECT ON INTERNAL DISPLACEMENT

The Brookings-LSE Project on Internal Displacement was created to promote a more effective response to the global problem of internal displacement and supports the work of the UN special rapporteur on the human rights of internally displaced persons. It conducts research, promotes the dissemination and application of the Guiding Principles on Internal Displacement, and works with governments, regional bodies, international organizations, and civil society to create more effective policies and institutional arrangements for the internally displaced.

The views expressed by the contributors to this volume are their
own, and do not necessarily reflect the views of the International
Center for Transitional Justice or the Brookings-LSE Project on
Internal Displacement.

Published by the Social Science Research Council
Printed in the United States of America

Series design by Julie Fry
Cover and typesetting by Debra Yoo
Cover illustration by Paolo Pellegrin / Magnum Photos

Library of Congress Cataloging-in-Publication Data

Transitional justice and displacement / edited by Roger Duthie.
    p. cm.
ISBN 978-0-911400-01-4
1. Transitional justice. 2. Human rights. I. Duthie, Roger.

JC571.T6993 2012
340'.114—dc23   2012024021

Contents

Acknowledgments

This book is the product of a collaborative research project of the International Center for Transitional Justice and the Brookings-LSE Project on Internal Displacement. On behalf of both institutions, I would first like to express our deep gratitude to the Swiss Federal Department of Foreign Affairs and the Canadian Department of Foreign Affairs and International Trade, which provided the funding that made this project possible.

Special thanks to the contributors to this volume and to the authors of the project working papers on which the chapters in the volume draw heavily: Paula Aponte Urdaneta, Rafael Barrantes Segura, Andrés Celís, Awa Dabo, Bina D'Costa, Madeline England, Tamy Guberek, Daniel Guzmán, Leila Hilal, Joanna Korner, Dilek Kurban, Barbara McCallin, Donny Meertens, Robert Muggah, Moses Chrispus Okello, William O'Neill, Romesh Silva, Roberto Vidal-López, and Luiz Vieira. Thanks also to the International Organization for Migration, which hosted an authors meeting in Geneva in October 2010; ICTJ's Bogotá office, which hosted an authors meeting in December 2010; and the Brookings Institution, which hosted an authors meeting in January 2011, as well as those who participated in the project meetings in various ways, including Victor de Currea-Lugo, Agnes Hurwitz, and Meghan Rhoad.

At the Brookings-LSE Project, I am extremely grateful to have had the opportunity to work in such a collaborative manner with Megan Bradley, Bryce Campbell, Elizabeth Ferris, Jacqueline Geis, and Andrew Solomon. At ICTJ, I owe my deep gratitude to a number of current and former staff, including Paige Arthur, Suliman Baldo, Camilo Bernal, Ruben Carranza, Cristián Correa, Amanda Lyons, Anne Massagee, Marcie Mersky, Kelli Muddell, Clara Ramírez-Barat, Michael Reed-Hurtado, Debbie Sharnak, Laura Smith, Shaina Wright, and especially Pablo de Greiff. At the Social Science Research Council, thanks to Alyson Metzger and Paul Price, and to Michael Simon for copyediting, and Julie Fry for design.

Roger Duthie
New York, February 2012

Incorporating Transitional Justice into the Response to Displacement

Roger Duthie

Transitional justice is often pursued in countries where massive numbers of people have been displaced from their homes and communities by armed conflict and human rights abuses.[1] Displacement is very much a human rights–related problem, and these contexts present significant challenges for the implementation of effective transitional justice measures. Transitional justice, however, has not addressed the issue of displacement as squarely as it has other types of abuses. Furthermore, large-scale displacement is a problem whose complexity and scope clearly make it unfeasible for transitional justice interventions to adequately address it on their own, and which therefore requires responses that draw closer links between the actions of a range of different actors, including those in transitional justice, human rights, humanitarianism, development, and peacebuilding. Yet practitioners, policymakers, and researchers who work on displacement in these fields are just beginning to consider the interactions between their activities. Little systematic research has been conducted on the ways in which transitional justice relates to displacement, to the justice claims of displaced persons, or to the actors that seek to resolve displacement.

In response to this knowledge gap, the International Center for Transitional Justice (ICTJ) and the Brookings-LSE Project on Internal Displacement collaborated on a research project to examine the relationship between transitional justice and displacement, both within and across national borders.[2] This edited volume is one of the products of that research. Taken together, the chapters in this book make a compelling case for incorporating transitional justice into the overall response to the problem of displacement in post-conflict and transitional contexts. In order to frame the arguments that lead to this conclusion, in this introduction I consider three initial sets of issues: (1) the reasons why displacement is a concern of transitional justice in the first place, (2) the ways in which transitional justice measures can address displacement and respond to the justice claims of displaced persons, and (3) the links that exist between transitional justice and interventions aimed more directly at resolving displacement. In thinking through the potential contributions that transitional justice can make to the resolution of displacement, I emphasize the challenges and tensions that may affect the implementation of transitional justice measures and consider how these may be faced. In the final section, I introduce each of the chapters in more detail.

DISPLACEMENT AS A CONCERN OF TRANSITIONAL JUSTICE

Displacement has not as of yet figured prominently in the literature or practice of transitional justice. Nor has transitional justice been a focus of research and policymaking on displacement. To begin with, then, it is worth asking why transitional justice should be concerned with the issue. *Transitional justice* refers to the set of measures that are designed and implemented to redress the legacies of massive human rights abuses that occur during armed conflict and under authoritarian regimes, and redressing these abuses entails, primarily, giving force to human rights norms that have been systematically violated.[3] The different measures that together make up a holistic approach to transitional justice (that is, one whose constituent elements are complementary both practically and conceptually) seek to provide recognition for victims, foster civic trust, and promote possibilities for democracy. They include criminal prosecutions of those most responsible for violations; reparations programs that distribute a mix of material and symbolic benefits to victims (such as compensation and apologies); restitution programs that seek to return housing, land, and property to those who were dispossessed; truth-telling initiatives that investigate, report, and officially acknowledge periods and patterns of past violations; and justice-sensitive security sector reform (SSR) that seeks to transform the military, police, and judiciary responsible for past violations through processes such as vetting.[4]

The term *transitional justice* emerged in the 1990s as a particular way of addressing serious human rights violations and facilitating the political transitions to democracy underway at that time in Latin America and Eastern Europe. As such, the particular violations it dealt with were civil and political and not economic and social (even though economic and social inequalities existed in such contexts). Since then, the measures associated with transitional justice have been increasingly applied in post-conflict contexts (as opposed to post-authoritarian ones) and in countries that have not undergone significant political transition, as well as in those that are still experiencing conflict. This expansion of the contexts in which transitional justice is applied means that it is more and more likely to be implemented in situations where problems such as massive displacement of people—linked to both civil/political and economic/social violations—are of significant concern.[5]

Displacement occurs when a person or group has been forced or obliged to flee or to leave their homes or places of habitual residence. The 1951 Refugee Convention defines a *refugee* as someone who flees across a border to avoid persecution,[6] but a broader definition has emerged since then, as reflected in the 1969 Organization of African Unity (OAU) Refugee Convention[7] and the 1984 Cartagena Declaration on Refugees, as someone trying to avoid the effects of armed conflict, situations of generalized violence, or violations of human rights. As laid out in the 1998 Guiding Principles on Internal Displacement, an "internally displaced person" (IDP) may be uprooted by similar causes as well as natural or human-made disasters.[8] "Durable solutions" to displacement include voluntary return, local integration, and resettlement in a third location or country.[9]

Displacement is integrally linked to massive human rights violations in several ways. Serious and widespread rights violations, such as mass killings, arbitrary arrests, torture, and rape, often cause displacement, while some violations, such as the destruction of homes and property, can be aimed at undercutting the possibility of a return home. Furthermore, when it is the result of intentional policy, displacement by itself can constitute a war crime or a crime against humanity.[10] In addition, displacement often leaves its victims vulnerable to other human rights violations; the displaced, without the basic protection provided by their homes, livelihoods, communities, and authority structures, are "especially vulnerable to acts of violence and human rights violations, including round-ups, forced conscription and sexual assault."[11]

Since transitional justice seeks to redress the legacies of massive human rights violations, it has reason to concern itself with displacement. Indeed, the achievement of its objectives would be undermined in certain contexts if it did not address displacement. Given these links, policymakers, practitioners, and researchers in the field of transitional justice have begun to address the issue.[12] Similarly, it is increasingly acknowledged in displacement discourse and practice that truly resolving displacement often requires not just a rights-based approach but also that *past* human rights abuses be specifically addressed. The actors that work most directly to achieve durable solutions—humanitarian, development, human rights, and peacebuilding actors—are realizing that they may not be able to achieve their aims without engaging the justice claims of the displaced.[13]

TRANSITIONAL JUSTICE RESPONSES TO DISPLACEMENT

International discourse in recent years has referenced the need for societies and actors struggling to resolve large-scale displacement crises to respond to the justice concerns these crises entail. The 2004 Report of the Secretary-General on the Rule of Law and Transitional Justice in Conflict and Post-conflict Societies, for example, calls for transitional justice to pay special attention to abuses committed against displaced persons, among other conflict-affected groups, and to "establish particular measures for their protection and redress in judicial and reconciliation processes." The 2011 report of the same title contains multiple mentions of displaced persons as well.[14] The UN Inter-Agency Standing Committee (IASC) 2010 Framework on Durable Solutions for Internally Displaced Persons also includes a section on access to effective remedies and justice—including transitional justice measures.[15] Asserting the importance of securing justice for displaced persons, the Framework argues that in some situations it is "necessary in order to achieve durable solutions to formally address past violations by holding perpetrators accountable, providing victims with reparations in a formal sense (including compensation), and/or providing information on the causes of displacement."[16]

Furthermore, and as is discussed in several of this book's chapters, contemporary understandings of a rights-based approach to humanitarian protection include a typology of three different types of action—responsive, remedial, and environment building. In distinguishing between these categories of action, the IASC's 2002 report *Growing the Sheltering Tree: Protecting Rights through Humanitarian Action* emphasizes the importance of the humanitarian community's support for remedial activities related to justice and reconciliation, including the work of truth commissions and the cultivation of "the concept of individual responsibility for serious crimes under international law."[17] Similarly, the 2009 African Union Convention for the Protection and Assistance of Internally Displaced Persons in Africa calls for the criminalization of acts of arbitrary displacement and the provision of effective remedies for the displaced, including "just and fair compensation and other forms of reparations."[18]

In practice, a number of transitional justice measures have directly addressed displacement. While earlier truth commissions did not, for the most part, include displacement in their mandates or focus on the issue in their reports, the trend among more recent commissions has been to depict displacement as a serious human rights problem. Commissions in Liberia and Sierra Leone, for example, reported that displacement was the most pervasive human rights violation in the armed conflicts in those countries. Timor-Leste's commission found that displacement caused more deaths than any other factor during Indonesia's occupation. And Guatemala's truth commission recognized the massive suffering and stigma endured by the displaced and the negative effect of state discrimination on their return and reintegration. Truth commissions have also made recommendations that respond to or are at least relevant to the specific concerns of displaced persons, such as the need for property restitution and land reform.[19]

Reparations programs can also respond to displacement by distributing benefits for the human rights violations that caused people to flee their homes, for the abuses they suffered while displaced, or for the crime of displacement. There have been only a few examples, though, of reparations programs providing compensation for displacement itself. Following the 1990–91 Gulf War, the UN Compensation Commission provided financial compensation to those who fled Kuwait and Iraq as a result of the latter's invasion of the former.[20] In Turkey, the 2004 Compensation Law provided compensation to IDPs for pecuniary losses, but while it has been described as a significant step toward addressing the country's displacement problem, serious problems of design and implementation have undermined its reparative effects.[21] In Timor-Leste, compensation was provided for property damage sustained in the 2006 displacement crisis, but the program specifically avoided using the term *reparations* because of its political implications.[22] In Guatemala and Peru, reparations programs treat displacement as a crime that merits reparation, and in Colombia the administrative reparations program recently established by the 2011 Victims' Law anticipates providing redress for displacement as such, but in none of these countries has compensation for displacement yet reached those who were displaced.[23] Reparations can also be tailored specifically to the needs and experiences of displaced persons. For instance, awarding benefits in the form of educational opportunities or health care may be particularly helpful to those who lacked adequate access to such services while displaced, and symbolic and collective forms of reparation may be appropriate when entire communities or groups were displaced because of their identities.[24]

Restitution of housing, land, and property in transitional contexts is a reparative measure that is clearly linked to displacement. After emerging as a practical tool for correcting injustice in Eastern Europe and South Africa at the end of the Cold War, restitution rose to prominence in the 1990s following the rash of armed conflicts involving ethnic cleansing campaigns; it was seen as "an integral response" to displacement-related human rights violations.[25] In postwar Bosnia, for example, as "an overtly human rights based remedy for resolving displacement," the restitution program processed two hundred thousand housing claims and supported the return of approximately half of those displaced by the armed conflict.[26] The utility of the "Bosnia model," however, has since been questioned in contexts such as Afghanistan, the Democratic Republic of Congo, and Timor-Leste, where restoring the property distribution patterns that existed prior to displacement would not necessarily be just. As Rhodri Williams explains in chapter 3, restitution has evolved from being seen as a mechanism meant to bring about return, to being recognized as a right in itself, to more aptly being considered one reparative but context-sensitive policy option among many in response to post-conflict property disputes.[27]

Criminal prosecutions can target the perpetrators of human rights violations that lead to the displacement of civilians, or they can target displacement as a crime itself. When it is the result of intentional policy, displacement can constitute a serious human rights violation.[28] According to the statutes of the International Criminal Tribunal for the former Yugoslavia and the International Criminal Court (ICC) and the Elements of Crimes of the Rome Statute, deportation and forcible transfer can constitute crimes against humanity, and unlawful deportation or transfer of a civilian is also a grave breach of the Geneva Conventions.[29] Displacement has also been the subject of prosecution by the Extraordinary Chambers in the Courts of Cambodia and in the Colombian judicial system.[30] The UN high commissioner for human rights has argued that criminal prosecution, through its potential deterrence effect, is "a very important aspect of the long-term solution to the problem of human rights and forced displacement."[31]

Some transitional justice measures, then, have in practice addressed the issue of displacement in various ways. The efficacy of any transitional justice response to displacement, however, may depend on the extent to which its processes are able to meaningfully engage with displaced persons through avenues such as outreach, consultation, and participation. Such engagement is important in ensuring that justice measures actually respond to the particular experiences, needs, and justice claims of the displaced.[32] Furthermore, given the prevalence of women and children among displaced populations, such engagement may be particularly important in redressing gender-based injustice and incorporating an overall gender perspective into transitional justice efforts.[33] If transitional justice processes do not engage with these groups, their concerns may not be adequately addressed.[34] Certain truth commissions, for example, have made specific efforts to involve displaced persons in their activities. Guatemala's commission was "one of the more successful in terms of integrating the perspectives of displaced persons," with investigators traveling throughout the country to interview thousands of the displaced.[35] Liberia's truth commission gathered statements from hundreds of refugees about such issues as "why they left home, the human rights abuses they suffered, opinions about the Liberian conflict, and what justice and reconciliation measures are needed."[36] And in Timor-Leste, displaced persons participated extensively in truth-telling by providing testimony in commission hearings that focused specifically on displacement and in the related community-based reconciliation processes.[37] Diasporas, including refugees, have participated in truth commissions in various ways, "as conceivers of the process, statement givers in the data collection process, advocates for justice."[38]

Responding to the issue of displacement and the justice needs of the displaced through transitional justice measures raises practical, legal, and methodological challenges. Displacement is often an immense problem in transitional countries, one whose sheer scale and complexity mean that transitional justice measures have a limited capacity to deal directly with the issue, let alone resolve the many hardships faced by displaced populations. This is particularly the case with measures that deal most directly with victims, such as reparations and restitution programs, because the large numbers of people displaced present significant resource and capacity challenges, whether the measures focus on immediate consequences of displacement-related human rights violations or on their root causes. Providing financial compensation for the lost property and suffering of thousands or even millions of displaced, for example, will often be unaffordable for transitional governments, particularly in developing countries, and assessing the socioeconomic situation of displaced populations and then distributing reparations benefits of greater complexity than compensation alone can be a serious technical and institutional challenge as well.[39] Furthermore, determining who qualifies as a victim of displacement and therefore as a potential beneficiary of a reparations program will be difficult: the legal status of "refugee" and the descriptive status of "internally displaced person" and their registration are unlikely to cover the full universe of victims of displacement, and so national reparations programs may need to get involved in developing additional categories.[40] Pursuing accountability for those responsible for causing displacement is challenging as well. Criminal justice efforts can be constrained because international jurisprudence is not as developed for the crime of displacement as it is for other crimes. And where the law does exist to prosecute, resource, political, evidentiary, or other constraints may lead prosecutors to prioritize more traditional crimes.[41]

Victims of displacement may face obstacles as well. In some cases, information about transitional justice measures is not available outside the country of implementation, which can prevent refugees from making claims.[42] In addition, whether people are displaced within or across borders, their frequent lack of documentation, which is often lost or confiscated, can create difficulties for restitution and reparations programs.[43] Problems of impoverishment, social marginalization, and physical inaccessibility can also be significant.[44] In Guatemala, the procedure for requesting compensation through the National Reparations Program is officially free, but "in practice, it demands a large monetary investment in travel, documentation, translators and so forth. Often, victims must incur debt to complete the process."[45] More structural constraints may also limit the ability of justice measures to effectively reach displaced persons, particularly groups disadvantaged on the basis of gender or ethnicity. In Colombia, for instance, legal and social practices shaped by historical discrimination against rural women and by patriarchal structures can mean that formerly displaced women face difficulties in proving land tenancy and therefore in accessing restitution and compensation.[46] In contexts of customary law or plural legal systems, which exist in most developing countries, additional challenges to justice efforts such as restitution arise in the form of the absence of legal certainty, restrictions on participation, and varying notions of land and property rights.[47]

The involvement of displaced persons in transitional justice processes also depends on the strength of their mobilization and the groups representing their interests. Mobilization early on can in particular lead to representation in peace negotiations and later transitional processes. However, displaced populations often face significant material and logistical challenges, including a lack of human and financial resources and weak levels of coordination.[48] Mobilization also represents a challenge that may vary according to whether displaced persons are IDPs or refugees, have returned or settled elsewhere, or remain in camps or in other urban or rural environments, as well as according to previous levels of organization within civil society.[49] (As discussed later, however, engagement with transitional justice measures can also serve to catalyze civil society organizations.) Gender dynamics in displacement contexts can also affect participation. Designing and implementing transitional justice processes with the meaningful participation of victims and other stakeholders is inherently difficult; it may be even more so when the victim population includes still or formerly displaced populations.[50]

Indeed, as a result of such obstacles, refugees and IDPs are "typically sidelined during reparations negotiations, and it is not surprising, therefore, that their concerns have so often been overlooked."[51] In Peru, one of the reasons that reparations have not been provided to displaced persons is that they have "not had significant input into the process."[52] Diaspora communities, it is argued, have the potential to play an important role in judicial processes and the fight against impunity—but it is a potential that has "not yet been fulfilled."[53] With such inadequate engagement with displaced persons, the use of transitional justice discourse and tools in displacement contexts may run the risk of overloading measures and raising expectations among victims beyond what the measures can deliver, particularly during ongoing conflicts. Lack of engagement may also have important consequences in the future, in that it may undermine the preventive goal of transitional justice. If justice measures have limited reach across borders, Bronwyn Harris argues, refugees "will automatically be excluded from the internal national focus on reconciliation. This holds the potential for conflict when such exiles eventually return home."[54]

If transitional justice is to be part of a sensible response to large-scale displacement, then practitioners in the field need to acknowledge such challenges and make efforts to overcome them to the extent possible. Doing so may require innovations in such areas as outreach, regional approaches, and the use of quantitative analyses. Outreach programs, for instance, can consider extending their functions across borders in refugee situations and approaching all displaced populations in contextually sensitive ways—as in Timor-Leste, where staff members and radio programs reached out directly to refugee camps in West Timor.[55] Other tools that can facilitate the participation of displaced persons include "remote hearings" in countries with large diasporas as well as the (as of yet limited and not unproblematic) use of the Internet and other technologies to record and share victim statements.[56] In contexts where conflict and displacement cross national borders, however, some suggest that, in addition to effective outreach, a regional approach to transitional justice measures may be needed. While no examples of such an approach exist as of yet, the desirability and feasibility of regional efforts would depend on a number of factors, including local and regional politics, identities, and histories. Regional approaches to reparations or truth-telling may represent important steps to improving the relevance of transitional justice to displacement-affected populations (including host communities), particularly in cases where the displaced resettle outside their home countries.[57] And finally, in meeting some of the evidentiary challenges that arise in working toward historical clarification and accountability for a phenomenon that can involve huge numbers of victims, certain methods of quantitative and demographic analysis may be able to provide a more accurate picture of the scope and dynamics of displacement, as was done in Timor-Leste and Kosovo, although these efforts also bring with them specific challenges.[58]

In addition to such innovations, it also makes sense for transitional justice processes that respond to displacement to involve those actors that work most directly on the issue. At the intersection of the fields of humanitarianism, transitional justice, and development, for example, restitution initiatives often elicit the actions and attention of a range of such actors. As Williams explains, the UN's Human Settlement Program is the formal lead agency on housing, land, and property issues, including restitution, within the "humanitarian reform" efforts aimed at increasing international coordination.[59] Additionally, the Office of the UN High Commissioner for Refugees (UNHCR) regularly engages with restitution issues in the field, the Norwegian Refugee Council has developed "unparalleled insights" into postdisplacement property claims through its legal advising programs, and important research programs on land and restitution have been conducted by organizations such as the Overseas Development Institute.[60]

Such direct involvement of displacement actors is less common in other justice processes. Humanitarian actors, for example, sometimes cooperate with reparations programs, but not nearly as much as they might. The International Organization for Migration often provides technical assistance and expert advice to governments implementing reparations programs,[61] and Doctors without Borders, a medical care provider, "can in some cases provide medical certification that certain crimes and acts of violence have occurred," which "helps to establish individuals' status as victims."[62] In general, information gathered by government or humanitarian agencies in registering displaced persons could be potentially valuable to reparations programs that provide benefits to the displaced. As Peter Van der Auweraert explains in chapter 4, reparations programs could in theory rely more than they do on information that is often already available about the socioeconomic situation of displaced populations and about who qualifies as a displaced person. In Colombia, for example, the government has set up procedures to register IDPs so they can receive assistance, and in most contexts international actors also register displaced persons for the provision of humanitarian aid; however, neither of these registries will likely be exhaustive in its inclusion of victims of displacement, because of constraints in access, capacity, and qualification criteria.[63]

Humanitarian actors also at times support truth-telling processes. As Megan Bradley points out in chapter 5, it should be less problematic for humanitarian actors to work and share information with truth commissions than with criminal justice processes (see below), because the former is less likely to lead to criminal punishment and so is seen to be less disruptive to humanitarian operations. UNHCR, for instance, has assisted truth commissions in Sierra

Leone, where it helped to facilitate refugee participation, and in Timor-Leste, where, together with the International Organization for Migration, it sought to promote return, reintegration, and reconciliation of displaced persons. Nevertheless, the actors that work most directly on displacement issues have not, historically, been deeply involved in truth-telling processes.[64]

Actors from different fields also sometimes work together on justice-sensitive SSR. In Chad, for example, a joint program run by the United Nations Development Program and UNHCR has provided funding, training, and equipment to a special national police unit set up to provide protection to displaced persons and escorts for humanitarians. Elsewhere, the Joint Task Force on Minorities, with representatives from a range of security, justice, and humanitarian actors, was, in the words of one observer, "vital to the effort to change the policing dynamic in Kosovo especially as it related to the displaced populations who were at great risk."[65] However, as Marina Caparini argues in chapter 7, greater coordination among those involved in the provision of immediate protection and humanitarian assistance and development efforts, including justice sector reforms, could significantly improve overall responses to the long-term justice needs of displaced persons.

The cooperation and participation of actors in different fields are least likely with criminal justice processes. When humanitarian actors work with displaced persons in conflict areas, they are likely to witness atrocities and therefore be potentially important providers of evidence, which is of interest to courts and tribunals. But while humanitarian organizations generally support and promote efforts to fight impunity for abuses, at the same time they worry about public cooperation with courts. Such cooperation, or even the perception of it, is often seen as potentially "compromising neutrality, forfeiting access and putting themselves and their staff at risk,"[66] which can inhibit their ability to provide protection and assistance to the displaced—as resulted from the ICC's involvement in northern Uganda and Darfur. Nevertheless, some degree of cooperation is possible. According to Assistant High Commissioner for Protection Erika Feller, UNHCR "is seen to have unique knowledge and capacities which can forward the fight against impunity" by criminal tribunals. "We do engage quite closely with them," she explains, "albeit that our cooperation has always to be tempered by concerns for the safety of refugees, the viability of our operations on the ground, and the security of our own staff."[67] A number of tools or protective measures can be used to minimize potential negative effects.[68]

Transitional justice measures, then, can respond to displacement and the justice claims of displaced persons in various ways. In the face of significant limitations and challenges, though, transitional justice actors need to innovate where possible and cooperate when appropriate with displacement actors. To conclude this section, it is worth making two additional points that may hold true for transitional justice generally and in contexts of displacement. First, the effectiveness of individual measures in responding to injustice may be reinforced by their relationships to each other. Transitional justice measures arguably have a better chance of achieving their goals if they are designed and implemented in a holistic manner—that is, if they are complementary to each other both practically and conceptually.[69] Just as victims of human rights violations may be less inclined to see reparations as an attempt to "buy them off" if those reparations are combined with measures to hold perpetrators accountable, acknowledge the truth, and reform institutions in order to prevent the recurrence of abuses, victims who receive reparations for or in response to their experiences of displacement may presumably be similarly less inclined if those other transitional justice measures also in some way address displacement. Furthermore, the likelihood that any particular justice measure does in fact respond to displacement may be higher if previous justice measures did so as well. For example, if truth commissions include displacement in their mandates, they may be more likely to recommend that subsequent transitional justice measures address the matter as well.[70]

Second, in order to understand the potential impact of a transitional justice response to displacement, it is critical to consider the extent to which that response is part of a broader set of reforms that address structural problems and injustices such as institutional incapacity, gender discrimination, poverty, and land insecurity. A truly gender-sensitive response to the justice claims of displaced (or nondisplaced) women, for example, often requires that transitional justice be accompanied by more transformative change. Transitional justice measures alone are unlikely to be transformative, but as Lucy Hovil argues in chapter 8, by addressing structural injustices they can at least avoid reinforcing them, contribute to long-term change, and draw attention to the need for broader reform. Security sector reform is another area where this general idea is illustrated. While it is difficult to point to examples of SSR—sensitive to transitional justice or not—that have sought to address the issue of displacement directly, it is clear that reforming justice and security institutions can be an important element of resolving displacement in a durable manner. But even where a justice-sensitive reform process can be argued to have played a role in protecting refugees or IDPs or in facilitating their sustainable return, as Caparini highlights, the success of that effort will be inherently limited if it is not part of a holistic approach to reform. Police reforms, for instance, will be undermined if the judiciary, the penal system, and government oversight are not reformed as well.[71] Transitional justice measures do not function in isolation, and broader change is necessary for them to achieve their goals. In the next section, I look at how justice measures relate at a broader level to the interventions of displacement actors.

TRANSITIONAL JUSTICE AND THE RESOLUTION OF DISPLACEMENT

The scope and complexity of displacement is generally such that resolving the problem requires the efforts of multiple sets of actors, including those operating in the fields of humanitarianism, peacebuilding, development, and human rights. Incorporating transitional justice measures into a comprehensive and effective response to displacement, then, requires drawing closer links between the activities of these various actors. In addition to the examples of direct cooperation between actors discussed in the previous section, the ICTJ-Brookings research project suggests a number of significant yet indirect ways in which transitional justice efforts can affect the resolution of displacement, and in which efforts to resolve displacement can affect the achievement of transitional justice aims.

As I discuss in more detail in chapter 1, arguably the most important long-term contribution that transitional justice can make to resolving displacement is facilitating the integration or reintegration of displaced persons. Integration and reintegration are key processes in achieving durable solutions, but they can be significantly hindered by the ways in which a legacy of past abuses can affect both individuals and their societies. Yet the primary actors working on displacement do not generally focus on dealing directly with past abuses and their impact. Transitional justice can therefore play a positive role here at the security, economic, social, and political levels in the following ways:

- Criminal justice and justice-sensitive SSR may facilitate integration/reintegration by improving the safety and security of formerly displaced persons and make integration/reintegration more durable by helping to prevent the recurrence of the abuses that led to displacement. They can do this by contributing to the reform of the institutions and in some cases removing the individuals responsible for such abuses.

- Reparations and restitution may facilitate economic integration/reintegration into and active participation in a community, enabling the rebuilding of sustainable livelihoods. Restitution in fact is seen by many to be a precondition for the durable solution of return precisely because it enables reintegration. Reparations and restitution can be especially crucial to the economic well-being of female-headed formerly displaced households.

· Truth-telling efforts may contribute to social integration/reintegration by reducing tensions between those who stayed and those who were displaced, revealing and validating the experiences of the different groups. Providing reparations to the nondisplaced who were victims of abuses may also reduce potential resentment toward returnees, thereby contributing to an environment in which integration/reintegration is less hindered.

· Transitional justice measures may facilitate the political integration/reintegration of formerly displaced persons at a broad level by reaffirming basic norms that were systematically violated and strengthening citizenship in general, more specifically by empowering the displaced through the inclusion of their voices and the restoration of their ability to make claims, and by catalyzing the organization of groups in civil society.

At the same time, attempts to achieve durable solutions to displacement can also facilitate transitional justice processes. By enabling refugees and IDPs to return home or settle elsewhere and helping them to rebuild livelihoods, the provision of assistance and protection can give displaced persons the opportunity and resources to participate in justice initiatives.[72] Furthermore, as Van der Auweraert suggests, a likely connection exists between the ineffectiveness of humanitarian assistance and economic development, on the one hand, and the unrealistically high expectations that victims of displacement may invest in compensation, on the other. "Addressing the social and economic marginalization of victims is not only necessary to reduce pressures on, and unrealistic expectations in, material reparations," he explains, "but it is also required to reduce the chances of vulnerable populations becoming victims of human rights violations again in the future"—which is a central goal of all transitional justice measures.[73]

Links between transitional justice measures and other responses to displacement will, of course, not always be positive or reinforcing. For example, in addition to risking the neutrality, access, and safety of humanitarian groups, criminal justice may also provide a disincentive to return. The *gacaca* courts in Rwanda, for instance, made some refugees who fled the country in 1994 reluctant to return out of a fear of being found guilty by association with the perpetrators of genocide.[74] On a quite different point, limitations on the number of victims who benefit from reparations may have a detrimental effect on integration/reintegration, as those displaced who feel they were victimized but do not receive the recognition as victims that other groups do may feel increased dissatisfaction. Two important points should be made here, though. First, some negative links may be the result of specific flaws in—rather than being inherent to—transitional justice measures, which means that steps can be taken to address (if not necessarily solve) the problem, such as strengthening due process guarantees or more accurately determining the universe of victims. Second, as Bryce Campbell points out in chapter 2, many of the legitimate concerns that other actors may have about the negative impact of transitional justice on efforts to resolve displacement are (a) about criminal justice and (b) magnified in situations of ongoing conflict and displacement. From a broader perspective, transitional justice is about more than just criminal justice, and its measures are usually implemented over a multiyear period. Short-term concerns should be addressed where possible, but the greatest impact that transitional justice measures have on durable solutions is likely to be in the long run.

That said, however, it is important to keep in mind that transitional justice and displacement actors do not always share the same goals, approaches, or priorities. Operating in the same environments and on similar issues can therefore reveal inherent tensions. As several contributors to the volume discuss in more detail, the differences between actors can be substantive and not merely based on technical obstacles or practical limitations. Transitional justice measures have been developed primarily as means to address serious human rights violations, as part of a rights-based approach to promoting accountability for perpetrators, acknowledgment of wrongdoing, and redress for victims. Humanitarian and development agencies, on the other hand, seek primarily to provide material assistance and legal protection to the displaced and to improve the socioeconomic conditions of the communities and societies in which the displaced or formerly displaced live.

Rights-based approaches, employed in the fields of humanitarianism and development, generally entail practitioners pursuing their objectives while treating individuals as rights-holders, using processes that respect human rights. However, the application of such approaches is contested. Among humanitarians, for example, a rights-based approach can be at odds with the objectives and methods of "classic" humanitarianism, which focus on immediate needs and saving lives while remaining neutral and impartial. As Caparini and Williams both point out, a rights-based approach may be more politically informed and strategic, and its critics see it as replicating the work of human rights organizations while risking the loss of neutrality and access to populations in need.[75] The classic approach to humanitarianism is embodied by the International Committee of the Red Cross, whose Anne-Marie La Rosa makes clear that "the purpose of humanitarian action is, above all else, to save lives, not to establish criminal responsibility."[76]

As emphasized earlier, incorporating transitional justice into responses to displacement is not just about employing a rights-based approach. Ideally, it is about seeking accountability for those people and institutions responsible for committing past human rights abuses that were associated with displacement and providing redress to the victims of those abuses. Using a transitional justice framework to address displacement may therefore further politicize the issue, which has potential advantages if in the long term it strengthens the relationship between displaced persons as citizens and their public institutions. But in the short term, using the discourse of redress and accountability or establishing links to the pursuit of justice (criminal or otherwise) may provoke increased political resistance to attempts to resolve displacement. Indeed, as Williams explains, restitution of land and property in itself can provoke resistance from powerful political, military, and economic actors that have much to lose from such measures—resistance that can be a factor in prolonging situations of protracted displacement. Furthermore, state actors that may otherwise support administrative property restitution may resist such programs if they fear that the disclosure of information and acknowledgment of dispossession may lead to criminal accountability for crimes related to displacement— crimes in which they may be implicated.[77] Political dynamics are also at play among the victims and beneficiaries of transitional justice efforts. A justice framework, for example, runs the risk of increasing competition or divisions between conflict-affected groups, particularly around the determination of "victim" status and qualification for benefits.[78] These types of political challenges should be expected with transitional justice processes in general, but the point here is that other actors working to resolve displacement may seek ways to avoid such debates or to limit the political repercussions for their own operations. There are some, however, who would argue that the further politicization of the space in which responses to displacement are implemented is necessary for the resolution of the problem.[79]

THEMATIC STUDIES

The chapters in this volume reflect the structure of the initial ICTJ-Brookings research project: six small working groups were formed, each one tasked with examining the relationship between displacement and a specific element of transitional justice—property restitution, reparations, truth-telling, criminal justice, justice-sensitive SSR, and gender justice. This working-group format allowed us to bring together experts from different fields—including transitional justice, humanitarianism, peacebuilding, and development—and to build on their diverse experiences, perspectives, and research. The members of the project's working groups each prepared a paper based on their practical experience with and research on their group's particular topic, and most of the topics focused on a specific region or country, including central Africa, Colombia, Israel and Palestine, Kosovo, Liberia, Peru, Timor-Leste, Turkey, and the former Yugoslavia. These working papers—available online[80]—provided an empirical basis for the development of the thematic studies that make up the chapters in this volume.

The project sought to collect and organize information about past experience, identify approaches and strategies that ought to be taken in the future, explore the potential for greater coordination and mutual reinforcement between the relevant actors, identify and warn of potential tensions and risks, and articulate the convergence of objectives and how this helps to provide guidance and to shape policy. These are among the issues addressed by the chapters in this volume.

The first two chapters are overview pieces that provide cross-cutting analysis of transitional justice and displacement from two different perspectives: transitional justice and humanitarianism. In chapter 1, I explore the potential contributions that transitional justice can make to achieving durable solutions, focusing specifically on how justice measures can facilitate the integration and reintegration of displaced IDPs and refugees into communities and societies. I argue that the success of integration and reintegration processes depends on numerous factors that are affected by the past, and particularly by past human rights abuses that were connected to displacement. Transitional justice can facilitate these processes by addressing those past abuses. Furthermore, this facilitation can occur at the security, economic, political, and social levels, which makes effective justice measures relevant to humanitarian, peacebuilding, and development actors. In chapter 2, Bryce Campbell addresses some of the main concerns that humanitarian actors (who work most directly with displaced persons) have about transitional justice. His focus is on two concerns in particular: the potential complications that transitional justice may create for humanitarians by provoking national authorities to restrict access to those in need and the inadequate involvement of displaced persons in justice processes. He argues that a multifaceted approach to transitional justice, which includes both judicial and nonjudicial measures, and the timing of those measures should mitigate these concerns.

The next two chapters examine the closely related justice measures of property restitution and reparations. In chapter 3, Rhodri Williams explores the evolving rationale for the restitution of housing, land, and property in displacement and transitional settings and how it relates conceptually through the framework of rights-based protection to the goals of humanitarian, development, and transitional justice responses. He also considers some of the main practical and conceptual challenges related to restitution, including those faced in the design and implementation of administrative restitution programs (dealing with mass claims, developing an evidentiary base, and facing political resistance) as well as questions about the extent to which those programs should attempt to address root causes of displacement and patterns of group exclusion. In chapter 4, Peter Van der Auweraert looks at reparations in the context of large-scale displacement, focusing on the potential for reparations programs to provide specific redress for displacement. He discusses the concept of reparations, whether the notion of displacement as it exists within the international protection discourse and practice can serve as a basis for reparations, the possible stakeholders in such an effort, and finally, what redress could be for in this context. Whether reparations for displacement are a good idea in a given transitional context, he contends, requires an understanding of the dynamics of how displacement has played out, how the experiences of the displaced and the nondisplaced have differed, and perceptions about and within the displaced population.

In chapter 5, Megan Bradley examines truth-telling processes and displacement. After identifying principles and frameworks that support the inclusion of displacement in the mandates of truth commissions, she analyzes how different commissions have in fact incorporated displacement into their work. She also explores the involvement of refugees and IDPs in truth commissions, highlighting international frameworks and principles that may facilitate their participation, obstacles to their equitable engagement, and innovations that can help to overcome these barriers. Bradley argues that although it is important not to overinflate expectations, the strategic and timely implementation of truth-telling can support the provision of durable and dignified solutions, while at the same time advancing the goals of transitional justice. Criminal justice and displacement are the subject of chapter 6 by Federico Andreu-Guzmán, who examines the issue from the international and national perspectives. As a potential serious crime under international law, he submits, "forced displacement" should ideally be prosecuted as other such crimes are. While the international legal framework for prosecuting displacement—as either a war crime or a crime against humanity—certainly exists, international jurisprudence for such violations is not as strong as for other serious crimes. National criminal justice systems, for their part, are generally not familiar with displacement. They tend to focus on the crimes connected to displacement rather than displacement itself, seeing the latter as a natural consequence of the former. Andreu-Guzmán thoroughly reviews the specific legal issues and challenges faced by efforts to prosecute this crime.

In chapter 7, Marina Caparini explores the underexamined intersection between transitional justice, displacement, and SSR. Specifically, her chapter looks at how justice-sensitive SSR processes can contribute to the protection of refugees and IDPs and support durable solutions to displacement. She argues that justice-sensitive SSR shares with those working to achieve durable solutions an interest in finding means of ensuring the longer-term safety, security, and justice needs of IDPs and refugees, and that efforts to improve the accountability (for past, current, and potential future abuses), legitimacy, integrity, and inclusiveness of security and justice arrangements are fundamental to meeting these needs. In chapter 8, Lucy Hovil argues that a gendered perspective on justice in the aftermath of conflict and displacement is important for those who have suffered specific gender-based injustice and for ensuring that transitional justice mechanisms are more fully engaged with their context. After exploring the many areas of gender injustice that characterize all stages of displacement, she outlines three areas of potential convergence between displacement and transitional justice from a gender perspective: promoting empowerment of the displaced by ensuring their voices are heard, engaging with discussions on durable solutions, and encouraging a transformative agenda.

Displacement is a complex human rights–related problem that is of concern to humanitarian, peacebuilding, development, human rights, and transitional justice actors, among others. In some contexts, the achievement of transitional justice objectives would be undermined if its measures did not address displacement. Similarly, resolving displacement may require that past human rights violations be addressed. But we must keep in mind that transitional justice and displacement actors also have different goals, approaches, and priorities, which can create tensions and suggest the need for appropriate divisions of labor. The chapters that follow, and the project working papers that they draw on, offer lessons learned from past experience and guidance in thinking about how to incorporate transitional justice into the overall response to displacement.

NOTES

1   Many thanks to Megan Bradley, Bryce Campbell, Pablo de Greiff, and Clara Ramírez-Barat for their comments on previous versions of this introduction. Some of the material contained here also appears in a different form in Roger Duthie, "Transitional Justice and Displacement," *International Journal of Transitional Justice* 5, no. 2 (2011): 241–61.

2   The Brookings-LSE Project on Internal Displacement was formerly the Brookings-Bern Project on Internal Displacement and is generally cited as such in the notes to this volume.

3   Pablo de Greiff, "Theorizing Transitional Justice," in *NOMOS LI: Transitional Justice*, ed. Melissa Williams, Rosemary Nagy, and Jon Elster (New York: New York University Press, 2012).

4   See International Center for Transitional Justice, "What is Transitional Justice?," http://ictj.org/about/transitional-justice, accessed December 20, 2011.

5   On the history of the concept of transitional justice, see Paige Arthur, "How 'Transitions' Reshaped Human Rights: A Conceptual History of Transitional Justice," *Human Rights Quarterly* 31, no. 2 (2009): 322–64; Jon Elster, *Closing the Books: Transitional Justice in Historical Perspective* (Cambridge: Cambridge University Press, 2004); and Ruti Teitel, "Transitional Justice Genealogy," *Harvard Human Rights Journal* 16 (2003): 69–94.

6   A refugee is a person who, "owing to wellfounded fear of being persecuted for reasons of race, religion, nationality, membership of a particular social group or political opinion, is outside the country of his nationality and is unable or, owing to such fear, is unwilling to avail himself of the protection of that country; or who, not having a nationality and being outside the country of his former habitual residence as a result of such events, is unable or, owing to such fear, is unwilling to return to it." Convention Relating to the Status of Refugees, July 28, 1951, 189 U.N.T.S. 150, art. 1, http://www.unhcr.org/3b66c2aa10.html.

7   OAU Convention Governing the Specific Aspects of Refugee Problems in Africa, September 10, 1969, 1001 U.N.T.S. 45.

8   IDPs are defined as "persons or groups of persons who have been forced or obliged to flee or to leave their homes or places of habitual residence, in particular as a result of or in order to avoid the effects of armed conflict, situations of generalized violence, viola-

tions of human rights or natural or human-made disasters, and who have not crossed an internationally recognized state border." United Nations Commission on Human Rights, "Human Rights, Mass Exoduses and Displaced Persons: Addendum–Guiding Principles on Internal Displacement," Report of the Representative of the Secretary-General, Mr. Francis M. Deng, E/CN.4/1998/53/Add.2, February 11, 1998.

9   For IDPs, the concept includes a rights-based element, with solutions considered "achieved when IDPs no longer have specific assistance and protection needs that are linked to their displacement and such persons can enjoy their human rights without discrimination resulting from their displacement." Brookings-Bern Project on Internal Displacement, *IASC Framework on Durable Solutions for Internally Displaced Persons* (Washington, DC: Brookings Institution / University of Bern, April 2010), 5.

10 See Federico Andreu-Guzmán, in this volume.

11 Erin Mooney, "The Concept of Internal Displacement and the Case for Internally Displaced Persons as a Category of Concern," *Refugee Law Quarterly* 24, no. 3 (2005): 17.

12 See, for example, Susan Harris Rimmer, "Reconceiving Refugees and Internally Displaced Persons as Transitional Justice Actors" (Research Paper no. 187, New Issues in Refugee Research, UNHCR, Geneva, April 2010); Megan Bradley, "The Conditions of Just Return: State Responsibility and Restitution for Refugees" (Working Paper no. 21, Refugee Studies Center, Department of International Development, University of Oxford, 2005); Duthie, "Transitional Justice and Displacement."

13 See, for example, Brookings-Bern Project on Internal Displacement, *Researching Internal Displacement: State of the Art and an Agenda for the Future* (Washington, DC: Brookings Institution / University of Bern, 2007); Andrew Solomon, "Justice, Accountability, and the Protection of Displaced Persons" (paper prepared for the Annual Course on Forced Migration, Mahanirban Calcutta Research Group, Kolkata, December 1, 2009). Transitional justice was one of the themes of the thirteenth conference of the International Association for the Study of Forced Migration, hosted by the Refugee Law Project, in Kampala, Uganda, July 3–6, 2011.

14 United Nations Security Council, "The Rule of Law and Transitional Justice in Conflict and Post-conflict Societies," Report of the Secretary-General, S/2004/616, 2004, 9; and "The Rule of Law and Transitional Justice in Conflict and Post-conflict Societies," Report of the Secretary-General, S/2011/634, 2011.

15 Brookings-Bern Project on Internal Displacement, *Framework on Durable Solutions*, 42–46.

16 Ibid., 43.

17 Inter-Agency Standing Committee, *Growing the Sheltering Tree: Protecting Rights through Humanitarian Action* (Geneva: IASC, 2002), 189. See also chapters by Rhodri Williams and Marina Caparini, in this volume.

18 African Union Convention for the Protection and Assistance of Internally Displaced Persons in Africa, Kampala, Uganda, 2009, arts. 3 and 12.

19   On truth commissions and displacement generally, see Megan Bradley, in this volume. On Liberia, see Awa Dabo, "In the Presence of Absence: Transitional Justice and Displacement in Liberia" (paper prepared for ICTJ / Brookings Project on Transitional Justice and Displacement, 2012); and on Timor-Leste, see Luiz Vieira, "The CAVR and the 2006 Displacement Crisis in East Timor: Reflections on Truth-Telling, Dialogue and Durable Solutions" (paper prepared for ICTJ / Brookings Project on Transitional Justice and Displacement, 2012).

20   See Peter Van der Auweraert, in this volume; and Hans van Houtte, Hans Das, and Bart Delmartino, "The United Nations Compensation Commission," in *The Handbook of Reparations*, ed. Pablo de Greiff (Oxford: Oxford University Press, 2006).

21   Turkish Economic and Social Studies Foundation and Norwegian Refugee Council / Internal Displacement Monitoring Centre, *Overcoming a Legacy of Mistrust: Towards Reconciliation between the State and the Displaced* (Geneva: TESEV/IDMC, 2006), 33. Dilek Kurban, "Reparations and Displacement in Turkey: Lessons Learned from the Compensation Law" (paper prepared for ICTJ / Brookings Project on Transitional Justice and Displacement, 2012).

22   See Peter Van der Auweraert, "Dealing with the 2006 Internal Displacement Crisis in Timor-Leste: Between Reparations and Humanitarian Policy-Making" (paper prepared for ICTJ / Brookings Project on Transitional Justice and Displacement, 2012).

23   See Claudia Paz y Paz Bailey, "Guatemala: Gender and Reparations for Human Rights Violations," in *What Happened to the Women? Gender and Reparations for Human Rights Violations*, ed. Ruth Rubio-Marín (New York: Social Science Research Council, 2006); and Rafael Barrantes Segura, "Reparations and Displacement in Peru" (paper prepared for ICTJ / Brookings Project on Transitional Justice and Displacement, 2012). On reparations generally, see Van de Auweraert, in this volume.

24   See chapters by Roger Duthie and Van der Auweraert, in this volume; and Barrantes Segura, "Reparations and Displacement in Peru."

25   Rhodri C. Williams, *The Contemporary Right to Property Restitution in the Context of Transitional Justice* (New York: ICTJ, 2007), 5.

26   Ibid., 47.

27   Williams, in this volume.

28   On criminal justice generally, see Andreu-Guzmán, in this volume; and on the former Yugoslavia, see Joanna Korner, "Criminal Justice and Forced Displacement in the Former Yugoslavia" (paper prepared for ICTJ / Brookings Project on Transitional Justice and Displacement, 2012).

29   United Nations Security Council, Resolution 827, "Statute of the International Criminal Tribunal for the Prosecution of Persons Responsible for Serious Violations of International Humanitarian Law Committed in the Territory of the Former Yugoslavia since 1991," S/RES/827, May 25, 1993, art. 5.d.1; United Nations General Assembly, Rome Stat-

ute of the International Criminal Court, A/CONF.183/9, July 17, 1998, art. 7.1.d; Geneva Convention Relative to the Protection of Civilian Persons in Time of War (Fourth Geneva Convention), August 12, 1949, 75 U.N.T.S. 287, art. 147. See also, Andreu-Guzmán, in this volume; Jan Willms, "Without Order, Anything Goes? The Prohibition of Forced Displacement in Non-international Armed Conflict," *International Review of the Red Cross* 91, no. 875 (2009): 547–65.

30 See Extraordinary Chambers in the Courts of Cambodia, "Press Release: Severance of Proceedings Ordered in Case 002," September 22, 2011; and Federico Andreu-Guzmán, "Criminal Justice and Displacement in Colombia" (paper prepared for ICTJ / Brookings Project on Transitional Justice and Displacement, 2012).

31 Navanethem Pillay, "International Criminal Tribunals as a Deterrent to Displacement," in *Human Rights and Forced Displacement*, ed. Anne F. Bayefsky and Joan Fitzpatrick (The Hague: Martin Nijhoff, 2000), 262. Pillay was president of the International Criminal Tribunal for Rwanda when she wrote this article.

32 Beyond Juba Project, *Violence, Exile, and Transitional Justice: Perspectives of Urban IDPs in Kampala* (Kampala, Uganda: RLP/HURIPEC, August 2009), 15. For a recent effort to document the views of refugees from Darfur on issues related to justice through a survey and interviews, see 24 Hours for Darfur, *Darfurian Voices: Documenting Darfurian Refugees' Views on Issues of Peace, Justice, and Reconciliation* (New York: 24 Hours for Darfur, July 2010).

33 Moses Chrispus Okello and Lucy Hovil, "Confronting the Reality of Gender-Based Violence in Northern Uganda," *International Journal of Transitional Justice* 1, no. 3 (2007): 433–43.

34 See Beyond Juba Project, "Why Being Able to Return Home Should Be Part of Transitional Justice: Urban IDPs in Kampala and Their Quest for a Durable Solution" (Working Paper no. 2, Refugee Law Project, Makerere University, Kampala, Uganda, March 2010).

35 Megan Bradley, "FMO Research Guide: Reparations, Reconciliation and Forced Migration," sec. 4.2, Forced Migration Online, October 2006, www.forcedmigration.org/guides/fmo044/fmo044.pdf, accessed March 30, 2011. See also Commission for Historical Clarification, "Conclusions and Recommendations," in *Guatemala: Memory of Silence: Report of the Commission for Historical Clarification* (CEH, 1999).

36 Laura A. Young and Rosalyn Park, "Engaging Diasporas in Truth Commissions: Lessons from the Liberia Truth and Reconciliation Commission Diaspora Project," *International Journal of Transitional Justice* 3, no. 3 (2009): 359.

37 See Bradley, in this volume.

38 Young and Park, "Engaging Diasporas in Truth Commissions," 349.

39 See Williams and Van der Auweraert, in this volume; Bradley, "FMO Research Guide," section 3.2; and Elizabeth Ferris, ed., "Internal Displacement and the Construction of Peace: Summary Report" (summary of proceedings from the conference on Internal Displacement and the Construction of Peace, Bogota, Colombia, November 11–12, 2008), 10.

40   See Van der Auweraert, in this volume.

41   See Andreu-Guzmán, in this volume.

42   Megan Bradley, "Redressing Refugees: The Emergence of International Norms on Reparations for Returnees" (paper prepared for the fiftieth International Studies Association Annual Conference, New York, February 15–18, 2009).

43   Mooney, "The Concept of Internal Displacement."

44   See Bradley, in this volume.

45   Lieselotte Viaene, "Life is Priceless: Mayan Q'eqchi' Voices on the Guatemalan National Reparations Program," *International Journal of Transitional Justice* 4, no. 1 (2010): 16.

46   Donny Meertens and Margarita Zambrano, "Citizenship Deferred: The Politics of Victimhood, Land Restitution and Gender Justice in the Colombian (Post?) Conflict," *International Journal of Transitional Justice* 4, no. 2 (2010): 189–206.

47   Barbara McCallin, "Transitional Justice, HLP Restitution and Legal Pluralism" (paper prepared for ICTJ / Brookings Project on Transitional Justice and Displacement, 2012).

48   Elyda Mey, *Cambodian Diaspora Communities in Transitional Justice* (New York: ICTJ, 2008).

49   See Duthie and Bradley, in this volume; and Dabo, "In the Presence of Absence."

50   See in particular Van der Auweraert, Bradley, and Lucy Hovil, in this volume.

51   Bradley, "Redressing Refugees," 4.

52   Internal Displacement Monitoring Centre, "Peru: Reparations Begin but IDPs Excluded" (Geneva: IDMC, January 8, 2009), 7.

53   Mey, *Cambodian Diaspora Communities*, 3.

54   Bronwyn Harris, *Between a Rock and a Hard Place: Violence, Transition and Democratisation: A Consolidated Review of the Violence and Transition Project* (Johannesburg: Centre for the Study of Violence and Reconciliation, 2006), 36.

55   Clara Ramírez-Barat, *Making an Impact: Guidelines on Designing and Implementing Outreach Programs for Transitional Justice* (New York: ICTJ, January 2011), 10, 26.

56   See Bradley, in this volume.

57   See Van der Auweraert and Bradley, in this volume. See also Iavor Rangelov, "A Regional Approach to Justice? Rethinking EU Justice Policies in Conflict and Transition" (Policy Brief, European Policy Centre, May 2011).

58   Romesh Silva, Daniel Guzmán, and Tamy Guberek, "Challenges and Opportunities in Incorporating Quantitative Analyses of Displacement into Transitional Justice Processes" (paper prepared for ICTJ / Brookings Project on Transitional Justice and Displacement, 2012); and Korner, "Criminal Justice and Forced Displacement in the Former Yugoslavia."

59   See "Humanitarian Reform and the Global Cluster Approach," OneResponse, August 15, 2011, http://oneresponse.info/COORDINATION/CLUSTERAPPROACH/Pages/Cluster%20Approach.aspx.

60   Williams, in this volume.

61   International Organization for Migration, "Reparations Programmes" (IOM Policy Brief, July 2009), www.iom.int/jahia/webdav/shared/shared/mainsite/policy_and_research/ policy_documents/policy_brief_reparation_programme.pdf; and *Property Restitution and Compensation: Practices and Experiences of Claims Programmes* (Geneva: IOM, 2008).

62   Françoise Bouchet-Saulnier and Fabien Dubuet, *Legal or Humanitarian Testimony? History of MSF's Interactions with Investigations and Judicial Proceedings* (Paris: Médecins Sans Frontières, 2007), 50.

63   Van der Auweraert, in this volume.

64   Bradley, in this volume.

65   William O'Neil, "Police Reform in Situations of Forced Displacement" (paper prepared for ICTJ / Brookings Project on Transitional Justice and Displacement, 2012).

66   Kate Mackintosh, "How Far Can Humanitarian Organisations Control Co-operation with International Tribunals," *Journal of Humanitarian Assistance* (May 1, 2005), http://jha. ac/articles/a175.pdf.

67   Erika Feller, "Giving Peace a Chance: Displacement and Rule of Law during Peacebuilding," *Refugee Survey Quarterly* 28, no. 1 (2009): 93.

68   Anne-Marie La Rosa, "Humanitarian Organizations and International Criminal Tribunals, or Trying to Square the Circle," *International Review of the Red Cross* 88, no. 861 (2006): 169–86.

69   De Greiff, "Theorizing Transitional Justice."

70   See Bryce Campbell, Williams, and Bradley, in this volume.

71   Caparini, in this volume.

72   See Campbell, in this volume.

73   Van der Auweraert, in this volume.

74   Lucy Hovil, "The Inter-Relationship Between Violence, Displacement and the Transition to Stability in the Great Lakes Region" (concept paper prepared for the Violence and Transition Project Roundtable, Centre for the Study of Violence and Reconciliation, Johannesburg, May 7–9, 2008). See also International Refugee Rights Initiative, "A Dangerous Impasse: Rwandan Refugees in Uganda" (Citizenship and Displacement in the Great Lakes Region Working Paper no. 4, June 2010).

75   Williams and Caparini, in this volume.

76   La Rosa, "Humanitarian Organizations and International Criminal Tribunals," 183.

77   Williams, in this volume.

78   See in particular Duthie, Van der Auweraert, and Bradley, in this volume.

79   See Duthie and Hovil, in this volume.

80   See http://ictj.org/our-work/research/transitional-justice-and-displacement and http:// www.brookings.edu/projects/idp.aspx.

CHAPTER 1

Contributing to Durable Solutions: Transitional Justice and the Integration and Reintegration of Displaced Persons

Roger Duthie

Transitional justice is not primarily an approach to solving displacement-related problems, and its measures have for the most part not prioritized issues related to displaced persons.[1] Transitional justice measures do, however, have a bearing on displaced persons' interests and on efforts to resolve displacement, in particular with regard to durable solutions, which include return and reintegration in one's place of origin, local integration in one's place of refuge, and resettlement elsewhere. Integration or reintegration is key to all three of these solutions. The Office of the UN High Commissioner for Refugees (UNHCR) states that the agency is actively involved in supporting transitional justice measures because "refugees, as victims of human rights abuses, have an interest in such activities, which will facilitate their process of re-integration."[2] Recognition of the relevance of transitional justice to displacement often focuses on the links between reintegration and the restoration of the rights of the displaced.[3] "Finding durable solutions is about restoring the human rights of IDPs," states the UN's Inter-Agency Standing Committee Framework on Durable Solutions for Internally Displaced Persons, which "may entail the right to reparation, justice, truth and closure for past injustices through transitional justice or other appropriate measures." The Framework goes on to argue that remedies for human rights violations associated with displacement can have a "major impact" on durable solutions, because the absence of such remedies can risk further displacement, impede reconciliation, and create a sense of injustice among the displaced.[4] Some have even suggested that transitional justice efforts have received support in recent decades in part because of their instrumentality in enabling return.[5]

In this chapter, I explore the contributions that transitional justice can make to achieving durable solutions, focusing specifically on some of the ways in which justice measures can facilitate the integration or reintegration of displaced persons into communities and societies. The first section reviews the notions of integration and reintegration, as well as others such as repatriation and reconciliation. While humanitarian, peacebuilding, and development actors have been the primary force in support of reintegration, most understandings of the notion suggest that there is space for transitional justice mechanisms to play an important role. I then discuss how transitional justice measures can facilitate integration/reintegration at the security, economic, political, and social levels. In the final section, I emphasize that while transitional justice may appear most relevant in situations of return, it can also play a role in cases of local integration and resettlement, both internally and across international borders.

My overall argument is that transitional justice can make a potentially positive contribution to durable solutions by facilitating the processes of integration and reintegration, which involve not only the displaced individuals themselves but also the groups with which they fled and the communities into which they are integrating or reintegrating. The success of these processes depends on many factors, including the actions taken by displaced individuals and groups, as well as the characteristics of and dynamics within the larger society; these factors are all affected by the past, and particularly by the human rights abuses that were connected to displacement. Transitional justice can therefore facilitate the processes of integration and reintegration, above all in the long term,[6] by addressing those past abuses, which makes it relevant to the concerns of humanitarian, peacebuilding, and development actors. Whatever its success, the contributions of transitional justice are likely to be modest and contingent, and most significant when part of a broader program of structural reform and development.

INTEGRATION AND REINTEGRATION

Durable solutions to the problem of internal displacement are achieved, on one account, when internally displaced persons (IDPs) "no longer have specific assistance and protection needs that are linked to their displacement and such persons can enjoy their human rights without discrimination resulting from their displacement." The notions of integration and reintegration are integral to such an understanding of durable solutions.[7] In refugee situations, those solutions are defined as repatriation to the country of origin, local integration in the country of refuge, or resettlement in a third country. In contexts of internal displacement, the solutions are defined as return and reintegration into the place of origin, local integration in the area of refuge, or resettlement and integration into another part of the country. According to UNHCR, "Reintegration is a process that should result in the disappearance of differences in legal rights and duties between returnees and their compatriots and the equal access of returnees to services, productive assets and opportunities" that address their legal, political, economic, and social needs.[8] It is elsewhere described as "the complex process by which returnees are gradually reincorporated within the social, economic and cultural fabric of their communities, and their rights as citizens restored to them,"[9] or a process enabling displaced persons to enjoy greater physical, social, legal, and material security.[10] Activities that support integration and reintegration can be viewed as a subset of "protection," which according to the International Committee of the Red Cross encompasses "all activities aimed at obtaining full respect for the rights of the individual in accordance with the letter and spirit of the relevant bodies of law, namely human rights law, international humanitarian law and refugee law."[11]

The term *reintegration* is sometimes criticized, because it implies that a person was integrated once before, which may not be the case. Often, the people who become displaced were previously among the more marginalized or vulnerable members of society. For example, the Nairobi Declaration on Women's and Girls' Right to a Remedy and Reparation argues that for women and girls, "reintegration and restitution by themselves are not sufficient goals of reparation, since the origins of violations of women's and girls' human rights predate the conflict situation."[12] Furthermore, it can also be problematic to assume that the displaced are necessarily "outside" of society, particularly when displacement is longstanding and refugees and IDPs may form communities of their own or become part of host communities. Many also maintain close links with their countries or communities of origin while displaced.[13]

In this chapter, I do not presume that all displaced persons were fully integrated before they were displaced. I also use the terms *integration* and *reintegration* to refer to processes that can involve integrating both into a physical community in a specific location and into a broader political community. I more frequently use the term *reintegration*, however, because (a) much of the displacement discourse highlights it (as a result of the prioritization by most relevant actors of return over other solutions) and (b) transitional justice can affect relations between citizens and their public institutions, as well as between citizens themselves, so it will likely have the most impact when people are returning to their communities of origin, where they will come in contact once again with the offices and representatives of those institutions that they may feel were responsible for their displacement. However, as I emphasize in the final section of this chapter, many of the dynamics at play (particularly those between citizens) are also relevant in situations where the displaced are not returning to their place of origin.

While precise definitions may vary, reintegration is generally seen as a long-term, complex process and a concern of actors in multiple fields. Humanitarian actors are primarily interested in providing protection and assistance to displaced persons while they are displaced and upon return or resettlement and in facilitating durable solutions, but they are inherently limited in the contributions they can make to the long-term process of reintegration. This is to be expected, since humanitarian assistance is by definition designed to be a short-term response to immediate, life-threatening conditions. By itself, it is widely acknowledged, humanitarian action is not enough to support the durable reintegration of massive numbers of people.[14]

As a long-term process, reintegration is also of concern to development and peacebuilding actors. As part of the "humanitarian reform process,"[15] reintegration of displaced persons is included in the work of the Cluster Working Group on Early Recovery, led by the United Nations Development Programme (UNDP). Early recovery is defined as a "multi-dimensional process, guided by development principles, that seeks to build upon humanitarian programmes and to catalyze sustainable development opportunities."[16] UNDP's concern with reintegration stems from its mission, which is to address poverty and human development and therefore includes working with "all categories of populations in helping them obtain access to reasonable choices in conducting their lives and promoting social inclusion," especially IDPs and returnees.[17] Another major development actor, the World Bank, is concerned with reintegration because displacement leads to the loss of housing, land, property, jobs, physical assets, social networks, and resources, as well as to food insecurity, increased morbidity and mortality, and social marginalization. Continued marginalization of this type may hinder economic and social progress, both in host and return or resettlement areas. The World Bank's policy objectives therefore call on it "to establish and/or preserve human, institutional, and/or social capital including economic reintegration of vulnerable people, who include refugees and IDPs."[18] It should be noted, however, that the articulation of these objectives among development actors is to a large degree aspirational; in practice, early recovery is acknowledged to be the weakest of the clusters, which most humanitarians see as part of a historical failure to address the transition between relief and development.[19]

Reintegration is also important to peacebuilding. A Brookings Institution report explains, for example, that achieving durable solutions for the displaced is necessary for peacebuilding because return and reintegration can help to address the root causes of conflict and prevent further displacement. A primary link here is through stability and security: unresolved problems of displacement can cause instability, and at the same time a minimum level of security is needed for durable solutions to be implemented. But reintegration can also allow people to contribute to processes of social rehabilitation, economic development, and legitimate governance.[20]

If such economic and security elements of the reintegration of displaced persons have been acknowledged in the discourse, for a long time the political side of the process has been underemphasized. According to Katy Long, in the 1980s attempts to find truly durable solutions for refugees were undermined because "repatriation" was understood to mean simply "return," with a focus more on geographical return than on the restoration of citizenship and the relationship between citizens and their state.[21] Refugees, however, suffer a breach of political trust that requires a political rejoining of the community— "the remaking of citizenship and consequent re-accessing of rights through reavailment of national protection in the country of action."[22] A major obstacle to repatriation is a lack of confidence among refugees—usually based on their past experience—in the ability of the state to guarantee basic security and dignity. "Repatriation is not just return," argues Long, "but involves complex, long-term and gradual processes of reintegration and reconciliation."[23] While the internally displaced do not have to repatriate to their countries of origin, it can be argued that their relationship with the state has suffered a similar breakdown that requires a similar repair process.[24]

There is a social element to reintegration as well. As Huma Haider puts it, sustainable return requires "renewed social relationships."[25] It is in this context that the connection between reintegration and reconciliation is often made. Reconciliation is another concept whose precise definition varies. According to UNHCR, in the context of durable solutions, reconciliation involves the promotion of equity between displaced persons and local residents, of structures and mechanisms to promote confidence building and coexistence.[26] B. S. Chimni defines reconciliation as the consolidation of constructive social relations between groups, including parties to the conflict. For him, reconciliation has to *precede* the full reintegration of displaced persons.[27] More specifically, according to Pablo de Greiff, reconciliation means that citizens can trust one another as citizens, "that they are sufficiently committed to the norms and values that motivate their ruling institutions, sufficiently confident that those who operate those institutions do so also on the basis of those norms and values, and sufficiently secure about their fellow citizens' commitment to abide by these basic norms and values."[28] An important point in the context of integration or reintegration, which will be revisited later, is that reconciliation does not involve only the displaced themselves but all those affected by conflict, including those who remained in their communities and those who left to become combatants. Equally important, though, for purposes of this argument, is the notion that reintegration depends on reconciliation between groups, which suggests a potential role for transitional justice.

This social element of reintegration, involving as it does social trust or capital, is also of relevance to the activities of development actors, who often seek to promote social inclusion through the implementation of development projects that build trust. In Guatemala, for example, microregional development committees that were formed by UNDP acted as "counterweights" to the Patrullas de Autodefensa Civil, which the army had used to control internally displaced persons, among others, and helped to "re-establish social trust."[29] The World Bank also provides support that may involve measures to promote social trust in contexts of displacement. "To provide the displaced with opportunities for equal participation and voice in local planning, alongside host populations or those in their home areas who never left or returned earlier," suggests one World Bank paper, "consultation and participation processes may draw on existing forms of social capital or may require creation of new arrangements that replace social fragmentation with cohesion."[30]

THE NEED TO CONFRONT THE PAST

As I have already mentioned, the success of these various elements of reintegration—security, economic, political, and social—all require the restoration or protection of the human rights of formerly displaced persons. However, a key argument of this chapter is that *successful integration and reintegration arguably must include not only the current and future protection of rights but also responses to past human rights violations.* "The sustainable reintegration of refugees and IDPs also has strong human rights components," explains Vicky Tennant. "The process of successful reintegration encompasses the reincorporation of those who have been failed by the state within a reshaped national identity, *a reckoning with the past*, and the elaboration of laws and reform of institutions such as the security sector, judiciary, and human rights commissions." Thus UNHCR's programming includes such activities as support to victims.[31] As Megan Bradley puts it, "The full restoration of refugees' rights is not only a forward-looking process. It must also take into account past violations of refugee rights."[32]

Why is it important that past abuses be addressed? Broadly, the violations of the past can have a significant impact both on the individual who is attempting to reintegrate and the community into which she or he is reintegrating.

One study of Guatemalan returnees, for example, showed that the success of reintegration was clearly related to the returnees' pasts, which in some cases included collective violence before and during the armed conflict. "Even if, at a later stage, the external conditions of peace and security are restored in the home country," writes Tania Ghanem, "it cannot be taken for granted that upon return the returnee will have forgotten the cause of his flight and exile, and go back to the same blithe existence that characterized his/her life before the events that caused him/her to flee." Return, she argues, to a certain extent forces a person to face his or her past.[33] It can bring with it, among other things, fear, anger, resentment, suspicion, and emotional pain, which may make joining the fabric of society more difficult. Moreover, some groups of displaced persons, such as women and girls, may be at risk of "double marginalization" during and after displacement. In addition to being displaced from their homes and communities, they are often denied access to whatever forms of justice are available in camps and settlements and stigmatized for the gender-based crimes committed against them.[34]

At the societal level as well, returnees may encounter significant economic, political, and social changes as the result of armed conflict or repression. In Argentina, for example, repression "produced a fear of any sort of association or gathering of people," leading to a reduction of social interactions that lasted into the postdictatorship period. In Chile, one returnee perceived the whole of society to be permeated by the ideology of authoritarianism. "All of these factors," writes Ghanem, "make identification with one's home country difficult for the returnee."[35] Such society-wide effects have broader implications for the reintegration process. As the World Bank has noted, when returnees are able to reach their areas of origin, "these areas frequently have limited economic growth and few economic opportunities since they are *characterized by the legacy of past conflict* or by ongoing low level conflict."[36] Whether displaced persons are returning to their former communities or settling elsewhere, the society around them may be changed in significant ways by the legacies of past human rights violations.

TRANSITIONAL JUSTICE MEASURES AND THE ELEMENTS OF INTEGRATION AND REINTEGRATION

There is, then, potential space for transitional justice measures to make a contribution to the processes of integration and reintegration. A legacy of past abuses can hinder the integration and reintegration of formerly displaced persons, yet the primary actors working on displacement—humanitarian, peacebuilding, development, and human rights—are not necessarily focused on dealing directly with past abuses and their impact. In this section, I map out some of the ways in which transitional justice efforts (including criminal justice, reparations, truth-telling, and justice-sensitive security sector reform) may serve to facilitate the different aspects of integration and reintegration. As Rhodri Williams argues in this volume, "Transitional justice seeks to reintegrate victims while simultaneously transforming the social framework they are to be reintegrated into."[37]

SAFETY AND SECURITY

Transitional justice measures, particularly criminal justice and justice-sensitive security sector reform (SSR) measures, may facilitate reintegration by improving the safety and security of—or the perception of safety and security among—formerly displaced persons. They may also make reintegration more durable by helping prevent the recurrence of the abuses that often lead to displacement,[38] even when such measures do not directly target the crime of forced displacement. As de Greiff has argued, prosecutorial initiatives and vetting measures likely serve a more preventive than deterrent function, in that one of their primary outcomes is the disabling of the institutional structures that allowed crimes to happen in the first place—that is, through the "disarticulation of criminal networks."[39] If such networks, which can include public institutions and government officials, committed or facilitated the crime of forced displacement or other abuses that led to displacement, then their visible disarticulation will likely make returning populations feel safer and more secure. This could be particularly important for women and girls, for whom the point of return is particularly dangerous, both psychologically and physically.[40]

Criminally prosecuting those whose abuses forced citizens into exile can be a "significant expression of state responsibility" and "may serve to reassure returnees that the state has reformed."[41] Prosecutions may also facilitate or encourage return by removing known perpetrators from security institutions or local communities, thereby increasing returnees' sense of safety and security. In Bosnia, Liberia, and Timor-Leste, for example, the return process "came up against deeply felt sentiments on the part of many that they could not return to a situation where the people directly responsible for the deaths of their relatives were living in the same village."[42] In Colombia, the representative of the UN secretary-general on the human rights of IDPs has noted a clear link between the reintegration with impunity of demobilized paramilitaries into specific areas and low returns of IDPs. "Where the perpetrators of forced displacement continue to stay in the areas where they have committed their crimes, people are wary of returning, since they do not feel safe."[43] Criminal prosecutions and justice-sensitive SSR, both of which can combat impunity, may make a difference here.

Diane Orentlicher's report on the impact of the International Criminal Tribunal for the Former Yugoslavia in Bosnia suggests that, while promoting return was not one of its main goals, the tribunal may have contributed to the return of those forcibly displaced during the conflict in two ways: first, because people felt safer with the knowledge of increased international scrutiny, and second, because some individuals who had committed crimes were no longer able to deter returns.[44] "When combined with other favorable factors," Orentlicher concludes, "the removal of notorious war criminals can contribute to displaced persons' willingness to return home and probably has had this effect, albeit to a limited extent."[45] Other evidence also suggests that the tribunal increased refugee returns—although possibly through its truth-telling effects more than its sentencing of criminals. Plea bargaining targeted at low-ranking perpetrators, according to one study, was more likely to increase refugee returns than indictments and sentencing of higher-ranking perpetrators, because of the contribution made by such pleas to truth-telling at the local level.[46]

However, since many perpetrators of the crimes connected to displacement do stay in the areas where they committed those crimes, and since criminal justice efforts will likely only reach a small number of people at most, the reform of security institutions, such as the police and military, may be an even more important factor in post-conflict return and reintegration. This will especially be the case if the reform is justice sensitive, involving such elements as the removal of human rights abusers and the redress of ethnic and gender imbalances in the security sector. If "previous structures of past leadership that threatened those who left are still in place," either locally or nationally, then "returning minorities may feel at risk, and rightfully so."[47] According to one report, "The presence of armed groups, whether belonging to regular forces or militias, may create a serious obstacle to return and may be considered as a threat by potential returnees due to their past behavior, ethnic origin or lack of discipline. This is especially true where these forces have caused the displacement suffered by returnees, for example in Colombia."[48] Similarly, in Iraq, where some of the almost 5 million displaced persons have begun the process of return, many find those responsible for their displacement in charge of neighborhood security, as members of the police, army, or Awakening Councils.[49]

According to Madeline England, justice-sensitive SSR can contribute to the reintegration of displaced persons in several ways. These include (1) providing physical protection for returnees and effective rule of law by police and military that act with integrity and are subject to accountability, thereby fostering an environment conducive to the returnees' reconciliation with the local population, and (2) building the legitimacy of the security sector in the eyes of returnees, by encouraging their empowerment by way of ownership of security institutions and increasing their representation.[50] In terms of legitimacy and ownership, while efforts to ensure mixed representation in the security sector in Kosovo were not intended to directly facilitate reintegration, they did so indirectly by fostering general reconciliation. When police officers represent minority returnees and speak their language, returnees feel that they understand their concerns.[51] In postwar Bosnia, the UN's police reform efforts included a minority recruitment policy that was specifically aimed at attracting the return of minority refugees.[52]

ECONOMIC INTEGRATION/REINTEGRATION

Reparations in the form of property restitution, compensation, or other benefits may facilitate reintegration into and active participation in the community, enabling the rebuilding of sustainable livelihoods.[53] Indeed, restitution of housing, land, and property is seen by many to be a precondition for durable solutions precisely because it enables reintegration.[54] Reparations and restitution can "make invaluable contributions towards increasing returnees' physical, legal and socio-economic security, while expanding the range of choices the refugee can make in the context of the return process."[55] According to the International Organization for Migration, reparations programs are an important component of durable solutions because they facilitate the voluntary return of displaced persons by "recognizing that injustice has occurred and providing material remedies that assist the integration of displaced persons in their places of origin."[56] Reparations and restitution can be crucial to economic well-being for formerly displaced families, especially female-headed households.[57] Truth commissions, for their part, can make recommendations for reparations and restitution programs that take into account the particular economic reintegration needs of the displaced.[58]

Despite the fact that possession of land, housing, and property is acknowledged to be essential to recovery and livelihoods, restitution and compensation for displaced persons represent a major challenge that in most situations has not been dealt with successfully.[59] In Bosnia, for example, because many of those responsible for ethnic cleansing remained in power after the conflict, minority returns were blocked by those tasked with carrying out the restitution process.[60] The absence of restitution and compensation programs, particularly when other returning groups such as ex-combatants receive assistance through disarmament, demobilization, and reintegration (DDR) programs, can disrupt the overall reintegration process. "If the broader goal of reintegration is to be achieved," argues Marina Caparini in this volume, "it is vital that an appropriate balance govern the provision of assistance to different parties, civilian and ex-combatant, who were affected by the conflict."

While in many cases of mass displacement it will be difficult if not impossible to provide material reparations, such as compensation, to displaced persons simply because they were displaced—as a result of resource limitations and other practical constraints, given the number of people involved[61]—it should nevertheless be possible to ensure that those benefits that are distributed are targeted to the actual needs of the displaced. In Turkey, the Compensation Law is not gender sensitive but "blind to the special needs of displaced women and the sexual crimes committed against them during the war."[62] In Peru, displaced persons' demands for assistance included two that were specific to their experiences of displacement: psychological assistance (normally not a priority among the poor when resources are scarce) and education (which their children had missed while displaced).[63] If groups of displaced are among those eligible for reparations, it makes sense to tailor the benefits according to such articulated needs. Collective reparations may be particularly appropriate when resource constraints would prevent all displaced from receiving individual benefits and possibly for indigenous and other strong, cohesive communities that were displaced together.

POLITICAL INTEGRATION/REINTEGRATION

Transitional justice measures may affect the political reintegration of formerly displaced persons at a broad, indirect level. To see this potential contribution, consider that the different elements of a comprehensive transitional justice policy are arguably meant to provide recognition to victims and to foster civic trust. They can be interpreted as efforts to institutionalize the recognition of individuals both as victims of human rights abuses and as rights bearers, as well as to promote civic trust between citizens and between them and their institutions.[64] In one sense, as de Greiff has argued, transitional justice can be thought of as comprising efforts to enable the activity and participation of citizens who were previously marginalized or excluded. This process of

integration, "of not just turning victims into citizens but thereby of strengthening inclusive citizenship," has an effect beyond the population of direct victims. By reaffirming basic norms, transitional justice efforts can strengthen
citizenship in general.[65]

This can have a specific bearing on the displaced, many of whom are
already marginalized. Those who are forcibly displaced during conflict often
suffer not as the unavoidable result of armed conflict but because their rights
are violated as a consequence of specific and intentional policies and actions,
as well as the inaction, of state and non-state actors. For such people, measures
taken to recognize them as rights bearers and to reestablish trust in fellow
citizens and government institutions may reinforce the positive outcomes of
other responses to displacement. As Megan Bradley explains, displaced persons can be among those with the least confidence in their states. Her notion of
"just return" therefore involves putting returning refugees on an equal footing
with others and establishing a new relationship of rights and duties between
the state and its returning citizens.[66]

The facilitation of political reintegration of displaced persons can happen in various ways. Engaging with the displaced at the political level is about
empowering them by including their voices and restoring their ability to make
claims. As England writes, "Including displaced voices in this SSR process is a
critical part of reintegration."[67] In Timor-Leste, the participatory nature of the
community reconciliation processes that were part of the truth commission's
work and their incorporation of traditional customs "strengthened governance
structures at the local level, which in turn facilitated reintegration and community reconstruction processes."[68] From a gender perspective, a transitional
justice measure such as reparations that engages with women and empowers
them to act can help overcome the perception of female displaced persons as
passive victims and recipients of aid.[69] More broadly, according to Bradley, a
transitional justice measure such as reparations can restore the refugee's ability to make claims against the state in several ways—in particular, it can "reposition the refugee as a citizen with legal and moral entitlements."[70]

At the same time, though, it is important to note that limitations on the
number of victims who actually benefit from transitional justice processes
(which can result from both resource constraints and political decisions) can
have a detrimental effect on integration: those who feel they were victimized but do not receive the recognition as victims that other groups do may
feel increased dissatisfaction. Furthermore, displaced persons may feel doubly wronged if transitional justice measures do not specifically acknowledge
them. In Colombia, for example, some IDPs felt wronged once because they

were displaced and a second time when other victims, such as relatives of the disappeared, received recognition and compensation.[71]

At a different level, transitional justice measures can facilitate political reintegration through their capacity to catalyze the organization of groups in civil society, or as de Greiff puts it, the "articulation of networks."[72] Justice measures such as reparations programs and truth commissions have been shown to play a role in catalyzing civil society organizations in countries such as Peru, South Africa, and Morocco.[73] This articulating capacity can also have an effect on those civil society organizations representing the interests of displaced persons. In Colombia, displaced women's groups have mobilized in response to rulings of the Constitutional Court on the government's obligations regarding displacement and the Justice and Peace Law. As Donny Meertens explains: "For the displaced women and their associations, 'being a victim' has acquired a new political and practical meaning, beyond the former status of 'displaced people.' They now want the government to go beyond the traditional parameters of humanitarian assistance. Women organized in victim's organizations in order to present their claims during the hearings with paramilitaries in the Justice and Peace process."[74]

The extent of this catalyzing effect, though, will likely be greater if there is some level of organization among the displaced population to begin with. In Guatemala, for example, returning refugees had been able to use their time outside the country, in Mexico, to organize and negotiate with the Guatemalan government. When the truth commission process began after their return, the returnees were able to participate, having already "created a precedent by their forthright manner of recounting their experiences." They therefore had the "capability to speak out."[75] This level of organization among the displaced may not always obtain, however. In Liberia, the truth commission did reach out in important ways to refugees and members of the diaspora, but it did not do the same for the country's internally displaced, in large part because civil society representation of internally displaced persons was almost nonexistent,[76] which also made it difficult for civil society to represent the displaced population's interests in the SSR process.[77]

Part of the issue here pertains to visibility, which may be different for refugees and IDPs. When their country of origin is under the rule of a repressive regime, refugees may find more political space and freedom to organize in their host country. In the case of armed conflict, refugees simply may be more visible than those who are internally displaced but remain among a much larger war-affected population. It has been pointed out, for example, that returnees are in general more difficult to study than refugees because "once they return to their country they are less visible, as they officially lose their refugee status and become part of the population again."[78] However, the opposite can also be true. Within Colombia, organizations representing IDPs are among the strongest victims groups, while Colombian refugees in Panama and Venezuela are much less visible.[79] Either way, the less visible and organized, the less likely groups of displaced persons will be to engage in transitional justice processes.

Furthermore, there may be significant obstacles to organizing in a context of displacement. Displaced populations often are geographically scattered, poorly educated or illiterate, speakers of different languages, mistrustful of other ethnic or religious groups even among themselves, absorbed by formidable daily challenges, and fearful of reprisals. One 2011 report claimed that more than sixty IDP leaders advocating for land rights in Colombia were murdered in recent years.[80] Lack of documentation and financial resources present additional obstacles. Problems may also lie in the design and implementation of transitional justice measures, which are much more likely to catalyze networks among displaced populations if they engage those populations directly and respond to their justice claims and needs. In Turkey, for example, the government did not consult the displaced at all before the enactment or during the implementation of the Compensation Law, which as a result has not catalyzed solidarity, with most civil society groups ignoring the law.[81]

The articulation of networks among the displaced through engagement with transitional justice measures can have important political and development-related outcomes, but the potentially negative consequences should not be ignored. For example, the displaced are not the only ones who organize in response to justice processes, and competition or tension between groups representing various interests can result, which may be harmful to levels of trust and reconciliation in a society. As Peter Van der Auweraert points out in this volume, in some contexts, such as Colombia, the displaced may be more advanced in their ability to politically organize than other, nondisplaced victims. This may contribute to a perception that international attention focuses exclusively on IDPs, which can cause "resentment and anger among other vulnerable groups," as well as "victim competition."[82] The nature of the civil society groups that mobilize around transitional justice should also not be taken for granted. Instead of legitimately and effectively representing the interests of the displaced, for example, they may turn out to be selective and exclusionary, elitist, ineffective, or unaccountable to their constituencies.[83]

SOCIAL INTEGRATION/REINTEGRATION

In many post-conflict situations, tensions can linger between those who were displaced and those who remained in their communities. Both groups may have suffered during the conflict, but their experiences will not necessarily be mutually understood. "Feelings of betrayal on the part of those left behind are a serious impediment to the process of social repair," writes Haider, "especially when those departing had knowledge of an impending assault on their town or village and said nothing. Return in postconflict societies requires such experiences to be overcome. Restoration of relationships, in turn, requires restoration of trust."[84] The displaced may be afraid of accusations that they deserted and avoided the suffering of those who stayed. Indeed, such perceptions among those who stayed behind may be based on a lack of knowledge and understanding of the experience of displacement or on the denial of the initial events and abuses that led to the displacement. One returnee spoke of a "culture of war" and a "culture of exile," in which the groups "did not recognize each other."[85]

In Bosnia and Herzegovina, for example, many refugees returning to Sarajevo reported facing resentment and discrimination, which led to feelings of marginalization and alienation, and difficulty establishing or finding housing, jobs, and livelihoods. "Many returnees," writes Anders Stefansson, felt "they [were] being accused by the stayees of betraying Sarajevo and BiH by fleeing abroad." At the same time, the experiences of the refugees and diaspora were for the most part missing from media coverage and public debate, to the point of "bordering on being a cultural taboo." Those who stayed in Sarajevo during the war were seen by some returnees as holding a "monopoly on suffering" and by others as inferior because of their experiences of "war, brutality and social degradation." All of this led to a "mental division" that made it "difficult for returnees to develop normal relations with stayees."[86] Similarly, in Guatemala, returnees experienced tensions with those who had remained at home, some of whom had suffered torture and other violence. "While the returnees had faced traumatic flights and endured difficult conditions in Mexican refugee camps," observe Ellen Long and Lynellyn D. Long, "they had escaped the daily control of the army and environment of terror." The resulting tensions between these groups led to disputes over such issues as land and property.[87]

In cases such as these, truth-telling efforts may serve to reduce tensions between those who stayed and those who were displaced by revealing and validating the experiences of the different groups, thereby potentially facilitating return/reintegration processes.[88] In Peru, the Truth and Reconciliation

Commission (Comisión de la Verdad y Reconciliación—CVR) helped to establish a better public understanding of the phenomenon of displacement. In cities, where many internally displaced ended up, they were often treated with contempt for having come from areas controlled by the insurgent group Shining Path and were therefore associated with "terrorism." The CVR played an important role in destigmatizing the displaced, that is, in letting people see what they had left behind in order to escape the Shining Path.[89] In Guatemala, the report of the Commission for Historical Clarification (Comisión para el Esclarecimiento Histórico—CEH) recognized the suffering and stigma experienced by the displaced, in addition to the negative impact of state discrimination on return and reintegration.[90]

Truth-telling may also facilitate return and reintegration of perpetrators of crimes. Participation in Timor-Leste's commission was seen as a way to encourage the return of refugees in West Timor camps.[91] Returning refugees who had committed "lesser crimes" could participate in the commission-facilitated community reconciliation processes—community-based hearings where perpetrators and members of the community came together to determine measures that would enable the perpetrators to reintegrate into the community. Several years later, following the crisis of 2006, dialogue and mediation teams (which could be seen as less formal truth-telling mechanisms) facilitated the social reintegration of displaced persons back into their communities.[92]

Reparations may also play a role in facilitating social reintegration by reducing resentment between groups. As discussed earlier, reparations benefits distributed to those who were displaced may help individuals rebuild their livelihoods. In addition, reparations to those who remained in their places of origin but were victims of other human right abuses could further facilitate reintegration for those who were displaced. Consider, for example, a case in which displaced persons returning to a community were to receive assistance in the form of humanitarian aid and returning ex-combatants were to receive benefits through a DDR program, while those who remained in the community but suffered from a series of violations received either no reparations or the mere promise of reparations somewhere down the line. It would be reasonable to expect some degree of resentment toward the returnees.

There is plenty of evidence that assistance provided to displaced persons can indeed foster such resentment. In Guatemala, for instance, UNHCR found that assistance to returnees "tended to set off the returnees from their non-repatriate neighbors and, in some cases, this caused resentment." On the other hand, in addition to jump-starting livelihoods, quick impact projects in some places contributed to reconciliation because the communities next to those of returnees believed that their needs were being considered as well.[93] Reintegration assistance is most effective, Tennant argues, when provided on a community-wide basis seeking to foster reconciliation.[94] Development actors such as UNDP and the World Bank have also emphasized the importance of a balance among aid to different groups. UNDP has observed that development programs exclusively covering certain population categories, such as IDPs and demobilized combatants, are often unsustainable because they tend to alienate other members of the local community.[95] The World Bank warns of the risk of "perceived marginalization" if all groups are not targeted with assistance.[96] In many situations, then, providing reparations to the nondisplaced who were victims of abuses could contribute to a more balanced environment in which reintegration is less hindered.

Of course, there is always the risk that reparations provided to displaced persons will also face resistance or incite competition, although that will depend on the specific context and the nature of the program. In Timor-Leste in 2006, compensation from the government was not called "reparations" in part because of the fear that the term would lead to divisions; this fear, however, stemmed from the fact that victims of human rights abuses in previous periods had not been awarded reparations benefits. The financial assistance that was provided to the displaced in 2006 was able to facilitate the reintegration of families without causing "social jealousy" partly because the beneficiaries took steps to share the money with others—in some cases giving those who had occupied their houses or lands in their absence a portion of the cash grant for "taking care" of the properties—and partly as a result of the work of the dialogue teams mentioned earlier.[97] In Turkey, however, the Compensation Law has been deeply divisive, because the number of applicants who are rejected and the different amounts awarded establishes a perceived hierarchy of victims.[98] Similarly, even the recommendations of truth commissions regarding potential reparations may foster competition, and if they go unimplemented, "may lead them [victims] to develop unrealistic expectations of the process" that could undermine reintegration and reconciliation efforts.[99]

LOCAL INTEGRATION AND RESETTLEMENT

Much of the discussion in this chapter about the ways in which transitional justice measures can facilitate reintegration of displaced persons seems most applicable in cases of return. Nevertheless, the dynamics under discussion can also play out in situations of local integration or resettlement elsewhere. No matter where the displaced integrate, they need to integrate into a community and a society, not just a physical place. The outcomes associated with transitional justice measures have to do not only with the relationships between citizens and their state institutions but also with relationships between citizens and groups. People displaced from a rural town to an urban center within their own country and who remain there, for example, may still need to be politically reintegrated. IDPs and refugees who integrate locally, wherever that may be, may still find their social integration hindered by the attitudes of the local community. Indeed, according to a recent Brookings Institution report, the factors affecting the success of local integration include the attitudes of the host community, how the members of that community view the causes of displacement, and how they view the displaced (for example, either as innocent victims or as responsible in some way for the conflict), as well as the attitudes of the displaced population, including their views of the host community and its involvement in the conflict and their own displacement.[100] As discussed earlier, these are factors that justice measures may affect.

Return has long been the preferred durable solution to displacement among policymakers and practitioners, but there is growing recognition that it is not always possible and that protracted situations of displacement[101] and processes such as urbanization[102] make a narrow focus on return unwise.[103] Displaced persons' preferences are also often affected by their experiences. As one recent report points out: "IDPs are not a monolithic group and their settlement preferences vary based on their personal experience and circumstances of war, even within one family. Individuals, families or groups from specific areas may have gone through traumatic experiences, which may make them opt for local integration even if return is considered possible by others."[104] In Colombia, for example, 80 percent of internally displaced persons wish to integrate locally.[105] Often, the displaced from rural areas settle in crowded urban centers, where they are not treated differently from other poor people: "Their particular reintegration needs, derived from consequences of their forced displacement and losses, are neither recognized nor addressed, leaving them vulnerable to abuse, subject to violence, and feeling that they have suffered injustice."[106]

It is important therefore that transitional justice not be seen as or become a tool of return—relevant only in cases of return—or a means of restricting the choices available to displaced persons.[107] Not only should transitional justice try to adhere to the idea that any return home must be a choice,[108] but some have argued that an important aspect of redress is the ability to choose a solution in itself.[109] "Part of the crime of forced migration is that it robs people of the chance to make choices about where and how they will live," writes

Bradley. "Focusing on choice as a key part of a dignified return is therefore itself a kind of redress."[110]

Restitution of housing, land, and property, and reparations in the form of compensation or other benefits provide the clearest examples of how justice measures can facilitate integration somewhere other than the community of origin. As noted by the World Bank, restitution can provide capital to help IDPs and refugees build a future elsewhere.[111] Patricia Weiss Fagan agrees: "Without surrendering their hopes of an eventual return to their original homes, such returnees probably will accept alternative locations if conditions are favorable. This is more likely if they are treated justly and are able to receive some form of compensation for their losses."[112] In Bosnia, property restitution was provided to beneficiaries whether they returned or not, thus affording them "income and assets (through sale, rental, or exchange of restituted properties) that could help them with local integration elsewhere."[113] Leila Hilal argues that a similar, noncoerced rights-based option, one that delinks return and restitution, would facilitate the resettlement of Palestinian refugees outside of Israel or allow them to return with the freedom to settle in urban locations. It would, she writes, "empower refugee families to make decisions regarding return without sacrificing all forms of justice."[114] In many cases, however, delinking restitution and return may be difficult because of the political or legal context. In customary systems, for example, it may be difficult to delink restitution from return because in such contexts the right to land is often understood to be integrally related to the use of that land.[115]

Other transitional justice measures may also facilitate local integration. As pointed out earlier, in Peru the truth commission process was able to destigmatize internal displacement, which had been associated with terrorist control of certain regions, thereby helping displaced persons to integrate into the cities where they had settled.[116] Justice-sensitive SSR processes that are implemented in the host country may also enable local integration. In Chad, for example, reform of the security sector there was aimed at the protection of refugees from Darfur—protection that may allow those refugees to make freer choices about where to integrate.[117]

CONCLUSION

In this chapter, I have tried to map out some of the ways in which transitional justice measures can contribute to achieving durable solutions for displaced persons. My focus has been on the ways in which transitional justice can, in modest but important ways, facilitate the integration or reintegration of displaced persons into society. These processes are complex and long term, so it is likely that the contributions of justice measures will be most pronounced in the long term. Transitional justice can help achieve the justice-related goals of providing recognition to victims, as both victims and citizens, and of fostering civic trust between citizens and between them and public institutions.[118] This indirect contribution, which has both political and social dimensions, does not necessarily require that justice measures directly address the issue of displacement (although the effect may be enhanced if they do so). Transitional justice can also affect reintegration in more direct ways, not only politically and socially, but also with regard to safety and security conditions and economic integration. While most of the examples discussed are most relevant in contexts of return, the dynamics of facilitating reintegration are similar when displaced persons integrate locally in their host communities or resettle in a third location.

Various contextual factors will affect the extent to which transitional justice can facilitate the integration and reintegration of displaced persons, as well as the extent to which the process of integrating into society is actually beneficial for the displaced. The society to which they return may not have been a very just one to begin with. For example, as Lucy Hovil explains, the pre-conflict context may have been profoundly biased against women, creating a need to address the already existing inequalities and discrimination.[119] The extent to which transitional justice can contribute to the transformation of a society is beyond the scope of this chapter, but it is clear that on their own, transitional justice measures can make only a modest contribution in this regard. As Williams argues, a purely corrective approach to restitution privileges return and restoration of property relations, while a development or distributive justice–oriented approach would require the actual transformation of legal and social relations.[120] For displaced persons to reintegrate into a just and peaceful society, that society will usually require a much broader program of institutional and structural reform and development. If transitional justice and efforts to deal with the past can be integrated in a coherent fashion into that broader program, then the process of reintegration may better serve the needs of the formerly displaced. At the same time, however, the implementation of transitional justice measures can serve as a signal to the displaced that a society has *already* begun to take steps toward reform, and that it is committed to becoming the kind of society they would want to live in.

NOTES

1   Many thanks to Megan Bradley, Bryce Campbell, Marina Caparini, Elizabeth Ferris, Pablo de Greiff, and Lucy Hovil for their comments on previous versions of this chapter. Versions of this chapter or the ideas contained in it were presented at the Conference on Displacement and Reconciliation (Conflict Research Centre, Saint Paul University, Ottawa, Canada, June 9–10, 2011); at the 13th Conference of the International Association for the Study of Forced Migration (Refugee Law Project, Kampala, Uganda, July 3–6, 2011); and at the International Seminar on Forced Displacement and Justice (Norwegian Refugee Council and the Fiscalía General de la Nación, Bogotá, Colombia, October 24–26, 2011); thanks to the participants in those events for their feedback.

2   Office of the United Nations High Commissioner for Refugees, "Rule of Law and Transitional Justice," http://www.unhcr.org/pages/4a293daf6.html.

3   Vicky Tennant, "Return and Reintegration," in *Post-conflict Peacebuilding: A Lexicon*, ed. Vincent Chetail (Oxford: Oxford University Press, 2009), 315.

4   Brookings-Bern Project on Internal Displacement, *IASC Framework on Durable Solutions for Internally Displaced Persons* (Washington, DC: Brookings Institution / University of Bern, April 2010), 5, 43, http://www.brookings.edu/reports/2010/04_durable_solutions.aspx.

5   Megan Bradley, "Redressing Refugees: The Emergence of International Norms on Reparations for Returnees" (paper prepared for the International Studies Association conference, New York, February 15–18, 2009), 7.

6   For a discussion of the short-term concerns of humanitarian actors about transitional justice, see Bryce Campbell, in this volume.

7   Brookings-Bern Project on Internal Displacement, *Framework on Durable Solutions*, 1. Little reliable data is available on the achievement of durable solutions for displaced persons, particularly IDPs, but much attention has been paid to the mechanisms through which durable solutions can and should be achieved. See Elizabeth Ferris, ed., *Resolving Internal Displacement: Prospects for Local Integration* (Washington, DC: Brookings Institution–London School of Economics Project on Internal Displacement / Internal Displacement Monitoring Centre, June 2011), 10, http://www.brookings.edu/reports/2011/0601_protracted_displace_local.aspx.

8   Office of the United Nations High Commissioner for Refugees, *Handbook for Repatriation and Reintegration Activities* (Geneva: UNHCR, 2004), 5.

9   Tennant, "Return and Reintegration," 307.

10 B. S. Chimni, "Post-conflict Peace-Building and the Return of Refugees: Concepts, Practices, and Institutions," in *Refugees and Forced Displacement: International Security, Human Vulnerability, and the State*, ed. Edward Newman and Joanne van Selm (Tokyo: UN University Press, 2003), 200–201.

11   International Committee of the Red Cross, *Strengthening Protection in War: A Search for Professional Standards* (Geneva: ICRC, 2001). See Rhodri Williams and Marina Caparini, in this volume, for broader discussions of the concept of protection and how justice measures relate to it. Also see Elizabeth G. Ferris, *The Politics of Protection: The Limits of Humanitarian Action* (Washington, DC: Brookings Institution Press, 2011).

12   Nairobi Declaration on Women's and Girls' Right to a Remedy and Reparation, (International Meeting on Women's and Girls' Right to a Remedy and Reparation, Nairobi, March 2007), declaration 3. For more on restitution, see Williams, in this volume.

13   Megan Bradley, communication with author, August 8, 2011.

14   Patricia Weiss Fagen, *Refugees and IDPs after Conflict: Why They Do Not Go Home*, United States Institute of Peace Special Report 268 (Washington, DC: USIP, April 2011), 2, http://www.usip.org/publications/refugees-and-idps-after-conflict.

15   "Humanitarian reform seeks to improve the effectiveness of humanitarian response by ensuring greater predictability, accountability and partnership. It is an ambitious effort by the international humanitarian community to reach more beneficiaries, with more comprehensive needs-based relief and protection, in a more effective and timely manner." See "Humanitarian Reform and the Global Cluster Approach," OneResponse, http://oneresponse.info/COORDINATION/CLUSTERAPPROACH/Pages/Cluster%20Approach.aspx.

16   Cluster Working Group on Early Recovery, quoted in Tennant, "Return and Reintegration," 318.

17   United Nations Development Programme, "Overview on UNDP's Involvement in the Reintegration of IDPs and Returnees in Post-Conflict Contexts" (New York: UNDP, 2003), 3.

18   Asger Christensen and Niels Harild, "Forced Displacement: The Development Challenge," (Washington, DC: World Bank, December 2009), 11–12; citing World Bank Operational Policy 8.00 on Rapid Response to Crises and Emergencies.

19   Elizabeth Ferris, communication with author, September 7, 2011.

20   Brookings-Bern Project on Internal Displacement, *Addressing Internal Displacement in Peace Processes, Peace Agreements and Peace Building* (Washington, DC: Brookings Institution / University of Bern, September 2007), 16, 43.

21   Katy Long, "State, Nation, Citizen: Rethinking Repatriation" (Working Paper no. 48, Refugee Studies Centre, University of Oxford, August 2008), 5, 7, 22.

22   Katy Long, *Home Alone? A Review of the Relationship between Repatriation, Mobility and Durable Solutions for Refugees* (Geneva: UNHCR, Policy Development and Evaluation Service, March 2010), 1, 3.

23   Ibid., 6, 9.

24   Tennant, "Return and Reintegration," 309.

25   Huma Haider, "The Politicisation of Humanitarian Assistance: Refugee and IDP Policy

in Bosnia and Herzegovina," *Journal of Humanitarian Assistance*, April 26, 2010, 5, 7, http://sites.tufts.edu/jha/archives/700.

26   UNHCR, *Handbook*, 4.

27   Chimni, "Post-conflict Peace-Building," 200–201.

28   Pablo de Greiff, "The Role of Apologies in National Reconciliation Processes," in *The Age of Apology: Facing Up to the Past*, ed. Mark Gibney et al. (Philadelphia: University of Pennsylvania Press, 2008), 126–27.

29   UNDP, "Overview on UNDP's Involvement," 13.

30   Christensen and Harild, "Forced Displacement," 14–15.

31   Tennant, "Return and Reintegration," 314 (emphasis added).

32   Megan Bradley, "Return in Dignity: A Neglected Protection Challenge" (Working Paper no. 40, Refugee Studies Centre, University of Oxford, June 2007), 9.

33   Tania Ghanem, "When Forced Migrants Return 'Home': The Psychological Difficulties Returnees Encounter in the Reintegration Process" (Working Paper No. 16, Refugee Studies Centre, University of Oxford, October 2003), 19, 23, 24.

34   See Lucy Hovil, in this volume.

35   Ghanem, "When Forced Migrants Return," 40–41.

36   Niels Harild and Asger Christensen, "The Development Challenge of Finding Durable Solutions for Refugees and Internally Displaced People," Background Note, *World Development Report 2011* (Washington, DC: World Bank, July 30, 2010), 3, http://wdr2011.worldbank.org/durable%20solutions (emphasis added).

37   Williams, in this volume.

38   See Federico Andreu-Guzmán, on criminal justice, and Caparini, on SSR, in this volume.

39   Pablo de Greiff, "Transitional Justice, Security, and Development," Background Paper, *World Development Report 2011* (Washington, DC: World Bank, October 29, 2010).

40   See Hovil, in this volume.

41   Megan Bradley, "The Conditions of Just Return: State Responsibility and Restitution for Refugees" (Working Paper No. 21, Refugee Studies Centre, University of Oxford, March 2005), 16.

42   Erika Feller, "Giving Peace a Chance: Displacement and Rule of Law during Peacebuilding," *Refugee Survey Quarterly* 28, no. 1 (2009): 93.

43   United Nations General Assembly, "Implementation of General Assembly Resolution 60/251 of 15 March 2006 Entitled 'Human Rights Council': Addendum–Mission to Columbia," Report of the Representative of the Secretary-General on the Human Rights of Internally Displaced Persons, Walter Kälin, A/HRC/4/38/Add.3, January 24, 2007, para. 57.

44   Diane F. Orentlicher, *That Someone Guilty Be Punished: The Impact of the ICTY in Bosnia* (New York: Open Society Institute, 2010), 79–80.

45 Ibid., 85.

46 Monika Nalepa, "Reconciliation, Refugee Returns, and the Impact of International Criminal Justice: The Case of Bosnia and Herzegovina," in *NOMOS LI: Transitional Justice*, ed. Melissa Williams, Rosemary Nagy, and Jon Elster (New York: New York University Press, 2012). See also Roger Duthie, "Transitional Justice and Displacement," *International Journal of Transitional Justice* 5, no. 2 (2011): 241–61.

47 Weiss Fagen, *Refugees and IDPs after Conflict*, 11.

48 Brookings-Bern Project on Internal Displacement, *Addressing Internal Displacement*, 44–45.

49 Deborah Isser and Peter Van der Auweraert, *Land, Property, and the Challenge of Return for Iraq's Displaced*, United States Institute of Peace Special Report 221 (Washington, DC: USIP, April 2009), 13. In Guatemala, early returns were hindered because of fears about personal safety and access to land stemming from the refugees' "traditional relationship with the Guatemalan state as oppressor rather than protector." Long, "State, Nation, Citizen," 27.

50 Madeline England, "Linkages between Justice-Sensitive Security-Sector Reform and Displacement: Examples from Liberia and Kosovo" (paper prepared for ICTJ / Brookings Project on Transitional Justice and Displacement, 2012).

51 Ibid.

52 See Gemma Collantes Celador, "Police Reform: Peacebuilding through 'Democratic Policing?,'" *International Peacekeeping* 12, no. 3 (2005): 364–76.

53 See Peter Van der Auweraert, in this volume.

54 See Williams, in this volume; and Leila Hilal, "Transitional Justice Reponses to Palestinian Dispossession: Focus on Restitution" (paper prepared for ICTJ / Brookings Project on Transitional Justice and Displacement, 2012).

55 Bradley, "Conditions of Just Return," 299, citing Rhodri Williams, "The Significance of Property Restitution to Sustainable Return in Bosnia and Herzegovina," *International Migration* 44, no. 3 (2006): 39–61.

56 International Organization for Migration, "Reparation Programmes" (IOM Policy Brief, July 2009), 1. See also Duthie, "Transitional Justice and Displacement."

57 See Hovil, in this volume.

58 See Bradley, in this volume.

59 Christensen and Harild, "Forced Displacement," 14.

60 Huma Haider, "(Re)Imagining Coexistence: Striving for Sustainable Return, Reintegration and Reconciliation in Bosnia and Herzegovina," *International Journal of Transitional Justice* 3, no. 1 (2009): 94.

61 See Van der Auweraert, in this volume.

62 Dilek Kurban, "Reparations and Displacement in Turkey: Lessons Learned from the Compensation Law" (paper prepared for ICTJ / Brookings Project on Transitional Justice and Displacement, 2012).

63 Rafael Barrantes, "Reparations and Displacement in Peru" (paper prepared for ICTJ / Brookings Project on Transitional Justice and Displacement, 2012).

64 Pablo de Greiff, "Theorizing Transitional Justice," in Williams, Nagy, and Elster, *NOMOS LI: Transitional Justice.*

65 Pablo de Greiff, "Articulating the Links between Transitional Justice and Development: Justice and Social Integration," in *Transitional Justice and Development: Making Connections,* ed. Pablo de Greiff and Roger Duthie (New York: Social Science Research Council, 2009), 62. See also Hovil, in this volume.

66 Bradley, "Conditions of Just Return," 286.

67 England, "Justice-Sensitive Security-Sector Reform."

68 Bradley, in this volume, paraphrasing Susan Harris Rimmer, "Women Cut in Half: Refugee Women and the Commission for Reception, Truth-Seeking and Reconciliation in Timor-Leste," *Refugee Survey Quarterly* 29, no. 2 (March 2010): 102–3.

69 See Hovil, in this volume.

70 Bradley, "Return in Dignity," 9.

71 Elizabeth Ferris, communication with author, September 7, 2011.

72 De Greiff, *Transitional Justice, Security, and Development.*

73 Ibid.

74 Donny Meertens, "Forced Displacement and Gender Justice in Colombia: Between Disproportional Effects of Violence and Historical Injustice" (paper prepared for ICTJ / Brookings Project on Transitional Justice and Displacement, 2012).

75 Paula Worby, "Lessons Learned from UNHCR's Involvement in the Guatemala Refugee Repatriation and Reintegration Programme (1987–1999)," rev. ed. October 2, 2000 (New York: UNHCR, Regional Bureau for the Americas and Evaluation and Policy Analysis Unit, December 1999), sec. 1.b.

76 Awa Dabo, "In the Presence of Absence: Transitional Justice and Displacement in Liberia" (paper prepared for ICTJ / Brookings Project on Transitional Justice and Displacement, 2012).

77 England, "Justice-Sensitive Security-Sector Reform."

78 Ghanem, "When Forced Migrants Return," 13.

79 See Van der Auweraert, in this volume.

80 International Displacement Monitoring Centre, "Colombia: Property Restitution in Sight but Integration Still Distant," September 5, 2011, 5, http://www.internal-displacement.org/countries/colombia.

81 Kurban, "Reparations and Displacement in Turkey."

82 Van der Auweraert, in this volume.

83 See Jennifer M. Brinkerhoff, Stephen C. Smith, and Hildy Teegen, "Beyond the 'Non': The Strategic Space for NGOs in Development," in *NGOs and the Millennium Development Goals: Citizen Action to Reduce Poverty,* ed. Jennifer M. Brinkerhoff, Stephen C. Smith, and

Hildy Teegen (New York: Palgrave Macmillan, 2007), 65. For a broader discussion of transitional justice and civil society, see Roger Duthie, *Building Trust and Capacity: Civil Society and Transitional Justice from a Development Perspective* (New York: ICTJ, November 2009), http://ictj.org/sites/default/files/ICTJ-Development-CivilSociety-FullPaper-2009-English.pdf.

84   Haider, "(Re)Imagining Coexistence," 99.

85   Ghanem, "When Forced Migrants Return," 44, 48.

86   Anders H. Stefansson, "Refugee Returns to Sarajevo and Their Challenge to Contemporary Narratives of Mobility," in *Coming Home? Refugees, Migrants, and Those Who Stayed Behind*, ed. Lynellyn D. Long and Ellen Oxfeld (Philadelphia: University of Pennsylvania Press: 2004), 172, 176–79.

87   Ellen Long and Lynellyn D. Long, "Introduction: An Ethnography of Return," in Long and Oxfeld, *Coming Home*, 13.

88   Eduardo Gonzalez, communication with author. See Bradley, in this volume.

89   Barrantes, "Reparations and Displacement in Peru."

90   See Bradley, in this volume.

91   Taina Järvinen, *Human Rights and Post-conflict Transitional Justice in East Timor* (Helsinki: Finnish Institute of International Affairs, 2004), 56.

92   Peter Van der Auweraert, "Dealing with the 2006 Internal Displacement Crisis in Timor-Leste: Between Reparations and Humanitarian Policy-Making" (paper prepared for ICTJ / Brookings Project on Transitional Justice and Displacement, 2012); and Luiz Vieira, "The CAVR and the 2006 Crisis: Reflections on Durable Solutions" (paper prepared for ICTJ / Brookings Project on Transitional Justice and Displacement, 2012).

93   Worby, *Lessons Learned*, secs. 3.b and 3.c.

94   Tennant, "Return and Reintegration," 315.

95   UNDP, "Overview on UNDP's Involvement," 5.

96   Christensen and Harild, "Forced Displacement," 12.

97   Van der Auweraert, "Internal Displacement Crisis in Timor-Leste"; and in this volume.

98   Kurban, "Reparations and Displacement in Turkey," 17.

99   Bradley, in this volume.

100   Ferris, *Resolving Internal Displacement*, 12.

101   Extended exile is the norm for a majority of refugees. Long, "Home Alone," 5. See also Brookings Institution–London School of Economics Project on Internal Displacement and Internal Displacement Monitoring Centre, *IDPs in Protracted Displacement: Is Local Integration a Solution?* (Washington, DC: Brookings-LSE Project on Internal Displacement / IDMC, May 2011), http://www.internal-displacement.org/publications/is-local-integration-a-solution.

102   Barrantes, "Reparations and Displacement in Peru." In Peru, those who sought refuge in large cities tended to stay there; those who were closer to home returned more often.

103   See Williams, in this volume.

104   Ferris, *Resolving Internal Displacement*, 13.

105   Ibid., 14.

106   Weiss Fagen, *Refugees and IDPs after Conflict*, 3.

107   This is arguably one of the main problems with the "Principles on Housing and Property Restitution for Refugees and Displaced Persons," United Nations Sub-Commission on the Promotion and Protection of Human Rights, Final Report of the Special Rapporteur, Paulo Sérgio Pinheiro, E/CN.4/Sub.2/2005/17, June 28, 2005. See Williams, in this volume, for a discussion.

108   Long, "Home Alone," 13.

109   Haider, "Politicisation of Humanitarian Assistance," 1.

110   Bradley, "Return in Dignity," 9.

111   Christensen and Harild, "Forced Displacement," 14.

112   Weiss Fagen, *Refugees and IDPs after Conflict*, 13.

113   Williams, in this volume.

114   Hilal, "Transitional Justice Responses to Palestinian Dispossession."

115   Barbara McCallin, "Transitional Justice, HLP Restitution and Legal Pluralism" (paper prepared for ICTJ / Brookings Project on Transitional Justice and Displacement, 2012).

116   Barrantes, "Reparations and Displacement in Peru."

117   England, "Justice-Sensitive Security-Sector Reform"; and William G. O'Neill, "Police Reform in Situations of Forced Displacement" (paper prepared for ICTJ / Brookings Project on Transitional Justice and Displacement, 2012).

118   De Greiff, "Theorizing Transitional Justice."

119   Hovil, in this volume.

120   Williams, in this volume.

CHAPTER 2

Addressing Concerns about Transitional Justice in Displacement Contexts: A Humanitarian Perspective

Bryce Campbell

This edited volume explores the connections between two fields—transitional justice and displacement—that have largely developed independently of one another. The impetus for the study includes increased contact in the field among a wide array of organizations,[1] including humanitarian organizations, development agencies, justice and human rights organizations, and peace-building actors, which are drawn to the same flash points of conflict, human rights violations, and states in need of rebuilding. Operating in common country contexts leads to increased opportunity for interactions between these various types of actors, which has sometimes led to tensions. While previous studies have explored relationships between development and transitional justice actors or displacement and peacemaking initiatives,[2] this project seeks, among other things, to address the challenges and opportunities presented by interactions between displacement and transitional justice actors.

In this chapter, I address the specific concerns of humanitarian actors regarding transitional justice in contexts of displacement. I begin with a description of the typical concerns of displacement actors, and the humanitarian community more broadly, toward transitional justice. In particular, my focus is on two concerns: (1) that displaced persons are inadequately involved in transitional justice processes, which as a result do not deliver enough concrete benefits to them, and (2) that transitional justice efforts can complicate or hinder the work of humanitarians by provoking national authorities to restrict access to those in need. I then set out suggestions for bridging, to some extent, the divide between displacement and transitional justice actors. My main argument is that a multifaceted approach to transitional justice, which includes both judicial and nonjudicial measures, should, in a number of ways, mitigate the concerns I have mentioned and in some instances even point the way toward potential cooperation. Furthermore, the timing of justice measures should also temper those concerns, and the fact that measures are often implemented sequentially rather than simultaneously may have positive implications for the engagement of the displaced. Displacement and justice actors often operate alongside each other and face common challenges, and the achievement of their long-term goals can be interdependent. It is therefore in the interests of both to attain a certain level of coexistence if not cooperation.

I use the term *displacement actors* interchangeably with *humanitarian actors* in this chapter, although there are organizations in the larger humanitarian community that do not act on displacement issues. Among the UN agencies and intergovernmental organizations serving refugees and internally displaced persons (IDPs) are the Office of the High Commissioner for Refugees (UNHCR), the International Organization for Migration, and the World Food Program. Other non-state humanitarian actors that provide assistance to displaced persons include the International Committee of the Red Cross (ICRC), Doctors without Borders, and the Norwegian Refugee Council. A wider range of organizations would fall under the umbrella term *humanitarian*, and the arguments in this chapter not pertaining specifically to displacement are intended to represent the general disposition of humanitarian organizations. Other actors that work to resolve problems associated with displacement include those in the fields of development, human rights, and peacebuilding. Each group in this diverse range may have its own particular set of concerns, but the arguments presented here should have some relevance for those actors as well.

References to *transitional justice actors* will encompass both actors and institutions tasked with carrying out various measures and mandates aimed at redressing the legacies of massive human rights violations. These include nongovernmental organizations (NGOs) such as the International Center for Transitional Justice as well as UN bodies such as the Office of the High Commissioner for Human Rights that promote accountability for human rights violations and other aspects of transitional justice. The International Criminal Court (ICC), the International Criminal Tribunal for the Former Yugoslavia (ICTY), the International Criminal Tribunal for Rwanda (ICTR), various truth commissions, and reparations and restitution programs are examples of bodies carrying out transitional justice mandates that will also be referred to below as transitional justice actors or institutions.

CONCERNS AMONG HUMANITARIAN ACTORS ABOUT TRANSITIONAL JUSTICE: ENGAGEMENT AND ACCESS

Transitional justice is not praised by all segments of the humanitarian community. Discrepancies between the objectives and approaches of the two fields can cause tensions around such issues as the participation of displaced persons and the access of humanitarian groups to those populations. Displacement actors, and humanitarians in general, have a more immediate and focused mandate than transitional justice proponents. Their fundamental objective is to save lives while remaining impartial and neutral; while they may be explicitly committed to particular values, including human rights principles, they typically do not take sides in political debates and conflicts. Humanitarians must be willing to work with, or around, state and non-state actors to deliver critical aid to those in need. In contrast, transitional justice actors are often perceived as taking sides in matters concerning state and non-state actors, which can create unease among humanitarians. Transitional justice is inherently a political process, one that calls for public recognition of wrongdoing and various forms of accountability, including criminal justice. It implicates individuals as well as institutions and therefore provokes political resistance. Despite these basic differences in approach, though, an increasing tendency of humanitarian actors to take a rights-based approach is leading to recognition of the interests they share with transitional justice actors.[3] Notions such as protection and durable solutions, for example, are predicated on the protection and restoration of human rights. However, this rights-based approach is contested by humanitarians because of the potential for its political nature to undermine neutrality.

The recognition of common interests between humanitarian and transitional justice actors, however, does not always lead to collaboration or cooperation. One reason for this is that humanitarian actors are often no longer present when transitional justice measures are implemented.[4] However, transitional justice is increasingly being applied in countries where conflict and displacement are ongoing, such as Colombia. But even when humanitarian organizations are still present, working together is not the norm. Furthermore, IDPs and refugees are unlikely to be involved in the design or implementation of transitional justice programs,[5] which may leave humanitarian actors reluctant to collaborate with these programs.

A number of factors explain the historical lack of involvement of displaced persons in transitional justice efforts, though the combination of geographic dispersion and limited government capacity are both significant. Displaced populations are not static—returns, secondary displacements, and local integration are likely to occur simultaneously—often making it difficult (even when there is political will) to involve them in planning and operating transitional justice programs. The location of IDPs and refugees when transitional justice measures are implemented has implications for the impact of those programs on displaced persons. In some instances, refugees and IDPs may be located far from capital cities where truth commissions and criminal tribunals typically carry out their work. Camps are the easiest sites for gathering information on displaced populations and where many humanitarian actors focus their assistance; however, being located outside capital cities does not automatically mean the displaced are in camps. Most refugees and IDPs are dispersed in either rural or urban areas outside of camps, where it is harder for humanitarian, government, or transitional justice actors to reach them. Furthermore, IDPs find it much more difficult to maintain organizational ties developed in camps once they have left,[6] which affects their ability to participate in transitional justice and other processes.[7] But regardless of where they settle during displacement, inclusion of IDPs and refugees has not been a significant component of transitional justice measures. This may particularly be the case in ongoing and protracted displacement contexts.

Displacement actors also often feel that transitional justice initiatives do not deliver enough concrete benefits for refugees and IDPs. It can be trying enough for the displaced to see what they perceive as preferential treatment for ex-combatants through the benefits of a disarmament, demobilization, and reintegration program or impunity for human rights violators who were either directly or indirectly responsible for their displacement.[8] When transitional justice measures are set up and displaced persons are excluded, such that their particular justice claims and experiences go unaddressed, this frustration can be even greater. This is one reason to encourage greater coordination between displacement and transitional justice actors when circumstances dictate that their paths will cross in a given country context.

At the same time, operating in the same countries or responding to the same crises as transitional justice practitioners can generate additional sources of concern for humanitarian actors. For instance, both groups rarely have sufficient funding to carry out their work and may see each other as competitors for funding from donors. Responding to humanitarian emergencies is an expensive undertaking, and from a displacement perspective, not enough aid finds its way to assisting IDPs and refugees. Thus, although displacement actors may see value in transitional justice measures, they will understandably continue to prioritize their own efforts[9] and may view justice processes as hindering those efforts by absorbing scarce resources.

In addition to their concerns over funding competition, humanitarian actors may find access to their target populations disrupted because of the actions of others in pursuit of justice. The ICC is one example of a transitional justice institution that regularly receives criticism from the humanitarian community. Although criminal prosecutions are only one aspect of transitional justice, they are frequently cited as being the sort of politically charged initiative that can affect the work of humanitarian actors. One clear example of this effect was when humanitarian workers in Uganda were attacked after the ICC issued arrest warrants for leaders of the Lord's Resistance Army.[10] In retaliation for the court's actions toward the rebel group, the group made the entire international community present in the region a target for reprisals. In a similar scenario, humanitarian organizations were pestered, interfered with, and in some cases expelled from Darfur in retaliation for the criminal charges leveled by the ICC against President Omar al-Bashir of Sudan.

The Uganda and Darfur examples demonstrate that humanitarian and other groups can be put at risk or expelled from operational space whether or not they are associated with the transitional justice measures that provoke such responses.[11] Concern is even greater when humanitarians choose or are forced to cooperate directly with those measures, particularly when they involve providing evidence to criminal justice processes. Humanitarian workers often see firsthand the consequences of human rights abuses—deaths, mutilations, rapes, displacement, families torn apart. They hear directly from affected people every day, and many on a personal level want to see those responsible punished for their crimes, so they usually support efforts to bring perpetrators to justice. But working for humanitarian organizations limits their ability to get involved in justice issues, particularly during ongoing conflicts.

Humanitarians often wish to limit or avoid participation in transitional justice efforts for good reason. While free to support transitional justice efforts, they are not generally eager to offer evidence in specific criminal cases, because of the risk it may bring to themselves, their access, or the people they are trying to reach. Nevertheless, sometimes humanitarians' participation in criminal justice proceedings against human rights violators is not voluntary. The ICTY and ICTR carry the weight of article 7 of the UN Charter, which compels states to support requests for evidence from the courts.[12] The broad mandates given to the ICTY and ICTR also give these bodies the power to ensure organizations and individual actors provide evidence when called for.[13] In response to the requirement to testify, humanitarians can take a number of steps: request that the sources of their testimony not be revealed, seek special protection measures for the safety of witnesses, or appeal for a leave of absence to produce a written testimony from outside the country rather than appear in person.[14] Exceptions to the rule have been made—the ICRC, for example, enjoys testimonial immunity at the ICC—while certain loopholes and organizational policies have created workarounds for some additional humanitarian actors as well. For instance, in addition to the states not party to the Rome Statute, which are not bound to cooperate with the ICC, humanitarian organizations can find a similar reprieve by proving that their information is confidential and not subject to subpoena. The ICTY and ICTR have both worked around different legal challenges to exempt various actors, including humanitarians, a journalist, and an interpreter, from being forced to testify, so there are some protective precedents for humanitarian organizations fearful of the risks of involvement in transitional justice efforts.[15]

In sum, while some humanitarian actors have confidentially turned over evidence and information to prosecutors at international tribunals such as the ICTY and ICTR,[16] most keep a healthy distance from criminal justice mechanisms. Not only do they wish to avoid collecting or presenting evidence, there is also recognition that even to explicitly support the establishment of these mechanisms can be seen as a political act. Moreover, humanitarian agencies recognize that they may have to work in the future with those committing atrocities in order to ensure the provision of humanitarian relief.[17] The concerns that humanitarians have about transitional justice need to be taken seriously. It is important to note, however, that these concerns often focus on one element of transitional justice—namely, criminal justice—and that they are heightened in the particular contexts of ongoing conflict and displacement.

ADDRESSING THE CONCERNS OF HUMANITARIAN ACTORS ABOUT TRANSITIONAL JUSTICE

In this section, I argue that some of the ways in which transitional justice measures are designed and implemented can lessen humanitarian actors' anxiety about working alongside or collaborating with these programs. The adoption of a multifaceted approach should mitigate some concerns by demonstrating that transitional justice is not just about criminal justice but also requires reparations, truth-telling, and institutional reform. Furthermore, the timing and sequential nature of transitional justice measures can help augment the involvement of displaced persons in those measures, thus mitigating humanitarian concerns about their effectiveness.

A MULTIFACETED APPROACH TO TRANSITIONAL JUSTICE

Given that many of the concerns expressed by humanitarian actors about transitional justice are specific to criminal prosecutions, the endorsement of a multifaceted approach to transitional justice is, from a displacement perspective, an important consideration. While the term *holistic approach* has different connotations to different actors, in transitional justice it refers to the implementation of a set of multiple measures that are complementary, both practically and conceptually. These measures can include but are not limited to criminal prosecutions, truth-telling processes, reparations and restitution programs, and various types of institutional reform, such as vetting. As former UN secretary-general Kofi Annan said, "Where transitional justice is required, strategies must be holistic, incorporating integrated attention to individual prosecutions, reparations, truth-seeking, institutional reform, vetting and dismissals, or an appropriately conceived combination thereof."[18] Here I explore the answers to two questions: why is it theoretically and practically important that transitional justice be approached holistically, and how does such an approach affect IDPs and refugees and the work of humanitarian actors?

Before considering how a holistic approach might impact displacement, it is important to describe its relevance from a transitional justice perspective. Many transitional justice proponents support a holistic approach for theoretical and empirical reasons. On the theoretical level, Pablo de Greiff explains that the importance of undertaking a holistic approach is in some ways based on the acknowledgment that no single transitional justice measure will ever be a complete success. Not every violation of human rights will be punished, not every victim will be compensated in proportion to their suffering, and so on. In fact, most transitional justice programs will not directly affect individuals. Implementing multiple programs at once offers a means of overcoming the shortcomings of separate individual transitional justice initiatives conducted in isolation. Transitional justice measures adopted "haphazardly, piecemeal, and in isolation from one another" are less likely to be perceived "as instances of justice, and more as instances of expediency at best."[19] The strength of transitional justice measures, it is argued, lies in mutual reinforcement. Reparations programs are more effective if the money given to victims is accompanied by prosecutions of perpetrators of human rights abuses or truth-telling measures. Rather than creating a perception of "buying off" the disgruntled, reparations in conjunction with other transitional justice measures can indicate a sincere attempt to recognize the suffering of individuals. At the same time, criminal justice proceedings that produce limited numbers of convictions are also seen in a better light if attempts are being made to address those crimes through other means, such as through security sector reform (SSR), reparations, or truth-telling.[20]

A second theoretical reason for supporting a holistic approach to transitional justice measures is that they serve the purpose of reestablishing fundamental norms. Massive human rights abuses signal a breakdown of society and the basic principles of the social contract. Transitional justice hopes to foster civic trust and eventually democracy[21] in part by reaffirming social norms. Convincing the public, political elites, the perpetrators of violence, and perhaps even the international community that the state is on the right course and that basic norms are respected again requires a multifaceted strategy, thus necessitating a holistic approach to transitional justice.

Support for a holistic approach to transitional justice has been found empirically as well. Improving human rights protections and promoting democracy—two key goals of transitional justice programs—have been found to correlate with a multiple-program approach. Tricia Olsen, Leigh Payne, and Andrew Reiter examined the implementation of five different transitional justice measures: trials, truth commissions, amnesties, reparations, and lustration (which involves purging or barring state officials from positions because of their involvement in past abuses). The authors tested the impact of these five transitional justice measures on levels of democracy and human rights protection in 161 countries transitioning from autocracy to democracy or in postconflict settings. They found a statistically significant relationship between trials, amnesties, and truth commissions in various combinations. However, reparations and lustration (considered an element of SSR in this book) were not found to correlate with improvements in either democracy levels or human rights. The statistical analyses did not account for restitution programs and focused on amnesties and vetting policies rather than a more inclusive definition of SSR. The study's main contribution is in determining that a sequenced, multi-initiative approach to transitional justice is the most effective.

Olsen, Payne, and Reiter suggest two possible explanations as to why a holistic approach improves the effectiveness of transitional justice mechanisms in contributing to democracy and human rights. The first explanation (the second will be discussed in the next subsection) is that the combination of measures offers a moderate solution—not too focused on criminal justice, not too lenient on offenders—that might "suggest fairness and pragmatism by not holding all perpetrators equally accountable, but it may also demonstrate its willingness to prosecute egregious misconduct."[22] Romania, for example, is cited for its successful progress in human rights and democracy following its progression of transitional justice measures, which included trials and amnesties.[23] While the nature of the transition in Romania differs from the typical post–civil war narrative, the basic tenet of the argument remains. By taking a balanced approach, the justice measures were more successfully implemented and beneficial.

From a displacement perspective, holistic programming is critical because it underlines that transitional justice is *multifaceted—that it is more than just criminal justice.* As stated previously, the fear of being forced to or perceived as cooperating with criminal justice proceedings produces anxiety for humanitarian actors. The ICRC, for example, has made clear that it will not participate in legal proceedings via documentation or testimony at the ICC, while other humanitarian organizations have agreed to submit reports without the authors testifying in court.[24] Concerns about criminal justice measures are certainly legitimate, especially during ongoing conflict and displacement. However, a holistic approach to transitional justice includes a wider spectrum of activities that are less threatening to displacement actors than the typical criminal justice initiative. For example, housing, land, and property issues are key components in finding durable solutions to displacement and can be addressed by transitional justice practitioners through reparations and restitution programs.[25] While some advocates of restitution in Colombia have been targeted with violence, there is much greater agreement between displacement actors and transitional justice proponents over the importance of dealing with housing, land, and property issues for long-term success. A similarly harmonized approach led the Norwegian Refugee Council to help traditional leaders in Uganda more formally establish their rules for adjudicating land disputes.[26] In another example, UNHCR recognizes the importance of "establishing and acknowledging the truth about the past through the work of truth commissions, and by creating memorials and other forms of remembrance."[27] Clearly then, there is room for coexistence when the transitional justice approach is a multifaceted one that shares desired outcomes with displacement actors.

Financial and resource considerations, judicial institutional capacity, and political resistance are among the reasons why states may pursue limited criminal justice procedures alongside amnesties. The decision to limit the scope of criminal proceedings can be advantageous because "by limiting the number of trials, they avoid exhausting their economies in retrospective justice projects. Indeed, they can devote more funds to developing new institutions to protect human rights and democracy."[28] A multifaceted set of transitional justice measures, with limited criminal justice, therefore, may also be more welcomed by humanitarian and other displacement actors because it would not interfere with—and may even support—other state-building capacities developing in parallel.[29] This would have direct implications for creating durable solutions for the displaced. For example, rebuilding schools or medical clinics in wartorn areas benefits entire communities and has been used to facilitate the return of IDPs in northern Uganda.[30] The point is that a multifaceted approach to transitional justice should not be viewed as necessarily incompatible with the work of displacement actors.

TIMING AND SEQUENCING

The specific implications of a holistic, multifaceted transitional justice pro-gram for displaced persons and displacement actors will also depend on the timing of that program and the individual measures that comprise it. Since the operations of transitional justice actors can create difficulties for humanitar-ians, one solution from the displacement perspective would be for transitional justice actors to wait until the fighting ends and displacement is resolved to begin their initiatives. Some proponents of transitional justice may under-standably balk at the suggestion of delay, pointing to the potential value of jus-tice measures in bringing conflict and abuses to an end. As mentioned above, transitional justice measures are increasingly being implemented in contexts, such as Colombia, where conflict and displacement are ongoing. Furthermore, it is widely understood that displacement does not end when the fighting stops. According to UNHCR, durable solutions for refugees are reached when voluntary repatriation, local integration, or third-country resettlement has occurred.[31] Durable solutions for IDPs, as laid out in the Inter-Agency Standing Committee Framework on Durable Solutions for Internally Displaced Persons, are "achieved when IDPs no longer have specific assistance and protection needs that are linked to their displacement and such persons can enjoy their human rights without discrimination resulting from their displacement."[32] However the displaced reach this point, the process rarely occurs immediately. This is also true of responses to refugees, particularly in the case of third-coun-try resettlement. So even if transitional justice measures are implemented once armed conflict is over and return processes are underway, truly resolving dis-placement is a long-term, complex process that will likely still be underway when later transitional justice measures are adopted. It is therefore important to consider the implications of timing in more detail.

If displacement and transitional justice actors both need to be active in the same country environments, one way to mitigate concerns of the former would be to employ transitional justice mechanisms when they can maxi-mize participation among the displaced. This raises the issue of sequencing. In addition to balance and moderation, Olsen, Payne, and Reiter argue in their book that the success of the holistic approach can also be attributed to mea-sures being properly "sequenced rather than simultaneous."[33] Their study lists the time frame in which the transitional justice measures under consid-eration were adopted, allowing for a more nuanced analysis. What they found was that, for a host of reasons, transitional justice measures usually are not implemented immediately following a political transition: lustration occurs on average 2.2 years after a transition, amnesties 2.5 years, trials 4.2 years, reparations 5.5 years, and truth commission processes 5.6 years.[34] Using this data, they lay out a hypothetical sequence for transitional justice measures:

> Amnesty might be offered in the first few years, as the findings suggest. Once democracy is established, trials may arrive in the form of delayed justice. By this point, spoilers have largely accommodated themselves with the new democratic government, weakening their capacity to destabilize the system. The truths gathered through trials and truth commissions, and the accountability signaled by the human rights trials, send a warning about future transgressions of domestic and international human rights laws.[35]

Even with the best of intentions and sophisticated domestic capacities and international support, most countries are unlikely to unfurl a five-pronged program of criminal proceedings, a truth commission, a reparations program, a restitution initiative, and SSR measures at the same time. More likely, programming will be prioritized. While a prescriptive approach from the perspective of displacement actors may not be feasible, it is worth considering the possible implications of various sequences of transitional justice measures.

To begin with, transitional justice measures are usually implemented several years after the political transition occurs, by which time many returns will already have occurred. In Burundi, Liberia, and Sierra Leone, for example, the highest annual levels of IDP and refugee returns took place before transitional justice initiatives in those states began.[36] This is, of course, not always the case. But it does mean that as time passes, (1) transitional justice should be less likely to disrupt humanitarian access, and (2) actual physical displacement should play less of a role in preventing people from engaging with justice processes. However, Olsen, Payne, and Reiter have also found that a connection exists between one transitional justice measure and those that follow. Granting amnesties today might lead to the political stability required to conduct criminal trials in the future, for example. Such a connection suggests that the involvement of the displaced in one transitional justice measure should have a positive effect on their involvement in later measures.

The interconnectivity of various transitional justice programs and the potential benefits of their sequenced nature are easy to imagine. Take, for example, the possible spillover effects of restitution programs. As Barbara McCallin notes, recognition of housing, land, and property rights is a precondition for successful peacebuilding in post-conflict settings.[37] The former representative of the UN secretary-general on the human rights of IDPs, Walter

Kälin, argues, "If IDPs are not able to recover their land or property or other-wise find solutions allowing them to live decent lives and when they feel that they have suffered injustice, reconciliation becomes more difficult."[38] Being recognized as a property owner and allowed to return home or given compen-sation for the loss of property can go a long way toward aiding the displaced in regaining or improving their livelihoods. Moreover, former IDPs and refugees may as a result come to feel their rights have been recognized and respected, which is important in promoting reconciliation with their neighbors.[39] But most important in relation to other transitional justice measures, restitution can facilitate participation. Restitution programs can restart livelihoods by allowing individuals and families to return to their homes or resettle elsewhere after being compensated for their loss of land or property. Such relatively sound footing, albeit far from being a guaranteed result of most restitution programs, would then theoretically allow the formerly displaced to contribute to truth commissions, follow criminal justice proceedings, and push their gov-ernment to continue SSR efforts.

The same interconnectivity and potential spillover benefits can just as eas-ily be seen in other combinations of sequenced measures. Indeed, while the success of restitution programs in initially facilitating return could be built on by other transitional justice measures, so too could other forms of transitional justice pave the way for a restitution program. As Rhodri Williams points out in this book, restitution programs should be predicated on knowledge of the situation prior to the conflict. Restitution mechanisms therefore would be aided greatly by earlier truth-telling efforts or criminal trials that documented the violence that drove the displaced from their homes.[40] This is largely due to the frequency of competing claims to housing and other property in post-displacement situations. Governments and other actors can set guidelines for adjudicating decisions between rival claimants for property, but there are limi-tations to how successful such frameworks can be in these situations. Compet-ing property claims and disputed truths will have an unavoidable impact on how quickly the displaced are able to return to their homes, that is, if they can reclaim their properties from secondary occupants at all.[41] Therefore, estab-lishing the truth behind rival property claims—as they existed prior to conflict and displacement—would greatly facilitate a successful restitution program.

While there may not be an ideal sequence for transitional justice measures, how those measures are arranged might affect the degree to which the dis-placed are involved in their design and implementation. This applies beyond restitution. For example, early SSR efforts or prosecutions of those respon-sible for committing human rights violations may also encourage sustainable return by signaling an end to impunity and increase security in communities to which refugees and IDPs return—thereby facilitating participation in later justice initiatives.[42] The participation of displaced or formerly displaced persons in an early truth commission may increase the likelihood that transitional justice overall will respond to their specific justice claims. On the other hand, the absence of displaced persons from truth-telling programs could also alter the trajectory of subsequent transitional justice programs, with implications for both humanitarian and transitional justice actors. A truth commission that does not incorporate the abuses involved in the displacement of civilian populations will have spillover effects on later programs: the displaced could be less likely to receive adequate compensation from reparations or restitution initiatives, and the perpetrators of crimes could be more likely to escape punishment through the criminal justice system. The exclusion of IDPs and refugees from initial transitional justice measures, then, may ultimately result in less success for transitional justice efforts overall.

Again, the interconnectedness of transitional justice measures, or what de Greiff calls "a thick web," explains their positive and negative repercussions.[43] For transitional justice practitioners, this stresses the importance of a well-formulated, multifaceted approach. For displacement actors and humanitarians, it drives home the point that, regardless of the particular sequence of measures, IDPs and refugees should ideally be included from the beginning of the justice process. This will make it much more likely that the transitional justice program overall will lead to outcomes that are in the interests of displaced persons. And this is something that those working directly with displaced persons can facilitate, by contributing to sustainable return and by supporting their participation in early justice measures. Transitional justice and displacement actors can agree that piecemeal approaches to transitional justice have not served the interests of the displaced to date. Going forward, then, there is a clear need to support the idea of a displacement-conscious, holistic approach to transitional justice. Such an approach would benefit the work of both humanitarian and transitional justice actors.

CONCLUSION

In theory, the end of a conflict should signify a transition from the involvement of humanitarian actors to the active engagement of development and peacebuilding actors. A move from a focus on immediate, life-saving needs to long-term assistance in support of the peace process is usually what is needed.

An ineffective transition can lead to an unraveling of progress toward peaceful reconciliation and development, and the unfortunate end result can be a return to conflict and yet more displacement.[44] A well-balanced approach can sustain a transition away from the worst of the violence to sustained peace. Transitional justice and displacement actors have unique roles in such a transition. However, they also have points of commonality, such as the need to negotiate with or confront warring parties in order to carry out their objectives, the need to prioritize the protection of their staff members operating in ongoing conflict and post-conflict settings,[45] and pressure from donor governments to achieve concrete results.

Long-term solutions to the problems targeted by both sets of actors are in many ways interdependent, and lasting results are increasingly seen as dependent on the connections between security, peace, and justice. For example, a peace settlement that does not include adequate security provisions and new institutional arrangements to more justly deal with conflict is more likely to regress back into violence.[46] In fact, displacement and transitional justice are connected around these three crucial elements,[47] and the displaced are at risk when any of them are neglected. IDPs and refugees are inherently in precarious situations and are frequently at risk of violence, so systemic changes to address their security, political, and human rights needs and provide a chance for them to live in peace are closely linked. In other words, transitional justice goals are well suited to provide the necessary conditions for the achievement of durable solutions for IDPs and refugees. States' goals of effective peacebuilding and development are also placed at risk by a lack of security, peace, or justice. Given the connection between these goals and the consequences of not achieving them, cooperation or, at a minimum, coexistence between humanitarian and transitional justice actors during conflict and throughout transition is essential.

As a whole, however, humanitarians have not enthusiastically supported transitional justice measures for a number of reasons. Central to their concerns are the lack of involvement of the displaced in typical transitional justice measures and the potential for transitional justice programming to interfere with the goals of humanitarian actors. There are also undeniable differences between the two sets of actors in their fundamental objectives and engagement with the communities they serve. Delivering life-saving assistance and fostering more democratic and just societies over time are both laudable objectives, but they require different approaches and methods. At times, humanitarian organizations have resented and resisted sharing operational space with transitional justice actors, and tensions between them can be augmented during conflict and by requests to assist in criminal justice proceedings by providing testimony or evidence. That being said, humanitarian and transitional justice actors have clear reasons to overcome these concerns to foster a healthier working arrangement. Approaches that consider the displaced in relation to the multifaceted nature, timing, and sequencing of transitional justice could go a long way toward addressing the concerns of displacement actors about transitional justice. In particular, the use of nonjudicial elements of transitional justice in tandem with criminal justice measures and the extended period over which these programs are implemented should mitigate some of these concerns and offer opportunities for collaboration. Hopefully, this discussion will serve as a starting point for further research to test these ideas on the ground.

NOTES

1   Whether the galvanizing force is the emergence of the "responsibility to protect" or simply a shared interest in assisting and empowering victims and vulnerable groups, more types of organizations are taking part in responses to mass human suffering. International Center for Transitional Justice, "Meeting on Transitional Justice and Humanitarian Concerns" (conference report, May 16–17, 2006), 2–3.

2   See Pablo de Greiff and Roger Duthie, eds., *Transitional Justice and Development: Making Connections* (New York: Social Science Research Council, 2009); and Brookings-Bern Project on Internal Displacement, *Addressing Internal Displacement in Peace Processes, Peace Agreements and Peace-Building* (Washington, DC: Brookings Institution / University of Bern, September 2007).

3   Peter D. Bell, "International Relief and Development NGOs and the International Justice System" (paper prepared for the Consultative Conference on International Criminal Justice, United Nations, New York, September 9–11, 2009), 2, http://reliefweb.int/sites/reliefweb.int/files/resources/3C4044C03B792832C12576340048C91D-intlcriminaljustice-session6.pdf.

4   Patricia Weiss Fagen, "Peace Processes and IDP Solutions," *Refugee Survey Quarterly* 28, no. 1 (2009): 32.

5   Ibid.

6 Ibid., 58.

7 See Awa Dabo, "In the Presence of Absence: Transitional Justice and Displacement in Liberia" (paper prepared for ICTJ / Brookings Project on Transitional Justice and Displacement, 2012).

8 Erika Feller, "Giving Peace a Chance: Displacement and Rule of Law During Peacebuilding," *Refugee Survey Quarterly* 28, no. 1 (2009): 86. See also Ana Cutter Patel, Pablo de Greiff, and Lars Waldorf, eds., *Disarming the Past: Transitional Justice and Ex-Combatants* (New York: Social Science Research Council, 2010).

9 Weiss Fagen, "Peace Processes," 57.

10 Anne-Marie La Rosa, "Humanitarian Organizations and International Criminal Tribunals, or Trying to Square the Circle," *International Review of the Red Cross* 88, no. 861 (March 2006): 170.

11 Governments have dozens of ways to make the lives of humanitarians difficult short of violence or expulsion: they can make the visa process more difficult for foreign aid workers, raise unnecessary bureaucratic procedures for getting relief supplies into the country, and manipulate exchange rates to make humanitarian efforts more expensive. The Sudanese government even read e-mails of international NGO staff. Elizabeth Ferris, interviews with NGO community.

12 Kate Mackintosh, "How Far Can Humanitarian Organisations Control Co-operation with International Tribunals?" *Journal of Humanitarian Assistance* (May 2005): 2–3.

13 La Rosa, "Humanitarian Organizations," 172.

14 Ibid., 172–73.

15 Ibid., 170–75. Doctors without Borders has pursued a similar approach, allowing it to provide evidence "to facilitate investigations, but not to build cases for prosecution." Françoise Bouchet-Saulnier and Fabien Dubuet, "Legal or Humanitarian Testimony? History of MSF's Interactions with Investigations and Judicial Proceedings," Cahiers du CRASH (Paris: Centre de Réflexion sur l'Action et les Savoirs Humanitaires / Fondation MSF, 2007), 12, http://www.msf-crash.org/en/publications/2009/05/25/130/legal-or-humanitarian-testimony-history-of-mfss-interactions-with-investigations-and-judicial-proceedings/.

16 Mackintosh, "Co-operation with International Tribunals," 8.

17 Larry Minear and Hazel Smith, eds., *Humanitarian Diplomacy: Practitioners and Their Craft* (New York: UN University Press, 2007).

18 United Nations Security Council, "The Rule of Law and Transitional Justice in Conflict and Post-conflict Societies," Report of the Secretary-General, S/2004.616, August 23, 2004, http://www.unhcr.org/4506bc494.html.

19 Pablo de Greiff, "Theorizing Transitional Justice," in *NOMOS LI: Transitional Justice*, ed. Melissa Williams, Rosemary Nagy, and Jon Elster (New York: New York University Press, 2012).

20 Ibid.

21 Ibid.

22 Tricia D. Olsen, Leigh A. Payne, and Andrew G. Reiter, *Transitional Justice in Balance: Comparing Processes, Weighing Efficacy* (Washington, DC: USIP Press, 2010), 147–48.

23 Ibid., 146–47.

24 The ICRC will, however, "provide to any party that requests them documents that have already been made public, something which has been done on a number of occasions." La Rosa, "Humanitarian Organizations," 171–72.

25 See Rhodri Williams, in this volume.

26 Barbara McCallin, "Transitional Justice, HLP Restitution, and Legal Pluralism" (paper prepared for ICTJ / Brookings Project on Transitional Justice and Displacement, 2012).

27 Feller, "Giving Peace a Chance," 93.

28 Olsen, Payne, and Reiter, *Transitional Justice in Balance*, 156.

29 See, for example, Naomi Roht-Arriaza and Katharine Orlovsky, "A Complementary Relationship: Reparations and Development," in de Greiff and Duthie, *Transitional Justice and Development*.

30 Charles Uma, District Disaster Management Committee chairperson, Gulu, interview with author, June 30, 2011.

31 Office of the United Nations High Commissioner for Refugees, "Durable Solutions," http://www.unhcr.org/pages/49c3646cf8.html

32 Brookings-Bern Project on Internal Displacement, *IASC Framework on Durable Solutions for Internally Displaced Persons* (Washington, DC: Brookings Institution / University of Bern, April 2010), 5, http://www.brookings.edu/reports/2010/04_durable_solutions.aspx.

33 Olsen, Payne, and Reiter, *Transitional Justice in Balance*, 148.

34 Ibid., 106–7.

35 Ibid., 147–49.

36 Return data based on UNHCR statistics. UNHCR Statistical Online Population Database, http://www.unhcr.org/pages/4a013eb06.html, accessed May 24, 2011.

37 McCallin, "Transitional Justice, HLP Restitution." Again, unfortunately, restitution programs were not included in the Olsen, Payne, and Reiter study, so future research will be required to determine the impact that restitution programs have in improving transitional justice outcomes from a quantitative empirical perspective.

38 Walter Kälin, "No Durable Solutions for the Displaced without Sustainable Peace— No Sustainable Peace without Durable Solutions" (speech on displaced populations and peace negotiations in Africa, UNHCR ExCom Side Event, Geneva, October 4, 2007), http://www.brookings.edu/~/media/Files/Projects/IDP/RSG%20Arts%20 Stmts/1004peace.pdf.

39 John Paul Lederach, *Building Peace: Sustainable Reconciliation in Divided Societies* (Washington, DC: USIP Press, 1997), 28.

40 Transitional justice actors should avoid a simple and potentially unjust return to the status quo ante that may have been a driving force behind the conflict. Williams, in this volume.

41 Rhodri C. Williams mentions that the displaced should be given the benefit of the doubt when possible. "The Contemporary Right to Property Restitution in the Context of Transitional Justice" (ICTJ Occasional Paper Series, International Center for Transitional Justice, New York, May 2007), http://www.brookings.edu/~/media/Files/rc/articles/2007/0531propertyrestitution_williams/20070531.pdf.

42 See Roger Duthie and Marina Caparini, in this volume.

43 De Greiff, "Theorizing Transitional Justice," 6.

44 Feller, "Giving Peace a Chance," 94.

45 Bell, "International Relief and Development NGOs," 3.

46 Caroline Hartzell, Matthew Hoddie, and Donald Rothchild, "Stabilizing the Peace after Civil War: An Investigation of Some Key Variables," *International Organization* 55, no. 1 (Winter 2001): 183–208.

47 Feller, "Giving Peace a Chance," 83. Another general threat is impunity. See William O'Neill, "Internal Displacement and Peacebuilding," *Refugee Survey Quarterly* 28, no. 1 (2009): 158–59.

CHAPTER 3

Protection in the Past Tense:
Restitution at the Juncture of Humanitarian
Response to Displacement and Transitional Justice

Rhodri C. Williams

Protection of individuals has come to play a central role across a range of fields concerned with ameliorating human suffering and bettering the human condition. The longstanding concept of protection as a fundamental obligation of states with regard to their citizens has been affirmed and progressively expanded by post–World War II developments such as the expansion of international law to protect civilians caught in conflicts as well as refugees fleeing persecution. Perhaps the most significant development during this period has been the establishment of human rights law and its post–Cold War amalgamation with related fields of activity ranging from humanitarian response to development. The adoption of rights-based approaches by actors in these fields has been accompanied by a new understanding that states are not merely expected but obligated to protect the lives, integrity, property, welfare, and dignity of individuals within their jurisdiction. Indeed, humanitarian responses to the post–Cold War phenomenon of internal displacement have been structured around the idea of "sovereignty as responsibility," which links state legitimacy to the protection of rights.[1]

The field of transitional justice can be viewed as a product of human rights promotion that is, as such, similarly infused with protection concerns. Transitional justice shares key attributes with both humanitarian response and development. In common with humanitarian response, transitional justice seeks to address the effects of past or ongoing violations and failures to protect individuals. However, transitional justice also posits that sustainable future protection requires the achievement of representative and accountable forms of democratic governance, in a manner that evokes normative developments in related fields.[2] For instance, the development field has been the cradle of the concept of "human security," which reorients the security concept from an exclusive focus on military protection against external threats to one that encompasses the social and economic protection of individuals and communities.[3] The human security concept, together with the principle of sovereignty as responsibility, formed the intellectual underpinnings for the UN General

Assembly's 2005 adoption of the "responsibility to protect" (R2P) doctrine.[4] By sanctioning the failure to protect civilian populations from atrocities with the threat of a UN-authorized intervention, the R2P doctrine represents the extent to which protection of rights has permeated international governance.

One relatively narrow area of normative development that has come to prominence during this period has been the assertion of a right to the restitution of housing, land, and property (HLP) assets in the wake of displacement of civilian populations. Restitution, in the form of the physical and legal restoration of wrongfully taken assets, was initially presented as a practical necessity for reversing the effects of ethnic cleansing in conflict settings such as Bosnia, but it rapidly came to be posited as a general post-conflict right of displaced persons through the dissemination of standards such as the 2005 "Pinheiro Principles."[5] Dominant contemporary understandings of the significance of restitution have been shaped by international responses to displacement and are primarily humanitarian in nature. However, restitution has its conceptual roots in traditional rules governing remedies for breaches of international law obligations and is related to transitional justice measures involving reparations for the victims of human rights abuses.[6]

In practice, humanitarian and transitional justice approaches to restitution appear to be converging around a shared reparations concept. This is demonstrated most clearly by the post–Cold War tendency of humanitarian actors to condemn egregious forms of displacement (such as ethnic cleansing) as violations of international law and to promote restitution explicitly as a "remedy for displacement."[7] Nevertheless, in both transitional justice and displacement settings, reparations in the form of property restitution present a number of common operational and conceptual challenges. In this chapter, I argue that while the operational challenges presented by restitution are susceptible to practical solutions, the conceptual challenges go to the heart of a fundamental question hanging over both transitional justice initiatives and humanitarian responses to displacement: whether such measures can and should attempt to deal with the root causes or merely the immediate results of systematic human rights violations.[8] A related, and more functional, question relates to whether restitution, as conceived of in humanitarian settings, can contribute to the transitional justice goals of retrospectively redressing violations and prospectively facilitating transition to democracy.

In both cases, I counsel caution. Measures such as restitution should be promoted based on the circumstances of a particular setting; the likelihood that they will contribute to the jointly held aims of humanitarian, transitional justice, and development actors; and the capacity and resources (both domestic and international) that are available to see them through. Calls for better coordination and complementarity reflect the need for such actors to mutually respect each other's broad areas of competence and avoid taking uncoordinated steps that could complicate each other's work.[9] Restitution has raised problematic issues in this context in part because it involves activities that straddle these three broad fields.[10] In this complicated institutional context, humanitarian conceptions of rights-based protection provide an analytical framework that highlights both distinctions and areas of overlap between humanitarian response and the complementary fields of transitional justice and development.

While humanitarians tend to focus on *responsive* measures meeting the immediate protection needs of the displaced, for instance, restitution represents an exceptional area in which humanitarian actors engage retrospectively with *remedial* questions related to addressing the effects of past violations involving displacement. Transitional justice practitioners view such remedial measures as a core activity but implement them with a view to simultaneously promoting prospective *environment-building* objectives related to reconciliation and democracy. Finally, development actors may support calls for restitution as a means of demonstrating respect for property rights or oppose them as the antithesis of necessary land tenure reforms, but they can rarely afford to ignore them, even in their largely prospectively oriented work.

In this chapter, I explore these issues from the perspective of the increasing engagement of humanitarian actors concerned with displacement with the principles and practices of transitional justice and development. The first section describes the evolving rationale for addressing property disputes in displacement settings, beginning with the early post–Cold War tendency to subordinate restitution to the physical return of displaced persons and moving to the later promotion of restitution as a right in itself, as well as more recent tendencies to treat it as equivalent to other forms of reparation. The next section explores the conceptual foundations of humanitarian response, transitional justice, and to a lesser extent development, describing where these areas overlap based on their respective modes of rights protection. As this analysis places restitution at the juncture of these three fields, the third section explores practical considerations related to restitution and how it can support the aims of transitional justice in light of these conceptual issues. I focus in particular on addressing root causes and prior patterns of group exclusion from the exercise of property rights. Throughout, I draw on relevant practice and scholarship in suggesting ways forward compatible with the aims of ending displacement and promoting transitional justice and broader development.

EVOLVING APPROACHES TO POST-CONFLICT PROPERTY RESTITUTION

The current prominence of restitution in post-conflict settings is a function of its embrace by humanitarian actors interested in addressing displacement. However, humanitarian responses to displacement can be divided into two phases that are quite distinct both chronologically and conceptually. The first, stretching from the interwar period through the end of the Cold War, was concerned mainly with the protection of refugees, or persons displaced across international borders. The rules of international refugee law that were developed during this period emphasize the duties of participating states to provide international protection to refugees coming from elsewhere, rather than imputing legal responsibility to the states of origin for having failed to provide protection. This approach is classically humanitarian in its responsive concern with alleviating current suffering rather than addressing root causes and was initially characterized by scant interest in restitution.

Since the end of the Cold War, humanitarian concerns have shifted to focus on internal displacement. Internally displaced persons (IDPs) share with refugees the essential vulnerability of having been uprooted from homes, livelihoods, and social networks, except that IDPs remain within their countries of origin. The response to internal displacement has emphasized the human rights aspects of displacement to a degree previously unprecedented in humanitarian activities. In fact, IDP advocacy has been one of the primary drivers of the new rights-based paradigm for humanitarianism. This approach emphasizes that even the provision of basic assistance, such as food and shelter, has important human rights protection overtones that humanitarian actors should be aware of and consciously incorporate in their work.[11] The human rights focus in the internal displacement field has in some respects made it a substantively different type of humanitarian response to displacement than classic international refugee law. While responses to internal displacement primarily focus on the current protection of IDPs' rights against immediate threats arising during displacement, they have consistently included a remedial element in the form of calls for restitution.

In fact, the emergence of post-conflict property restitution is closely linked to the simultaneous post–Cold War development of humanitarian responses to internal displacement, as reflected by its prominence in the Guiding Principles on Internal Displacement. Although early steps toward institutionalizing restitution as a response to mass displacement were taken in the course of early 1990s peacebuilding processes, the Guiding Principles represented the first general assertion of a state duty to restore property or provide compensation to displaced persons. Notably, the manner in which this obligation was phrased identified it clearly as remedial—that is, as a form of "just reparation."[12] As acceptance of post-conflict restitution spread, a new UN standard-setting process formalized this remedial approach further through the 2005 promulgation of the Pinheiro Principles.[13] In the meantime, even the international refugee law discourse, which traditionally eschewed discussion of state-of-origin responsibilities in favor of reinforcing international protection by refugee-hosting states, has embraced restitution as a means of ensuring the sustainability of repatriation processes.[14]

General support for restitution as a response to displacement and an element of peacebuilding has remained high, and mechanisms for restitution have become a nearly standard component of peace agreements. However, an extensive debate has also focused on the proper scope and nature of restitution, as well as its effectiveness in meeting various postdisplacement justice claims. This section traces the evolution of restitution norms, approaches, and understandings from the early 1990s to the present date, tracing three phases during which restitution programs shifted, respectively, from being understood purely as a mechanism for bringing about the humanitarian aim of durable solutions (and return in particular), to being viewed as a per se right (one aptly applied as a remedy to displacement), to their most recent incarnation as one policy option among many in remedial responses to post-conflict property disputes that may require either distributive or corrective approaches.

EARLY RESTITUTION AND THE DEVELOPMENT OF THE BOSNIA MODEL

The origins of contemporary understandings of human rights–based reparations and restitution can in part be found in the model of interstate reparations for breaches of international law. Such reparations were meant to discourage states from violating their obligations to each other by restoring the status quo ante as though the breach had never happened. This corrective policy motivated a preference for the actual restitution of disputed assets over alternative remedies such as compensation. This preference was famously expressed by the interwar Permanent Court of International Justice in a 1928 ruling, *Factory at Chorzow (Germany v. Poland)*:

> The essential principle contained in the actual notion of an illegal act ... is that reparation must, as far as possible, wipe out all the consequences of the illegal act and reestablish the situation which would, in all probability, have existed if that act had not been committed.[15]

The UN's embrace of human rights, and particularly the adoption of the Universal Declaration of Human Rights in 1948, saw the migration of this concept from interstate disputes to the domestic, constitutional relationship between states and their citizens.[16] The "right to a domestic remedy" (for human rights violations) established in article 8 of the declaration and reproduced in many subsequent global and regional human rights treaties focused on procedural remedies—that is, access to an impartial adjudicator.[17] With time, however, an obligation to provide substantive remedies such as restitution has also come to be understood as a component of the right to a remedy in human rights law. This new understanding was formalized in 2005 through the adoption of the "Van Boven-Bassiouni Principles," which assert rights to both procedural and substantive reparations.[18]

In parallel to these normative developments, property restitution also emerged as a practical tool for correcting injustice during the sweeping political changes in Eastern Europe and South Africa at the end of the Cold War. In Eastern Europe, restitution was employed as a means of symbolically wiping out the Cold War era by seeking to restore a set of property relations that preceded it.[19] As critics later noted, restitution on these terms was not only selective, frequently on the basis of ethnicity, but also liable to arbitrary implementation in practice.[20] Meanwhile, in South Africa, a restrained approach to property restitution was applied, with white owners of confiscated land initially entitled to be bought out at market prices.[21] In both Eastern Europe and South Africa, property restitution programs went forward as key components of transitional justice programs that included elements of truth-telling, prosecution, and institutional reform but largely neglected reparations for victims of non-property-related abuses.[22]

European and South African programs raised the profile of restitution, giving it credence as a policy response that could be applied in post-conflict settings as well.[23] The perceived need for such approaches increased during the 1990s, as increased levels of migration and an economic downturn in industrialized countries eroded political support for generous asylum policies. These factors contributed to a shift in emphasis in international refugee policy from assuming that refugees would be unable to return to their countries of origin to assuming the opposite as a matter of course. A new emphasis on repatriation as the preferred durable solution for refugees was accompanied by policies designed to make it more difficult for refugees to enter countries of asylum and easier to repatriate them (even at the risk of returning them to internal displacement, in some cases). In the context of these shifts in refugee policy, it was both practically and morally expedient to seek ways to make repatriation and return sustainable, and restitution of homes offered one of the most obvious means of reanchoring displaced persons in a social fabric that might prevent them from being uprooted again.[24]

A succession of peace agreements in the early 1990s included provisions on repatriation and return and bolstered them with increasingly concrete obligations to address the property claims of returnees. The watershed came with the 1995 General Framework Agreement for Peace (GFAP) that ended the conflict in Bosnia and established restitution as a practical mechanism for achieving the overriding goal of the return of displaced persons to their places of origin. This relationship was implicit in the phrasing of annex 7 of the GFAP, which regulated displacement issues:

> All refugees and displaced persons have the right freely to return to their homes of origin. They shall have the right to have restored to them property of which they were deprived in the course of hostilities since 1991 and to be compensated for any property that cannot be restored to them. The early return of refugees and displaced persons is an important objective of the settlement of the conflict in Bosnia.[25]

Property restitution commitments in the GFAP were promoted with the unambiguous aim of achieving sustainable return and reconstituting a multiethnic country. In pursuing this goal, international actors largely ignored provisions of the GFAP allowing for monetary compensation under some circumstances and protecting the right of displaced persons to make voluntary decisions on return.[26] However, international monitors soon observed that the subordination of restitution rights to a return policy posed the risk that displaced persons would be arbitrarily dispossessed if they did not choose to return.[27] As a result, property restitution was reframed as a freestanding legal right to be given effect without regard to decisions by beneficiaries on whether to return.[28] This new approach still favored restitution as the only legal remedy capable of supporting truly voluntary decisions on durable solutions. Restitution, it was argued, not only facilitated return but also afforded displaced persons income and assets (through sale, rental, or exchange of restituted properties) that could help them with local integration elsewhere. By contrast, remedies based solely on compensation allowed local integration but precluded return. In part as a result of this policy, the Bosnian authorities achieved the extraordinary accomplishment of processing two hundred thousand restitution claims within a decade of the end of the war. However, the emphasis on restitution led to the neglect of compensation-based remedies for persons whose properties were impossible to restore.[29]

As the potential relevance of the lessons learned in Bosnia to other post-conflict settings began to sink in, restitution there came to stand for two principles. First, decisions on durable solutions were to be made in an informed and voluntary manner by the displaced rather than imposed by national elites or international administrators based on policy preferences.[30] Second, however, restitution was to be prioritized over compensation and other alternative remedies for loss of property rights during displacement, on the theory that restitution alone creates the conditions for meaningful choice of durable solutions. The ascendance of this "Bosnia model" for return and restitution coincided with emerging consciousness among transitional justice practitioners of the need to give greater attention to reparations for victims.[31] Restitution began to take the form of a common frame of reference as key international standards that anchored the Bosnia model in broader humanitarian practice presented it explicitly in terms of reparations for displacement-related rights violations.

The first of these documents was the Guiding Principles on Internal Displacement, which set out for the first time a general state obligation to provide restitution for property left behind by IDPs. Although the duty asserted in principle 29 was only one among a myriad of provisions protecting IDPs' rights, its inclusion represented the single most progressive element in a standard that broke new ground in many respects.[32] The Guiding Principles reflect lessons drawn from the Bosnia experience in both affirming the voluntary nature of durable solutions (principle 28) and prioritizing restitution over compensation through the proviso that such subsidiary forms of reparation should only be considered in case restitution was not possible (principle 29). The drafters of the Guiding Principles derived their authority on these points by reference to both practice in Bosnia and to the broader right to a remedy, including reparations, in international human rights law.[33] In doing so, they explicitly identified both restitution and compensation as forms of just reparation to dispossessed IDPs.

The elements of the Bosnia model—as well as its professed relationship to reparations—were most clearly spelled out seven years later. In 2005 UN special rapporteur Paulo Sergio Pinheiro presented Principles on Housing and Property Restitution for Refugees and Displaced Persons (the Pinheiro Principles) to the UN Sub-Commission on Human Rights. Unlike the Guiding Principles on Internal Displacement, the Pinheiro Principles focus exclusively on property issues and aspire to "assist all relevant actors ... in addressing the legal and technical issues surrounding ... restitution in [displacement] situations."[34] In their central prescriptions, the Pinheiro Principles again reflect the key conclusions drawn from Bosnian restitution, anchored in the discourses of both displacement and reparations. Most obviously, they support voluntary durable solutions, affirming restitution as a distinct right, "prejudiced neither by the actual return nor non-return of refugees and displaced persons."[35] However, the Pinheiro Principles also go considerably further than other standards by exhorting states to "demonstrably prioritize the right to restitution as the preferred remedy for displacement and as a key element of restorative justice" and concluding that compensation should only be permissible for "property that is factually impossible to restore as determined by an independent, impartial tribunal."[36] Later, this standard is defined as relating primarily to "material impossibility" in the limited situations in which the property at stake "is destroyed or when it no longer exists."[37]

International reception of the two documents has also followed different trajectories, in part because of the nature of the advocacy campaigns that have served to promote them. The Guiding Principles were presented in 1998 to the UN Human Rights Commission.[38] Despite concerns that member states had been denied a role in drafting them, the principles were "taken note of" by the commission.[39] This cool but essentially positive reception laid the ground for the Guiding Principles to become the centerpiece of a concerted advocacy effort that targeted states affected by displacement. This campaign was characterized by a technical capacity-building approach that sought to convince states that partnership with international agencies in addressing displacement was in their interests and fully compatible with respect for their sovereignty.[40] The office of the representative of the UN secretary-general on the human rights of IDPs has also been central to advocacy for the Guiding Principles.[41] As a result of these factors, the principles have won broad recognition. They have been operationalized by UN and other international humanitarian actors,[42] promoted by numerous regional organizations, incorporated in the world's first regional treaty on internal displacement in 2009,[43] and applied through domestic law and policies on displacement by several dozen states.[44]

By contrast, the Pinheiro Principles have lacked both a UN-mandated advocate along the lines of the representative of the secretary-general and a similarly clear advocacy strategy toward the states responsible for their application.[45] Despite winning significant support in a number of peacebuilding settings, they have yet to be widely applied through national laws and policies reflecting their provisions.[46] As a result, the most significant achievement of the Pinheiro Principles to date may be the manner in which they initially came to dominate the humanitarian discourse on restitution. UNHCR and the UN Human Settlement Program (UN-HABITAT) were early advocates of more systematic approaches to property issues and the incorporation of the Pinheiro Principles into UN operations.[47] UNHCR regularly engages with restitution issues in the field but has been reluctant to take an interagency lead on such matters given the numerous other protection issues requiring its attention.[48] UN-HABITAT received a formal lead on HLP issues (including restitution) in the context of ongoing humanitarian reform efforts aimed at greater international coordination.[49] Despite the progress represented by formal recognition of the significance of HLP issues in humanitarian settings, however, the practical impact of these efforts has been limited to date.[50]

In the decade following the end of the war in Bosnia, restitution went from humble beginnings as a policy mechanism to help promote the return of displaced persons to being accepted as an emerging right. Restitution was still central to voluntary durable solutions for displaced persons (whether return or resettlement elsewhere) but was also arguably mandatory in cases where acts causing displacement and related usurpation of property gave rise to an obligation to provide reparations to victims. However, at this stage restitution also remained largely untested.

REASSESSING RESTITUTION

In 2007 the UN secretary-general proposed a number of concrete measures to improve responses to post-conflict property issues.[51] The following year, a meeting was held in Oslo to celebrate the broad acceptance achieved by the Guiding Principles on Internal Displacement during its first decade.[52] However, it was noted at the time that whatever the merits of the Bosnia model for property restitution in theory, practice on the ground remained thin and inconsistent.[53] Indeed, during the same year, the third major initiative to provide property restitution to IDPs in Colombia collapsed,[54] and a promising restitution program in Iraq began to visibly stall, with one observer subsequently estimating that "many more years, if not decades," would be required to complete the remaining caseload.[55]

The utility of restitution had, by this time, already been questioned in a number of humanitarian settings characterized by significantly different outset conditions than those encountered in Bosnia. For instance, Daniel Fitzpatrick noted early on that property relations had been so fiercely contested for such a long time in Timor-Leste that there might not be any mutually agreeable "status quo ante" that all parties would feel should be restored through a corrective restitution program.[56] Similarly, land tenure expert Liz Alden Wily questioned the value of restitution in the context of repatriation of refugees to Afghanistan in 2004, pointing out that many if not most of the displaced had been landless or land hungry prior to displacement.[57] Meanwhile, Koen Vlassenroot and Chris Huggins noted that conflict in the eastern Democratic Republic of Congo had swept away a pattern of corrupt and highly inequitable land relations that hardly merited being restored.[58] Although subsequent violence and displacement has emphasized the disputed and unstable nature of land relations in all of these settings, strict insistence on a return to the pre-conflict status quo does not stand out as the optimal outcome in any of them.

Meanwhile, the Norwegian Refugee Council, which has developed unparalleled insights into postdisplacement property claims as a result of its numerous legal advising programs in post-conflict countries, frequently found itself forced to abandon unrealistic restitution paradigms in favor of negotiating agreements before customary dispute resolution bodies by which displaced communities would share their lands with subsequent occupiers.[59] As noted by Barbara McCallin, such land-sharing arrangements run counter to the spirit of the Pinheiro Principles but tend to predominate in settings where weak or discredited state capacities leave local customary bodies as the sole effective recourse—and where customary norms tying valid possession of land to uninterrupted use support current users in seeking a compromise with displaced claimants.[60]

Mounting unease with the corrective approach embodied by the Pinheiro Principles found its most forceful expression in the conclusions of a research program initiated by the Overseas Development Institute (ODI) in London.[61] Among the contributors, land tenure experts familiar with development practice dismissed the Pinheiro Principles as shortsighted, dogmatic, and potentially counterproductive in humanitarian settings.[62] Some of these criticisms missed the point by equating restitution of property with return of people (the same mistake that early humanitarian actors made in Bosnia). However, while the Pinheiro Principles do not condition restitution on return, as discussed earlier, they do arguably reflect a residual return bias in the notion of restitution as "the preferred remedy for displacement and as a key element of restorative justice."[63] This corrective approach regards the legal reconstruction of predisplacement property relations as a precondition for those affected by displacement to make free choices regarding return.

The ODI authors, by contrast, introduced a distributive viewpoint in querying whether justice may best be served in some cases by transforming pre-conflict land relations rather than restoring them. They also noted that the corrective outlook embodied in the Bosnia model is built on a set of assumptions about land relations relevant to the European countries where this approach was forged that do not apply to the many postcolonial, developing, and agrarian economies currently most closely correlated with violent conflict and displacement. The central issue in such settings is typically the need to move beyond the conditions that prevailed before displacement rather than to recreate them.

The clearest distributive justice arguments arise in development settings where land relations have been a chronic source of conflict. Examples include Latin American countries where land has been concentrated in the hands of postcolonial elites to the detriment of both indigenous peoples and ordinary *campesinos* long since relegated to tenant-farmer or seasonal-laborer status.[64] Where, as in much of Africa, subsistence farmers have maintained possession of land but without formal recognition of any legal rights, they are denied the full value of their land and live under the constant threat of eviction. Finally, where, again as in Africa, ostensibly nonautochthonous groups deemed to have arrived more recently to a region or country are arbitrarily denied land rights, conflict can ensue.[65] In such settings, strictly corrective restitution programs could end up inadvertently recreating land relations that development experts had been seeking to transform, precisely because they were so unjust or unsustainable that conflict could ensue.

ODI contributors questioned broader humanitarian assumptions, such as the implicit supposition that displacement is inherently of a temporary or exceptional nature. Several authors noted that displacement often simply represents a brutal acceleration of longstanding urbanization trends in developing settings, rather than an easily reversible aberration.[66] Others elaborated on conflict-sensitive concerns about restitution, noting that the inflexibility of the Pinheiro Principles reduces the discretion of parties to conflicts to make concessions in this area that would achieve the overarching goal of peace.[67] While critics of the Bosnia model did not uniformly deny that restitution remains an appropriate response in many settings, they accused humanitarians of having succumbed to a form of "displacement bias" that obscured the need to consider other, more distributive approaches in settings where reform was more badly needed than corrective justice. Against this background, they argued that it was not only counterproductive but also "dangerous to limit engagement on land and property issues to the mechanical application of the Pinheiro Principles."[68]

Such doubts about the wisdom of prioritizing restitution over other remedial responses quickly made their mark on humanitarian policy, as reflected by the December 2009 Framework on Durable Solutions for IDPs.[69] The Framework stipulates that a credible mechanism for addressing property rights violations is a necessity for the achievement of durable solutions. As the document is meant to give effect to the Guiding Principles on Internal Displacement, one would expect it to adopt the same approach taken in Guiding Principle 29—namely, restitution whenever possible, or else compensation. However, in specifying how such a mechanism should operate, the Framework distances itself from the impossibility standard:

> Addressing housing, land and property rights issues requires a comprehensive perspective. In principle, restitution is the preferred remedy. But in some cases it may be more equitable, after weighing different interests, to compensate the displaced owner instead of restoring his or her property.[70]

From the perspective of human rights law, as well, the strong preference for restitution expressed through the extremely narrow "material impossibility" standard for compensation in the Pinheiro Principles is increasingly questionable. Most human rights treaties express the right to a remedy in procedural terms as a right to access impartial tribunals, rather than establishing a list (let alone a hierarchy) of substantive forms of reparation such as restitution or compensation that should be provided by such tribunals. In 2005 the UN General Assembly adopted the Van Boven-Bassiouni Principles, an authoritative set of guidelines on remedies for human rights violations, which failed to express any preference for restitution, stating only that substantive remedies should be weighted in accordance with contextual circumstances.[71] These trends received a judicial validation in March 2010, when the European Court of Human Rights issued its ruling in *Demopoulos v. Turkey*.[72] The court in this case confirmed the effectiveness of remedies provided by a Turkish Cypriot property commission for the properties left behind in 1974 by Greek Cypriot displaced persons—even though the commission's rules prioritized compensation and exchange of properties over restitution. In doing so, the court rejected a "material impossibility" standard for restitution:[73]

> The Court's case-law indicates that if the nature of the breach allows *restitutio in integrum*, it is for the respondent State to implement it. However, if it is not possible to restore the position, the Court, as a matter of constant practice, has imposed the alternative requirement on the Contracting State to pay compensation for the value of the property. This is because the Contracting Parties to a case are in principle free to choose the means whereby they will comply with a judgment in which the Court has found a breach.[74]

While this formulation is unclear on the extent to which states are still required to prioritize restitution even in principle, one possible reading is that the court has retained the impossibility standard but opened it up for much broader interpretation by state authorities applying it than was foreseen in the Pinheiro Principles. As I have argued elsewhere, a reasonable interpretation of this statement is that while the freedom of choice of states in redressing breaches of the European Human Rights Convention is significantly restricted by the court's express preference for restitution in theory, states nevertheless retain a degree of discretion to specify conditions under which restitution is deemed impossible in practice.[75]

Since the early 1990s, then, restitution programs have evolved from being understood as a mere mechanism for bringing about the humanitarian aim of durable solutions (and particularly return), to being recognized as a per se right in displacement settings, to being considered one policy option among many in response to post-conflict property disputes that may require either distributive or corrective approaches. In the next section, I consider restitution at the more conceptual level and how it relates to the goals of humanitarianism, transitional justice, and development.

THE PROTECTION OF RIGHTS: RESTITUTION IN TRANSITIONAL JUSTICE AND RESPONSES TO DISPLACEMENT

Much of the current debate surrounding restitution arises because it involves measures that impinge simultaneously (but not necessarily uniformly) on the aims of humanitarian, transitional justice, and development actors. As a retrospective, remedial effort to at least partially address the causes as well as the consequences of displacement, restitution truly stands out from other humanitarian responses, which tend to focus on alleviating the symptoms of vulnerability. Restitution "came of age" as a humanitarian response, but given the focus transitional justice places on retrospective redress for victims of human rights abuses, restitution presents a fit with transitional reparations as well. While restitution can serve as an important means of achieving the remedial aims of both fields, it can also come into tension with the parallel responsive goals of humanitarians and the emphasis placed on environment building in transitional justice settings. In development practice, restitution has periodically been promoted as a means of restoring respect for property rights—or discouraged as inimical to necessary reforms. In either case, restitution measures clearly set important outset conditions for prospective development programming.

In attempting to map the significance of restitution with respect to these three fields of activity—humanitarian action, transitional justice, and development—the framework of protection provides a lens that relates all three fields back to a fundamental joint concern: the rights and agency of individuals. The contemporary humanitarian definition of protection takes in "all activities aimed at obtaining full respect for the rights of the individual in accordance with the letter and spirit of the relevant bodies of law, namely human rights law, international humanitarian law and refugee law."[76] This definition has been criticized for extending the concept of humanitarian protection far beyond its traditional core concerns and potentially watering it down.[77] By incorporating the entire spectrum of human rights law, the definition not only includes core humanitarian activities such as life-saving aid provision but also redress for rights violations, promotion of democracy, and rights-based aspects of development. These various functions, and the manner in which the protection concept links them, are further highlighted by the contemporary humanitarian typology of protection activities. This typology divides protection activities into three categories:

1. *Responsive action* consists of "any immediate activity undertaken in connection with an emerging or established pattern of violation and aimed at preventing its recurrence, putting a stop to it, and/or alleviating its immediate effects."[78]

2. *Remedial action* is "aimed at restoring people's dignity and ensuring adequate living conditions subsequent to a pattern of violation, through rehabilitation, restitution, compensation and repair."[79] Such measures can include tracing family members, health care, livelihood support, housing, education, and judicial investigations and redress.

3. *Environment-building action* is "aimed at creating and/or consolidating an environment—political, social, cultural, economic and legal—conducive to full respect for the rights of the individual [by means of] a deeper, more structural process that challenges society as a whole by aiming to change policy, attitude, belief and behavior."[80]

This typology vividly demonstrates how thoroughly the concept of humanitarian protection has been transformed through the post–Cold War adoption of rights-based approaches. Of the three listed fields of activity, only the first, responsive measures, corresponds to traditional modes of humanitarian action based on the fundamental principle of humanity (the prevention and alleviation of human suffering without ulterior motives).[81] The second category, remedial action, almost immediately passes out of the traditional humanitarian comfort zone by implying attention to causes of violations rather than simply amelioration of their effects. Although some specific activities listed as remedial actions correspond to traditional humanitarian activities (most notably, family tracing and health care and shelter provision), others such as prosecution and reparations are core human rights and transitional justice concerns. These types of measures remain controversial in humanitarian practice as they necessarily entail the attribution of responsibility for violations and can therefore negate the perception of neutrality that humanitarians have traditionally relied on in order to secure access to persons in need.[82]

The emphasis of environment-building actions on preventing future violations by building up a culture of respect for rights aligns closely with transitional justice aims related to reconciliation and democracy, as well as development policy, which tends to be framed in prospective and transformative terms. Unlike remedial measures, which retrospectively address past violations, environment-building actions are prospective and seek to prevent future violations. The prospective focus of environment-building measures renders them less politically sensitive and therefore more amenable to the traditional humanitarian mandate.[83] However, such measures also presuppose a level of expertise and long-term engagement not envisioned in the classic humanitarian model of quick deployment to crisis areas and rapid withdrawal as they stabilize. Humanitarian action has clearly moved beyond such traditional approaches, as indicated by the scope and ambition of the new humanitarian protection paradigm. Nevertheless, humanitarian actors also recognize that upholding this paradigm is a shared responsibility, and that a good deal of the work involved entails coordination with other post-conflict actors, respecting their mandates and expertise, and ensuring complementary programming. This is evident in the recent articulation of early recovery as a means of overcoming the gap that frequently arises between the departure of humanitarian agencies and the arrival of development expertise:

> Early recovery is a multidimensional process guided by development principles that begins in a humanitarian setting, and seeks to build on humanitarian programmes and catalyze sustainable development opportunities. ... It encompasses the restoration of basic services, livelihoods, transitional shelter, governance, security and rule of law, environment and other socio-economic dimensions, including the reintegration of displaced populations. It strengthens human security and aims to begin addressing the underlying causes of the crisis.[84]

It is also worth noting that the expansion of humanitarian programming into activities associated with other fields has come as a natural response to changing patterns of displacement. One example is the increasingly common phenomenon of protracted internal displacement, in which the search for voluntary durable solutions has stalled, frequently because of frozen conflict situations. Under such circumstances, humanitarian actors often find that programming still technically qualified as aid provision begins to take on long-term, development-related characteristics (for example, where shelter needs are met through the provision of permanent housing). A recent expert meeting on protracted internal displacement concluded that durable solutions were both a humanitarian and development issue and could best be achieved through better coordination.[85]

Nevertheless, humanitarian response to displacement remains primarily responsive in nature, despite its post–Cold War embrace of an explicitly rights-based approach. The key exception to this pattern is restitution, a remedial activity that has been extensively promoted by humanitarian actors in light of its centrality to the achievement of durable solutions. Meanwhile, transitional justice straddles both remedial and environment-building activities, given its dual emphasis on redressing violations and promoting democracy. Recent scholarship on transitional justice indicates that the field's most distinctive contributions are in the remedial area, given the significant but relatively indirect influence transitional justice measures are likely to have on the longer-term goal of democratic rule of law in any given setting.[86] This inference is reinforced by the recognition that environment building—in the form of the distributive justice goals frequently urged on transitional justice practitioners—may be best achieved through development work.[87] As a largely and perhaps even primarily remedial field, transitional justice has a legitimate role in shaping the future of restitution as a response to violations involving displacement. Most notably, transitional justice actors may be best placed to find a way out of the current impasse between humanitarian actors, who have forcefully and successfully promoted restitution as an adjunct to their responsive activities against displacement, and development actors, who have evinced skepticism about restitution's effects on their environment-building goals.

RESTITUTION AND THE GOALS OF TRANSITIONAL JUSTICE

Despite the proliferation of transitional justice practice and scholarship since the end of the Cold War, debates persist over the definition of transitional justice and its aims. Paige Arthur has suggested that the field is distinguished by its simultaneous embrace of two "normative aims"—namely, justice for victims of violations and a political transition to democracy.[88] De Greiff has more recently proposed a normative conception of transitional justice that refines the nature and scope of these aims and establishes their relationship to the measures—prosecution, truth-telling, institutional reform, and reparations—that have come to define the field. According to him, these measures aim to redress the legacies of massive human rights abuses by "giving force to human rights norms that were systematically violated." They qualify as "part of transitional justice in virtue of sharing two mediate goals (providing recognition to victims and fostering civic trust) and two final goals (contributing to reconciliation and to democratization)."[89] The "final goals" promoted by transitional justice measures correspond to Arthur's "normative aims." Most obviously, transitional justice entails justice in the form of redress for past violations (including, in de Greiff's formulation, measures that "restore the rights that were so brutally violated and affirm victims' standing as full citizens").[90] However, the factor that distinguishes the field from human rights advocacy is its second normative aim—namely, transition, in the specific sense of promoting political change oriented toward democratic rule of law.

It is now relatively well established that transitional justice's "domain of application" has extended "from its original context—namely, societies emerging from authoritarianism—to societies emerging from conflict."[91] Many observers have also called for transitional justice mechanisms to make the additional jump to addressing violations of social and economic rights.[92] New openness to addressing conflict and inequality has in turn facilitated exploration of the relationship between development and transitional justice.[93] Researchers now attribute to both fields a common set of long-term, essentially environment-building goals "that involve transforming society."[94] De Greiff distinguishes transitional justice from development, though, by placing them, respectively, at the ends of a continuum between "corrective justice," which is concerned with addressing harms, and "distributive justice," which is concerned with equitable outcomes.[95]

For transitional justice mechanisms characterized by a generally retrospective orientation toward past violations, the humanitarian term *remedial protection* is largely equivalent in meaning to "corrective justice" as de Greiff uses it. However, this broad concept of remedial or corrective justice can be contrasted with a stricter view frequently promoted in restitution contexts. For instance, rigorously corrective approaches to restitution as applied by the Permanent Court of International Justice in the *Chorzow* case aspire to "wipe out all the consequences of the illegal act and reestablish the situation which would, in all probability, have existed if that act had not been committed."[96] Given the firmly established principle that transitional justice measures cannot fully redress the harm caused by massive human rights abuses (and are bound to result in disappointed expectations when they aspire to), strict corrective justice in this sense can hardly be compatible with the transitional justice goals of reaffirming subverted human rights norms and rebuilding civic trust in institutions.[97]

Justice claims related to land and property may be remedial without being corrective in the strict sense promoted by standards such as the Pinheiro Principles (which implicitly assume the existence of fair and equitable predisplacement property relations overturned by acts of dispossession in clear violation of international law). For instance, financial compensation represents an approach that is remedial in the sense that it addresses the direct effects of wrongful property confiscations without being strictly corrective in the sense of undoing them. Despite the difference between strict forms of restitution and compensation, both clearly fall within the ambit of the established transitional justice mechanism of reparations. By contrast, truly distributive measures may be motivated by the need to address the effects of past violations but do so indirectly, channeling resources to marginalized groups based first and foremost on the fact of their marginalization rather than on whether it arises as a result of past violations. In the terms of the humanitarian protection framework, such measures are environment building rather than remedial. In practice, they imply recourse to reform-oriented measures that do not correspond to the traditional set of transitional justice mechanisms.

By way of example, land reform in South Africa includes both elements—with two components of reparations (restitution and compensation) serving as a remedial response to the direct effects of dispossession of nonwhites since 1913, and separate measures to facilitate acquisition of land by nonwhites serving as a distributive means of addressing the indirect effects of earlier confiscations (in the form of racial disparities in landownership).[98] In either case, justice claims to land and property have the potential to not only transform society but also disrupt both political and economic life. Addressing such claims may also involve the acceptance of short-term instability as necessary in a bid for long-term stability and legal certainty. In analyzing the potential of distributive measures such as land tenure reform to promote transitional justice goals, Huggins and others observe that the level of complexity and political calculation they entail argue for leveraging immediate-term transitional justice mechanisms to facilitate longer-term distributive change rather than conflating the two.[99] However, in cases where land and property claims are essentially remedial, and relate to broader patterns of violations that are the subject of transitional justice measures, it is hard to conceive of a principled reason for failing to seek their resolution through reparation measures.

RESTITUTION AND HUMANITARIAN RESPONSE TO DISPLACEMENT

Post–Cold War advocacy for an effective response to the needs of IDPs has been remarkably successful, both in terms of its effect on the broader humanitarian discourse and in terms of its acceptance in practice by state authorities. However, this success may by its nature complicate efforts to address the root causes of displacement. Modes of human rights advocacy tend to run along a spectrum, with public denunciation of violations by intransigent state actors at one end and capacity building and support to more tractable national counterparts at the other.[100] Given that the Guiding Principles affirm that arbitrary displacement is a violation of international law, they present an ample basis for denunciation of acts of displacement as well as demands for accountability and reparations for victims. However, denunciation tends to preempt the possibility of dialogue, and IDP advocates have historically calculated that their impact will be greatest if they avoid confrontation with intransigent states and instead focus their efforts on supporting positive tendencies in states at least partially receptive to the message of sovereignty as responsibility.[101]

While this approach has been demonstrably effective in improving the day-to-day lives of IDPs in many countries worldwide, it may not succeed in permanently ending displacement or addressing its underlying causes in such settings without being accompanied by more overtly political acts of national reconciliation and redistribution. It is now generally recognized that the effects of armed conflict are often exacerbated by longstanding patterns of inequality, injustice, and discrimination. In such circumstances, addressing displacement is not always the same as addressing its root causes and aggravating factors. However, the Guiding Principles primarily reflect a responsive, rather than a remedial approach; they are designed to close the protection gap resulting directly from displacement, rather than any protection gaps that may have led to displacement. As an advocacy strategy, putting states on notice that they may be found responsible *in the future* for failures to address the present vulnerability experienced by IDPs is more calculated to succeed than pressing them to account for *past* acts or omissions that led to displacement. The most important Guiding Principles—and the ones that have been most forcefully promoted by humanitarian advocates—are those that take displacement as a given and focus on addressing its immediate effects.[102]

Rights based or not, this approach remains broadly consistent with the humanitarian tradition of responsive action. International refugee law, as the starting point for humanitarian responses to displacement, pursued the sole aim of providing durable solutions.[103] The form of protection entailed by this approach was essentially responsive, in that it aimed to prospectively ameliorate the suffering of refugees by restoring the nominal protection of a state rather than to retrospectively redress the persecution that caused displacement. The post–Cold War rights-based approach to IDP protection was built on recognition that the territorial link between the duty-bearing state and rights-holding individuals remained unbroken by the latter's displacement within their home state. However, the main protection focus arguably remained responsive, rather than remedial.[104]

Claims involving retrospective justice for past human rights violations raise a set of issues that did not register in traditional humanitarian practice. This is perhaps most clearly indicated by the paucity of retrospectively oriented measures in the Guiding Principles. While the principles abound with recommendations on measures that can be taken to avoid human rights violations that could result from displacement, they have relatively little to say about what measures should be taken when such violations occur. Even the obligation to allow IDPs to return to their places of origin tends to be portrayed as an exercise in fulfilling the right to freedom of movement and choice of residence rather than purely as a remedy for earlier arbitrary displacement.[105] It is here that property restitution (as called for in Guiding Principle 29) has always stood out as something of an exception, as the sole unambiguously retrospective and remedial measure called for in the Guiding Principles. However, the scope of even this measure, which is limited to restoring property that IDPs "left behind or were dispossessed of upon their displacement," is retrospective only to the point of addressing violations directly related to displacement, rather than the root-cause violations that create underlying vulnerability to displacement.

This is not to say that the Guiding Principles do not have a place in addressing root causes. For instance, their legal focus creates a perhaps undervalued opportunity to reframe sensitive and entrenched political issues as technical questions to be resolved by the application of international law. For instance, simply labeling a particular group of people in legal terms (as IDPs) rather than in political terms (as an ostensibly secessionist minority) may give greater scope to national authorities to engage with the humanitarian needs of such a group. This, in turn, may build confidence, creating new space to negotiate a lasting solution to the underlying political disputes. However, there is also a risk that such reframing may present states with an opportunity to deflect attention from any responsibility they may bear for failures to address historical grievances, deferring sustainable political solutions in favor of humanitarian responses to the symptoms of political grievance.[106]

Since the adoption of the Guiding Principles in 1998, greater awareness of the significance of addressing root causes of displacement appears to have taken hold. This is most obviously reflected in recent standards related to internal displacement such as the Framework on Durable Solutions for Internally Displaced Persons. While confirming the central importance of restoring property rights, for instance, the Framework goes on to recognize the importance of broader transitional justice measures "including access to justice, reparations and information about the causes of violations."[107] Strikingly, the Framework also relates socioeconomic grievances to the sustainability of durable solutions, implying the need to consider distributive approaches.[108] However, the Framework also confirms the rule that human rights violations that were the immediate cause of displacement or resulted directly from it are the primary concern of humanitarian actors. For instance, the Framework focuses on the need to redress international law violations "which caused displacement, or which occurred during displacement," without explicitly referencing categories of violations that may have created the conditions for displacement without directly triggering it.[109] Likewise, durable solutions are deemed to have been achieved even where socioeconomic or political inequalities that may have constituted root causes of displacement remain unaddressed:

> IDPs who have achieved a durable solution may still face needs or human rights concerns that are not displacement-specific, e.g. when IDPs return or relocate to an area that was neglected and impoverished even before their displacement or where the wider population faces the same challenges as IDPs to participate in elections or other public affairs.[110]

The ambiguity surrounding root causes of displacement in humanitarian discourses is understandable. For humanitarian actors, restitution represents something of a remedial aberration from a largely responsive modus operandi, but one that is intimately connected with the goal of achieving durable solutions. Until recently, the corrective nature of restitution in displacement settings distinguished it from less doctrinaire and more context-sensitive approaches to reparations that have come to characterize human rights and transitional justice approaches to remedial justice. However, as described earlier, recent developments have blunted this corrective approach. This has come about in part because development experts have noted that restoring the status quo ante risks actually reinforcing root causes of displacement rather than addressing them. On the other hand, the reduced emphasis on corrective measures also represents the recent insight among humanitarians that insisting on the primacy of restitution in protracted displacement settings where the conditions for it may never be achieved may hinder the ability of affected persons to pursue local integration. While remedial action remains crucial to securing durable solutions (and relevant to root causes) in both protracted and more transient displacement settings, framing it in strict corrective terms would be counterproductive.

CHALLENGES TO RESTITUTION IN TRANSITIONAL SETTINGS

Given the gradual but significant evolution in thinking about the nature of restitution in displacement settings, protracted and otherwise, it may be possible to conclude that "just reparations" for property violations, rather than restitution per se, is now seen as the main remedial precondition for achieving durable solutions.[111] Restitution as a "preferred remedy" for displacement, as conceived of in the Pinheiro Principles, represented something of an aberration from the tendency of broader human rights documents, such as the Van Boven-Bassiouni Principles, to eschew any explicit general preference among the various forms of reparations. If, as it now seems, the impossibility standard has been abandoned—or at least more clearly subordinated to contextual and policy considerations, as implied in the European Court of Human Rights ruling in *Demopoulos*—then restitution is no longer absolutely prioritized over other remedies even in the case of property violations associated with displacement. Indeed, the court's allowance of state discretion "to assess the practicalities, priorities and conflicting interests on a domestic level"[112] corresponds intuitively to the Van Boven-Bassiouni Principles' recommendation to choose reparations modalities "as appropriate and proportional to the gravity of the violation and the circumstances of each case."[113] It also reflects the UN secretary-general's 2004 observation that giving force to victims' own conceptions of justice may rule out a strict hierarchical approach:

> No single form of reparation is likely to be satisfactory to victims. Instead, appropriately conceived combinations of reparations measures will usually be required, as a complement to the proceedings of criminal tribunals and truth commissions.[114]

To the extent that property restitution in humanitarian settings is now seen as equivalent, rather than hierarchically superior, to other forms of reparations, remedial humanitarian responses have aligned themselves with broader human rights practice. As such, postdisplacement restitution no longer involves activities that are categorically distinct from reparations, as one of the four core mechanisms for transitional justice (the other three being prosecution, truth-telling, and institutional reform). The current convergence of post-conflict property restitution and human rights reparations suggests that restitution is now clearly understood as a means of redressing violations. However, the extent to which such restitution can contribute to transitional justice remains contingent on its ability to support democratic rule of law, another aim of transitional justice.

One means of examining the role of restitution in bringing about political change is to examine some of the main challenges that have arisen in designing and implementing restitution programs, as well as broader reparations programs with property restitution elements. We can begin with issues in restitution and reparations programs that highlight their relationship with the goals of recognition and civic trust. However, a related set of challenges raise the broader issue of the extent to which restitution and reparations programming can and should seek to address the underlying root causes of land and property grievances and vulnerability to being dispossessed. Here, again, evolving understandings of the role of restitution as a form of reparations may be crucial, not least because the alternatives to restitution, such as compensation, are not strictly corrective in nature and therefore allow for remedial approaches to take on a more prospective character related to environment-building goals such as political transformation or economic development. Depending on the context, balancing restitution more flexibly with other reparations measures may also contribute to transitional justice goals by allowing the effects of past harms to be redressed without risking recreation of the conditions that made them possible.

DESIGN AND IMPLEMENTATION OF RESTITUTION PROGRAMS

The practical challenges to designing and implementing property restitution programming in post-conflict settings are numerous and frequently context specific, but a good deal of guidance already exists on how such problems can be overcome, and a number of issues stand out. Among these are (1) the issue of addressing massive numbers of claims rooted in common and historically specific patterns of rights violations, and (2) the need to develop a reliable evidentiary base in support of programmatic responses to such violations. In both cases, redress can be provided in a manner that promotes the transitional justice goals of civic trust and recognition. However, restitution also shares the propensity of other post-conflict remedial measures to destabilize the perceived wartime gains of the parties, giving rise to (3) a distinct surge of political resistance.

The issue of mass claims to property arises in situations where large groups of people have been displaced and dispossessed (or have suffered other human rights violations) under similar circumstances. Referring such large and often politically controversial bodies of claims to ordinary adjudicatory institutions may be counterproductive both for those institutions, which may be overwhelmed, and for claimants, whose claims are likely to be delayed. In cases where existing adjudicatory bodies with a clear basis for jurisdiction lack capacity (and perhaps legitimacy) to process restitution claims, ad hoc, provisional bodies have frequently been proposed as a means of providing quick and effective redress. This is a familiar issue for transitional justice practitioners in the context of reparations. For instance, de Greiff has described such choices in transitional reparations settings as falling between "juridical" approaches based on the application of legal standards to individual claims and "programmatic" or "administrative" approaches that offer standardized but rapid redress based on a political determination that doing so is in the best interests of society.[115]

In arguing for programmatic approaches, de Greiff begins by detailing the inherent disadvantages of ordinary adjudicatory systems in dealing with massive and systematic violations.[116] Likewise, Jaime Malamud-Goti and Lucas Grosman distinguish between judicial "tort law" approaches and "administrative compensation," detailing many advantages of the latter in mass-claims settings.[117] Humanitarian actors responding to displacement have come to similar conclusions, in part based on the positive outcomes of the provisional programmatic approach and expedited administrative procedures adopted in Bosnia. Significant elements of this approach were also included in the Pinheiro Principles and expanded on in a 2008 manual meant to assist in the drafting of domestic laws and policies on internal displacement:

> Procedures before ordinary courts and adjudicatory bodies tend to place the primary burden of proof on the initiator of a case ... who must bring evidence and establish the facts in that particular case. Such procedures normally involve elaborate and time-consuming fact-finding and may be subject to multiple appeals. In situations of mass displacement in

which patterns of dispossession are similar across cases and generally can be documented, such elaborate fact-finding procedures not only are unnecessary but also impose a high burden in terms of production of formal evidence, expense, time, and uncertainty on claimants who often are already impoverished and traumatized by their experience.[118]

However, in keeping with the dual aspirations of transitional justice, namely, redress and democratization, de Greiff has described administrative reparations as not only superior to judicial approaches in achieving redress for victims but also justified as a means of promoting political change favoring democracy.[119] Specifically, he notes that reparations can constitute a material form of recognition affirming the moral standing and equal citizenship of victims as well as a material manifestation of the aspiration of fellow citizens and official institutions to trustworthiness (as an element of civic trust) and part of a "new 'social contract' in which [victims'] dignity and their interests are amply recognized."[120]

Administrative property restitution, viewed as a form of transitional reparations, can similarly support these goals. However, it may have a particularly strong relationship with the question of recognition. As de Greiff notes, recognition of the moral standing of victims requires acceptance of the fact that special treatment of victims is necessary to reestablish conditions of equality between citizens that were upended by human rights abuses.[121] It is hard to imagine an area where the relationship between redress and equality would be as intuitive as in the restoration of the right to a home, a sphere of privacy and intimacy, the fundamental importance of which to human and social life is universally acknowledged. At a symbolic level, efforts to restore homes to those wrongfully dispossessed of them signals an intention to restore the equal citizenship of displaced persons in the same manner as the original usurpation of homes represents a revocation of citizenship rights. It is for precisely this reason that noncorrective remedial approaches to dispossession such as compensation have never shared the same intuitive sense of justice as that evoked by restitution of property. Except in settings where displaced persons actively seek compensation, denial of restitution can easily be construed as denial of recognition of the unique suffering caused by the loss of homes and homelands.

Acceptance of the utility of programmatic approaches to mass claims for restitution raises a second practical issue—namely, *how to develop an evidentiary base* in support of such programs. As noted earlier, one of the main advantages of programmatic reparations is the fact that they relieve claimants of the obligation to provide evidence proving all details of the violations they have suffered in each individual case. This is particularly important for displaced persons, who frequently lose access to personal documents, including those that would establish their property rights, and who might also face risks of retaliation or being retraumatized by the experience of testifying in adversarial proceedings. However, if the victims are not required to bring evidence of such abuses, where is such evidence to be derived?

While this may seem like an overly scrupulous question in the wake of mass atrocities, it is worth recalling that administrative reparations programs represent significant incursions into the ordinary functioning of adjudicatory systems. They frequently rely on devices such as waived prescription laws, reduced evidentiary requirements, and the reversal of the ordinary burden of proof, in effect allowing victims' claims to be vindicated based on evidence of little more than their identity and the most basic indications of the harms they suffered. Moreover, even standardized reparations payments can impose a significant cumulative cost on society, while restitution programs present individuals and households occupying claimed property with the threat of evictions. The proven advantages of administrative approaches notwithstanding, such measures must be based on the most reliable evidence possible in order to be credible.

Malamud-Goti and Grosman note that one of the disadvantages of administrative reparations is that they lack the "truth-finding virtues" of individual judicial proceedings, and they suggest that the two systems might complement each other through the use of small numbers of court proceedings to establish a "basis for understanding the truth" that would benefit victims more generally.[122] In fact, there are a number of ways in which an evidentiary base can be fashioned for administrative restitution and reparations programs. These range from the use of precedent judicial decisions to establish common patterns of facts that can be assumed in other similarly situated cases to legislative inquiries and fact-finding efforts that allow general determinations to be made—and relied on in subsequent administrative procedures—regarding what happened when and where, who was victimized, and who was responsible.

Such solutions may be particularly effective in that they leverage the extraordinary nature of mass abuses. De Greiff observes that ordinary adjudicatory bodies "work on the assumption that norm-breaking behavior is more or less exceptional," rendering them less capable of addressing categories of abuses that were temporarily the norm as reflected by their massive and systematic nature.[123] However, it is precisely the widespread and systematic nature of such abuses that may facilitate the identification of general patterns that can be confirmed at the global level to speed programmatic reparations, rather than leaving it for victims to prove in each individual case.

For instance, in the case of a 2008 reparations bill in Colombia, the Victims' Law (which failed to pass but became part of the basis for a successful later effort in 2011), the provision of reparations to victims of violence was meant to be based on the "principle of good faith," meaning that victims' assertions were to be lent evidentiary weight essentially because they were made by victims.[124] A report by the nongovernmental organization Displacement Solutions noted that a more solid legal case for such a program would be the official documentation of the "systematic and documented patterns" of abuses that had given rise to property claims.[125] The report went on to note that the findings of a proposed truth commission on land issues in Colombia might "not only serve the functions of historical memory and recognition of violations and abuses, but could actually be accorded evidentiary weight in identifying times and places in which, for instance, transactions of land could be presumed to have taken place under duress."[126]

What is striking about proposals like this one is the manner in which they highlight linkages between property restitution and the aims and measures of transitional justice. At a broad level, use of official determinations or the results of inquiries such as truth commissions as the basis for expedited restitution procedures would clearly serve the aim of recognition, particularly where such information was freely disclosed by state authorities (rather than wrung from victims in judicial proceedings). At a narrower level, the proposal would result in considerable coherence between the transitional justice measures of truth-telling and reparations.

In positing a normative conception of transitional justice, de Greiff argues that the achievement of the aim of "giving force to human rights norms that were systematically violated" requires "external coherence" between transitional justice mechanisms, consisting of their conception and implementation in a manner "not as discrete and independent initiatives but rather as parts of an integrated policy."[127] Transitional justice measures must be seen to be credible attempts along numerous fronts to restore a normative order severely compromised by past abuses, rather than isolated one-offs. However, there is also an instrumental aspect to the argument for external coherence given that the proper functioning of any one mechanism may create conditions conducive for the others. Theo Van Boven elaborated this dynamic as early as 1993 in a study accompanying the precursor to the Van Boven-Bassiouni Principles.[128] In discussing the link between impunity and reparations, he identified investigations of systematic human rights violations—truth-telling—as "the first requirement of justice" and the linchpin guaranteeing an evidentiary basis for the functioning of prosecutions and reparations mechanisms.[129]

As anticipated by Van Boven, the most significant linkage between restitution and transitional mechanisms other than reparations arguably relates to truth-telling. This connection is particularly likely to arise in mass-claims contexts, where the factors described earlier argue in favor of an administrative program, necessitating official recognition in the form of the voluntary adoption by public authorities of general findings on the nature of the underlying violations. In order to provide a clear legal basis for expedited programmatic reparations, such recognition should be adopted by the legislative branch, either through a direct legislative determination regarding patterns of violations, or through legislative endorsement of the findings of bodies such as truth commissions. Given the political tensions that typically attend discussions of wartime violations, this step alone will require significant political capital and gives rise to the risk of incomplete or distorted official "admissions" of what happened.

Corrective reparations efforts involving restitution programs typically involve even *greater political tensions*, as restoring formerly owned property to the displaced can destabilize the post-conflict demographic status quo. In the past, wars were almost uniformly waged with the aim of securing territory, and control of territory still represents one of the most fundamental attributes of states. In post-conflict settings, land and natural resources are often treated at least implicitly as spoils of war and may represent some of the only immediate sources of revenue and wealth available. Accordingly, restitution programs pose an inherent challenge for post-conflict regimes that represent political, military, and business actors with much to lose from reversing the post-conflict situation. Political resistance to restitution and return frequently fuels protracted displacement, in which remedial responses to property violations remain blocked despite the development of norms specifying that restitution should proceed independently of formal peace agreements.[130] As noted by Leila Hilal, the Israeli-Palestinian conflict provides a virtually paradigmatic case of the "property issue" being too closely associated with the "territory issue" dividing the parties to be resolved without a broader resolution of the conflict.[131]

Indeed, the tension between individuals' claims to lands they consider their homes and the state's claim to land it considers its territory (often manifested through the claims of secondary occupants to remain in contested properties) is often a sticking point—one that still distinguishes restitution from broader reparations. While there may be numerous political obstacles to the implementation of reparations in the form of compensation, for instance, the money paid to victims is ultimately a fungible resource. Land, by contrast, is not only valuable but also inherently scarce. Each parcel of land is unique, and its location, characteristics, history, and associations may lend it an aura of irreplaceable economic, strategic, spiritual, cultural, or sentimental value. Where land is contested, there is the potential for conflict at the individual level and between communities, as well as between government and individual or community interests.

Another significant political challenge in all reparations settings (whether restitution is involved or not) is the potential for official determinations of fact made in support of such programs to fuel other more politically charged transitional justice claims such as calls for prosecution. Although the Guiding Principles on Internal Displacement largely focus on prospective amelioration of the condition of IDPs, recent advocacy has emphasized the need for countries facing displacement to adopt domestic legislation recognizing, as international law does, that arbitrary displacement is a crime.[132] As a result, state actors face increasing criminal liability not only for more traditionally recognized war crimes, such as murder and looting, that tend to accompany forced displacement but also for displacement itself.[133] This state of affairs may pose a dilemma for advocates of remedial approaches to property violations. Simply put, where state actors have been accused of complicity in arbitrary displacement, this may lead to fears that disclosure of information necessary to develop remedial property programming may also fuel the prosecution of state agents.

From the point of view of human rights and holistic conceptions of transitional justice, such investigations and prosecutions are a natural part of responding to systematic violations. However, the perceived or real risk of parties to the conflict being prosecuted may prevent state actors from supporting restitution programs through disclosure or official acknowledgment of facts that support the claims of displaced persons or other victims. In this sense, administrative responses to property violations may pose something of a dilemma. On one hand, restitution and reparations programs that are not built on acknowledgment and disclosure are likely neither to be effective in their own terms nor to contribute to the broader norm-restoring goals promoted through a holistic approach to transitional justice. On the other hand, where the state refuses to cooperate at all for fear of accountability, displaced persons and other victims may be denied redress and left without the prospect of durable solutions.

The importance of political calculations in determining whether reparations programs go forward and succeed is undeniable, despite the rapid development of international law norms constraining state discretion in principle.[134] However, while the development of standards such as the Pinheiro Principles can "lead the horse to water"—property restitution obligations, for instance, are virtually a standard component of contemporary peace agreements and refugee repatriation regimes—they cannot always make it drink, in the sense that many, if not most, of these commitments remain unfulfilled.

The failure of past efforts to promote reparations and restitution in Colombia provides an example of the extent to which such efforts may face obstacles precisely because of their potential to implicate state responsibility and invoke the need for broader approaches, including prosecution and institutional reform. For instance, the failure of the 2008 reparations bill in Colombia resulted in part from the government's insistence that its application should be limited to redress for victims of non-state actors. Prior to discussion of the 2008 bill, two other reparations systems for victims of the conflict in Colombia had already been set up. However, the first, Law 975 of 2005, focused on the demobilization of right-wing paramilitaries and provided a reparations process exclusively for victims of this group. A subsequent "administrative reparations" program set up under a 2008 decree explicitly excluded redress for acts attributable to agents of the state.[135] Both measures were, in any case, left largely unimplemented, in a state of affairs that motivated the proposal of the failed 2008 bill and the passage of the Victims' Law in 2011. Although the new law provides for reparations for all victims "regardless of who was responsible" for the crimes inflicted on them,[136] one of the main remaining political objections to the law is its failure to explicitly recognize the role of the state in human rights abuses.[137] Thus, the controversy dogging reparations in Colombia to date reflects de Greiff's concern that the failure of states to be seen to promote external coherence between transitional justice mechanisms may undermine even strongly supported individual mechanisms.

Political obstacles to restitution present a genuine dilemma, but one where consensus across sectors has emerged. Humanitarian actors, human rights advocates, transitional justice proponents, and development experts agree on the larger point that failing to respond to conflict-related land and property issues may set the stage for further conflict. Disagreements tend to arise over matters of emphasis. As set out earlier, development actors have objected to a tendency in recent human rights and humanitarian responses to focus on displacement to the near exclusion of other concerns and assume that restitution is always an appropriate default response. For transitional justice actors, who are concerned with achieving whatever redress is possible and with fostering political transformation, the tendency toward greater context sensitivity in current restitution thinking will likely be seen as germane.

ROOT CAUSES AND PATTERNS OF GROUP EXCLUSION

Two questions raising conceptual challenges to restitution programs may be particularly helpful in defining their relationship with transitional justice aims and measures: to what extent is it possible for postdisplacement restitution programs to address root causes of displacement, and to what extent can they mitigate the risk of perpetuating patterns of group exclusion from equal access to and exercise of property rights? Beginning with the issue of root causes, there is no denying the attraction of an appeal to fully redress displacement and other violations by removing the underlying patterns of discrimination and marginalization that gave rise to conflict and rendered affected populations particularly vulnerable to both being displaced and suffering disproportionately as a result. The question is whether restitution—or even broader reparations—can contribute to achieving this goal. Fully addressing root causes is beyond the scope of the responsive humanitarian goal of achieving durable solutions to displacement and the remedial aims pursued by transitional justice, as both are currently understood.

Neither the remedial nor the corrective approach requires looking behind the "triggering" violations it responds to in order to transform the underlying conditions that both increased their likelihood and intensified their effect on victims. Addressing root causes falls more clearly within the scope of environment-building activities, including those going beyond the political goals of transitional justice and raising central distributive concerns addressed by development (and in this case, land tenure) practitioners. In dealing with these issues, development actors have recourse to a broad range of measures that may include elements related to reparations and restitution but also involve prospective reform in areas such as land tenure, taxation, and title registration. Such measures are clearly beyond the scope of humanitarian expertise and were explicitly rejected by early practitioners of transitional justice.[138] Huggins notes that the political and technical complications inherent in land reform issues still counsel against their inclusion as central mechanisms for transitional justice programming.[139] Practicalities aside, the fact that development measures respond to poverty rather than victimhood per se has tended to demarcate the environment-building aims of the former field from the remedial aims of transitional reparations.

However, addressing land-related root causes is of specific concern to two groups rendered particularly vulnerable to the effects of displacement—namely, women and indigenous peoples. Indeed, for these groups as well as others that suffer from similar vulnerabilities, addressing root causes related to land may not only be a precondition for durable solutions but also constitute a crucial form of recognition for transitional justice purposes. Thus, even if the general rule in humanitarian and transitional practice remains that remedial measures should address the effects of violations involving displacement rather than their root causes, these two categories exemplify a possible exception.

Women and girls tend to face discrimination in both accessing land and property and exercising rights to it normally enjoyed by men.[140] This problem is most typically associated with customary rules and institutions for administering land, which remain prevalent in much of the developing world. As McCallin notes, discrimination against women in such settings can take many different forms, but the most problematic in displacement settings are rules that prevent married women from retaining tenure over land when their husbands have died or disappeared and other male relatives assert claims.[141] Given the prevalence of female-headed households in many displacement settings, such obstacles to accessing land once held in common with missing or dead husbands can pose a serious obstacle to their social and economic reintegration. The issue of discrimination against women regarding access to and enjoyment of property rights is also frequently a problem in "formal" systems, such as Colombia's, where land is administered through statutory rules applied by bureaucratic institutions.[142] While domestic legislation can itself have discriminatory aspects, even formally adequate guarantees of equality may be ignored or interpreted away in practice, leaving women exposed to discrimination.

The gap that persists between international standards such as those set out in the 1979 Convention on the Elimination of All Forms of Discrimination Against Women (CEDAW)[143] and actual practice worldwide has led to the recognition of a form of nested vulnerability in displacement settings, whereby women not only share a "protection gap" with other displaced persons but also face particular obstacles to the enjoyment of their rights based on gender. The Guiding Principles on Internal Displacement recognizes this state of affairs by prescribing treatment for particularly vulnerable IDPs—including female heads of household—that "takes into account their special needs."[144] Meanwhile, a similar dynamic of "double marginalization" has been observed in transitional justice settings, prompting calls for reparations measures to address root causes of women's vulnerability. For instance, Ruth Rubio-Marín, in introducing a study on gender and reparations, queries the extent to which such measures can "help to either reinforce or subvert some of the pre-existing structural gender inequalities that are commonly built into the social tissue of civil society resulting in women's systematic discrimination."[145] The Nairobi Declaration, adopted at a 2007 International Meeting on Women's and Girls' Right to a Remedy and Reparation, presents a forceful assertion that reparations programs can and should address root causes:

> Reparation must drive post-conflict transformation of socio-cultural injustices, and political and structural inequalities that shape the lives of women and girls; ... reintegration and restitution by themselves are not sufficient goals of reparation, since the origins of violations of women's and girls' human rights predate the conflict situation.[146]

A second group with an arguable claim to restitution measures that take into account land-related root causes of marginalization includes ethnic minorities, indigenous peoples, and others that share "a special dependency on and attachment to their lands."[147] While women have historically suffered continuous discrimination in accessing land and enjoying property rights, indigenous peoples and analogous groups have typically suffered specific historical injustices such as colonial-era dispossession and continue to face threats in the form of lack of recognition of their rights to lands they still hold, resulting in insecurity of tenure and new displacement. International norms recognize the existential threat this state of affairs poses to both the identity and the livelihoods of affected groups, and documents such as the 2007 UN Declaration on the Rights of Indigenous Peoples assert the rights of such groups to both recognition and the prospective protection of current landholdings, as well as the restitution of previously confiscated land.[148]

In the internal displacement discourse, the central importance of land rights to the protection of marginalized groups is clearly recognized as a matter of prevention of arbitrary displacement, with states placed under "a particular obligation to protect against the displacement of indigenous peoples, minorities, peasants, pastoralists and other groups with a special dependency on and attachment to their lands."[149] However, Guiding Principle 29 simply asserts a general duty to provide remedies for the loss of property by all IDPs, without distinguishing the special vulnerability of some or positing a corresponding "particular obligation" to provide an effective remedy for their dispossession. Nevertheless, key decisions by the inter-American and African regional human rights systems have implied such rights.

Most recently, in February 2010, the African Commission on Human and Peoples' Rights issued a groundbreaking decision in a case brought on behalf of the Endorois tribal people against Kenya.[150] If the European Court's *Demopoulos* ruling suggests that restitution has been downgraded to one of a number of acceptable substantive remedies in ordinary cases, the African system's *Endorois* case appears to set out an important exception for particularly vulnerable categories of victims.[151] While it is now possible to argue that restitution may remain a preferred remedy for indigenous peoples and others with a special dependency on and attachment to their lands, this still does not imply that post-conflict restitution in humanitarian settings is required to go beyond redressing dispossessions directly related to the conflict and displacement. Historical dispossessions that constitute root causes of both conflict and the vulnerability of indigenous peoples and analogous groups remain, in other words, beyond the clear scope of humanitarian responses to displacement.

In cases where the current vulnerability of particular groups is in part the result of historical patterns of exclusion or dispossession, an important departure point is the need for realistic expectations regarding what humanitarian actors can achieve. If, as described earlier, humanitarian approaches are still struggling nearly a decade after Bosnian restitution to consistently repeat its feat of redressing property violations directly related to displacement, the timing hardly seems propitious for such responses to be burdened with the additional expectation of taking on earlier property violations that shaped particular vulnerability to displacement and its effects. Indeed, taking on such ambitions in humanitarian settings would risk creating entirely unrealistic expectations on the part of displaced persons, straining both the mandate and capacities even of rights-based humanitarian actors beyond reasonable bounds.

While some ambiguity continues to prevail regarding the extent to which transitional justice actors should take on root-cause issues generally, a cautious assessment appears to be ascendant with regard to the narrower question of land. In discussing land tenure reform as a means of addressing historical claims involving dispossession or lack of recognition, Huggins counsels caution; given the ongoing debates among development practitioners regarding the proper aims and modalities of such reforms, transitional measures should merely seek to facilitate domestic political processes, not predetermine their outcome.[152] Meanwhile, in the case of women's land rights, Rubio-Marín has noted that an excessive focus on property restitution as a component of reparations may risk "having a disparate impact on women, who tend to be underrepresented among land or property owners."[153] While one might argue that such underrepresentation is precisely one of the root causes that reparations might be extended to address, Rubio-Marín observes that female victims of

rights abuses themselves tend to privilege "the future-oriented notion of rehabilitation or reintegration of the victim" over "notions of compensation or restitution, which seems to require the identification of discrete and easily quanti-
fiable losses and/or the realization of the status quo ante."[154]

Human Rights Watch and other observers have argued for approaching
historical injustice—that which took place beyond living memory—by essentially distributive rather than corrective means.[155] Such an approach involves
prioritizing the contemporary disadvantages suffered by the descendants of
direct victims of abuse. Such disadvantages are usually of a social and economic nature, implying that appropriate remedies will be of a distributive
nature, in the form of prospective assistance in achieving a better social and
economic standard. In fact, direct restitution of property is generally complicated by the passage of time because of factors such as loss of evidence, the difficulty of identifying claimants, and the development of legitimate competing
rights on the part of long-time good-faith occupants.[156] In many cases, direct
restitution may no longer be desirable to the dispossessed, underscoring the
importance of the increasingly context-sensitive approach to evaluating which
forms of reparations may be most appropriate in any given situation.

All this is not to say that humanitarian responses to displacement should
avoid seeking to address root causes in favor of a narrow focus on addressing
its consequences. However, as implied in the Framework on Durable Solutions,
efforts to address the direct effects of displacement should be prioritized, with
root causes taken up where capacity exists and a clear opportunity presents
itself. Ultimately, given the political sensitivities that typically surround root-
cause issues, truly sustainable resolutions will emerge only from domestic
political processes, particularly those that result from a transition to democratic
rule of law, which transitional justice is meant to encourage and strengthen.

However, even without directly tackling root causes, restitution programs
can still seek to address the effects of prior discrimination and marginalization
along with the direct effects of displacement. Indeed, failing to do so would, in
some cases, risk perpetuating patterns of group exclusion from equal access
to and exercise of property rights. While the desire to engage in post-conflict
restitution may be driven in large part by international norms and standards,
the practical details of restitution programs are often based almost exclusively
on domestic law and practice. As a result, there is a significant risk that such
programs may exclude de facto land and property rights exercised by marginalized groups without de jure legal recognition and protection from the state.
This lack of recognition is a root cause of vulnerability to displacement, as
the resulting land tenure insecurity leaves affected persons at constant risk of

eviction, and as they are unable to invest in property (for example, by using it as collateral) in order to achieve greater self-reliance.

When restitution programs proceed entirely from domestic law, without inquiring as to the de facto land relations that may lie behind the formal rules, this can have the ironic effect of transforming the de jure nonrecognition of such rights into a de facto—and permanent—dispossession. Denied an official redress for the confiscation of their land because they never enjoyed official recognition of their possession of it, displaced persons in this situation risk severe impoverishment and dependence. The Pinheiro Principles seek to address this dynamic by recommending that restitution programs include "positive measures to ensure that women are able to participate on a fully equal basis" and to "recognize the rights of possession of indigenous and traditional communities to collective lands."[157] In implementing such programs, states are also advised to implement "measures to ensure registration or demarcation" of restored property "as is necessary to ensure legal security of tenure."[158] The 2008 *Manual for Law and Policymakers: Protecting Internally Displaced Persons* makes a similar point in relation to the recognition of women's property rights:

> International human rights law requires that all citizens be treated equally before the law and in particular that men and women have equal rights to acquire and administer property. When such guarantees were not fully incorporated in domestic law at the time that IDPs were displaced, that should not prevent particular categories of IDPs from having access to remedies for loss or denial of access to homes, lands, and properties on the same basis as all other displaced.[159]

The manual invokes the fact that states will have already violated the spirit of international human rights law through their failure to recognize and protect the property rights of certain protected groups (at a minimum, women and indigenous peoples) prior to displacement. The compounding of this violation through the failure to prevent displacement surely cannot constitute grounds for excluding such groups from legal remedies. Indeed, this point is perhaps most emphatically made in the African Commission decision in the *Endorois* case, which not only states that international legal recognition of indigenous titles obligates states to recognize such titles as well but also asserts that wrongful dispossession cannot be used to extinguish them.[160]

CONCLUSION

Restitution is a point of overlap between transitional justice discourses and humanitarian responses to displacement. While restitution has been of marginal interest to the transitional justice field, comprising one of several forms that reparations measures can take, it has been central to the post–Cold War development of responses to internal displacement and the broader tendency toward rights-based humanitarianism. However, even rights-based humanitarianism is based on more modest and responsive goals than those that motivate transitional justice. While both fields nominally pursue remedial aims such as redress for violations, the defining goal of humanitarianism (in displacement contexts) is ending displacement through the reintegration of affected individuals and households into a protective social framework. However, the defining goal of transitional justice has always been much broader. By aspiring to support both accountability and political change, transitional justice seeks to reintegrate victims while simultaneously transforming the social framework they are to be reintegrated into.

Humanitarian responses to displacement can contribute to transitional justice aims, most notably through reparative measures related to the property and other rights of the displaced, which can serve as recognition not only of their victimization but also of their restoration as equal citizens and reintegration into society. However, humanitarian actors are ultimately far more dependent on the results of transitional justice processes as a means of ensuring the ultimate sustainability of their efforts to end displacement and prevent it from reoccurring. By restoring social expectations of respect for human rights obligations, transitional justice measures correspond to the baseline prescription set out in the Guiding Principles for avoiding arbitrary displacement—namely, the commitment of "all authorities and international actors [to] respect and ensure respect for their obligations under international law, including human rights and humanitarian law, in all circumstances."[161]

Both internal displacement and transitional justice discourses seek to achieve their objectives primarily by influencing and supporting states in taking steps that, at a minimum, prevent future violations. While the human rights aims of both fields presume the need for effective redress for past violations, this element has not been emphasized as strongly as prospective prevention in the internal displacement field. Restitution has been a signal exception to this rule, particularly in light of its early corrective focus on undoing the physical effects of displacement. However, humanitarian thinking on restitution has shifted toward acceptance of development actors' assertions that justice may in some cases be better served by transforming the unjust or unsustainable conditions that prevailed prior to displacement rather than restoring them. In this way, the environment-building perspective of development experts has helped make restitution more compatible with transitional justice goals related to reconciliation and democratic transformation.

This new emphasis may allow more focused attention on how durable solutions to displacement can facilitate the longer-term processes of equitable development and political transformation that will be crucial to preventing its repetition. However, while humanitarian practitioners' new context sensitivity operates by limiting the circumstances in which strictly corrective restitution is to be prioritized over more broadly remedial measures, the transitional justice goals of recognition and civic trust militate for retaining a corrective approach in exceptional cases, such as when addressing the vulnerabilities of displaced women and indigenous groups. However, the new general emphasis on promoting effective reparative measures rather than restitution per se in humanitarian practice may also reduce the likelihood that restitution will be treated as an entirely separate category from reparations or needlessly divert resources and attention from other transitional justice measures.

NOTES

1   "National authorities have the primary duty and responsibility to provide protection and humanitarian assistance to internally displaced persons within their jurisdiction." United Nations Commission on Human Rights, "Human Rights, Mass Exoduses and Displaced Persons: Addendum–Guiding Principles on Internal Displacement," Report of the Representative of the Secretary-General, Mr. Francis M. Deng, E/CN.4/1998/53/ Add.2, February 11, 1998, principle 3.1 ("Guiding Principles").

2   See, for example, United Nations Development Programme, *Human Development Report 2002: Deepening Democracy in a Fragmented World* (New York: Oxford University Press, 2002).

3   United Nations Development Programme, *Human Development Report 1994: New Dimensions of Human Security* (New York: Oxford University Press, 1994).

4   United Nations General Assembly, "2005 World Summit Outcome," A/60/L.1, September 15, 2005, paras. 138–39.

5   United Nations Sub-commission on the Promotion and Protection of Human Rights, "Principles on Housing and Property Restitution for Refugees and Displaced Persons," Final Report of the Special Rapporteur, Paulo Sérgio Pinheiro, E/CN.4/Sub.2/2005/17, June 28, 2005 ("Pinheiro Principles").

6   Rhodri C. Williams, "The Contemporary Right to Property Restitution in the Context of Transitional Justice" (ICTJ Occasional Paper Series, International Center for Transitional Justice, New York, May 2007).

7   UN Sub-commission on the Promotion and Protection of Human Rights, Pinheiro Principles, principle 2.2.

8   These dilemmas are posed most vividly in the case of groups such as indigenous peoples and categories of victims such as women that may have faced systematic discrimination and marginalization prior to displacement, exacerbating displacement's negative effects and raising concerns about the utility of corrective legal remedies that would simply restore an unsatisfactory status quo ante.

9   The need to address the gap that typically arises between the departure of humanitarian relief actors from post-conflict settings and the arrival of development actors has been acknowledged through the development of "early recovery" approaches emphasizing complementarity between these fields. Cluster Working Group on Early Recovery, *Guidance Note on Early Recovery* (Geneva: CWGER, April 2008). Meanwhile, the relationship between transitional justice and development has been explored in a recent research project by the International Center on Transitional Justice. Pablo de Greiff and Roger Duthie, eds., *Transitional Justice and Development: Making Connections* (New York: Social Science Research Council, 2009).

10   This chapter could treat human rights promotion as a fourth key field of activity in postdisplacement settings but does not for several reasons. First, human rights is a very broad field related to almost all aspects of human life in both conflict and peacetime settings, and unlike the other three fields, it has not involved predictable interventions in postdisplacement settings by operational actors (although the increasing level of post-conflict field engagement by the Office of the UN High Commissioner for Human Rights may require reassessment of this position). Second, human rights approaches are increasingly becoming mainstream in humanitarian and development work and are integral to transitional justice. Finally, human rights standards can be used to argue for both corrective approaches such as restitution and distributive approaches. This means that while human rights–based arguments suffuse debates about restitution, "human rights promotion" as a field of activity does not have a clear stake in the debate being resolved one way or the other.

11   Hugo Slim and Andrew Bonwick, *Protection: An ALNAP Guide for Humanitarian Agencies* (London: Overseas Development Institute, 2005).

12   UN Commission on Human Rights, Guiding Principles, principle 29.2.

13 UN Sub-commission on the Promotion and Protection of Human Rights, Pinheiro Principles.

14 UNHCR Executive Committee, "Conclusion on Legal Safety Issues in the Context of Voluntary Repatriation of Refugees," *EXCOM Conclusions*, no. 101 (LV) (October 8, 2004): para. h.

15 Factory at Chorzow (Germany v. Poland), P.C.I.J., series A, no. 17, judgment no. 13 (1928), 47, http://www.worldcourts.com/pcij/eng/decisions/1928.09.13_chorzow1.htm.

16 Richard Falk, "Reparations, International Law and Global Justice: A New Frontier," in *The Handbook of Reparations*, ed. Pablo de Greiff (Oxford: Oxford University Press, 2006), 483.

17 Article 8 of the declaration reads as follows: "Everyone has the right to an effective remedy by the competent national tribunals for acts violating the fundamental rights granted him by the constitution or by law." United Nations General Assembly, Resolution 217 A (III), "Universal Declaration of Human Rights," A/RES/3/217A, December 10, 1948, http://www.un-documents.net/a3r217a.htm.

18 Antoine Buyse, *Post-conflict Housing Restitution: The European Human Rights Perspective, with a Case-Study on Bosnia and Herzegovina* (Cambridge: Intersentia, 2008), 118–25.

19 For a contemporary depiction of this phenomenon, see Merje Feldmann, "Justice in Space? The Restitution of Property Rights in Tallinn, Estonia," *Cultural Geographies* 6, no. 2 (1999): 165–82.

20 See, for example, Elazar Barkan, *The Guilt of Nations: Restitution and Negotiating Historical Injustices* (New York: Norton, 2000).

21 Williams, "Contemporary Right to Property Restitution," 25. This policy reflected splits within the newly ascendant African National Congress over whether the goal of such measures should be to undo the effects of apartheid land confiscations entirely or to progressively change the racial composition of the powerful commercial agriculture sector without jeopardizing food security.

22 See, for example, Christopher J. Colvin, "Overview of the Reparations Program in South Africa," in de Greiff, *Handbook of Reparations*.

23 Human rights advocates have sought to distinguish post-conflict restitution from its openly ideological Eastern European antecedents. Scott Leckie, "New Directions in Housing and Property Restitution," in *Returning Home: Housing and Property Restitution Rights of Refugees and Displaced Persons*, ed. Scott Leckie (Ardsley, NY: Transnational, 2003), 25–26.

24 Richard Black and Saskia Gent, "Sustainable Return in Post-conflict Contexts," *International Migration* 44, no. 3 (2006): 15–38.

25 General Framework Agreement for Peace in Bosnia and Herzegovina, Paris, December 14, 1995, annex 7, chapter 1, art. 1.1, http://www.nato.int/sfor/basic/gfap.htm.

26 Ibid., annex 7, chapter 1, art. 1.1; and chapter 2, art. 12.6 (setting out the possibility of compensation). See also chapter 1, art. 1.4: "Choice of destination shall be up to the individual or family, and the principle of the unity of the family shall be preserved. The Par-

ties shall not interfere with the returnees' choice of destination, nor shall they compel them to remain in or move to situations of serious danger or insecurity, or to areas lacking in the basic infrastructure necessary to resume a normal life."

27 Williams, "Contemporary Right to Property Restitution," 38.

28 Office of the High Representative, "PLIP Inter-Agency Framework Document," October 15, 2000, http://www.ohr.int/plip/key-doc/default.asp?content_id=5510.

29 For instance, the cases of some categories of claimants barred from restitution programs in Bosnia but not provided with compensation have now been treated by regional human rights mechanisms. See Dokic v. Bosnia and Herzegovina, judgment, app. no. 6518/04, European Court of Human Rights, May 27, 2010.

30 The rules on durable solutions are different with regard to refugees, who may be involuntarily repatriated to their countries of origin in accordance with international refugee law but afterward enjoy the same rights to choice of residence as IDPs. See, for example, Convention Relating to the Status of Refugees, July 28, 1951, 189 U.N.T.S. 150, art. 1.c.5, http://www.unhcr.org/3b66c2aa10.html.

31 See, generally, de Greiff, *Handbook of Reparations*. See also Paige Arthur, "How 'Transitions' Reshaped Human Rights: A Conceptual History of Transitional Justice," *Human Rights Quarterly* 31, no. 2 (2009): 356–57 (noting that reparations remained the "least developed theme" of a seminal conference on transitional justice).

32 Simon Bagshaw, "Property Restitution for Internally Displaced Persons: Developments in the Normative Framework," in Leckie, *Returning Home*.

33 Walter Kälin, *Guiding Principles on Internal Displacement: Annotations*, Studies in Transnational Legal Policy no. 38 (Washington, DC: American Society of International Law, 2000), 72–74.

34 UN Sub-commission on the Promotion and Protection of Human Rights, Pinheiro Principles, principle 1.1.

35 Ibid., principle 2.2.

36 Ibid., principles 2.2 and 2.1, respectively.

37 While principle 2.1 prescribes compensation only where claimed properties are "factually impossible to restore as determined by an independent, impartial tribunal," principle 21.2 clarifies that "states should ensure, as a rule, that restitution is only deemed factually impossible in exceptional circumstances, namely when housing, land and/ or property is destroyed or when it no longer exists, as determined by an independent, impartial tribunal."

38 In 2006 the UN Human Rights Commission was replaced by the Human Rights Council, which has a mandate to strengthen human rights protection worldwide. See the council's website at http://www2.ohchr.org/english/bodies/hrcouncil/.

39 UN Human Rights Commission, Resolution 1998/50, April 17, 1998, para. 1.

40   Thomas G. Weiss and David A. Korn, *Internal Displacement: Conceptualization and Its Conse-quences* (New York: Routledge, 2006).

41   All three office holders, Francis Deng (1992–2004), Walter Kälin (2004–10), and Chaloka Beyani (2010–present), have been supported by a unit within the US-based Brookings Institution, which is currently referred to as the Brookings-LSE Project on Internal Dis-placement. See the project website at http://www.brookings.edu/projects/idp.aspx.

42   Global Protection Cluster Working Group, *Handbook for the Protection of Internally Dis-placed Persons* (Geneva: Inter-Agency Standing Committee, 2010), http://www.unhcr.org/refworld/docid/4790cbc02.html.

43   African Union Convention for the Protection and Assistance of Internally Displaced Persons in Africa, Kampala, Uganda, October 23, 2009, http://www.unhcr.org/refworld/docid/4ae572d82.html.

44   Brookings-Bern Project on Internal Displacement, *Protecting Internally Displaced Persons: A Manual for Law and Policymakers* (Washington, DC: Brookings Institution / Univer-sity of Bern, October 2008), http://www.brookings.edu/papers/2008/1016_internal_displacement.aspx. In light of recent developments such as the UN General Assembly's 2005 endorsement of the Guiding Principles, there are indications that they may even-tually come to be seen as binding on states in the form of customary international law. United Nations General Assembly, Report of the Representative of the Secretary-Gen-eral on the Human Rights of Internally Displaced Persons, Walter Kälin, A/HRC/13/21, January 5, 2010, para. 11.

45   The drafter of the principles, Paulo Sergio Pinheiro, submitted them along with his final report upon the expiry of his mandate. Meanwhile, the United Nations Sub-commis-sion on the Promotion and Protection of Human Rights, which endorsed the principles in 2005, is an expert body without member state representation.

46   The three most significant breakthroughs—incorporation of the principles in the Iraqi national policy on internal displacement, a Colombian Constitutional Court decision on the rights of the displaced, and a protocol to the Great Lakes Pact on Security, Stability and Development in East Africa—have all come in regions where actual implementa-tion of restitution programs has been mixed at best to date.

47   See Scott Leckie, *Housing, Land and Property Rights in Post-conflict Societies: Proposals for a New United Nations Institutional and Policy Framework*, Legal and Protection Policy Research Series, PPLA/2005/01 (Geneva: UNCHR, March 2005).

48   In November 2001, for instance, UNHCR adopted a restitution checklist, but it is not clear whether this has been widely used in the field. *Checklist on the Restitution of Housing and Property* (Geneva: UNHCR, November 28, 2001).

49   General information on the humanitarian reform process and the resulting coordina-tion structures led by UN-HABITAT, as well as specific information on HLP respon-

sibilities, can be found on a dedicated interagency website: OneResponse, http://
oneresponse.info/Pages/default.aspx.

50 UN-HABITAT's tenure as coordinator of the Land, Housing and Property Working
Group has been subject to criticism. See Barbara McCallin, "Housing, Land and Property Issues within the Global Protection Cluster: Making a New Start," *Displacement Solutions Global Update*, no. 3 (October 2009).

51 United Nations Security Council, Report of the Secretary-General on the Protection of
Civilians in Armed Conflict, S/2007/643, October 28, 2007, http://daccess-ods.un.org/
TMP/3090565.50264359.html.

52 See Marion Couldrey and Maurice Herson, eds., "Ten Years of the Guiding Principles on
Internal Displacement," special issue, *Forced Migration Review*, December 2008.

53 Rhodri C. Williams, "Guiding Principle 29 and the Right to Restitution," in Couldrey
and Herson, "Ten Years of the Guiding Principles on Internal Displacement," 23–24.

54 Jakob Rothing and Richard Skretteberg, "NRC: One Last Chance for Colombia's Victims," *Forced Migration Review* 32 (April 2009): 72.

55 Peter Van der Auweraert, "Policy Challenges for Property Restitution in Transition—
the Example of Iraq," in *Reparations for Victims of Genocide, War Crimes and Crimes against
Humanity: Systems in Place and Systems in the Making*, ed. Carla Ferstman, Mariana Goetz,
and Alan Stephens (Leiden: Martinus Nijhoff, 2009), 468.

56 Daniel Fitzpatrick, "Land Policy in Post-conflict Circumstances: Some Lessons from
East Timor," (Working Paper no. 58, New Issues in Refugee Research, Evaluation and
Policy Analysis Unit, UNHCR, Geneva, February 2002).

57 Liz Alden Wily, "Rural Land Relations in Conflict: A Way Forward" (briefing paper,
Afghanistan Research and Evaluation Unit, Kabul, August 2004).

58 Koen Vlassenroot and Chris Huggins, "Land, Migration and Conflict in Eastern DRC," in
From the Ground Up: Land Rights, Conflict and Peace in Sub-Saharan Africa, ed. Chris Huggins
and Jenny Clover (Pretoria: African Center for Technology Studies, 2005).

59 Ingunn Sofie Aursnes and Conor Foley, "Property Restitution in Practice: The Norwegian Refugee Council's Experience" (paper written in connection with the Expert Consultation on the Draft Principles on Housing and Property Restitution for Refugees and
Displaced Persons, Brown University, Providence, Rhode Island, April 21–22, 2005).

60 Barbara McCallin, "Transitional Justice, HLP Restitution and Legal Pluralism" (paper
prepared for ICTJ / Brookings Project on Transitional Justice and Displacement, 2012).

61 See Sara Pantuliano and Samir Elhawary, "Uncharted Territory: Land, Conflict and
Humanitarian Action" (HPG Policy Brief 39, Humanitarian Policy Group, Overseas
Development Institute, London, November 2009).

62 Sara Pantuliano, ed., *Uncharted Territory: Land, Conflict and Humanitarian Action* (Rugby,
UK: Practical Action, 2009).

63 UN Sub-commission on the Promotion and Protection of Human Rights, Pinheiro Principles, principle 2.2.

64 Klaus Deininger, *Land Policies for Growth and Poverty Reduction* (Washington, DC: World Bank, 2003), 11–15.

65 Internal Displacement Monitoring Center, *Whose Land Is This? Land Disputes and Forced Displacement in the Western Forest Area of Côte d'Ivoire* (Geneva: IDMC, October 2009).

66 See, especially, Alex de Waal, "Why Humanitarian Organizations Need to Tackle Land Issues," in Pantuliano, *Uncharted Territory*.

67 John W. Bruce, "International Standards, Improvisation and the Role of International Humanitarian Organizations in the Return of Land in Post-conflict Rwanda," in Pantuliano, *Uncharted Territory*.

68 Pantuliano and Elhawary, "Uncharted Territory," 3.

69 Brookings-Bern Project on Internal Displacement, *IASC Framework on Durable Solutions for Internally Displaced Persons* (Washington, DC: Brookings Institution / University of Bern, April 2010), http://www.brookings.edu/reports/2010/04_durable_solutions.aspx.

70 Ibid., 38.

71 United Nations General Assembly, Resolution 60/147, "Basic Principles and Guidelines on the Right to a Remedy and Reparation for Victims of Gross Violations of International Human Rights Law and Serious Violations of International Humanitarian Law," A/RES/60/147, March 21, 2006, para. 18. While some observers attribute the abandonment of any preference between reparations modalities in the principles to political sensitivities, there are also clear functional justifications for adopting this approach, given that many, if not most, violations of human rights (and humanitarian) law do not involve the taking of a tangible thing that can be restored as such. Williams, "Contemporary Right to Property Restitution," 4–5.

72 Demopoulos and Others v. Turkey, decision on admissibility, app. nos. 46113/99, 3843/02, 13751/02, 13466/03, 10200/04, 14163/04, 19993/04, 21819/04, European Court of Human Rights, March 1, 2010.

73 Although the court based this approach in part on the passage of time since the original displacement, as well as the resulting rights of occupants of claimed property, the decision also allows general discretion to states "to assess the practicalities, priorities and conflicting interests on a domestic level even in a situation such as that pertaining in the northern part of Cyprus." Ibid., para. 119.

74 Ibid., para. 114.

75 Rhodri C. Williams, "Introductory Note—European Court of Human Rights: Demopoulos v. Turkey," *International Legal Materials* 49, no. 3 (May 2010): 819.

76 International Committee of the Red Cross, *Strengthening Protection in War: A Search for Professional Standards* (Geneva: ICRC, 2001). This definition was subsequently endorsed by

the Inter-Agency Standing Committee, which coordinates the work of key humanitarian actors and agencies.

77   Elizabeth G. Ferris, *The Politics of Protection: The Limits of Humanitarian Action* (Washington, DC: Brookings Institution, 2011), 5.

78   Inter-Agency Standing Committee, *Growing the Sheltering Tree: Protecting Rights through Humanitarian Action* (Geneva: IASC, 2002), 115. This tripartite framework for protection activities is often referred to as the "egg model" in light of the concentric approach implied (from a narrow focus on response outward to broader environment-building activities).

79   Ibid.

80   Ibid.

81   Ferris, *Politics of Protection*, 11.

82   Marc Du Bois, "Protection: Fig Leaves and Other Delusions," *Humanitarian Exchange Magazine* 46 (March 2010): 2–4. See also Bryce Campbell, in this volume.

83   In practice, the implementation of environment-building measures in humanitarian settings tends to involve changing the emphasis of existing programming rather than developing new programming. For instance, recent guidance on humanitarian assistance recommends that health care interventions be structured in a manner that adds permanent capacity to existing health care services and facilities rather than duplicating it. Sphere Project, *Humanitarian Charter and Minimum Standards in Humanitarian Response* (Rugby, UK: Practical Action, 2011). Similarly, encouraging beneficiaries to participate in the design of humanitarian programming is increasingly seen as an opportunity to prepare marginalized communities for more effective political participation and encourage mobilization within communities to end inequitable or discriminatory practices. Global Protection Cluster Working Group, *Handbook for the Protection of Internally Displaced Persons*, 416.

84   Cluster Working Group on Early Recovery, *Guidance Note on Early Recovery*, 9.

85   Brookings Institution–London School of Economics Project on Internal Displacement and Internal Displacement Monitoring Centre, *IDPs in Protracted Displacement: Is Local Integration a Solution?* (Washington, DC: Brookings-LSE Project on Internal Displacement / IDMC, May 2011), 8, http://www.internal-displacement.org/publications/is-local-integration-a-solution.

86   Pablo de Greiff, "Theorizing Transitional Justice," in *NOMOS LI: Transitional Justice*, ed. Melissa Williams, Rosemary Nagy, and Jon Elster (New York: New York University Press, 2012).

87   Pablo de Greiff, "Articulating the Links between Transitional Justice and Development: Justice and Social Integration," in de Greiff and Duthie, *Transitional Justice and Development*, 63.

88   Arthur, "How 'Transitions' Reshaped Human Rights," 357.

89   De Greiff, "Theorizing Transitional Justice."

90   Ibid.

91   De Greiff, "Justice and Social Integration," 29.

92   Social and economic rights have been recognized as indivisible from civil and political rights—which are currently the primary object of concern in transitional justice—since the end of the Cold War. Louise Arbour, "Economic and Social Justice for Societies in Transition," *New York University Journal of International Law and Politics* 40, no. 1 (2007): 1–27.

93   "The majority of armed conflicts today occur in countries at low levels of development. Poverty, inequality, and underdevelopment may not in themselves cause armed conflict and human rights abuses, but they can be contributing or enabling factors. Moreover, armed conflict and authoritarianism, and the humanitarian disasters and massive human rights abuses that accompany them, can have an immensely negative and longlasting effect on development. As a result, transitional justice is often pursued in a context of severely underdeveloped economic and social institutions, widespread scarcity of resources, and myriad competing needs." Roger Duthie, introduction to de Greiff and Duthie, *Transitional Justice and Development*, 19.

94   Ibid., 22.

95   "Justice … understood in a broad sense, precisely the sense that deep social transformation calls for, has both corrective and distributive dimensions. Transitional justice is functionally designed to address issues in the sphere of corrective justice, and development can also deal with issues in the 'distributive' side of justice." De Greiff, "Justice and Social Integration," 63.

96   *Factory at Chorzow (Germany v. Poland)*, series A, no. 17, 47. For an example of restitution programming based explicitly on the corrective rationale, see Feldmann, "Justice in Space."

97   There are serious questions about both the feasibility and desirability of a strict corrective approach in settings characterized by mass violations. Pablo de Greiff, "Justice and Reparations," in de Greiff, *Handbook of Reparations*. However, in the case of virtually all transitional justice measures, the goal remains to promote a prospective transition as well as retrospective justice. As a result, even highly retrospective measures such as reparations aim to provide redress in a manner that builds confidence in the capacity of the system to prospectively guarantee equal citizenship and enjoyment of rights. De Greiff, "Theorizing Transitional Justice."

98   Williams, "Contemporary Right to Property Restitution," section 3.b.

99   Chris Huggins, "Linking Broad Constellations of Ideas: Transitional Justice, Land Tenure Reform, and Development," in de Greiff and Duthie, *Transitional Justice and Development*.

100 See, for example, Slim and Bonwick, *Protection: An ALNAP Guide*, 79–101.

101 Weiss and Korn, *Internal Displacement*, 34–35.

102 UN Commission on Human Rights, Guiding Principles, section 3.

103 This is not to say that support for the emergence of international refugee law in the West was without an underlying ideological agenda, nor that refugee status determinations have never been influenced by foreign policy considerations. However, such motivations have typically been denied precisely because they would contradict the stated humanitarian rationale for international protection of refugees.

104 These circumstances are particularly pronounced in internal displacement settings where fallback on international protection by other state authorities is not an option.

105 UN Commission on Human Rights, Guiding Principles, principle 28.1; Walter Kälin, *Guiding Principles on Internal Displacement: Annotations*, rev. ed. (Washington, DC: American Society of International Law, 2008), 126.

106 The fact that minority and indigenous rights tend to be viewed as political concerns as much as legal ones underscores both the difficulty and the necessity of taking them into account in order to sustainably end many of the world's displacement situations. See Thomas Hammarberg, "Persons Displaced During Conflicts Have the Right to Return," press release, Council of Europe Commissioner for Human Rights, 2008. For an account of this dynamic in Turkey, see Bilgin Ayata and Deniz Yükseker, "A Belated Awakening: National and International Responses to the Internal Displacement of Kurds in Turkey," *New Perspectives on Turkey*, no. 32 (2005): 5–42.

107 Brookings-Bern Project on Internal Displacement, *Framework on Durable Solutions*, Quick Reference Guide, A4.

108 "Where there are large disparities between displacement-affected areas and other parts of the country (which could be a source of renewed tension and displacement) tangible commitments on the part of the authorities and partners should be made to progressively realize the economic, social and cultural rights of both IDPs and other affected populations. In many cases, it is necessary to 'build back better' and address root causes of displacement." Brookings-Bern Project on Internal Displacement, *Framework on Durable Solutions*, 69.

109 Ibid., 43.

110 Ibid., 6.

111 The Guiding Principles privilege restitution wherever it is possible but require that some form of "just reparations" be provided in all cases (principle 29.2).

112 *Demopoulos*, European Court of Human Rights, para. 119.

113 UN General Assembly, Resolution 60/147, principle 18.

114 United Nations Security Council, "The Rule of Law and Transitional Justice in Conflict and Post-conflict Societies," Report of the Secretary-General, S/2004/616, August 23, 2004, paras. 54–55, http://www.unhcr.org/4506bc494.html.

115 De Greiff, "Justice and Reparations." See also Peter Van der Auweraert in this volume.

116 De Greiff, "Justice and Reparations," 455–59. De Greiff notes that the expectations generated by isolated judgments based on the application of legal standards that calculate

compensation in direct proportion to harm would be impossible to meet in mass violations settings within the resources typically available to post-conflict states. He also raises procedural concerns related to the likelihood that similarly situated victims in settings where each case must be pursued individually will have differential access to courts and face arbitrary variations in compensation awards.

117 Jaime E. Malamud-Goti and Lucas S. Grosman, "Compensation for Human Rights Abuse: Exploring the Possibilities of Reparative Justice in Transitional Democracies," in de Greiff, *Handbook of Reparations*. Among other things, the authors note that claims in such cases come in high numbers, typically directed at a single set of defendants with limited ability to pay; that judicial approaches may be slow, traumatic for victims, difficult to access, and antagonistic; and that administrative procedures can be crafted to overcome legal impediments such as prescription statutes that would hinder court action.

118 Brookings-Bern Project on Internal Displacement, *Protecting Internally Displaced Persons*, 378.

119 De Greiff, "Justice and Reparations," 460–66.

120 Ibid., 464–65.

121 Ibid., 460–61.

122 Malamud-Goti and Grosman, "Compensation for Human Rights Abuse," 552.

123 De Greiff, "Justice and Reparations," 454.

124 Colombia, Ley 1448 de víctimas y restitución de tierras [Law 1448 on victims and land restitution], draft, 2008, art. 1.

125 Displacement Solutions, *Comments on the Proposed Victims' Law and National Restitution Plan: Respecting and Protecting the Housing, Land and Property Restitution Rights of All Internally Displaced Persons in Colombia* (Geneva: Displacement Solutions, December 22, 2008), para. 53.

126 Ibid., para. 47.

127 De Greiff, "Justice and Reparations."

128 United Nations Sub-commission on the Promotion and Protection of Human Rights, "Study Concerning the Right to Restitution, Compensation and Rehabilitation for Victims of Gross Violations of Human Rights and Fundamental Freedoms," Final Report Submitted by Mr. Theo van Boven, Special Rapporteur, E/CN.4/Sub.2/1993/8, July 2, 1993.

129 Ibid., paras. 127–29 and 134.

130 See, for example, Parliamentary Assembly of the Council of Europe, Resolution 1708, 2010, "Solving Property Issues of Refugees and Displaced Persons," January 28, 2010, paras. 10–10.1: "Bearing in mind these relevant international standards and the experience of property restitution and compensation programmes carried out in Europe to date, member states are invited to ... guarantee timely and effective redress for the loss of access and rights to housing, land and property abandoned by refugees and IDPs

without regard to pending negotiations concerning the resolution of armed conflicts or the status of a particular territory."

131 Leila Hilal, "Transitional Justice Reponses to Palestinian Dispossession: Focus on Restitution" (paper prepared for ICTJ / Brookings Project on Transitional Justice and Displacement, 2012).

132 Brookings-Bern Project on Internal Displacement, *Protecting Internally Displaced Persons*, 48–49.

133 See Federico Andreu-Guzmán, in this volume.

134 Falk, "Reparations, International Law, and Global Justice."

135 Colombia, Decreto 1290 de 2008 crea el programa de reparación individual por vía administrativa para las víctimas de los grupos armados organizados al margen de la ley [Decree 1290 of 2008], April 22, 2008, art. 2.

136 Colombia, Ley de víctimas y de restitución de tierras, art. 9.

137 Author discussions with victims and experts at an international seminar, Desafíos para la reparación integral a las víctimas del conflicto armado interno en Colombia [Challenges for integral reparation to the victims of the internal armed conflict in Colombia], Bogota, October 5–7, 2011.

138 Arthur, "How 'Transitions' Reshaped Human Rights," 341–42.

139 Huggins, "Linking Broad Constellations of Ideas," 364.

140 For a discussion of gender justice and displacement, see Lucy Hovil, in this volume.

141 McCallin, "Transitional Justice, HLP Restitution and Legal Pluralism."

142 See Donny Meertens, "Forced Displacement and Gender Justice in Colombia: Between Disproportional Effects of Violence and Historical Injustice" (paper prepared for ICTJ / Brookings Project on Transitional Justice and Displacement, 2012).

143 CEDAW is a global human rights convention that includes a number of safeguards for women's property rights. Most prominent among these are guarantees of women's equality before the law, including "equal rights to conclude contracts and to administer property" and protection of the equal rights of spouses "in respect of the ownership, acquisition, management, administration, enjoyment and disposition of property, whether free of charge or for a valuable consideration." United Nations General Assembly, Resolution 34/180, "Convention on the Elimination of All Forms of Discrimination against Women," A/Res/34/180, December 18, 1979, arts. 15.2 and 16.1.h, http://www.un.org/womenwatch/daw/cedaw/text/econvention.htm. CEDAW also recognizes "the particular problems faced by rural women and the significant roles which rural women play in the economic survival of their families" and prescribes specific protections, including equal benefits from rural development and "access to agricultural credit and loans, marketing facilities, appropriate technology and equal treatment in land and agrarian reform as well as in land resettlement schemes." Ibid., arts. 14.1 and 14.2.g.

144 UN Commission on Human Rights, Guiding Principles, principle 4.2.

145 Ruth Rubio-Marín, "The Gender of Reparations: Setting the Agenda," in *What Happened to the Women? Gender and Reparations for Human Rights Violations*, ed. Ruth Rubio-Marín (New York: Social Science Research Council, 2006), 25.

146 Nairobi Declaration on Women's and Girls' Right to a Remedy and Reparation (International Meeting on Women's and Girls' Right to a Remedy and Reparation, Nairobi, March 2007), declaration 3.

147 UN Commission on Human Rights, Guiding Principles, principle 9.

148 The declaration asserts not only a clear duty to "give legal recognition and protection" to the current lands, territories, and resources of indigenous peoples but also to redress historical confiscations: "Indigenous peoples have the right to redress, by means that can include restitution or, when this is not possible, just, fair and equitable compensation, for the lands, territories and resources which they have traditionally owned or otherwise occupied or used, and which have been confiscated, taken, occupied, used or damaged without their free, prior and informed consent." United Nations General Assembly, Resolution 61/295, "United Nations Declaration on the Rights of Indigenous Peoples," A/RES/61/295, October 2, 2007, paras. 26.3 and 28.

149 UN Commission on Human Rights, Guiding Principles, principle 9.

150 Centre for Minority Rights Development (Kenya) and Minority Rights Group International on Behalf of Endorois Welfare Council v. Kenya, 276/2003, African Commission on Human and Peoples' Rights, February 4, 2010.

151 The ruling concerns the fate of a pastoralist group removed from its traditional lands to make way for a nature reserve in the 1970s. Drawing heavily on precedents from the inter-American system, the African Commission recognized the fundamental connection between the Endorois and their land, as well as the radical insecurity that resulted from displacement. The commission asserted a state obligation to recognize the inherent title of indigenous peoples to their traditional lands, found this duty violated with regard to the Endorois, and ordered restitution, along with other forms of reparations.

152 Huggins, "Linking Broad Constellations of Ideas," 364.

153 Rubio-Marín, "Gender of Reparations," 33.

154 Ibid., 30.

155 Human Rights Watch, "An Approach to Reparations," July 19, 2001, http://www.hrw.org/news/2001/07/19/approach-reparations.

156 I have argued that the last of these factors may have been decisive in the *Demopoulos* decision by the European Court of Human Rights. Rhodri C. Williams and Ayla Gürel, "The European Court of Human Rights and the Cyprus Property Issue: Charting a Way Forward" (Paper 1/2011, Peace Research Institute Oslo, October 2011).

157 UN Sub-commission on the Promotion and Protection of Human Rights, Pinheiro Principles, principles 13.2 and 15.3.

158 Ibid., principle 15.2.

159 Brookings-Bern Project on Internal Displacement, *Protecting Internally Displaced Persons*, 186.

160 *Endorois Welfare Council*, African Commission on Human and Peoples' Rights, para. 209.

161 UN Commission on Human Rights, Guiding Principles, principle 5.

CHAPTER 4

The Potential for Redress: Reparations and Large-Scale Displacement

Peter Van der Auweraert

In the past two decades, both transitional justice and displacement—especially internal displacement—have attracted significant attention as central issues to be addressed in international peacebuilding and postcrisis stabilization efforts.[1] In part, this stands as testimony to the political efforts and success of a loose coalition of international scholars, nongovernmental organizations, international civil servants, and progressive politicians, diplomats, and government officials that have worked tirelessly to get and keep these issues on the international agenda. Historically, the two issues have come to international prominence together, supported by different communities of activists. It is only recently that these communities have started to engage with each other on how to connect their fields of political action, and discussions remain in the early stages.[2] One focus of this shared attention has been on how reparations efforts in transitional contexts should extend to displacement, in addition to the other violations and crimes such efforts usually cover. That these initial contacts are timely and relevant is underscored by the multiple situations around the world where massive violations of international humanitarian and human rights law have gone hand in hand with large-scale displacement, both of which need to be addressed in the context of peacemaking, peacebuilding, and transitional measures following regime change.

While much of this mutual engagement has been at the international policy and advocacy level, some reparations programs have in fact engaged with displacement.[3] Prominent national experiences include the compensation program established in 2004 by Law 5233 in Turkey (which compensates the displaced for their inability to access assets during displacement)[4] and the administrative reparations program established by the recent Victims' Law in Colombia (which after long and arduous political discussions now foresees redress for displacement as such).[5] The Property Claims Commission in Iraq also deserves mentioning here, especially the provisions in its mandate specifying access to its restitution and compensation program for Iraq's large diaspora.[6] While it cannot be qualified as a transitional justice effort, the United

Nations Compensation Commission (UNCC) can serve as an example of a compensation scheme that provides redress for large-scale displacement. Created by the UN Security Council in the aftermath of the first Gulf War (1990–91), the UNCC provided financial compensation to, among others, those who fled Kuwait and Iraq because of the latter's invasion of the former.[7]

Against this background, in this chapter I take a closer look at reparations in the context of large-scale displacement, focusing in particular on the idea that reparations programs should provide specific redress for displacement, independent from redress for other human rights violations. I focus on four central themes or questions connected to the idea of reparations for displacement: (1) what reparations should look like in the context of redress for large-scale displacement, (2) how to define *displacement* and whether the concept as it currently exists within the international protection discourse and practice can serve as a basis for reparations, (3) who the stakeholders are in a reparations effort, and (4) what the redress should be for (material losses, psychological suffering, etc.). In the last section, I discuss the wisdom and feasibility of reparations for large-scale displacement in fragile state contexts and in situations where extreme poverty and widespread deprivation prevail.

FROM JURIDICAL REPARATIONS TO REPARATIONS AS BENEFITS FOR VICTIMS

Juridical reparations refers to measures that "may be employed to redress the various types of harms that victims may have suffered as a consequence of certain crimes."[8] The "Van Boven-Bassiouni Principles," adopted by the UN in 2005, define those measures as including "restitution, compensation, rehabilitation, satisfaction and guarantees of non-repetition."[9] Juridical reparations are part and parcel of contemporary international human rights law, international humanitarian law, and international criminal law, as evidenced, for example, by the Rome Statute of the International Criminal Court.[10] The concept has been primarily developed through international, regional, and national courts and tribunals, and the European and Inter-American Courts of Human Rights have played a preponderant and often trailblazing role. Today a rich treasure of jurisprudence exists, setting out the scope and nature of the reparations measures to which victims of different types of human rights and humanitarian law violations are entitled.

The objective of juridical reparations is full restitution, or returning the victims to the situation they were in before the violations took place. This is achieved by undoing or, if that is impossible, compensating all forms of material and physical harm inflicted on the victims. Methodologically, full restitution requires the identification and evaluation of the particular harm each individual victim has suffered. This requires an individualized process and a quite intensive use of different types of evidence (documentary evidence, expert valuations, witnesses statements, and so on), as it is crucial for full restitution to establish exactly what losses and harms each victim has sustained. By definition, in the context of juridical reparations, measures of redress will tend to differ from case to case, as two victims will rarely have been in identical situations before the violations (even if they suffered from the same type of violations). The judicial processes used by courts and tribunals are well adapted to implement juridical reparations, and even if a special-purpose body is established to provide reparations for a specific caseload, the use of an individualized, judicial-style process will be unavoidable if full restitution is the aim. Inherently, judicial processes dealing with reparations for human rights violations tend to be time- and resource-consuming and hence quite demanding on the victims who need to participate in the identification, verification, and valuation of the exact violations and losses that were inflicted on them. More often than not, professional legal representation is indispensable for effective participation in such processes.

When the issue is redress for a very large number of people, juridical reparations, and the objective of full, or integral, restitution, is usually neither a viable nor, as will be argued further, a desirable option. Juridical reparations can work well in contexts where human rights violations are the exception rather than the rule and where as a consequence the universe of victims is limited. Similarly, the individualized approach to determining reparations demanded by integral restitution is possible in contexts where the number of victims is small, the specific human rights violations from which they suffered are relatively easy to establish, and the evidence to prove the particular damages each victim sustained is not too problematic to come by. None of these conditions exist in contexts where, over a prolonged period time, human rights and humanitarian law violations were the rule rather than the exception, and where many thousands of people were affected as victims of those violations, including displacement. This is even more the case if such violations occurred in environments characterized by great informality, where document trails of birth certificates, identity cards, and evidence of residence or property rights are simply unavailable for most people. In such situations, full restitution and the individualized approach that needs to accompany it tend to be impossible from both an operational and a fiscal perspective.[11] The selected country examples in the box below serve as a reminder of the size and scope of several displacement situations, many of which are informal (with the notable exception of Iraq, with its long bureaucratic tradition of documenting nearly everything).[12] It is clear that the opportunities and limitations for reparations in such contexts will be shaped by the sheer number of people the programs are intended to serve.

- ✓ **Afghanistan**: more than 300,000 IDPs and 3 million refugees
- ✓ **Colombia**: between 3.6 and 5 million IDPs and more than 100,000 recognized refugees[13]
- ✓ **Democratic Republic of Congo**: about 1.7 million IDPs and around 500,000 refugees
- ✓ **Iraq**: an estimated 2.8 million IDPs and about 1 million refugees
- ✓ **Palestine**: 4.7 million refugees registered with the UN Relief and Works Agency for the Palestinian Refugees in the Near East[14]
- ✓ **Pakistan**: close to 1 million IDPs and more than 30,000 refugees
- ✓ **Somalia**: about 1.5 million IDPs and more than 700,000 refugees

---

In contexts of mass human rights violations, it is more useful to understand reparations as referring to "attempts to provide benefits directly to the victims of certain types of crime."[15] From a material perspective, this type of reparations does not aim for integral restitution but rather for the apparently more modest objective of delivering benefits that are adequate and fair and that, under most circumstances, will fall short of making up for the total losses victims sustained. Procedurally, this type of reparations does not require an individualized judicial or quasi-judicial process[16] and can be implemented through much lighter and faster procedures with, crucially, much more flexible evidentiary standards.[17] While at first sight this type of reparations may seem to short-change victims, in reality the (material) trade-off it appears to involve can be quite desirable from a transitional justice as well as a social justice perspective. Whereas juridical reparations tend to be available only to the relatively few victims who have the resources, education, evidence, and stamina to file and succeed a claim in court, reparations programs focusing on delivering benefits to victims have the potential to provide redress to, if not all, then at least the majority of victims, including the most vulnerable and needy among them. What distinguishes this type of reparations program from others aimed at victims' assistance are its "roots as a legal entitlement based on an obligation to repair harm, and ... an element of recognition of wrongdoing as well as harm, atonement or making good."[18]

In terms of the benefits reparations programs of this type can deliver, no benefits need be excluded on a principled basis alone (although, arguably, the choice of benefits is limited by the "adequate and fair" criterion, which will be explained further). Benefits can be symbolic, material, or both. Examples of symbolic benefits include "official apologies, rehabilitation, the change of names of public spaces, the establishment of days of commemoration, the creation of museums and parks dedicated to the memory of victims."[19] The process of adopting and implementing a reparations program can contain an important symbolic element, even if it formally only provides material benefits, provided it is done properly (itself a criteria that is highly contextual). A common material benefit that so far has been a component in all large-scale reparations programs is monetary compensation for individual victims, which can be delivered in cash (single payment or installments), in the form of a pension or allowance, or through shares in microfinance institutions.[20] Alternatives to cash are preferential or priority access to certain types of public services or support, such as psychosocial support, targeted physical health services,[21] social housing or housing allowances, free education, and other types of livelihood support. Finally, reparations programs can provide benefits to individual victims ("individual reparations") or collectives ("community" or "collective" reparations[22]). While the latter form appears to be gathering support among transitional justice advocates, questions linger as to whether "community reparations" can ever be scaled up sufficiently to deal with a large universe of victims and affected communities and whether "such measures can be sufficiently differentiated from development programs."[23]

Given that reparations that provide benefits for victims do not have integral restitution as an objective and guideline to determine what redress should look like, the questions that arise are how to then determine that the reparations effort is indeed sufficient from a material point of view and whether a formula exists that can distinguish "worthy" from "unworthy" reparations efforts. What can and will eventually be done depends on a myriad of highly contextual legal and nonlegal factors, which include the relative political prominence of the issue of victims' reparations in comparison with other pressing matters, such as the demobilization of ex-combatants; the balance of power between local political actors (and their respective positions on victims' reparations); the level of organization and political influence of victims' organizations and other civil society actors (and, indeed, their particular priorities and demands); and the international community's influence or lack thereof on local political decisionmaking, as well as that community's priorities and preferences in the given transitional situation. An additional factor is the extent to which displacement itself is on the political radar and, indeed, from what perspective it is viewed by different political actors (it may well be that the reparations angle is simply neither used nor advocated for by the relevant local actors). Moreover, the extent to which a large-scale reparations program is subject to judicial oversight or interference may also have an impact on the benefits it eventually provides. In practice, the level of judicial control depends on the activism and attitudes of the local judiciary, the influence of international law on the domestic legal framework, domestic law, and the willingness and ability of victims' organizations to use the courts for reparations purposes.

In terms of what reparations suffice, then, no magic formula exists. However, in the context of large-scale reparations programs, the benefits provided to the victims should at least be adequate and fair. While it is difficult to pin down in the abstract what benefits can be regarded as adequate and fair, as views and standards vary from context to context, this can be a useable criterion when considered against the background of a specific situation. The more complex question is in whose eyes this adequate-and-fair standard should be met and to what extent it is possible (and important) that a consensus around this is formed. First, unless most victims perceive the benefits provided by a reparations program as adequate and fair,[24] the program is unlikely to bring full political closure to the reparations issue. Witness, for example, how long World War II victims of forced labor kept their reparations demands alive in light of the failure of (mostly) German companies that had profited from this forced labor to provide reparations that the victims considered adequate and fair.[25] Second, reparations programs also have the potential to divide the victim population from within. What is adequate and fair for one segment of that population may be seen as inappropriate and unfair by another segment. This relates to a general, and sometimes overlooked, point that the universe of victims is seldom uniform. Usually, it will be as diverse in its opinions and views, including those about the specifics of reparations and transitional justice, as the wider population in the society. But more specifically, reparations policies can themselves divide victims, and in the context of displacement, perceptions about diasporas and internally displaced populations can vary quite starkly among victims of human rights violations who never left their homes, which will be discussed in more detail later. Third, the perceptions of the broader population also matter, arguably to a lesser degree than that of the victims, although it is difficult to conceive of a successful reparations program that would not be accepted by the broader society.

Beyond underscoring that "adequate and fair" is a contextual yardstick that faces its ultimate test in victims' perceptions, it is worth underlining that the extent to which reparative benefits allow victims to overcome social exclusion, reduce their vulnerability, and reconstruct their lives is likely to play a big role in how they think about the effort. Displaced persons in Kenya expressing the desire to have "their lives restored to normality"[26] when asked about their reparative demands is just one indication of how important it is for a reparations program to be about the future as well as about the past. This is especially true in contexts where those who are now victims were poor and destitute before the human rights violations took place. For such victims, a reparations program focusing on integral restitution—and hence looking at the past as a measurement to determine what to do today—would yield little in terms of opportunities to construct a better, more humane and dignified life.[27] They instead require a forward-looking effort, just like victims whose protracted displacement, lasting years if not decades, has pushed them (further) into poverty and despair and for whom the prior situation is not more than a distant, often idealized memory. Simplified, large-scale reparations should not seek to recreate society as it existed before the conflict or the human rights violations (this was, after all, the environment in which conflict and violations found a fertile breeding ground) but rather aim to positively contribute to the development of a new society that, in some significant way, is better than the one that existed before. It is difficult to see, then, how reparations could be successful without being connected to progressive politics, in the nonpartisan sense of trying to create a more just society with less despair and more shared "social hope."[28]

Working toward a reparations policy that meaningfully increases victims' ability to construct better lives for themselves almost invariably requires taking two steps. First, policymakers need access to up-to-date and reliable information about the broad, socioeconomic make-up and situation of the victim population and, ideally, how they compare to the overall population. Without knowing much about the victim population's (relative) levels of poverty, education, employment, and access to shelter and health services, for example, policymakers will find it difficult to design and target reparative benefits in the best possible way. When a reparations policy is being discussed, this information may already be available, as it is not uncommon for international humanitarian organizations to carry out detailed assessments of the displaced population during a crisis or conflict.[29] Academic studies may also be able to help policymakers get a clearer picture of the background and situation of the victim population.[30] This type of information collection can be complementary to the work carried out by truth commissions, which tend to focus on the nature and truth of the violations, rather than the socioeconomic profile of the victim population. Second, policymakers and lawmakers working to turn the reparative demands of victims into a real policy need to have a grasp of the developmental effects that different benefits are likely to have. Moreover, reparations policies may work best in terms of lifting people out of poverty if they are coordinated with, or are an integral part of, a broader strategy for pro-poor economic growth and development.[31] This is necessary to ensure that reparations fulfill their forward-looking potential, but it is also a matter of good governance. In a context of scarce resources and multiple needs, it would be irresponsible to spend significant amounts of public funds on reparations without ensuring that they provide the highest possible economic return, for the victims as well as for the broader society. Integrating these economic aspects into the design of a reparations policy can be a challenge, as those who drive reparations policymaking often tend to have a legal and human rights background and limited knowledge about how to generate economic growth and development. To overcome this hurdle, a multidisciplinary approach must be adopted from the outset at both the level of policy development (where national and international experts may be consulted) and at the institutional level (for example, within a truth commission that has a mandate to make recommendations on reparations).

The types of crimes or violations a reparations program can provide redress for is, of course, dependent on the types of violations that occurred. What a program ends up covering is, however, also invariably a product of the specific politics involved in bringing it about. Relevant political actors, in this respect, can include the main political parties; civil society actors, including religious organizations; victims' communities and their organizations; the international community; and international, regional, or national courts. The jurisprudence of such courts has sometimes proved to be one of the catalysts for governments to establish reparations programs and, indeed, bring certain crimes and violations to the forefront of the political agenda.[32] Truth commissions require a special mention, as they have played a key role in calling for reparations in a number of countries, including Morocco, Chile, Guatemala, Peru, and, possibly soon, Nepal. In practice, reparations programs have focused on serious violations of basic civil and political rights and international humanitarian law, providing redress for, among other crimes, unlawful killings and assassinations, torture and unlawful imprisonment, gender-based violence, forced disappearances, forced and slave labor, and illegal seizure of land and property. Displacement was, as I have already indicated, included as a separate violation in the UNCC mandate,[33] the Turkish Law 5233,[34] and the recent Victims' Law in Colombia.[35] In addition, the Comprehensive Reparations Program in Peru regards those who suffered from forced displacement as conflict victims eligible for reparations.[36] Whether displacement is treated as a separate violation in future reparations programs will depend on local political contingencies, including the extent to which international actors advocate this as a desirable practice.[37]

In addition to the core objective of delivering benefits that are adequate and fair to victims of certain crimes,[38] reparations programs can serve at least two additional objectives: to recognize and acknowledge the victims and what they went through and to contribute to reestablishing "civic trust."[39] As already indicated, it is the element of recognition and acknowledgment that sets a reparations program fully apart from humanitarian assistance, development aid, and ordinary social policies.[40] This is a complex matter, but it suffices here to emphasize that whether victims feel that there is genuine recognition and acknowledgment will affect how they perceive the reparations effort as whole. Civic trust refers to shared normative expectations and the ability to trust that institutions and fellow citizens are acting on the basis of shared values, norms, and principles.[41] Massive human rights violations tend to leave a legacy of mistrust between the victims and the state and, more broadly, a very low level of civic trust. Reparations programs can contribute to improving trust between the state and the victims (although a serious effort in this respect may well require nothing less than a full overhaul of state institutions' internal cultures and management), and they can also, through the affirmation of certain fundamental norms such as respect for basic human rights, have a positive impact on relationships between citizens (although each context would require empirical research to determine whether this is indeed the case). Finally, reparations policies should aim to avoid causing new grievances or social divisions, especially in countries that have just emerged from internal conflict. As will be discussed later on, this can be a particularly relevant issue in the context of reparations for displacement.

DEFINING DISPLACEMENT IN THE CONTEXT OF REPARATIONS

Defining displacement is central to developing a reparations program and determining who can benefit from it. The challenge is how to delineate displacement from other types of migration or population movement that should not be included in the effort to provide redress. At the international level at least, the determination of what displacement means in the context of transitional justice has so far received only limited attention. Advocates and supporters of reparations for displacement have mostly defined it as referring to internally displaced persons (IDPs) and, to a lesser extent, refugees.[42] This is in line with the current international protection framework and discourse, which focuses mostly on these two categories, with a shift in emphasis from refugees to IDPs over the past two decades, usually defended by reference to the greater (and increasing) number of IDPs and the smaller (and decreasing) number of refugees worldwide.[43] This section's point of discussion concerns the extent to which policymakers can regard this international framework—and its implied view of migration—as a sufficiently sound basis for constructing and implementing national reparations policies.

EXTERNAL DISPLACEMENT AND INTERNATIONAL PROTECTION: REFUGEES

We live in an international system constructed around the concept of state sovereignty—that is, the idea that the state has the liberty to do what it wants within its own territory.[44] In reality, the concept of state sovereignty is more complex (and, indeed, limited) than that, but this basic description structures many of the debates and policies in the international realm. [45] Despite globalization and an ever-shrinking world, sovereignty continues to function as a description of statehood, a norm that needs to be respected in international relations, and a status many continue to aspire to (witness the population's jubilation at the independence of South Sudan in 2011). In this system, the management of migration and, more broadly, cross-border movements of people is an integral part of each state's sovereign powers. The regulation of who can enter or stay in a state's territory and the connected activity of border protection are among the most jealously guarded prerogatives of sovereign states. Notice, for example, how the International Covenant on Civil and Political Rights carefully protects the right to free movement and choice of residence within one state only for those who are "lawfully" within that state[46] and limits states' right to expulse aliens only on the condition that such expulsion should be in accordance with national law.[47] Similarly, the covenant accords anyone the right to leave any state, including one's own, but fails to provide a corresponding right to access the territory of any state other than one's own.[48] This background underscores the exceptional nature of the system established by the 1951 UN Convention on the Status of Refugees.

The Refugee Convention establishes an international protection regime that obliges all state parties to the convention to allow any "migrant" who falls within its refugee definition to remain in their territory and enjoy their protection. Article 1.a.2 defines a refugee as a person who,

> owing to well-founded fear of being persecuted for reasons of race, religion, nationality, membership of a particular social group or political opinion, is outside the country of his nationality and is unable or, owing to such fear, is unwilling to avail himself of the protection of that country; or who, not having a nationality and being outside the country of his former habitual residence as a result of such events, is unable or, owing to such fear, is unwilling to return to it.[49]

Central to the convention's protection regime is the allocation of a particular legal status—"refugee status"—through an individual asylum process, carried out by either the national authorities of the host state or the UN High Commissioner for Refugees (UNHCR), the international agency mandated with the protection of refugees.[50] Obtaining refugee status is a formal confirmation that the person in question did indeed have a "well-founded fear of being persecuted" and hence has the right to remain in the territory of the host state. While the 1951 Refugee Convention has had (and continues to have) its critics, the fact remains that, sixty years after it came about, it continues to be a source of protection for many thousands of people around the world.

The question most relevant for the discussion here, however, is whether policymakers working on reparations for displacement can assume that, at least in the vast majority of cases, the convention's concept of a refugee adequately captures the category of people who have been displaced beyond the borders of their countries of habitual residence. There are at least two reasons for exercising caution in relying on this definition in the context of a reparations effort and transitional justice programming more generally.

The first reason has to do with the changed nature of migration crises in recent decades and the increased gulf between the premises on which the 1951 Refugee Convention was based and the reality of displacement in the twenty-first century. Historically, the protection regime established through the convention was created to address a very clear problem: how to protect people who are persecuted by their own states for political, religious, or other reasons. It also found its origins in the Cold War and the need to protect those "persecuted by Communist regimes."[51] The core image underlying the convention—one that many people used to associate with the term *refugee*—was that of the lone opponent of an oppressive regime who, after a heroic fight for democracy and human rights, was forced to flee across borders in fear of his or her life. Looking at population movements in the past twenty years, however, it is clear this image no longer reflects the majority of people who flee. Rather than a small stream of individuals seeking protection from persecution by their governments, present-day migration crises are characterized by large groups crossing national borders because of a combination of drivers. Events such as the ongoing exodus of thousands of people from Somalia into northeastern Kenya and Ethiopia,[52] the flight of tens of thousands of people from Libya into neighboring Egypt and Tunisia during the uprising against Gadhafi,[53] and the mass exodus from Zimbabwe to South Africa involving an estimated 2 million people between 2005 and 2009[54] all raise important issues of international protection but do not easily fit within, and have little to do with, the parameters of the 1951 Refugee Convention.

There is a vivid debate within the field of refugee studies about what the changed face of forced migration means for the current international refugee protection framework.[55] In many, if not most, contemporary contexts, only a few of those who flee across national borders are likely to be able to show an individual, well-founded fear of persecution as demanded by the 1951 Refugee Convention. In short, the risk is that a reparations effort for displacement that limits its scope to the 1951 definition of a refugee would end up excluding the majority of those who left their countries during periods of violent conflict, repression, or widespread human rights violations. Clearly, the extent to which this risk becomes reality and the degree to which such exclusion matters from a transitional justice perspective depend on the context and the reparations policy in question; however, it remains a factor to be kept in mind when discussing how to define displacement in the context of reparations.

The second reason for caution has to do with the evolving and frequently disputed meaning of the 1951 definition of a refugee. There are two interrelated components to this. First, the 1951 refugee concept has been subject to interpretations that, at both the national and international level, have evolved over time in conjunction with changes in the broader political, social, and cultural environments. Witness, for example, how awareness and practice around the gendered use and application of the 1951 definition have evolved over the past decades.[56] In the 1950s and 1960s, the questions of whether women qualify as a social group under the Refugee Convention and whether a well-founded fear of persecution for being a women could be a sufficient ground for refugee status were simply not topics of discussion. In contrast, various national jurisdictions now extend protection to certain categories of female refugees.[57] Second, interpretations of the 1951 refugee concept differ between, but also within, national settings, with some states interpreting the concept liberally and broadly and others interpreting it restrictively. Even fundamental issues, such as whether persecution by a non-state actor can give rise to refugee status, can receive different answers in different jurisdictions.[58] Within states, different authorities, courts, tribunals, and administrative entities involved in the asylum process frequently disagree with each other about the exact scope and content of the 1951 refugee concept.[59] Finally, UNHCR and state parties to the convention at times also find themselves at odds over the right interpretation of the concept.[60]

In terms of reparations for displacement, we can draw two conclusions from the reality of competing interpretations of the 1951 refugee concept. First, if policymakers decide to include the 1951 refugee definition in their legal framework for reparations, they should clarify and further define certain elements in the definition to avoid unintentionally excluding certain victims (for example, in a situation where the majority of victims suffered from persecution at the hands of non-state actors, it may be important to explicitly mention that this is deemed to be covered by the 1951 refugee definition). Second, the fact that different national asylum procedures can lead to different outcomes for similar cases puts into question whether a reparations program should ever rely solely on refugee status as recognized in the host states to which the relevant population has fled. While refugees from countries such as Colombia, Iraq, and Somalia (all countries that have diasporas scattered around the world) may have fled similar situations, whether they eventually obtain refugee status will depend on the interpretation used by the asylum process of the country where they end up.

The broader political environment in the host countries may also influence how refugees from the same country fare. For example, out of an estimated 455,000 Colombian refugees worldwide, an estimated 86 percent live in Ecuador, Panama, and Venezuela.[61] Despite having fled under broadly similar circumstances, the Colombian refugees' formal legal situation differs widely depending on which of the three countries they ended up in. In Panama and Venezuela, "the majority of Colombians in need of international protection remain 'invisible', not seeking international protection and instead remaining undocumented or using alternative migratory routes," while in Ecuador, "generally the most receptive of these countries to refugees," many have been formally recognized and documented as refugees.[62] In situations like these, a national reparations program should reinvestigate whether those involved have indeed been displaced under conditions amounting to persecution.

A final comment here concerns the fact that a significant number of countries have not ratified the 1951 Refugee Convention, especially in Asia and the Middle East.[63] The Palestinian refugees are not covered by the 1951 Refugee

Convention but instead fall under the mandate of the UN Relief and Works Agency for Palestinian Refugees in the Near East.[64] Arguably, the Palestinian refugee situation is the one that has seen the most research on the question of reparations and, especially, land restitution.[65] This further underscores the limited scope for directly applying the 1951 refugee definition in the context of reparations programs.

INTERNAL DISPLACEMENT AND INTERNATIONAL PROTECTION: IDPs

Attempts to develop a specific international protection regime for IDPs came to the fore in the 1990s, eventually leading to what has become the key international document in this regard—the UN Guiding Principles on Internal Displacement. Presented by the representative of the secretary-general on the human rights of IDPs to the UN Commission on Human Rights in April 1998, the Guiding Principles have been gathering increased recognition ever since.[66] Roberta Cohen, one of the protagonists in the political struggle to bring the plight of IDPs to the forefront of international attention, points to four reasons why the idea that IDPs needed international protection eventually got traction among key governments and within the United Nations.[67] These include a growing realization of the security context of internal displacement and, especially, of how large-scale internal population movements not only can disrupt the stability of the affected country but also frequently undermine regional and international security. Moreover, the change in the notion of sovereignty after the end of the Cold War created a new possibility for crossing borders and reaching people in need. Also, the growth in the number of IDPs was an important factor: "In 1982, 1.2 million people were found to be uprooted in their home countries. Four years later the total had grown to 14 million. By 1995, there were an estimated 20 to 25 million in more than 40 countries, twice as many as refugees."[68] Finally, the asylum agenda had an influence on the increasing willingness of the international community to look at international protection for IDPs. The post–Cold War increase in refugees, especially from the Global South, brought to the fore the idea that protecting and assisting people within their own borders was the first line of defense against ever larger refugee flows and rising asylum applications. In short, assisting IDPs in their own countries was seen as a way to avoid the same people becoming refugees.

From a legal perspective, there are significant differences between the international protection regime for refugees and the one for IDPs. Whereas the former is enshrined in an international convention, the latter is laid down in an international "soft law" instrument[69] developed by a group of international experts but never negotiated and formally adopted by the international community of states.[70] In principle, then, the Guiding Principles are not legally binding on states. The proponents of the principles maintain, however, that the practical impact of this difference is less than meets the eye, given that the principles "are consistent with international human rights law and international humanitarian law and to a large extent thus codify and make explicit guarantees protecting internally displaced persons that are inherent in these bodies of law."[71] In that sense, they only repeat obligations that governments already had based on the international "hard law" contained in human rights treaties, the Geneva Conventions, and international customary law. The Guiding Principles have in fact become the dominant framework through which international actors tend to approach crisis situations involving large internal population movements.[72] Similarly, an increasing number of national governments have incorporated the principles into their legislation and displacement policies.[73] Finally, a number of regional efforts have strengthened the legal and political standing of the Guiding Principles, including the Great Lakes Protocol on the Protection and Assistance to Internally Displaced Persons, which obliges signatory governments to incorporate the Guiding Principles into their national laws,[74] and the African Union Convention on the Protection and Assistance of Internally Displaced Persons in Africa, which is broadly based on the Guiding Principles.[75]

Can the international protection framework's conception of displacement be used as a basis for a reparations program? The definition of an IDP is much broader than the 1951 definition of a refugee and therefore much more grounded in the reality of today's migration crises. The Guiding Principles define IDPs as "persons or groups of persons who have been forced or obliged to flee or to leave their homes or places of habitual residence, in particular as a result of or in order to avoid the effects of armed conflict, situations of generalized violence, violations of human rights or natural or human-made disasters, and who have not crossed an internally recognized state border."[76] Using this definition in the context of a reparations program for displacement, then, is unlikely to lead to the same level of exclusion as the 1951 refugee concept would. In that sense, the former may often be more useful to policymakers than the latter. However, reparations programs will likely still have to undertake efforts to identify who is an IDP in a given context.

It is worth emphasizing here that the term *internally displaced person*, unlike *refugee*, does not denote a legal status, at least as it is intended in the Guiding Principles. As the *Handbook for the Protection of Internally Displaced Persons* puts it, "The IDP definition is a descriptive definition rather than a legal definition," one that "simply describes the factual situation of a person being uprooted within his/her country of habitual residence" and "does not confer a special status or rights in the same way that recognition as a refugee does."[77] One implication of this is that, from an international perspective, there is no need for an equivalent to the asylum process in an IDP context. In practice, however, information is often available about IDPs that reparations programs can rely on, at least as a starting point. For example, in countries such as Colombia, official procedures exist to register IDPs, usually in the context of programs intended to provide specific support or assistance to the displaced population.[78] Furthermore, in most contexts where large-scale displacement is taking place, international humanitarian actors will register IDPs as part of their efforts to manage and target humanitarian aid. One caveat, however, is that both official and international registration efforts may not be exhaustive. For official procedures, access may be an issue, especially for the most vulnerable IDPs, as may be the capacity of national institutions responsible for registration. International registration efforts tend to focus on IDPs in camps, leaving out those living with host families or in rented accommodations in urban settings. Another caveat, which applies especially to international humanitarian efforts to register IDPs, concerns the criteria that are used to decide who to register and how "tight" the registration process is. Humanitarian registration is not an official administrative process, nor is it intended to be. However, the extent to which this hinders a reparations program's adoption of IDP registration as sufficient evidence for its purposes is a contextual issue that needs to be thought through ahead of time. Notwithstanding earlier registration efforts, this may be another reason for reparations programs to get involved in determining who is an IDP.

DISTINGUISHING BETWEEN VOLUNTARY MIGRATION AND DISPLACEMENT

Providing benefits to victims through a reparations program inevitably involves a decision as to who can and who cannot be considered a victim. Such choices need to be made at the policy level—that is, at the moment the program mandate is being debated and developed—and at the operational level— that is, when the categories and their respective definitions contained in the mandate need to be applied to real-life cases and claims. Two important pitfalls exist in respect of this exercise: the program can be so restrictive that victims that reasonably should have been included in the effort to provide redress find themselves excluded, or it can be so broad in its mandate or lax in the concrete application of the victims' categories that the program includes people who cannot reasonably be considered victims. If not managed properly, these issues have the potential to undermine a reparations effort.

Following the international protection framework for forced displacement, the key distinction to be made here is between those who voluntarily migrate across or within national borders and those who, against their will, become displaced. The protection regimes for both IDPs and refugees want to distinguish their own target populations from migrants who leave their homes behind to seek a better life abroad or elsewhere in the same country. There may be disagreements among advocates and practitioners about the scope and application of the Guiding Principles, but "it is clear that [the principles] do not apply to persons who move voluntarily from one place to another solely in order to improve their economic circumstances."[79] Both the practicability of distinguishing between voluntary migration and displacement and the routine emphasis on socioeconomic migrants as "the other" from whom IDPs and refugees need to be distinguished pose challenges for reparations and tend to be especially difficult in countries affected by so-called complex emergencies[80] and in contexts where a combination of factors such as state failure, violent conflict, human rights violations, livelihood collapse, and environmental degradation drive people to migrate elsewhere in the country or across borders. The more protracted a crisis or displacement situation becomes, the more difficult it is to neatly divide people who left their habitual places of residence behind into categories such as IDPs, economic migrants, and refugees.

The Democratic Republic of Congo (DRC) offers a case in point. Decades of mismanagement, repeated foreign interventions, widespread internal conflict, and brutal violence have been accompanied by multiple waves of displacement of entire communities across and within national borders.[81] Years into the transition from war to peace (which officially started in 2003), a large portion of the Congolese population struggles to survive in a country where, in large parts of the territory, formal institutions have all but ceased to exist and violence and displacement continue to be part of daily life.[82] As indicated in the table earlier in the chapter, many thousands have been affected and are now living away from their original homes and villages. Nevertheless, it would be extremely difficult to determine who in this population would qualify as displaced. As an International Committee of the Red Cross official working in the DRC recently wrote: "The labels 'refugee', 'urban IDP', 'host family' and 'economic migrant' may be convenient for aid workers and policymakers but they can often be misleading in that they seldom describe a person's overall situation."[83] How, she asks, do you categorize "a family from a village in North Kivu which has some members who commute between Goma town and

Rwanda selling produce, and others who left after an armed attack and moved to Kinshasa in search of a safer and better life"? Are people who share their time between Goma and Rwanda "refugees or internally displaced people"? And "what about the group of people from a village that has been looted who decide to go to a bigger town, having heard that displaced people can make money there"? Are their motives "economic or related to armed violence"?[84] Similar conundrums emerge when one takes a closer look at the refugee and migration crises affecting countries such as Afghanistan, Iraq, Somalia, and Sudan,[85] among others, making it very difficult for any future reparations programs in these places to determine who should be in and who should be out.

Two final considerations have to do with the almost routine exclusion of voluntary, or socioeconomic, migrants from the category of displacement. First, in many contexts socioeconomic drivers play a role in the decision to move either abroad or elsewhere in the same country (the most common example, in this respect, is people moving from rural to urban areas during conflict).[86] Iraqis who fled post–Saddam Hussein Iraq or moved within the country did so for political as well as socioeconomic reasons, including political and religious persecution mostly by non-state actors (especially relevant for members of Iraq's small minorities);[87] the collapse of law and order and the generalized insecurity and violence it engendered; the further deterioration and, in some areas, collapse of basic public services such as water, electricity, health care, and education;[88] the lack of economic opportunities and the rapid deterioration of the labor market; and a fundamental pessimism about where the country was heading.[89] Concepts such as "survival migration"[90] and "mixed migration flows"[91] have been developed to express the complexity of migratory movements during crisis situations, but the bottom line is that in many circumstances, the dichotomy between political and economic migrants simply fails to reflect reality and is unsuitable as the basis for a reparations program once the crisis is over.

Second, it is debatable whether reparations programs should always endorse and reproduce the routine exclusion of socioeconomic deprivation as specific and stand-alone grounds for considering displacement nonvoluntary, as is done in the context of the international protection framework. There are certainly scenarios imaginable where a transition requires coming to terms with the fact that a former regime deliberately refused to invest in education, health care, and other basic services, siphoned money away from the country into private bank accounts (for example, in the context of the exploitation of high-value natural resources), and never did anything to save people from poverty and disease. In such circumstances, reparations benefits for the displaced, such as the official recognition of their suffering, the acknowledgment of their rights, and the restoration of civic trust, may need to be extended to victims of economic deprivation, including those who had to leave their homes behind to survive. Of course, doing so may be difficult if the available resources are limited, but this is more a matter of how different violations (and categories of victims) are prioritized than a matter of resources per se.

Given that the causes of displacement and the movement of people themselves are often diverse and characterized by "mixed flows, multifarious motivations and multiple labels," [92] policymakers and experts alike are well advised to keep the concept of displacement open, at least at the outset of the policy development process. Automatically assuming that the categories and distinctions emanating from the international protection framework are adequate for the local context may mean excluding people who should be included in any reparations effort for displacement. A careful analysis of the local realities of both external and internal displacement is indispensable before deciding how the reparations policy in question should define displacement and whether displacement is, in the particular transitional context, an adequate ground for reparations. Discussing, negotiating, and determining what displacement is and means in the given context needs to be a central component of the participatory process of establishing a reparations program. Whether such an exercise can establish a clear line between voluntary migration and displacement that does not exclude some of the displaced while including those who are not displaced and that can be realistically applied depends on the context. In many of the countries listed in the table earlier in the chapter, achieving such results would not be easy.

REPARATIONS FOR DISPLACEMENT AND PARTICIPATION

It is often said that the quality of the process of coming to a reparations program can be as important as the quality of the program itself. The thinking is that broad participation in the discussion and decisionmaking about what reparations policies are necessary in a particular context may in itself be a powerful signifier that from now on, governance and community relations will be different from what went on in the period before the transition. Whereas, it is argued, a reparations policy put together by a small, closed group of decisionmakers with little or no consultation with the victims or the wider population may signal that the transition is really just "more of the same" and the reparations program is more an attempt to appease than a genuine effort to provide redress. Moreover, participatory processes are also seen as a means to encourage victims' ownership of the reparations program and as having a "potential healing effect on victims and communities."[93] Similarly, it is often argued that a process leading up to a reparations program in which victims are consulted and treated as full citizens and rights' bearers can in and of itself be an important step in achieving the symbolic goals of reparations. Finally, consultation is seen as a "virtue that will make reparations more responsive to reality and thus more effective."[94]

While using a participatory process to develop a reparations program is commonly seen as good practice, real participation can be difficult to achieve, even in contexts where no large-scale displacement has taken place.[95] What, for example, does meaningful participation consist of in contexts such as Colombia or the DRC, where hundreds of thousands of people have been affected by violence and human rights violations? Truth commissions have demonstrated they can fulfill an important role in engaging with victims' communities[96] but may not be in a position to reach more than a fraction of the victim population in situations where numbers run into the hundreds of thousands. Involving victims' organizations, nongovernmental organizations, and civil society groups is another way of trying to ensure that a reparations program reflects victims' needs and concerns, but their representativeness of the wider victim population is not always a given. Moreover, such groups tend to be heterogeneous in terms of the types of violations they focus on, and strong differences in political clout or sympathy, cultural approaches, and levels of negotiating experience often exist among victims' organizations.[97] This can lead to conflict and disputes between organizations around, for example, the nature and scope of the desired reparations effort. Surveys may be a good way of gauging what victims' perceptions of justice and reparations are in contexts where numbers or local circumstances do not allow for actual engagement, but this remains quite far removed from a real participatory process.[98] Finally, creative solutions involving customary forms of social mobilization, grassroots conferences, and other bottom-up consultation processes[99] can be useful, but achieving real participation is invariably a big challenge, especially when it comes to the most vulnerable victims.

Experience has shown that in contexts where displacement has occurred on a massive scale, the engagement of all relevant actors tends to be even more complicated than normal, both politically and logistically. In practice, "sufficient engagement with displaced persons has often not been the case," although a number of truth commissions, including the ones in Guatemala and Liberia, have engaged with refugees and internally displaced persons.[100]

Moreover, beyond participation in the determination of what a reparations effort should look like in a given context, large-scale displacement also tends to raise specific operational and technical challenges related to the displaced population's access to reparations. In Iraq, for example, the Property Claims Commission has so far been unable to process the approximately 5,000 claims it received from Iraqis living outside the country because of a lack of specific rules and procedures for engaging with claimants who live abroad. In Colombia, the extent to which refugees will be able to claim reparations under the recent Victims' Law remains to be seen, but there is no doubt that significant obstacles exist.[101] Common hurdles are related to documentation and evidence, a lack of financial and human resources, and difficulties in coordination and management.[102] While these can be formidable, the remainder of this section will focus more on participation in the development of reparations policies.

ENGAGING THE DIASPORA

Recent advances in technology have expanded the ways diaspora communities can interact with the home country. Cheaper and faster communications accessible to a broader swath of the population have quite literally shortened distances between those who remained and those who left. More researchers than ever before are now studying the diaspora-conflict-peace nexus,[103] although so far they have paid only limited attention to how diaspora communities can contribute to (or, indeed, undermine) transitional justice efforts in their countries of origin.[104] The diaspora concept itself is quite fuzzy and can have different meanings depending on the context and who is using it,[105] but for our purposes the concept is most usefully understood as including political refugees, alien residents, guest workers, immigrants, and overseas communities more broadly. This can be complemented with the notion that the diaspora concept is best seen as building on three criteria: "dispersal; settlement in multiple locations; and the idea of a 'homeland.'"[106]

Concerning the possible involvement of members of a diaspora in the development of reparations policies (whether or not they eventually include reparations for displacement), a number of factors are important to keep in mind. First is the heterogeneous nature of most, if not all, diaspora groups in terms of socioeconomic stratification, political views and allegiances, levels of social and political organization, and remaining connections and interests with the homeland.[107] Members of the diaspora may, for instance, disagree about what peace and transitional justice in the home country should look like. The makeup of diaspora groups can also vary strongly from host country to host country. These differences may have been there from the outset (for example, the socioeconomic background of Iraqis fleeing to Jordan between 2003 and 2006 tended to differ somewhat from the background of those leaving Iraq for Syria)[108] or may arise from the different experiences provided by life in different host countries (for example, whether Palestinian refugees live in a camp in Lebanon or in a nice neighborhood of New York will inevitably have some influence on their outlook on life). Similarly, the politics of different host countries toward the diaspora or the diaspora's home country also tends to be a factor of influence regarding the scope of diaspora engagement in peacebuilding and transitional justice.

Good reasons exist to involve the diaspora in the development of transitional justice initiatives beyond the fact that at least some of its members will have been victims of persecution or human rights violations. If it is indeed true that, as a number of researchers have argued, diasporas can often play a negative role in perpetuating conflict or increasing the risk of a recurrence of conflict, then obtaining their political engagement in peacebuilding, post-conflict recovery, and transitional justice may be crucial for a sustained peace.[109] Moreover, it may also facilitate their eventual reintegration into the home country, if they eventually decide to return. Such engagement with the diaspora is, however, best seen as a multidimensional effort that needs to include but also go beyond simple outreach by the home state government.[110] It may require the political mobilization of diaspora communities around a set of common goals; engagement with host states, which may look suspiciously at any political activity with or in the diaspora; and outreach by diaspora victims to those victims who remained behind in the home state to try to foster a shared transitional justice project. Finally, it is important to underscore that the positive impact of diaspora engagement is not a given. The effect of transnational peacebuilding activities "remains less than clear," as "the existing literature relies to a large extent on speculations and hypotheses to assess impact."[111]

In practice, then, some risks are attached to the involvement of the diaspora, which, depending on the context, may require careful management (posing the difficult question of who would be able to perform such management). One element to highlight is that the diaspora's involvement in the policy development of reparations may be driven by a small group of its members who want to seize the opportunity of the transition to get their wealth back. As such, this may not be problematic, except that the immediate aftermath of the cessation of violence or the change of a regime may give this group a comparative advantage to push through a reparations program that primarily serves its own interests, which may or may not be aligned with those of the victims who never left or the less wealthy among the diaspora victims. The establishment of the Iraq Property Claims Commission, for example, had originally more to do with the advocacy and lobbying by a small group of Iraqi exiles (who had been able to organize themselves during their years abroad, including some spent in the United States) than with any consultations with or endorsement by the victims who had remained in Saddam Hussein's Iraq (who had had little opportunity to organize themselves and formulate their desired transitional justice policies). While the diaspora's role as a transitional justice front-runner can be a good thing, it can also deepen tensions between diaspora actors and those who were never able to leave. Arguably, this risk is heightened in situations where displacement was protracted and exile was spent in countries that were much better off economically than the homeland (think, for example, of Somali exiles living in London or Helsinki versus those living through the conflict in Somalia).

PARTICIPATION OF IDPs: BUSINESS AS USUAL?

In principle, the participation of IDPs in the development of reparations policies should not raise challenges that, politically and operationally, differ greatly from those related to ensuring that the wider victim population is fully engaged. The fact they remained within national borders means that, at least theoretically, they remain within reach of the national authorities. Practical hurdles such as a lack of documentation (including official identity documents and birth certificates) may affect IDPs as well as other types of victims, especially in countries where the state apparatus is rather weak and underdeveloped. Moreover, the common assumption that IDPs are necessarily the most vulnerable victims—and hence the most difficult to reach and engage in participatory processes to establish a national reparations policy—does not always hold true and needs to be reassessed in each context.[112] Also, in terms of their ability to politically organize themselves, IDPs may be stronger and more advanced than other, nondisplaced victims. This is the case in Colombia, where the strongest victims' organizations tend to be those representing IDPs.[113] Finally, the reality or perception of international humanitarian attention focusing exclusively on IDPs can cause resentment and anger among other vulnerable groups. Where that is the case, centering the subsequent reparations debate on the displaced (who may be the largest group within the universe of victims) can lead to victim competition, which may hinder the objectives of reparations.

MIGRANTS IN TRANSITION CONTEXTS: A FORGOTTEN GROUP?

Recent events in Libya have brought migrants, and especially migrant workers, onto the radar screen of the international protection community. Before the uprising against the Gadhafi regime, Libya counted an estimated 2.5 million foreign workers in the country, employed in the oil industry, construction, and the informal sector.[114] In the recent conflict, reports indicate, migrants from sub-Saharan Africa suffered abuse and human rights violations "at the hand both of the rebels and of Gadhafi loyalists," under the accusation of being "foreign mercenaries."[115] As of November 14, 2011, close to 770,000 of those migrants had fled Libya either to neighboring countries or, often with international assistance, back home farther afield.[116] Many observers have argued that this crisis "highlighted a gap in the international regime for protection of IDPs and in particular migrant workers" and further "called into question the relevance to modern humanitarian crises of a dated refugee definition."[117] Some have criticized the lack of clarity about whether migrant workers who are displaced within the country where they work are actually covered by the Guiding Principles on Internal Displacement. This lack of attention to the fate of migrants during crises is symptomatic of the broader reluctance at the international level to seriously engage with the human rights of migrants, during war and peace. It is no coincidence that the International Convention on the Protection of Rights of All Migrant Workers and Members of Their Families has seen the "slowest progress between initial adoption and ultimate entry into force, and the smallest number of participating countries" of any international treaty.[118] This, in turn, is a further confirmation of socioeconomic migrants as the "other" in international protection discourse and practice in relation to displacement, as discussed earlier in the chapter.

The events in Libya have shown, however, that in a globalized world, regular and irregular migrant workers are increasingly affected by conflict and widespread human rights violations. Beyond the challenge of international protection, this poses the question of how and to what extent reparations programs can and should take this group into account, both as participants and as eventual beneficiaries. This applies to reparations programs providing redress for displacement in situations, such as Libya, where migrant workers are forced to flee the country in which they work, sometimes under direct threats and as victims of looting and extortion. It is also relevant for reparations efforts focusing on human rights violations more broadly—for example, when migrant workers are among the victims of a brutal dictatorship, as most likely is the case in Libya. Many challenges may exist to achieving redress, including resistance from the "indigenous" to the inclusion of migrants in local transitional justice efforts, the logistical difficulties of reaching out to people who have returned home (possibly temporarily),[119] and the challenge of how to deal with irregular migrant workers who, as in the Libyan context, made up the majority of migrant workers in the country. In addition, there is always the danger of overloading reparations and other transitional justice measures with more issues than they can handle. At the same time, however, if labor and other migrants are permanent features of the transitional society in question, it is difficult to see how the objectives of reparations could be achieved without including them, as they form an integral part of the local social fabric.

INTERNATIONAL ASPECTS OF DISPLACEMENT AND REPARATIONS

Another issue is how a reparations effort can address the international features of displacement, which are easiest to observe when large numbers of refugees cross borders into neighboring countries. At the local level, the communities living in the areas where refugees settle will invariably be affected by this new population. Mass displacement tends to have "a profound effect on ecosystems and consequently on livelihoods and state stability" and hence on the likelihood of human rights violations and, indeed, further displacement.[120] Things may become especially complicated when, over time, those refugees become independent players in the local political landscape or an integral part of local conflict and strife. The Palestinian refugees in Lebanon and their role in the civil war there may be an extreme, but in no way isolated, example of how the destinies of a refugee community and a host community can become intimately connected.[121] The international drivers of displacement both inside and outside national borders are often connected to the nature of contemporary conflict. "Conflict in the Global South has been shown to spill into neighboring states through the spread of small arms, the movement of armed groups and the policies of neighboring states," whereby population movements are clearly "linked to the regionalization of conflict."[122] The reality that communities can be victims of multiple instances of displacement involving movement both within and across national borders further underscores that the phenomenon cannot always be explained by reference to national factors (and actors) alone.

In such situations, focusing on reparations at the national level risks divorcing those efforts from the reality of what people went through, as well as potentially excluding actors that can be considered victims of displacement (for instance, host communities in neighboring countries that eventually become displaced themselves because of pressures from the arriving refugees). Whether a regional approach is desirable and feasible depends on the existing linkages between the states involved and the people living in those states, their joint histories and political evolutions, the presence of an identity of regional belonging overlaying national and local identities, and the extent to which regional displacement is interconnected as a whole. While there are as yet no real examples of regional reparations programs,[123] recent policy initiatives such as the International Conference on the Great Lakes Region in eastern and central Africa and the ensuing Great Lakes Pact can serve as examples in this respect. The pact, which grew out of a realization that people living in the Great Lakes area are so "interlinked ethnically, culturally and linguistically that the instability initially generated by purely internal causes in each country quickly spread to generate and maintain the dynamic conflict in the entire region,"[124] was adopted by regional governments on December 15, 2006, and set out new norms, standards, and mechanisms for protecting displaced persons.[125] While the process through which the pact came about can serve as an example (involving governments, civil society actors, and international and national experts), the difficulties related to its subsequent implementation, including the lack of sustained political will and the barriers caused by weak and dysfunctional state institutions, point toward the possible limitations of a regional approach. At the same time, in contexts where resources are extremely limited, the regional pooling of resources may be one (partial) step forward.

REPARATIONS FOR FORCED DISPLACEMENT: REMEDIES

As explained at the outset, large-scale human rights violations usually call for reparations to be approached as a matter of providing benefits directly to victims rather than as an attempt to achieve full restitution. Concerning what those benefits should be, there is no magic formula that can be applied in every situation. As a general minimum standard, those benefits should at least be adequate and fair, and where appropriate, they should be targeted to reduce victims' overall socioeconomic vulnerability. When it comes to material benefits, this standard does not require a direct link between the actual material losses victims sustained and the eventual benefits the reparations program provides to them. Of course, victims may well dismiss benefits as unfair and inadequate if no such link exists, but this is not always the case. One example is the German Forced Labor Compensation Program, which between 2000 and 2006 provided former forced and slave laborers from the Nazi era with monetary compensation.[126] Despite the fact that the compensation amounts were very low compared to the material, physical, and psychological losses many victims had sustained, the program appears to have been generally accepted as adequate and fair and, indeed, a legitimate way to bring closure to this particular reparations issue politically.[127] It is hence a good example of a reparations effort where a remedy not directly connected to the actual loss (and also never presented as such) provided some measure of justice to the victims. As regards the symbolic benefits of recognition and acknowledgment, these relate, by their very nature, more to the violations than the ensuing losses (although officially recognizing and acknowledging those violations often involves a simultaneous reference to the losses victims sustained as a consequence). In broad terms, the options and limitations (fiscal and otherwise) regarding the types of benefits that can be provided in the context of large-scale reparations for displacement are not substantially different from those in the context of reparations for other human rights violations, although underlying needs may, of course, be somewhat different.

One particularly sensitive issue is how to rank material reparations for displacement among redress measures for other violations. In large-scale reparations programs, benefits are best tied to violations, rather than to the actual material losses of individual victims. Unless the same material redress is provided for each type of violation, a reparations program has to somehow rank the different types of violations it covers, so as to decide what benefits to attach to what violation. For example, if the material redress is compensation, then the issue is what violation should be granted the highest amount of compensation, which one the second highest, and so on all the way down to the violation that will be granted the lowest amount. The alternative of providing the same amount to all victims independent of the type of violation they have suffered has, at least to my knowledge, never been put into practice, possibly because it would be perceived as unfair and unjust (even if we can agree that all victims of human rights violations in a particular country have suffered, we usually also can agree that certain violations cause graver suffering than others). Any ranking needs to conform to the prevailing moral code and sensibilities of the society, and of course, whose code and sensibilities should prevail will likely be a source of disagreement. Arguably, those whose moral code and sensibilities matter most are the victims themselves, and ideally, a reparations program would appeal to the largest possible number of victims in this respect, avoiding creating new or deepening existing divisions among victims.[128]

Displacement may be more difficult to rank or even accept as a separate violation than other abuses, such as torture and murder, and this has to do with the perception of victims who did not leave regarding those who did. In the eyes of the former, it is not always true that the latter suffered more. Indeed, those who did not leave may see those who left as the lucky ones and may have little enthusiasm for creating a specific material remedy for the displaced. While there are no universally applicable rules here, mixed sentiments may more likely be felt about a diaspora than an internally displaced population, especially after a protracted period of displacement. It is not uncommon for real tensions to exist between those who lived through years or decades of repression, human rights violations, or conflict and those who spent those same years as refugees living elsewhere.[129]

A number of points should be made concerning what types of restitution would be suitable for displaced populations. First, the preferences and priorities of the displaced—often informed by their socioeconomic situation—must be considered, so that where victim populations are poor and vulnerable, the emphasis will lie on measures that help reestablish living conditions and economic security.[130] Cash compensation frequently makes it to the top of the list of victims' preferred benefits,[131] sometimes driven by a lack of faith that the government will deliver on other, more long-term reparative measures. In Timor-Leste, for example, IDPs showed little faith in the government's promise to build new houses, instead preferring immediate cash payments as a condition for their leaving the camps.[132] Notably, these priorities often reflect pressing needs rather than specific ideas victims may have about what reparations should offer them as distinct from humanitarian aid, social services, or state support, broadly speaking.[133] As argued earlier, these preferences then need to be counterbalanced with considerations related to the economic effectiveness of benefits and their ability to lift victims out of poverty and vulnerability. The latter consideration may point toward measures that increase long-term self-sufficiency for the victims, such as improved access to higher education, livelihood support, and also cash grants, with or without incentives to spend this money on services and items that have a durable effect. Second, the Framework on Durable Solutions for Internally Displaced Persons can also provide guidance on the choice of benefits.[134] It defines a durable solution as having been achieved when IDPs "no longer have any specific assistance and protection needs that are linked to their displacement and can enjoy their human rights without discrimination resulting from their displacement."[135] In addition to pointing toward measures that can assist IDPs with return, local integration, or resettlement, the Framework provides eight criteria that can be used to determine the extent to which a durable solution has been achieved, which can guide policymakers considering what reparative benefits are the most adequate for victims of displacement.[136]

As argued earlier, one crucial step in designing a reparations program that can make a real contribution to pro-poor growth and development is to carry out an assessment of the overall socioeconomic situation of the victim population, including the extent to which it has access to basic services. Such assessments should also include a comparative element, so that the situation of the displaced population is evaluated against that of the overall population. In Colombia, studies have demonstrated "the precarious living conditions of displaced households ... in comparison to the rest of the Colombian population living in poverty, and specifically in relation to the non-displaced neighboring households of the same economic stratum."[137] Findings such as this not only help quantify the negative impact of displacement on those affected but can also play a positive role in building political support for a reparations effort that includes the displaced, as well as increasing understanding and acknowledgment of what this population has experienced. Where governments lack the capacity to carry out such assessments, international support is often available in the form of institutional capacity building or as part of international humanitarian or development assistance programs.

The idea that reparations for displacement should help victims overcome its consequences raises the issue of how reparations efforts differ from humanitarian assistance, early recovery support, and development aid.[138] Conceptually, reparations efforts sit closer to early recovery than humanitarian aid, at least if humanitarian efforts include only immediate life-saving support such as the distribution of food and water and the provision of tents. The Cluster Working Group on Early Recovery defines early recovery as "a multidimensional process" that "begins early in humanitarian settings," is "guided by development principles," and aims to "generate self-sustaining nationally owned and resilient processes for post-crisis recovery."[139] In terms of activities, it covers "the restoration of basic services, livelihoods, shelter, governance, security and the rule of law, environment and social dimensions, including the reintegration of displaced populations."[140] Early recovery activities are mostly carried out by the same national and international actors that provide humanitarian assistance. While it would be beyond the scope of this chapter to exhaustively discuss possible overlaps and differences between early recovery, on the one hand, and reparations, on the other, the following considerations arise.

The principal distinction between reparations measures and early recovery support does not lie in the type of benefits national and international actors can use to achieve their respective goals. Any benefit that can be used to repair victims' lives (compensation, preferential access to basic services, allocation of land and housing, the provision of psychosocial support) can, at least in principle, also be used by actors trying to foster the early recovery of communities and individuals affected by crisis. The Timor-Leste National Recovery Strategy adopted to address the 2006 internal displacement crisis, for example, provided IDPs with cash grants to cover the destruction, looting, or damaging of their homes. Presented in a different language—as compensation for a violation of rights—this strategy could, from a benefits perspective alone, easily have qualified as a reparations effort, even though it was not.[141] Nor does the distinction necessarily lie in the process through which reparations and early recovery come about. Reparations and early recovery guidelines and manuals emphasize the need to use participatory processes that bring to light the priorities and demands of the victims or beneficiaries themselves, even if those processes are often flouted in practice. Clearly, it can also not just be a matter of what language or discourse is used to describe the effort: it is unlikely that victims would accept a government simply requalifying social or humanitarian assistance as "reparations" (on the other hand, deliberately not defining cash grants as compensation or reparations does, inevitably, disqualify an effort for the reparations label).[142] Instead, the main distinction between reparations and early recovery can be found in the broader political context, including the public discourse around the efforts, whether they are treated as official acknowledgments of past violations and are openly intended to provide justice for past suffering, and the perceived good faith of decisionmakers. The distinction also has to do with what other measures a government takes to address past violations, including efforts to unearth the truth, promote and achieve accountability, and engage in genuine institutional reforms.[143] Not all these measures need to happen simultaneously,[144] but a broader transitional justice process of sorts is required to elevate a benefits-for-victims program above the "ordinary" provision of humanitarian assistance or social support.

LIMITATIONS OF REPARATIONS FOR DISPLACEMENT: FRAGILE STATES AND EXTREME POVERTY

As the table earlier in the chapter testifies, displacement often occurs in contexts where poverty is widespread, the most basic of needs remain unmet for important portions of the population, and state and governance structures are weak or in some parts of the territory nonexistent. Developing effective reparations measures in such contexts can be challenging, in part because of the sheer number of people affected by displacement and hence the size of the universe of victims that a reparations program needs to cover. The two main challenges to be overcome in such contexts are (1) where to find the financial resources to fund the administration and implementation of a large-scale reparations effort and (2) how to operationalize the provision of benefits to tens or hundreds of thousands of victims in a more or less efficient and fair manner.

The issue of material resources is one of absolute scarcity and prioritization of available means. Absolute scarcity occurs in situations where the state, as the entity responsible for providing effective remedies to victims of human rights violations, has no resources to cover a reparations effort for all the victims. Funding by the international community may be an alternative, but examples where international funds have actually been used for providing reparations remain scarce, although attitudes may slowly be shifting in this respect.[145] The prioritization of available means is possible when at least some material resources are available but spending more on reparations is likely to require spending less on something else. This dilemma (which needs to be looked at carefully in each situation, as it is open to abuse by those opposing reparations for political reasons) is starkest when widespread poverty also requires increased spending on basic needs. While it is well beyond this chapter to discuss this (potential) dilemma in depth,[146] two related points are worth emphasizing.

In situations where victims are mostly poor—for example, in Colombia[147]—the apparent tension between development and reparations spending can be reduced (if not resolved) by tailoring benefits with their developmental impact in mind.[148] If benefits provided to victims by a reparations program also allow them to escape poverty in a durable manner, then the goals of both development and reparations may have been met. If benefits are designed with a vulnerability- and poverty-reduction goal in mind, then implementing reparations not only has a fiscal cost but also offers fiscal benefits through an eventual reduction in expenditures on humanitarian assistance, social aid, and so on. This needs to be carefully looked at in each situation, but as a starting point, reparations are best seen as potentially generating both fiscal costs and fiscal benefits.

The institutional challenges related to the implementation of a reparations program involving tens or hundreds of thousands of displaced persons inside and across national borders may be as formidable as the material resource challenge in contexts where state institutions are fragile. Issues of transparency, corruption, central control, political bias, and a lack of state presence in parts of the territory may individually or collectively render the implementation of a reparations program extremely challenging. The need to involve embassies, consular offices, and host governments to reach refugees and other displaced populations can further complicate the picture of how to achieve this where state institutions struggle to even carry out the most basic tasks. International support and capacity building can help, but institutional building is inherently a long-term process. As a rule, practicability needs to be a central concern from the beginning: it is no good designing or advocating for measures of redress that go well beyond what local institutions can implement.

Material and institutional constraints should not, however, be an excuse for not doing anything at all in terms of reparations for displacement. They do not, for instance, prevent governments from implementing symbolic reparations efforts in line with victims' demands.[149] There are multiple, displacement-focused symbolic measures that can be conceived, and what can be done is limited primarily by what victims themselves consider to be real and meaningful efforts. Examples include the official recognition that displacement did take place, that it was caused by the deliberate acts of concrete actors, and that displaced people were also victims of human rights violations.[150] Official accounts that simply blame displacement on generalized violence and instability, and suggest that no identifiable actors can be held accountable for the fact that so many people had to leave their homes and livelihoods behind, are unlikely to achieve the restorative goals sought by reparations and other transitional justice efforts.[151] Memorialization and the inclusion of the experience and causes of displacement in the official posttransitional historical narrative can be meaningful, although the dangers of an excessive politicization of the "new" national history are always present in transitional situations.[152] Similarly, the systematic revision of official rules and practices concerning how the state responds to the particular needs and circumstances of the formerly displaced population can make a positive contribution, especially if it occurs against the background of a broader transitional justice effort. Finally, symbolic reparations can also involve supporting particular ceremonies (traditional or otherwise),[153] changing the names of streets or institutions,[154] and erecting monuments or artworks connected to the displacement experience. In and of themselves, symbolic reparations may not answer to all the victims' expectations, but a genuine effort does have the potential to make a meaningful difference. It can also make a significant contribution to—and be an integral part of—restoring confidence in the state and transforming state institutions, a necessary ingredient of any policy aimed at breaking the cycle of violent conflict that affects so many fragile states.[155]

It is also important to keep in mind the connection between the success of humanitarian assistance and economic development, on the one hand, and demands for material reparations, on the other. As pointed out earlier, victims' concrete reparations demands will often be closely connected to their socio-economic situation. To somewhat oversimplify: the more victims are affected by poverty, a lack of livelihood opportunities, and overall vulnerability, the more likely their reparative demands will focus on material and livelihood support measures. The high expectations that victims invest in material reparations can also reflect the lack of other avenues available to them for improving their circumstances. While somewhat speculative, it is difficult not to see a relationship between Colombian civil society actors' strong advocacy for, and high political investment in, demands for material reparations for IDPs and the continued poverty of IDPs in both absolute and relative terms compared to the overall Colombian population.[156] When past assistance and ongoing economic development policies fail to bring people out of their misery, the displaced may invest reparations measures with hopes and expectations that they cannot really fulfill. This further underscores the need to make effective victims' assistance, as well as pro-poor economic development that includes the targeting of victims of past violations, a central part of the overall transitional effort. Addressing the social and economic marginalization of victims is not only necessary to reduce pressures on, and unrealistic expectations in, material reparations, but it is also required to reduce the chances of vulnerable populations becoming victims of human rights violations again in the future.

CONCLUSION

Displacement in situations of conflict, oppression, and widespread human rights violations is a complex phenomenon that cannot be easily reduced to a matter of refugees and IDPs alone. A key understanding of how displacement has played out in a given context, how the experiences of the displaced and the nondisplaced have differed, and perceptions of and within the displaced population is essential in determining whether reparations for displacement are appropriate. Whether they are deemed appropriate or not will (and should) usually be determined by local, inclusive politics, but to the extent that international advocacy has a role to play in this determination, it should start by understanding how displacement fits within the broader local cultural, social, economic, and political context, as assumptions about who is vulnerable and who should be considered a victim may bring more problems than assistance to the displaced. Even the use of the term *victim* to describe the displaced population may not fit well with dominant self-perceptions and identities in a particular situation. Finally, thinking about reparations for displacement also brings to the fore how reparations can integrate the realities of today's globalized world, where national causes are frequently insufficient to explain crises, and where reparations may need to reach those beyond a given national community. When oppression and human rights violations happen in Libya, communities in countries as far afield as Bangladesh feel the effects and, indeed, have victims in their midst. How reparations measures, and transitional justice more broadly, can grapple with these issues without sinking under expectations they will never be able to fulfill remains one of the main challenges ahead for the field.

NOTES

1   I would like to thank Marwan Shehadi and Emilie Arnaud for their efficient and effective research assistance and the editors for their pointed comments and suggestions. The opinions expressed in this chapter are mine alone.

2   For a similar observation regarding displacement and transitional justice more broadly, see Roger Duthie, "Transitional Justice and Displacement," *International Journal of Transitional Justice* 5, no. 2 (2011): 242–61. For a plea to conduct research on how to connect transitional justice and displacement, see Susan Harris Rimmer, "Reconceiving Refugees and Internally Displaced Persons as Transitional Justice Actors," (Research Paper no. 187, New Issues in Refugee Research, UNHCR, Geneva, April 2010).

3   Other transitional justice measures have also engaged with forced displacement, including truth commissions in Timor-Leste and Sierra Leone and land restitution efforts in Colombia, Bosnia, and Iraq. See Commission for Reception, Truth, and Reconciliation in East Timor, "Forced Displacement and Famine," in *Chega! Final Report of the Commission for Reception, Truth and Reconciliation in East Timor* (Dili: CAVR, 2005); Sierra Leone Truth and Reconciliation Commission, *Witness to Truth: Final Report of the Sierra Leone Truth and Reconciliation Commission*, 2 vols. (Accra: GPL Press, 2004); Rodrigo Umprimny-Yepes and Nelson Camilo Sanchez, "Los dilemas de la restitución de tierras en Colombia," *Revista estudios socio-jurídicos* 12, no. 2 (2010): 305–42; Rhodri Williams, "Post-conflict Property Restitution and Property Return in Bosnia and Herzegovina: Implications for

International Standard-Setting and Practice," *New York University Journal of International Law and Politics* 37, no. 3 (2005): 442–553; and Peter Van der Auweraert, "Policy Challenge for Property Restitution in Transition," in *Reparations for Victims of Genocide, War Crimes and Crimes against Humanity*, ed. Carla Ferstman, Mariana Goetz, and Alan Stephens (The Hague: Martinus Nijhoff, 2009), 459–82.

4   Turkey, Law 5233 on the Compensation of Damages that Occurred Due to Terror and the Fight against Terror, July 2004, http://www.brookings.edu/projects/idp/Laws-and-Policies/turkey.aspx. The beneficiaries of this law are not limited to the displaced, although "it was evident from the debates in the parliament that the law was to be adopted *for* the displaced." Dilek Kurban, "Reparations and Displacement in Turkey: Lessons Learned from the Compensation Law" (paper prepared for ICTJ / Brookings Project on Transitional Justice and Displacement, 2012).

5   Colombia, Ley 1448 de víctimas y restitución de tierras [Law 1448 on victims and land restitution], June 10, 2011, http://www.archivogeneral.gov.co/index.php?idcategoria=4419#.

6   Iraq, Statute of the Commission for the Resolution of Real Property Disputes, January 9, 2006, art. 30, http://www.brookings.edu/projects/idp/Laws-and-Policies/iraq.aspx.

7   Ibid., 335.

8   Pablo de Greiff, "Justice and Reparations," in *The Handbook of Reparations*, ed. Pablo de Greiff (Oxford: Oxford University Press, 2006), 451.

9   United Nations General Assembly, Resolution 60/147, "Basic Principles and Guidelines on the Right to a Remedy and Reparation for Victims of Gross Violations of International Human Rights Law and Serious Violations of International Humanitarian Law," A/RES/60/147/, March 21, 2006, art. 18.

10   United Nations General Assembly, Rome Statute of the International Criminal Court, A/CONF. 183/9, July 17, 1998, art. 75.

11   Caution is warranted in assessing fiscal arguments either against reparations or as a basis to limit reparations. They are easily misused by those who, for other more political reasons, do not wish to see a reparations program come to light, and they are best judged against the background of solid cost assessments for different types of reparations, public expenditure in other areas, the overall state budget, and the types of competing needs.

12   Unless indicated otherwise, the figures were taken from Internal Displacement Monitoring Centre, "Global Statistics," http://www.internal-displacement.org.

13   The official number is 3.6 million individuals, or seven hundred thousand households, which reflects the number of people registered in the information system on the displaced population. Civil society organizations such as CODHES claim that "the official figures do not reflect the total number of displaced persons as there is a perceptible percentage of under-registration amongst this population." CODHES estimates the total number to be around 4.5 million IDPs. See Luis Jorge Garay Salamanca, Fernando Barberi Gomez, and Clara Rimirez Gomez, *The Humanitarian Tragedy of Forced Displace-*

ment in Colombia (Bogota: CODHES, January 15, 2011), 1, http://www.codhes.org/index.php?option=com_content&task=view&id=39&Itemid=52.

14 See United Nations Relief and Works Agency for Palestinian Refugees in the Near East, *UNRWA in Figures* (Gaza: UNRWA, July 2011), http://www.unrwa.org/userfiles/2011092751539.pdf. The population registered with the agency is only a proportion of the total Palestinian refugee population around the world.

15 De Greiff, "Justice and Reparations," 451. One component of large-scale reparations can be the restitution of land and property, as is the case in Colombia. For more on land and property restitution, see Rhodri Williams, in this volume.

16 As David Cantor points out, there is an international legal obligation that a remedy provided by the state with respect to human rights violations should be judicial in nature and "effective in practice as well as in law." David Cantor, "Restitution, Compensation, Satisfaction: Transnational Reparations and Colombia's Victims' Law," (Working Paper no. 215, New Issues in Refugee Research, Evaluation and Policy Analysis Unit, UNHCR, August 2011), 29.

17 For a broad discussion of technical issues of large-scale administrative processes, including issues of evidence, see Permanent Court of Arbitration, ed., *Redressing Injustices through Mass Claims Processes: Innovative Responses to Unique Challenges* (Oxford: Oxford University Press, 2006). See also International Organization for Migration, *Property Restitution and Compensation: Practices and Experiences of Claims Programs* (Geneva: IOM, 2009), especially 117–51.

18 Naomi Roht-Arriaza and Katharine Orlovsky, "A Complementary Relationship: Reparations and Development," in *Transitional Justice and Development: Making Connections*, ed. Pablo de Greiff and Roger Duthie (New York: Social Science Research Council, 2009), 172.

19 De Greiff, "Justice and Reparations," 453.

20 See Andre Armstrong and Hans Dieter Seibel, "Reparations and Microfinance Schemes" in de Greiff, *Handbook of Reparations*, 676–98.

21 This was the case in the reparations program in Sierra Leone. See International Organization for Migration, "IOM Provides Technical Assistance to Reparations Programme for Victims of Sexual Violence in Sierra Leone," press briefing, March 23, 2010, www.iom.int/jahia/Jahia/media/press-briefing-notes/pbnAF/cache/offonce?entryId=27138.

22 For more on collective reparations, see International Center for Transitional Justice, *The Rabat Report: The Concept and Challenges of Collective Reparations* (Rabat: ICTJ, 2009), http://ictj.org/sites/default/files/ICTJ-Morocco-Reparations-Report-2009-English.pdf.

23 Pablo de Greiff, "Articulating the Links between Transitional Justice and Development: Justice and Social Integration," in de Greiff and Duthie, *Transitional Justice and Development*, 38.

24 Although this is sometimes overlooked, victims are rarely a homogenous group, and they are often as politically diverse as the population as a whole, so that when it comes

to redress for the violations they suffered, they frequently have diverging opinions.

25 In the late 1990s, more than four decades after the violations took place, victims and victims' organizations filed lawsuits in the United States and elsewhere against high-profile German companies they accused of having used forced labor during World War II and of never having provided "adequate and fair" reparations to the victims. Under pressure, the German government and private sector eventually established a fund under the management of the Foundation "Remembrance, Responsibility and Future" that by the end of 2006 had paid out a total of EUR 4.37 billion in compensation to more than 1.66 million former forced laborers and other victims of National Socialism in ninety-eight countries (see www.stiftung-evz.de). On this program, see John Authers, "Making Good Again: German Compensation for Forced and Slave Laborers," in de Greiff, *Handbook of Reparations*, 420–48; and Peter Van der Auweraert, "The Practicalities of Forced Labor Compensation," in *NS-Forced Labor: Remembrance and Responsibility: Legal and Historical Observations*, ed. Peer Zumbansen (Baden-Baden: Nomos, 2002), 301–18.

26 An IDP in a camp in the Rift Valley, Kenya, quoted in Simon Robins, *"To Live as Other Kenyans Do": A Study of the Reparative Demands of Kenyan Victims of Human Rights Violations* (New York: ICTJ, 2011), 21.

27 See Rhodri Williams, in this volume, for a discussion of this issue in regard to property restitution.

28 See Richard Rorty, *Philosophy and Social Hope* (London: Penguin Books, 1999). Arguably, this applies less in contexts where the victims targeted by a reparations program are "more or less well-off." However, the countries in which today's conflicts and large-scale, systematic human rights violations play out make this scenario the exception rather than the rule.

29 Among many possible examples from the International Organization for Migration and UNHCR, see the regular needs assessments carried out by the former regarding the displaced population in Iraq at www.iom-iraq.net.

30 For studies in the Turkish context, see Internal Displacement Monitoring Centre and Turkish Economic and Social Studies Foundation, *Overcoming a Legacy of Mistrust: Towards Reconciliation between the State and the Displaced* (Geneva/Istanbul: IDMC / TESEV, 2006).

31 See Overseas Development Institute, "Pro-poor Growth and Development" (Briefing Paper no. 33, ODI, London, January 2008), http://www.odi.org.uk/resources/docs/825. pdf. See also Roht-Arriaza and Orlovsky, "A Complementary Relationship."

32 This has been the case in both Colombia and Turkey. Regarding the latter, the consistent jurisprudence of the European Court for Human Rights ordering Turkey to pay compensation to individual victims played an important role in the creation of Law 5233. See Dilek Kurban, "Reparations and Displacement in Turkey," 16.

33 For an overview of how the UNCC was created by the UN Security Council and, especially, the different decisions made by the UNCC Governing Council, see www.uncc.ch/ decision.htm.

34   Turkey, Law 5233.

35   Colombia, Ley de victimas y restitución de tierras.

36   Rafael Barrantes Segura, "Reparations and Displacement in Peru" (paper prepared for ICTJ / Brookings Project on Transitional Justice and Displacement, 2012).

37   There are of course instances of ongoing conflict where it is impossible to imagine a durable peace without some form of reparations for displacement, with the Israeli-Palestinian conflict being the most emblematic example. See Leila Hilal, "Transitional Justice Responses to Palestinian Dispossession: Focus on Restitution" (paper prepared for ICTJ / Brookings Project on Transitional Justice and Displacement, 2012).

38   Actual delivery should be central to reparations from the outset. Too often, the reality of implementation lags behind the lofty reparations principles contained in the laws and policy documents that are supposed to frame the reparations effort. The result is not infrequently a revictimization of the very people reparations are intended to serve. Take the example of Sierra Leone, where only some of the victims of sexual violence received reparations, while others who went through the same ordeals received nothing because of a lack of funds.

39   De Greiff, "Articulating the Links."

40   Arguably, this was absent in the Turkish case. See Dilek Kurban, "Reparations and Displacement in Turkey," 8. Conversely, however, acknowledgment does not necessarily turn a support program into a reparations effort. See Peter Van der Auweraert, "Dealing with the 2006 Internal Displacement Crisis in Timor-Leste: Between Reparations and Humanitarian Policy-Making" (paper prepared for ICTJ / Brookings Project on Transitional Justice and Displacement, 2012), 25.

41   De Greiff, "Articulating the Links," 46.

42   See for example, Harris Rimmer, "Reconceiving Refugees," which refers to the need to conceive of "refugees and IDPs" as transitional justice actors.

43   According to UNHCR, at the end of 2010 some 43.7 million people worldwide were displaced because of conflict and persecution, the highest number in more than fifteen years. This included 15.4 million refugees and 27.5 million IDPs, as well as over eight hundred thousand people whose asylum applications had not yet been adjudicated by the end of the reporting period. For the latest figures, see www.unhcr.org.

44   See article 2.7 of the UN Charter, which emphasizes that "nothing contained in the present Charter shall authorize the United Nations to intervene in matters which are essentially within the domestic jurisdiction of any state." For an interesting historical contextualization of the sovereignty concept in international law, see Philip Allott, *The Health of Nations: Society and Law beyond the State* (Cambridge: Cambridge University Press, 2002), especially 342–80.

45   For a critical discussion of the concept of state sovereignty and its ever fleeting content, see Martti Koskenniemi, *From Apology to Utopia* (Helsinki: Finnish Lawyers' Publishing Company, 1989), 192–263.

46 International Covenant on Civil and Political Rights, 999 U.N.T.S. 171, A/6316, December 16, 1966, art. 12.1.

47 Ibid., art. 13. The distinction between "aliens" and "nationals" is relevant to the discussion of reparations for displacement, as will be discussed further.

48 "Everyone shall be free to leave any country, including his own." Ibid., art. 12.2.

49 Convention Relating to the Status of Refugees, July 28, 1951, 189 U.N.T.S. 150, art. 1.a.2, http://www.unhcr.org/3b66c2aa10.html. For an introductory discussion of the interpretation and meaning of the different elements of the definition as well as a basic explanation of the concept of cessation of refugee status, see Office of the United Nations High Commissioner for Refugees, *An Introduction to International Protection: Protecting Persons of Concern to UNHCR* (Geneva: UNHCR, 2005), 55–59.

50 For a recent discussion of the role of UNHCR in global refugee protection, see Gil Loescher and James Milner, "UNHCR and the Global Governance of Refugees," in *Global Migration Governance*, ed. Alexander Betts (Oxford: Oxford University Press, 2011), 189–209. UNHCR is not, however, responsible for the protection of the Palestinian refugees, who fall under the United Nations Relief and Works Agency for Palestinian Refugees in the Near East. For an extensive overview, see Ricardo Bocco and Lex Takkenberg, eds., "UNRWA and the Palestinians Refugees 60 Years Later," special issue, *Refugee Survey Quarterly* 28, nos. 2 and 3 (2009).

51 For a discussion of the origins and post–Cold War shifts in the approach to international refugee law and the protection mechanisms it created, see B. S. Chimni, "The Geopolitics of Refugee Studies: A View from the South," *Journal of Refugee Studies* 11, no. 4 (December 1998): 350–74. For a brief description of historical shifts, see also Loescher and Milner, "UNHCR and the Global Governance of Refugees," 193–95.

52 UNHCR, "Almost 320,000 Civilians Flee Somalia This Year, Including 20,000 to Yemen," October 21, 2011, http://www.unhcr.org/4ea185356.html.

53 By November 27, 2011, close to eight hundred thousand people (mostly migrants) had left Libya since the start of the crisis. For the latest updated figures compiled by the International Organization for Migration, see http://www.migration-crisis.com/libya/page/index/2.

54 Alexander Betts and Esra Kaytaz, "National and International Responses to the Zimbabwean Exodus: Implications for the Refugee Protection Regime," (Working Paper no. 175, New Issues in Refugee Research, Evaluation and Policy Analysis Unit, UNHCR, 2009).

55 See for example, Guy Goodwin-Gill, "After the Cold War: Asylum and the Refugee Concept Move On," *Forced Migration Review* 10 (April 2001): 14.

56 See, for example, Carol Bohmer and Amy Shuman, "Gender and Political Asylum," *Foreign Policy Blogs*, April 13, 2011, http://foreignpolicyblogs.com/2011/04/13/gender-political-asylum/; Nahla Valji, Lee Anne De La Hunt, and Hellen Moffet, "Where Are the Women? Gender Discrimination in Refugee Policies and Practices," in *Refugee Law Reader Syllabus*, 3rd ed., ed. Rosemary Byrne (Budapest: UNHCR, 2005), 30; and Jaqueline Great-

batch, "The Gender Difference: Feminist Critiques of Refugee Discourse," *International Journal of Refugee Law* 1, no. 4 (1989): 518–27.

57 See, for example, Nicole LaViolette, "Gender-Related Refugee Claims: Expanding the Scope of the Canadian Guidelines," *International Journal of Refugee Law* 19, no. 2 (2007): 169–214.

58 See Karin Landren, "The Future of Refugee Protection: Four Challenges," *Journal of Refugee Studies* 11, no. 4 (1998), especially 417–20. For a comparative case study of differences in national practices, see Ekaterina Yahyaoui Krivenka, "Muslim Women's Claims to Refugee Status within the Context of Child Custody upon Divorce under Islamic Law," *International Journal of Refugee Law* 22, no. 1 (2010): 48–71, which finds strong discrepancies between Great Britain, on the one hand, and Canada and New Zealand, on the other.

59 For a discussion of the differences between various European asylum procedures, see Liza Schutser, "A Comparative Analysis of the Asylum Policy of Seven European Governments," *Journal of Refugee Studies* 12, no. 1 (2000): 118–32.

60 See Michael Kagan, "The Beleaguered Gatekeeper: Protection Challenges Posed by UNHCR Refugee Status Determination," *International Journal of Refugee Law* 18, no. 1 (2006): 1–29.

61 David Cantor, "Restitution, Compensation, Satisfaction," 29.

62 Ibid., 30.

63 Asian countries that have not ratified the convention include Bangladesh, India, Indonesia, Malaysia, Nepal, and Pakistan. No Middle Eastern countries have become state parties to the convention.

64 See www.unrwa.org.

65 Out of many studies, see, for example, Shahira Sami, *Reparations to Palestinian Refugees: A Comparative Perspective* (London: Routledge, 2010); and Hilal, "Transitional Justice Responses to Palestinian Dispossession."

66 United Nations Commission on Human Rights, "Human Rights, Mass Exoduses and Displaced Persons: Addendum–Guiding Principles on Internal Displacement," Report of the Representative of the Secretary-General, Mr. Francis M. Deng, E/CN.4/1998/53/Add.2, February 11, 1998 ("Guiding Principles").

67 See Roberta Cohen, "Nowhere to Run, No Place to Hide," *Bulletin of Atomic Scientists* 58, no. 6 (November/December 2002): 37–45, http://www.brookings.edu/articles/2002/11humanrights_cohen.aspx.

68 Ibid. See also Roberta Cohen, "The Guiding Principles on Internal Displacement: A New Instrument for International Organizations and NGOs," *Forced Migration Review* 2 (August 1998): 31–33.

69 On international soft law instruments, see Kenneth W. Abbott and Duncan Snidal, "Hard and Soft Law in International Governance," *International Organizations* 54, no. 3 (2000): 421–56.

THE POTENTIAL FOR REDRESS

70 For a discussion of the reasons why this route was chosen over the development of a UN convention for IDPs, see Khaled Koser, "Internally Displaced Persons," in Betts, *Global Migration Governance*, 219. For an argument that it would still be wrong to push for a convention, see Walter Kälin, "The Future of the Guiding Principles," in "Ten Years of the Guiding Principles on Internal Displacement," ed. Marion Couldrey and Maurice Herson, special issue, *Forced Migration Review*, December 2008, 38–40.

71 Walter Kälin, *Guiding Principles on Internal Displacement: Annotations*, Studies in Transnational Legal Policy no. 38 (Washington, DC: American Society of International Law, 2008), viii.

72 The Guiding Principles have also spawned a whole range of tools and instruments intended to assist international actors with protecting internally displaced populations. A key example is the Inter-Agency Standing Committee's *Handbook for the Protection of Internally Displaced Persons* (Geneva: IASC, June 2010), www.unhcr.org/refworld/docid/4790cbc02.html.

73 In October 2000, Angola was the first country to enact elements of the Guiding Principles directly into its national law. For other examples and an overview of national legislation on internal displacement more broadly, see http://www.brookings.edu/projects/idp/Laws-and-Policies/idp_policies_index.aspx.

74 The pact is the first multilateral instrument to commit member states to adopting and implementing the Guiding Principles as a framework. It also addresses some specific concerns that have arisen from the experience of internal displacement in the African Great Lakes region, such as protection measures for pastoralists, host communities, and families of mixed ethnic identity. Furthermore, it strengthens the legal basis for IDPs to claim their rights, including the right to access to information, to be consulted about and participate in decisions that affect their lives, and to receive humanitarian assistance. The full text can be retrieved at www.internal-displacement.org/greatlakes.

75 African Union Convention for the Protection and Assistance of Internally Displaced Persons in Africa, Kampala, Uganda, 2009, www.unhcr.org/refworld/docid/4ae572d82.html.

76 UN Commission on Human Rights, Guiding Principles, preamble, art. 3.

77 Inter-Agency Standing Committee, *Handbook for the Protection of Internally Displaced Persons*, 8.

78 See Karina Wong, *Colombia: A Case Study in the Role of the Affected State in Humanitarian Action* (London: Overseas Development Institute, 2008), especially 12–17.

79 Kälin, *Guiding Principles on Internal Displacement*, 4.

80 The Inter-Agency Standing Committee defines a complex emergency as "a humanitarian crisis in a country, region, or society where there is a total or considerable breakdown of authority resulting from internal or external conflict and which requires an international response that goes beyond the mandate or capacity of any single agency and/or the ongoing UN country program." See ReliefWeb, *Glossary of Humanitarian Terms* (ReliefWeb, August 2008), 18.

81   For background, see Gérard Prunier, *Africa's World War: Congo, the Rwandan Genocide and the Making of a Continental Catastrophe* (Oxford: Oxford University Press, 2009).

82   Séverine Autesserre, *The Trouble with the Congo: Local Violence and the Failure of International Peacebuilding* (Cambridge: Cambridge University Press, 2010).

83   Veronika Talviste, "ICRC: Careful Analysis Is the Key," *Forced Migration Review* 36 (November 2010): 43.

84   Ibid.

85   See Hiram A. Ruiz, "Afghanistan: Conflict and Displacement, 1978 to 2001," *Forced Migration Review* 13 (2004): 8–10; Géraldine Chatelard, "What Visibility Conceals: Re-embedding Refugee Migration from Iraq," in *Dispossession and Displacement: Forced Migration in the Middle East and Africa*, ed. Dawn Chatty and Bill Finlayson (New York: Oxford University Press, 2010), 17–44; Hassan Noor, "Emergency within an Emergency: Somali IDPs," *Forced Migration Review* 28 (2007): 29–31; Anna Lindley, "Crisis and Displacement in Somalia," *Forced Migration Review* 33 (2009): 18–19; and Colin Thomas-Jensen, *Crisis and Opportunity: Protracted Displacement in Sudan* (Middle East Institute / Foundation pour la Recherche Stratégique, May 2011), www.refugeecooperation.org/publications/sudan/pdf/09_thomas.pdf. For an older overview on Sudan, see Eltigani E. Eltigani, ed., *War and Drought in Sudan: Essays on Population Displacement* (Gainesville: University of Florida Press, 1994).

86   Colombia and Turkey are two examples where violence in the rural areas led to an accelerated urbanization process that, in all likelihood, will turn out to be irreversible.

87   See Chris Chapman and Preti Taneja, *Uncertain Refuge and Dangerous Return: Iraq's Uprooted Minorities* (London: Minority Rights Group International, 2009), http://www.aina.org/reports/mrgiraq200909.pdf.

88   In the final decade of Saddam Hussein's rule, basic services had already declined to a very low level. See Peter Van der Auweraert, *Displacement and National Institutions: Reflections on the Iraqi Experience* (Middle East Institute / Foundation pour la Recherche Stratégique, June 2011), 8–11, www.refugeecooperation.org/publications/Iraq/08_auweraert.php.

89   All of these reasons were mentioned repeatedly by Iraqi refugees and IDPs during focus group discussions with the author. See also Géraldine Chatelard, *Iraqi Refugees and IDPs: From Humanitarian Intervention to Durable Solutions* (Middle East Institute / Foundation pour la Recherche Stratégique, June 2011), 22.

90   See Alexander Betts, "Survival Migration: A New Protection Framework," *Global Governance* 16, no. 3 (2010): 362. He defines "survival migrants" as people who are "outside their country of origin because of an existential threat for which they have no access to a domestic remedy or resolution," where the "existential threat" includes livelihood collapse and broader socioeconomic drivers.

91   This term is used to refer to migration flows that are made up of "refugees, asylum-seekers, survival migrants, economic migrants, victims of trafficking, and other migrants"

and that often accompany protracted conflicts or repression. International Organization for Migration, "Irregular Migration and Mixed Flows: IOM's Approach," IOM Council, 98th session, MC/ONG/297, October 19, 2009, 1.

92 Talviste, "ICRC: Careful Analysis," 43.

93 See, for example Maria Suchkova, *The Importance of a Participatory Reparations Process and Its Relationship to the Principles of Reparations* (Briefing Paper no. 5, Reparations Unit, Transitional Justice Network, University of Essex, 2011), 2.

94 Lisa Magarrell, "Outreach to and Engagement of Victims on Reparations: Lessons Learned from Truth and Reconciliation Processes" (presentation made at the conference Reparations for Victims of Genocide, Crimes Against Humanity and War Crimes: Systems in Place and Systems in the Making, The Hague, March 1–2, 2007), 2, http://www.redress.org/downloads/events/OutreachEngagementLM.pdf.

95 For a discussion, see also Cristián Correa, Julie Guillerot, and Lisa Magarrell, "Reparations and Victim Participation: A Look at the Truth Commission Experience," in Ferstman, Goetz, and Stephens, *Reparations for Victims of Genocide*, 385–414.

96 Office of the United Nations High Commissioner for Human Rights, *Rule of Law Tools for Post-conflict States: Reparations Programs* (New York: OHCHR, 2008), 11.

97 Magarrell, "Outreach to and Engagement of Victims," 4.

98 For an example, see Phoung Pham et al., *Forgotten Voices: A Population-Based Survey on Attitudes about Peace and Justice in Northern Uganda* (New York: ICTJ, 2005), http://reliefweb.int/sites/reliefweb.int/files/resources/A1AABC919BF22E384925704A0022B98D-hrc-uga-25jul.pdf.

99 For examples in the context of peacebuilding, see Autesserre, *Trouble with the Congo*, 247.

100 Duthie, "Transitional Justice and Displacement," 248.

101 For a discussion, see Cantor, "Restitution, Compensation, Satisfaction."

102 See also Duthie, "Transitional Justice and Displacement," 249.

103 For an overview, see Päivi Pirkkalainen and Mahdi Abdile, *The Diaspora-Conflict-Peace Nexus: A Literature Review* (Jyväskylä, Finland: DIASPEACE, March 2009). Among many case studies, see, for example, Cindy Horst and Mohammed Hussein Gaas, "Diaspora Organizations from the Horn of Africa in Norway: Contributions to Peacebuilding?" (Policy Brief 2, International Peace Research Institute, Oslo, 2009); and R. Cheran, *Diaspora Circulation and Transnationalism as Agents for Change in the Post-conflict Zones of Sri Lanka* (Berlin: Berghof Foundation for Conflict Management, 2004). See also Hazel Smith and Paul Stares, eds., *Diasporas in Conflict: Peace-Makers or Peace-Wreckers* (Tokyo: United Nations University Press, 2007).

104 For an exception, see Elyda Mey, *Cambodian Diaspora Communities in Transitional Justice* (New York: ICTJ, March 2008).

105 See, for example, Judith T. Shuval, "Diaspora Migration: Definitional Ambiguities and a Theoretical Paradigm," *International Migration* 38, no. 5 (December 2000): 41–56.

106 Pirkkalainen and Abdile, *Diaspora-Conflict-Peace Nexus*, 8.

107 See Pnina Werbner, "The Place Which Is Diaspora: Citizenship, Religion and Gender in the Making of Chaordic Transnationalism," *Journal of Ethnic and Migration Studies* 28 (2002): 119–33.

108 See Géraldine Chatelard and Mohamed Kamei Dorai, "La présence Irakienne en Syrie et en Jordanie : Dynamiques sociales et spatiales, et mode de gestion par les pays d'accueil," *Revue française Maghreb-Machrek* 199 (2009): 43–60, http://hal.archives-ouvertes.fr/docs/00/39/62/77/PDF/Maghreb_Machrek_Chatelard_Dorai.pdf.

109 "A large diaspora considerably increases the risk of further conflict." Paul Collier and Anke Hoeffler, "Greed and Grievance in Civil War" (Policy Research Working Paper 2355, World Bank, Washington, DC, 2000), 21. See also Pirkkalainen and Abdile, *Diaspora-Conflict-Peace Nexus*, 5.

110 The obligation to inform the diaspora of reparations programs is laid down in various international and national legal instruments. Examples include article 204 of the new Colombian Victims' Law, which obliges the Ministry of Foreign Affairs to ensure that Colombians living abroad are correctly informed about the law, and principle 13.4 of the Pinheiro Principles, which recommends making information about reparations programs available to the countries of asylum or wherever victims have fled. There is also jurisprudence confirming that an obligation to inform exists; see Cantor, "Restitution, Compensation, Satisfaction," 11. However, these examples cover access to existing reparations programs, rather than (political) participation in the development of the policies that bring them about.

111 Pirkkalainen and Abdile, *Diaspora-Conflict-Peace Nexus*, 7.

112 In Timor-Leste, for example, the socioeconomic situation of the population in the IDP camps following the 2006 crisis was, on average, not different from that of the general population (despite initial assumptions by the international community to the contrary). See Peter Van der Auweraert, "Dealing with the 2006 Internal Displacement Crisis," 9.

113 One of the strongest organizations in this respect is undoubtedly the Consultorio para Los Derechos Humanos y Desplazamiento (Codhes). See www.codhes.org.

114 See Anna Di Bartolomeo, Thibaut Jaulin, and Delphine Perrin, "Carim Migration Profile Libya" (European University Institute and Robert Schuman Center for Advanced Studies, 2011), 2, http://www.carim.org/public/migrationprofiles/MP_Libya_EN.pdf.

115 Khalid Koser, "Responding to Migration from Complex Humanitarian Emergencies: Lessons Learned from Libya" (Chatham House Briefing Paper, Royal Institute of International Affairs, London, November 2011), 3.

116 For regularly updated figures, see http://www.migration-crisis.com/libya/reports.

117 Koser, "Lessons Learned From Libya," 1.

118 Graziano Battistella, "Migration and Human Rights: The Uneasy but Essential Relationship," in *Migration and Human Rights: The United Nations Convention on Migrant Workers'*

Rights, ed. Ryszard Cholewinksi, Paul de Guchteneire, and Antoine Pécoud (Cambridge: Cambridge University Press, 2009), 47.

119   In Libya, some of the migrant workers who fled the violence quickly returned to take up their former (or other) jobs.

120   Refugee Studies Center, *Forced Migration Research and Policy: Overview of Current Trends and Future Directions* (Oxford: Refugees Studies Centre / University of Oxford, April 2010), 12.

121   The standard work on the Lebanese civil war is without a doubt Robert Fisk's *Pity the Nation: The Abduction of Lebanon* (New York: Nation Books, 2002). See also Rebecca Roberts, *Palestinian Refugees in Lebanon: Living with Long-Term Displacement* (London: Tauris, 2010).

122   Refugee Studies Center, *Forced Migration Research and Policy,* 6.

123   Arguably, one (so far) missed opportunity in this respect is the former Yugoslavia, where an approach to reparations for civilian victims of the war also would have reconciliatory potential. On victims' reparations in the former Yugoslavia, see Djordje Djordjević , *A Casualty of Politics: Overview of Acts and Projects of Reparation on the Territory of the Former Yugoslavia* (New York: ICTJ, July 2002), http://www.ictj.org/publication/casualty-politics-overview-acts-and-projects-reparation-territory-former-yugoslavia.

124   "International Conference on Peace, Security, Democracy and Development in the Great Lakes Region: A Concept Paper," quoted in International Displacement Monitoring Center, *The Great Lakes Pact and the Rights of Displaced People: A Guide for Civil Society* (Geneva: IDMC, 2008), 9.

125   Ibid.

126   See Peter Van der Auweraert, "The Practicalities of Forced Labor Compensation," in Zumbansen, *NS-Forced Labor,* 301–18. For a similar program related to Swiss bank holdings belonging to Holocaust survivors, see Peter Van der Auweraert, "Holocaust Reparations Claims Fifty Years After: The Swiss Banks Litigation," *Nordic Journal of International Law* 71, no. 4 (2002): 557–83.

127   The Foundation "Remembrance, Responsibility and Future" has commissioned a broad study on the perceptions of beneficiaries and the impact of the compensation program, the results of which are forthcoming.

128   The provision of humanitarian aid can also lead to divisions among victims. See "Drought Causing Divisions Amongst Victims," www.youtube.com/watch?v=VrxICQhxTxc, where Kenyan victims of drought complain they are being ignored by international aid agencies while Somali refugees get all the attention and support.

129   Many factors can play a role in the tensions between those who left and those who stayed behind, including the circumstances under which people became displaced—for example, instances where people fled following targeted persecution in the context of ethnic cleansing versus situations where people fled generalized violence or insecurity. Such tensions played out in Iraq after Saddam Hussein was overthrown. They also

existed when Yasser Arafat returned to Palestine, and those who had spent their time in exile in Tunis immediately clashed with local leaders who had remained in the West Bank and Gaza. See Maher El-Sheikh, "Arafat's Homecoming: Hopes and Fears," *Palestine-Israel Journal of Politics, Economics and Culture* 1, no. 3 (1994).

130 See, for example, Robins, *"To Live as Other Kenyans Do,"* 21; and Rafael Barrantes Segura, "Reparations and Displacement in Peru," 15; which refers to the findings in Peru that two priority reparative measures for displaced persons were "economic assistance or help with schooling materials" and "employment opportunities." In Cambodia, surveys show a strong support and preference for livelihood and social support as reparative measures for victims of the Khmer Rouge. See www.peacebuildingdata.org/cambodia/results/reparations.

131 This was true also in the Kenyan case; see Robins, *"To Live as Other Kenyans Do,"* 21, 22. The Kenyan study also shows the link between the socioeconomic situation of the victims and their reparative preferences. As the author writes, "Only a small minority of victims who were financially secure (and largely educated and urban) saw issues of truth and justice as of a higher priority than compensation."

132 Van der Auweraert, "Dealing with the 2006 Internal Displacement Crisis."

133 In Iraq, for example, 75 percent of IDPs identified access to work as their highest-priority need in interviews. See International Organization for Migration, *Five Years after the Samarra Bombing: Review of Displacement and Return in Iraq* (Baghdad: IOM-Iraq, February 2011), 8. While there has been no participatory process regarding reparations for post-2003 displacement, focus group discussions and informal conversations the author participated in suggest that were such a process to be organized, results in terms of reparations' priority measures would be quite similar.

134 See Brookings-Bern Project on Internal Displacement, *IASC Framework on Durable Solutions for Internally Displaced Persons* (Washington, DC: Brookings Institution / University of Bern Project on Internal Displacement, April 2010).

135 Ibid., 1.

136 These criteria are safety and security; an adequate standard of living; access to livelihoods; restoration of housing, land, and property; access to documentation; family reunification; participation in public affairs; and access to effective remedies and justice. Ibid., 4.

137 See Garay Salamanca, Barberi Gomez, and Rimirez Gomez, *Humanitarian Tragedy*, 9.

138 On the links with development aid, see especially Marcus Lenzen, "Roads Less Traveled? Conceptual Pathways (and Stumbling Blocks) for Development and Transitional Justice," in de Greiff and Duthie, *Transitional Justice and Development*, 76–109.

139 "Early Recover Cluster Overview," OneResponse, http://oneresponse.info/GLOBALCLUSTERS/EARLY%20RECOVERY/Pages/default.aspx.

140 Ibid.

141 Van der Auweraert, "Dealing with the 2006 Internal Displacement Crisis."

142 This is, indeed, the key reason why the already mentioned National Recovery Strategy in Timor-Leste cannot be considered a reparations program. Ibid.

143 The criticism that, for example, Dilek Kurban formulates toward Law 5233 in Turkey is that such a "broader package" wasn't included in the legislation. See Dilek Kurban, "Reparations and Displacement in Turkey," 19.

144 Indeed, there may be advantages from a displacement perspective when measures are sequential rather than simultaneous. See Bryce Campbell, in this volume.

145 One example where the international community did provide the (initial) funding for reparations is Sierra Leone. In this case, the funding came from the UN Peacebuilding Fund. Compared to the instances of forced displacement listed at the outset of the chapter, however, the number of victims covered here was relatively small (thirty-three thousand registered victims). See International Organization for Migration, "Support for the Sierra Leone Reparations Program," http://www.iom.ch/jahia/Jahia/support-for-the-sierra-leone-reparations-programme.

146 The framing of the discussion as reparations versus spending on basic needs is already a political move, especially in circumstances where significant budgetary provisions must be made for many other matters, like military spending. Whether a reparations-versus-basic-needs dilemma exists needs to be assessed against the background of full government expenditure. For an exhaustive treatment of the links between development and transitional justice more broadly, see de Greiff and Duthie, *Transitional Justice and Development*.

147 On the socioeconomic characteristics of the displaced population in Colombia, see Garay Salamanca, Barberi Gomez and Rimirez Gomez, *Humanitarian Tragedy*, 9.

148 For a discussion of the relationship between financial compensation and poverty in the context of large-scale development projects, see Michael M. Cernea and Hari Mohan Mathur, eds., *Can Compensation Prevent Impoverishment? Reforming Resettlement through Investments and Benefit-Sharing* (Oxford: Oxford University Press, 2008).

149 A survey in Cambodia, for example, found that 91 percent of those surveyed believed it was important to provide symbolic reparations to victims of the Khmer Rouge or their families. See www.peacebuildingdata.org/cambodia/results/reparations.

150 On truth-telling and displacement, see Megan Bradley, in this volume.

151 For the argument that this is where the Turkish effort with Law 5233 fell short, see Kurban, "Reparations and Displacement in Turkey."

152 See, for example, Ereshnee Naidu, *Symbolic Reparations: A Fractured Opportunity* (Cape Town: Center for the Study of Violence and Reconciliation, 2004), which focuses on the experience in South Africa.

153 For an example in Sierra Leone, see Hope–Sierra Leone, *Sierra Leone Reparations Program 2009: Report of Symbolic Reparations (Memorials and Reburials), Bomaru, Kailahun District, 21–23 March 2009* (Freetown: Hope–Sierra Leone, 2009).

154 See Mia Swart, "Name Changes as Symbolic Reparations after Transition: The Examples of Germany and South Africa," *German Law Journal* 9 (2008): 105–21.

155 See World Bank, *World Development Report 2011* (Washington, DC: World Bank, 2011), especially 99–117, http://wdr2011.worldbank.org/sites/default/files/pdfs/WDR2011_Full_Text.pdf.

156 On the poverty and vulnerability of Colombian IDPs, see Garay Salamanca, Barberi Gomez, and Rimirez Gomez, *Humanitarian Tragedy*.

CHAPTER 5

Truth-Telling and Displacement: Patterns and Prospects

Megan Bradley

In the aftermath of conflict, repression, and large-scale human rights abuses, survivors have a right to know the truth about the violations inflicted on them, their families, and their communities.[1] In recent decades, more than forty truth commissions have been established around the world to investigate atrocities and support transitions from conflict to peace.[2] Often directly affected by the crimes that these commissions seek to expose, refugees and internally displaced persons (IDPs) have a major stake in the success of transitional justice processes, which can shape the stability of post-conflict communities as well as the prospects for safe, dignified, and durable solutions to displacement. However, in many cases displaced persons have not been recognized as critical stakeholders in truth-telling processes, and truth commissions have often failed to substantively address forced migration as a human rights violation.

In this chapter, I examine efforts to address displacement through truth-telling processes and to engage the displaced as key players in truth commissions. I first identify frameworks and principles supporting the inclusion of displacement in truth commission mandates and analyze the ways in which different truth commissions have incorporated displacement into their reports and recommendations. I then explore the direct involvement of refugees and IDPs in truth commissions, highlighting international frameworks and principles that may inform efforts to facilitate their participation, obstacles to their equitable engagement, and innovations that have helped to overcome these barriers. This analysis suggests that while many truth commissions have historically failed to devote sufficient attention to forced migration and have struggled to meaningfully engage refugees and IDPs, displacement is now increasingly recognized as a significant concern meriting the attention of such institutions. At the same time, displaced populations are increasingly being acknowledged by the international community as important stakeholders who not only have a right to participate in transitional justice initiatives but can also make valuable contributions to the success of truth-telling processes. Finally, I discuss the relationship between truth-telling and the resolution of displacement, arguing that while it is important not to overinflate expectations of truth-telling processes, the strategic and timely implementation of truth-telling mechanisms may support the provision of durable, dignified solutions to refugees and IDPs while also advancing the broader goals of transitional justice processes, such as the recognition of past abuses, the promotion of accountability for violations, and the restoration of trust between neighbors and between citizens and the state.

ADDRESSING DISPLACEMENT IN TRUTH-TELLING PROCESSES: FRAMEWORKS AND PRINCIPLES

Priscilla Hayner offers a widely accepted definition of a truth commission as an institution that: "(1) is focused on past, rather than ongoing, events; (2) investigates a pattern of events that took place over a period of time; (3) engages directly and broadly with the affected population, gathering information on their experiences; (4) is a temporary body, with the aim of concluding with a final report; and (5) is officially authorized or empowered by the state under review."[3] While I focus in this chapter predominantly on official truth commissions, there are many other types of truth-telling processes in which displaced persons may also have a stake, including commemorations,[4] exhumations,[5] and the revision of school curricula.[6] Trials also have a significant truth-telling function, which, in conjunction with the removal of offenders from return communities, may play an important role in opening up durable solutions for refugees and IDPs.[7] It is important to recognize not only the diversity of approaches to truth-telling but also the connections between truth commissions and other forms of transitional justice. For example, truth commissions may serve as a stepping stone toward trials, commemorations, or the provision of compensation for survivors. Including displaced persons and their concerns in the focus of truth commissions may help ensure that refugees and IDPs benefit from the other forms of redress that often flow from the recommendations of truth commissions.

As truth commissions are ad hoc institutions, the architects of each of these bodies must make difficult decisions about the crimes that will be investigated and the particular populations the commission will seek to engage. However, there are a number of crosscutting international frameworks and principles that support the equitable participation of displaced persons in the work of truth commissions and the inclusion of forced-migration issues in the mandates of commissions in countries affected by large-scale displacement.

While most of the frameworks linking displacement and truth-telling processes focus on IDPs rather than refugees,[8] the logic that supports addressing internal displacement through truth-telling processes also applies to refugees (although some elements of refugee situations can complicate matters, such as when refugees remain outside national borders during truth-telling, making engagement and participation, as well as political dynamics, more complex.)

First, the 2004 report of the UN secretary-general "The Rule of Law and Transitional Justice in Conflict and Post-conflict Societies" underlines the importance of "comprehensive" rule-of-law and transitional justice strategies that "pay special attention to abuses committed against groups most affected by conflict, such as … displaced persons and refugees, and establish particular measures for their protection and redress in judicial and reconciliation processes."[9]

Second, the Guiding Principles on Internal Displacement, developed by the UN Commission on Human Rights, provides strong grounds for recognizing IDPs' central stake in the work of truth commissions. According to Guiding Principle 16, "All internally displaced persons have the right to know the fate and whereabouts of missing relatives." It also indicates, "The authorities concerned shall endeavor to establish the fate and whereabouts of internally displaced persons reported missing." Guiding Principle 28 also backstops the view that truth commissions should both actively engage displaced populations and substantively address forced migration as a human rights violation: "Competent authorities have the primary duty and responsibility to establish conditions, as well as provide the means, which allow internally displaced persons to return voluntarily, in safety and with dignity, to their homes or places of habitual residence, or to resettle voluntarily in another part of the country. Such authorities shall endeavor to facilitate the reintegration of returned or resettled internally displaced persons."[10] Knowing the truth about the human rights violations at the root of their displacement is a vital precondition to a dignified return for displaced persons. Similarly, as I will discuss later in this chapter, honest recognition of the abuses that forced refugees and IDPs from their homes may play an important role in enabling sustainable and just reintegration processes.[11]

Third, the Framework on Durable Solutions for Internally Displaced Persons, developed by the former representative of the UN secretary-general on the human rights of IDPs, offers focused recommendations on maximizing the positive linkages between peace processes, transitional justice, and the resolution of displacement. The Framework recognizes that durable solutions "should be a specific goal of peace agreements" and calls for peace agreements to tackle "the specific needs of IDPs, including … reconciliation and peace-building … [and] remedies for violations suffered."[12] Furthermore, it acknowledges that "community reconciliation and confidence-building mechanisms are often necessary, in particular where IDPs and the resident population or different groups within the IDP population are seen as having been associated with opposing sides in the conflict, but now live side by side."[13] Perhaps most important for advocates wanting to see truth commissions respond more effectively to forced migration, the Framework asserts that displaced persons "who have been victims of violations of international human rights or humanitarian law, including arbitrary displacement must have full and non-discriminatory access to effective remedies and access to justice, including, where appropriate, access to existing transitional-justice mechanisms, reparations and information on the causes of violations."[14]

Complementing these provisions, transitional justice expert Pablo de Greiff offers a general account of the attributes of well-designed reparations programs for the survivors of large-scale human rights violations, which I would argue, could also be applied to the development of truth-telling processes. The principles de Greiff identifies support the notion that it is important both to include forced migration in the investigatory mandates of truth commissions and to ensure that displaced persons themselves are able to participate in truth commissions and benefit from any other forms of redress, such as compensation, that may emerge as a result of commissions' recommendations.[15]

According to de Greiff, the three primary goals of reparations programs are to (1) recognize past wrongs and victims' individual worth, (2) build civic trust, and (3) develop social solidarity, all with a view to returning individuals to the status of citizens within trusting, trustworthy, and empathetic political communities.[16] To accomplish these goals, reparations programs must be appropriately *comprehensive* and *complete*. While comprehensiveness refers to the specific types of crimes these programs attempt to redress, completeness denotes an initiative's ability to "cover, at the limit, the whole universe of potential beneficiaries." De Greiff argues that it "goes without saying that completeness is a desirable characteristic in a reparations program." However, when the actors involved in a conflict have carried out a litany of abuses, from murder and torture to ethnic cleansing, forced sterilization, and rape, it may be difficult to address each type of crime in a meaningful manner. Yet "all things considered, comprehensiveness is a desirable characteristic. It is better, both morally and practically, to repair as many categories of crime as feasible. … Leaving important categories of victims unaddressed not only deprives a transitional administration of the gains in legitimacy that it might accrue by establishing a comprehensive reparations program but it also virtually guarantees that the issue of reparations will continue to be on the political agenda."[17]

De Greiff's arguments on comprehensiveness and completeness give rise to a range of persuasive reasons to consider refugees and IDPs an "important category of victim" in the context of truth-telling initiatives launched in the aftermath of violence that has caused large-scale displacement.[18] First, in many cases the uprooting of people is the result of violations, such as torture and rape, that have traditionally been at the center of truth commission investigations. Second, refugees and IDPs often continue to be subjected to grave human rights abuses even after they have fled their communities, as belligerents may attack displaced persons' camps in order to intimidate the displaced, discourage their return, and quell militants who may seek shelter and regroup in civilian camps. Third, forced migration itself represents a serious abuse that merits attention in its own right. For many displaced persons, losing their homes and enduring forced exile causes significant suffering that should be recognized in the context of efforts to develop comprehensive narratives of a community's or nation's experiences of repression and conflict. Fourth, displaced populations often have particular reintegration needs and justice claims (particularly relating to lost property); incorporating these concerns into the recommendations developed by truth commissions may fortify efforts to ensure that they are taken seriously and dealt with effectively by transitional governments and their international supporters.

However, labeling displaced persons "victims" for the purpose of truth-telling processes raises a host of challenges. Refugees and IDPs are clearly not only victims but also survivors of human rights violations. The potentially disempowering effects of "victimhood" discourses are well documented, and it is arguably more productive, accurate, and respectful to stress displaced persons' resiliency rather than their victimhood. Indeed, many displaced individuals and communities reject the victim label and may even refuse to identify themselves as refugees, owing to that term's close connotation with ideas of helplessness and lack of political agency.[19] *Displaced persons* and *victims* may even in some cases be made into mutually exclusive legal categories. For example, the Colombian government has instituted a legal distinction between "victims" of paramilitary violence, who have a right to access redress through transitional justice mechanisms, and the country's four million registered IDPs. This definitional maneuver limits the government's responsibility for redressing this large number of potential claimants, who in many cases have been victimized not only by paramilitary violence but also by state mining and agribusiness policies.

For conflicts, such as the Liberian civil war, where the majority of citizens were directly affected by displacement, the extent to which it is helpful and appropriate, from a transitional justice standpoint, to define the majority of a country's population as victims is an open question. Counting refugees and IDPs as victims to be included in truth-telling processes may raise expectations for participation and tangible outcomes, such as compensation, that cannot ultimately be realized and may exacerbate competition between different types of victims, particularly when the distribution of material benefits results from the recommendations of truth commission reports. This leads to a general question about capacity: to what extent will a truth commission have the expertise and resources to address a problem on the scale of massive displacement? It will of course depend on the commission in question, but as with other matters, such as socioeconomic development, the more truth commissions expand their mandates, the greater the risk of institutional overload, watered-down recommendations, and unmet expectations.

Given these considerations, identifying displaced persons as victims of interest in truth-telling processes becomes a much more contentious decision. However, as I demonstrate in the following section, it is now increasingly common for truth commissions to be mandated to engage with displaced populations as an important category of victims. Despite the risk of competition between victims and the challenges associated with prioritizing different victim groups and ensuring that the victimhood discourse does not undercut displaced persons' agency and dignity, this is ultimately a positive development. If displaced persons are not recognized as critical stakeholders in truth-telling processes, the narratives and recommendations that emerge from these initiatives will inevitably be incomplete, consigning the displaced to remain on the margins of their societies.

TRENDS IN TRUTH COMMISSION MANDATES, REPORTS, AND RECOMMENDATIONS

Historically, the crime of forced migration and the abuses endured by displaced populations have not been included in truth commission mandates and have not figured prominently in the reports and recommendations issued by these institutions. However, as I demonstrate in the following section, this trend is gradually changing.

MANDATES

A truth commission's mandate shapes the extent to which it can effectively address particular human rights violations, such as arbitrary displacement,[20] although some truth commissions may address displacement as a specific human rights concern or as a broader contextual factor without being specifically mandated to do so. Many early truth commissions were charged with very narrow mandates that precluded investigation of displacement. For example, the Argentinean and Chilean truth commissions focused on "disappearances" and torture, discounting the experiences of flight and exile that many dissidents endured in order to escape these fates. South Africa's Truth and Reconciliation Commission (TRC) did not have a mandate to examine displacement, despite the fact that the apartheid system was fundamentally predicated on forced migration, which relegated millions of black South Africans to infertile lands. Instead, the TRC examined "gross human rights violations," defined as "killing, abduction, torture, and severe ill-treatment."[21] Critics such as Mahmood Mamdani argue that by excluding apartheid practices that affected ordinary South Africans, the TRC proffered a "compromised truth" that "has written the vast majority of victims out of history."[22]

Despite the exclusion of displacement from the mandates of these early truth commissions, it appears that the trend is now toward broader mandates amenable to addressing a wider range of abusive practices and human rights violations, including forced migration. This broadening of mandates poses challenges of its own, as truth commissions are expected to accomplish more without parallel increases in budgets or time frames.[23] For example, truth commissions that are mandated to investigate displacement will likely have to engage with a much larger population of survivors, who may be geographically dispersed and difficult to contact. Refugees in protracted displacement situations may have taken on the language of their host communities and may not speak the working language of the truth commission, necessitating the use of translators. Nonetheless, Hayner argues, "as a general rule, terms of reference should be sufficiently broad and flexible to allow investigation into all forms of rights abuses, leaving to the commission the decision of what specific cases or practices to investigate and report."[24] There is no ideal truth commission, and what is preferable in terms of scope and powers for a commission will depend on many factors, including the political context in which the commission operates. However, as argued earlier, it is in the interests of survivors and transitional societies more broadly for truth commissions to strive for comprehensiveness and completeness, which requires that they be empowered not only to compile technical details but also to investigate how and why violations such as forced migration occurred.

The flexible approach to truth commission mandates advocated by Hayner does not guarantee that forced migration concerns will be addressed adequately. Indeed, while many recent, broadly mandated truth commissions have had the opportunity to investigate displacement, they have approached this challenge "in an ad hoc or constricted manner, and without a conscious strategy."[25] For example, the Liberian truth commission addressed the widespread displacement that characterized the country's civil war, but it lacked a conscious strategy for engaging IDPs and ensuring that their contributions and concerns were reflected in the final commission reports. However, several recent and ongoing truth commissions have specifically incorporated forced migration and related crimes into their mandates. Morocco's Equity and Reconciliation Commission (2004–5) was mandated to do the following: "Assess, research, investigate, arbitrate and make recommendations about gross human rights violations ... [including] forced disappearances, arbitrary detention, torture, sexual abuse and deprivation of the right to life, as a result of unrestrained and inadequate use of state force and coerced exile."[26] Various bodies, including the truth commissions for Mauritius (2009–present), the Solomon Islands (2009–present), Ghana (2003–4), and Kenya (2009–present), have concertedly focused on the dispossession of land. The Solomon Islands Truth and Reconciliation Commission is mandated to investigate "the destruction of property, deprivation of rights to own property and the right to settle and make a living."[27] Timor-Leste's Commission for Reception, Truth and Reconciliation (Comissão de Acolhimento, Verdade e Reconciliação de Timor-Leste—CAVR) was also mandated to investigate displacement but suffered from blind spots in its treatment of the issue: although it specifically aimed to investigate forced migration and contribute to the resolution of displacement through the return and reintegration of IDPs and refugees from West Timor, the commission failed to engage or address in detail the situation of the many refugees who sought asylum outside the Indonesian archipelago.[28] The factors that lead to the formal inclusion of forced migration in truth commission mandates vary; however, it appears that in general when forced migration and the dispossession of land represent significant, current concerns for the international community and local elites, commissions are more likely to be directed to investigate these issues. When the displaced and dispossessed have no prominent backers, or when displacement crises have been sustainably resolved without the establishment of a truth commission, there is much less pressure for truth-telling initiatives to tackle these concerns.

Ensuring that truth commissions are mandated to investigate displacement has important implications for gender equity and the equal treatment of different age groups. While both men and women are subjected to abuses such as extrajudicial executions and arbitrary imprisonment, which have historically been the focus of truth commissions, these violations disproportionately affect young and middle-aged men. The majority of those uprooted, on the other hand, are women, children, and elderly people. By purposefully mandating truth commissions to investigate displacement, the architects of these bodies can ensure that their work more comprehensively reflects the experiences and suffering of the entire population.[29]

REPORTS AND RECOMMENDATIONS

Reports are the major tangible outcome of truth commissions and can have a definitive impact on the construction of post-conflict national narratives. Consequently, the acknowledgment and examination of displacement and exile in truth commission reports may significantly affect whether the experiences and suffering of refugees and IDPs are broadly recognized as a critical part of a conflicted country's history.

Of the thirty-two truth commission reports publicly released to date, at least nine of them address displacement, if only briefly,[30] and at least eight were prepared by commissions operating under restricted mandates that precluded examination of displacement. Several of the reports that address displacement do so in commendable detail. For example, the reports for Liberia and Sierra Leone indicate that forced migration was the most pervasive human rights violation in these interlinked conflicts, accounting for 36 percent of reported violations in Liberia and almost 20 percent of reported abuses in Sierra Leone.[31] *Chega! The Final Report of the Commission for Reception, Truth and Reconciliation in East Timor* addresses displacement in extensive detail and finds that forced migration resulted in more deaths than any other factor during Indonesia's occupation of Timor-Leste.[32] Guatemala's Commission for Historical Clarification (Comisión para el Esclarecimiento Histórico—CEH) focused on the social conditions surrounding the displacement of swaths of the country's indigenous population, and its report specifically recognizes the suffering and stigma endured by the displaced, as well as the detrimental impact of state discrimination on return and reintegration. The CEH report also documents more than a dozen cases of occupation of refugee lands.[33] Many of these reports address displacement as a consequence of other human rights violations, such as killing, torture, and rape, as a violation in and of itself, and as a condition that rendered victims more vulnerable to further abuses, such as exploitation and violence in refugee camps.

Truth commission reports often include recommendations for reforms and reparations programs; however, Hayner notes that those "countries that have crafted a reparations program independent of a broader truth-telling exercise have found a much cooler reception from victims."[34] Therefore, integrating the issue of forced migration into the work of truth commissions may help ensure that the recommended reparations programs include and are effective for displaced beneficiaries. Various commissions have made specific efforts to craft recommendations that respond to displaced persons' specific concerns, such as the need for property restitution or land reform, the acceptance of dual nationality for those who have obtained another passport while in exile, the recognition of foreign qualifications, and the acceptance of the diaspora's participation in peacebuilding and development activities. Ghana's National Reconciliation Commission, for example, recommended the restitution of confiscated property,[35] while the report of the Guatemalan CEH advanced perhaps the most comprehensive set of recommendations to date relevant to redressing and resolving displacement.

The CEH report set a clear remedial standard, stating that the government must undertake "measures for the restoration of material possessions so that, as far as possible, the situation existing before the violation [is] re-established, particularly in the case of land ownership."[36] The report also called for financial compensation for the most serious injuries, as well as psychological rehabilitation; medical, legal, and social services; and moral and symbolic reparations. Although these different forms of redress were not, for the most part, specifically employed with a view to supporting the resolution of displacement, many of these remedial tools were highly relevant to the needs and concerns of the displaced.[37] However, implementation of reparations has faced numerous delays and obstacles. After extensive negotiations, the Reparations Commission and National Reparations Program were agreed on in 2003, but implementation did not actually begin until 2005, and the program has been drastically underfinanced: approximately US$3.6 million was to be allotted annually over ten years, significantly less than the US$48 million that advocates argued was required. Furthermore, in most of the years following 2005, the actual allocation within the national budget did not come close to the $3.6 million that was promised. According to the director of the National Reparations Program, some thirty thousand victims have received compensation since the program began,[38] but the amounts have been extremely limited, with cases of extrajudicial executions and disappearances receiving less than

US$3,000. The National Council of Displaced Guatemalans (Consejo Nacional de Desplazados de Guatemala—CONDEG) states that no IDPs have received settlements through the program, despite the fact that forced migration is one of the crimes eligible for compensation.[39]

In addition to individual reparations, the CEH report called for collective redress initiatives in war-affected communities that would "promote reconciliation, so that in addition to addressing reparations [they] ... favor the entire population, without distinction between victims and perpetrators" and other community members.[40] This approach fit with the Guatemalan government's strategy of providing assistance to the displaced alongside the broader landless population, rather than through targeted programs.[41] However, these attempts to provide redress and assistance without taking into account the particular experiences, claims, and concerns of the potential beneficiaries resulted in "neglect of the special needs of displaced persons, and an overall lack of justice and restitution for the displacement that they suffered."[42] More broadly, this approach to collective redress raised significant normative problems: although the reincorporation of perpetrators into society is essential to post-conflict transformation, transitional justice processes must make a moral and legal distinction between the actions of offenders and the offended; they should strive to rectify injustices experienced by victims, rather than reap benefits for the abusers.[43]

CONSULTATION AND PARTICIPATION OF DISPLACED PERSONS IN TRUTH-TELLING PROCESSES

As Diane Orentlicher, the United Nations independent expert on impunity, attests, the establishment of a truth commission "should be based upon broad public consultations in which the views of victims and survivors especially are sought."[44] Historically, however, debates on the creation and operation of truth commissions and other transitional justice initiatives have left out IDPs, refugees, and other members of the diaspora. Yet as I suggest in the following section, a range of internationally negotiated frameworks and principles underpin the view that displaced persons are among the central stakeholders that must be engaged in truth-telling processes. At the same time, the involvement of displaced populations in truth commissions in countries including Liberia, Sierra Leone, and Timor-Leste offer insights that may inform efforts to engage refugees and IDPs in future truth-telling processes.

FRAMEWORKS AND PRINCIPLES INFORMING THE ENGAGEMENT OF DISPLACED PERSONS

A range of international frameworks and principles bolster the view that refugees and IDPs should have the opportunity to participate actively in truth-telling processes, from the consultation stage to the implementation of recommendations flowing from truth commission reports.[45] First and foremost, the United Nations Basic Principles and Guidelines on the Right to a Remedy and Reparation for Victims of Gross Violations of International Human Rights Law and Serious Violations of International Humanitarian Law, which recognizes that truth-telling processes may be an important aspect of efforts to remedy injustices, states that the principles must be applied "without any discrimination of any kind or on any ground, without exception."[46] It is therefore unacceptable to exclude potential participants on the basis of arbitrary factors such as their being outside the country or internally displaced.

The Guiding Principles on Internal Displacement and the Framework on Durable Solutions for Internally Displaced Persons also backstop IDPs' right to be included in truth-telling processes. Principle 22 of the Guiding Principles says that IDPs have the right to "participate equally in community affairs" and in "governmental and public affairs."[47] Principle 28.2 also speaks to the issue of participation: "Special efforts should be made to ensure the full participation of internally displaced persons in the planning and management of their return or resettlement and reintegration."[48] Since truth commissions bear on community, governmental, and public affairs and may have significant bearing on return and reintegration processes (discussed later), IDPs clearly have a strong claim to participate actively in them. Indeed, as principle 28.2 suggests, it is incumbent on those responsible for truth commissions to institute special measures, if needed, to ensure that these bodies are accessible to displaced populations. This view is echoed in the Framework on Durable Solutions, which states that IDPs "need to be fully informed about existing remedies," such as truth commissions, "and should be involved in their design, implementation and evaluation."[49] As the Framework indicates, involving the displaced in these initiatives "contributes to providing a greater sense of justice and dignity and helps in redressing the relationship between the victims and the State."[50] The Report of the Secretary-General on the Rule of Law and Transitional Justice also recognizes refugees and IDPs as key stakeholders in transitional justice processes and calls for authorities to do the following:

> Recognize and respect the rights of both victims and accused persons, in accordance with international standards, with particular attention

to groups most affected by conflict and a breakdown of the rule of law, among them children, women, minorities, prisoners and displaced persons, and *ensure that proceedings for the redress of grievances include specific measures for their participation and protection.*[51]

PARTICIPATION IN TRUTH COMMISSIONS

IDPs, refugees, and other diaspora groups have engaged in truth commission processes in a range of ways—"as conceivers of the process, statement givers in the data collection process, advocates for justice or ... as participants in all phases."[52] Displaced and diaspora populations have helped to establish truth commissions in countries such as Haiti, where the admittedly abortive National Truth and Justice Commission (1994–96) was created in part through the work of exiled Haitians.[53] Refugees and IDPs from countries such as Guatemala and Liberia helped to gather testimonies from other survivors, which were then fed into truth commission reports.[54] In various cases, displaced persons have also served as witnesses in public truth commission sessions. The participation of displaced persons has been particularly extensive in commissions such as the CAVR, which held hearings specifically focused on forced migration, with testimony from those displaced internally and across borders. The CAVR's community-level "reception function" used the truth-telling process to facilitate the return and reintegration of displaced low-level offenders, who participated as confessors seeking the opportunity to make amends and return to their homes; community members, many of whom were returnees themselves, served as decisionmakers responsible for determining both whether the offender was telling the truth and the forms of redress he or she would have to make before being absolved of past crimes and welcomed back into the community.[55]

It is difficult to assess the significance for displaced persons of these different approaches to participating in the work of truth commissions. In the last section of this chapter, I examine the potential significance of truth-telling processes, including truth commissions, for the resolution of displacement. But beyond potentially facilitating the attainment of durable solutions, has participation in truth commissions proved to be personally meaningful for the displaced? Has it contributed to reconciliation on interpersonal, community, or national levels? The answers to such questions will of course vary among cases and people. In Guatemala, many victims indicated that they found testifying before the CEH and attending the release of the truth commission report to be powerful experiences. However, since many refugees and IDPs returned to remote regions of the country, their opportunities to participate were typically "brief and superficial," limited not only by their remote location but also by fear of reprisals.[56] Some CEH investigators who hiked into the remote highlands to interview displaced civilians found that many people did not realize the war had ended or that a truth commission had been established. This experience underscores that the active and meaningful participation of the displaced is contingent upon effective outreach and awareness-raising activities. Once they were informed about the goals of the CEH, many displaced Guatemalans were eager to participate; indeed, the commission lacked the capacity to record the testimonies of all those who wanted to register their experiences.[57]

When truth commissions have limited resources to carry out their mandates, collective testimonies that present communities' experiences are an important way to make participation accessible to as many survivors as possible. Although refugee and IDP camps are typically temporary communities that disband when their residents have access to durable solutions, such as voluntary return or local integration, these communities often endure significant abuses, such as cross-border military attacks and infiltration by armed elements. Enlisting current and former residents of these camps in the production of collective testimonies may be a valuable avenue for increasing the participation of displaced persons and ensuring that the unique experiences of these impermanent communities are included in the historical record.

PARTICIPATION IN OTHER FORMS OF TRUTH-TELLING

Beyond truth commissions, displaced persons have also participated actively in truth-telling processes such as the exhumation, identification, and reburial of the bodies of those killed in genocidal violence. In the aftermath of the Srebrenica massacre in Bosnia, the information obtained through exhumation and identification processes played an important role in establishing the truth about this event. Many refugees and IDPs from Srebrenica returned, even if only temporarily, to participate in the reburial of their family members, which was an important way of publicly marking the genocide that took place there in July 1995.[58] In Turkey, IDP groups such as the Saturday Mothers, who have successfully advocated for the exhumation of clandestine graves and the identification of the remains of disappeared family members, have also been pushing—so far without success—for the establishment of a national truth commission to examine abuses against the Kurdish population. Despite major political opposition to the creation of a truth commission in Turkey, the information gained through these exhumations adds credence to IDPs' calls for a more comprehensive investigation of the government's involvement in crimes such as displacement, torture, murder, and disappearances.[59]

The return process itself can also be a powerful act of truth-telling. For example, before settling down on the land set aside for them, the first group of collectively organized Guatemalan refugees to return from Mexico undertook a three-week, cross-country journey by caravan to raise awareness of their experiences and their goal of reclaiming their homeland and to renegotiate their relationship with the Guatemalan state. The "grand tour" was both a "symbolic reappropriation of citizenship" and an astute strategy based on the returnees' recognition that their security depended on "popular support and visibility in (the very limited) public opinion."[60] Before the returnees' cross-country tour in 1993 (four years prior to the establishment of the CEH), many Guatemalans indicated that they had no idea of the scope and severity of the violations inflicted on the country's indigenous communities during the war, suggesting that the caravan had an important truth-telling function, one that paved the way for the country's official truth commission.

Refugees and IDPs have also participated in commemoration efforts that acknowledge experiences of displacement and other human rights violations. In some cases, commemorative activities such as the creation of memorials grow out of the recommendations of truth commissions; in others, they are instigated independently by the members of displaced communities and their supporters; but in both instances, they serve an important truth-telling function, as they direct public attention toward histories of forced migration and abuse. The preserved sections of the Berlin Wall where East Germans were killed while attempting to flee to the West is one of the most well-known examples of a memorial linked to the flight of refugees. In the early euphoria after the fall of East Germany, large segments of the wall were ripped down before authorities recognized that its preservation was essential to telling the history of the divided city and remembering the victims of the Communist regime. The Palestinian Ministry of Development and Planning has taken heed of this near-oversight by planning, in the event of a solution to the Israeli-Palestinian conflict, to preserve certain refugee camps in Gaza and the West Bank as memorials to the refugees' losses and resilience. The Israeli nongovernmental organization (NGO) Zochrot is already involved in complementing these plans by erecting small memorials in Israel recognizing the Palestinian villages that were abandoned in 1948 and subsequently razed, while the descendants of Palestinians displaced from the village of Lifta in 1948 are campaigning publicly and in court to halt the proposed development of the site as an upscale housing project. While the former residents and their families realize that the Israeli government will not restore their properties to them, they want the ruins to stand as a "site of memory."[61] In Cape Town, the District Six Museum commemorates the more than sixty thousand black South Africans who were forcibly relocated to the barren Cape Flats when the apartheid government declared District Six to be a "white" neighborhood. The museum aims to "keep alive the memories of District Six and displaced people everywhere" and was developed with the active participation of the families of the displaced.[62]

These examples demonstrate that commemorative activities, including the creation of memorials and museums, serve as a form of truth-telling about both different experiences of displacement and governments' responses to forced migrants at different phases of the displacement cycle. Displaced populations and the descendants of the displaced participate in these commemorative activities in a variety of ways. For example, the displaced may be involved in initiating and designing commemorative projects, participating in visits to and services at commemorative sites, and serving as staff or facilitators at memorials and museums, communicating their own stories of displacement and the experiences of their communities. Further research is required to better understand how such commemorative activities may be made as meaningful as possible for the survivors of displacement and other human rights violations whose histories are being recognized.

OBSTACLES TO PARTICIPATION

Despite clear calls for their participation, the actual engagement of refugees and IDPs in the work of truth commissions has generally been lackluster. In some instances, refugees have not been involved because participation in the process was purposefully limited to those within the country, as in the case of the Brazilian truth commission.[63] Even if displaced persons are not technically barred from participating, however, they may lack national identity documents that confirm their eligibility to participate in truth commission hearings. Furthermore, the physical inaccessibility of truth commission meetings can be another significant obstacle. Displaced persons who have sought refuge outside the country or in remote regions may not be able to travel to the cities where truth commissions typically meet. While some recent commissions have convened "satellite" hearings in countries with large diaspora populations and have sent investigators to gather testimony in refugee camps, these activities depend on the willingness of host states to provide access to those within their borders. In contexts where relations between refugees, host states, and states of origin are strained, such access may not be forthcoming.

Problems of impoverishment and social marginalization in displaced communities mean that even if refugees and IDPs can physically access truth commission hearings, they may not feel comfortable participating or may simply be too focused on making ends meet to be able to participate. As survivors of human rights violations often committed by state agents, refugees and IDPs may be fearful or distrustful of official institutions such as truth commissions and may be reluctant to "forego their anonymity" by testifying.[64] Indeed, testifying before a truth commission may provoke reprisals in divided return communities and may compel witnesses to flee their homes anew. To date, attacks against witnesses have been a more pressing concern during formal trials, but without effective precautions and protections, truth commission witnesses can also be intimidated, attacked, or forced to flee. This may be a significant deterrent for refugees and IDPs struggling to resolve their initial displacement.

Lack of appropriate outreach and effective civil society engagement represent two of the foremost obstacles to the participation of displaced persons in truth commissions. In many cases, information about truth-telling processes may not be widely distributed outside the country or in remote areas where IDPs may be living. As pointed out earlier, this was a problem in Guatemala. Furthermore, as I will discuss, engaging humanitarian, peacebuilding, and development actors who work closely with displaced populations may be essential to effective outreach to forced migrants. Equally, local and national civil society organizations may play a central role in crafting and executing effective, innovative outreach strategies. For example, in light of the CAVR's emphasis on return and reintegration, concerted efforts were directed toward enabling the participation of refugees in West Timor in the commission's work. To reach out to this group, the CAVR sent eighteen representatives from a range of NGOs into the refugee camps in West Timor for six months to raise awareness of the CAVR process using tools such as radio programs tailored to address the refugees' concerns.[65]

Civil society organizations composed of refugees and IDPs and dedicated to advocating on their behalf may play critical roles not only in terms of outreach but also in first getting displacement on truth commission agendas and then promoting the implementation of truth commission recommendations related to forced migrants' concerns. For example, Peru's national truth commission investigated displacement after concerted lobbying from displaced persons' organizations and civil society groups such as the National Committee for the Displaced (Mesa Nacional de Desplazados—MENADES).[66] However, organization and mobilization among displaced populations is often limited because of factors such as fear, government repression, and lack of resources and training. In countries such as Colombia, organizational efforts among the displaced are marked by a serious tension: IDPs organize in order to advocate their rights and thereby increase their collective security, but by challenging the state, paramilitaries, and powerful corporations, they become more insecure because of threats and violence from these actors.[67]

Events in Liberia demonstrate the importance of organizing early in order to ensure that the concerns of displaced persons are addressed in both peace negotiations and truth-telling processes. Because internal displacement in particular was so ubiquitous during the war, no civil society group represented the IDPs in the Liberian peace negotiations. Rather, the assumption was that because such large numbers were affected by displacement, the concerns associated with forced migration would naturally be addressed in the process. In practice, this assumption did not hold: while Liberian refugees were effectively represented in the peace negotiations, and special efforts were made to engage them in the national truth commission, those for whom internal displacement was particularly prolonged and problematic did not have their concerns concertedly addressed. After the Liberian IDPs were marginalized in the peace negotiations, it became difficult to meaningfully integrate their concerns in the truth-telling process. This case underlines the fact that displacement does not entail a uniform level of vulnerability; responding effectively to those who have not recovered from the insecurities associated with displacement necessitates early organization to communicate these concerns and ensure that they are taken seriously.[68]

Although the lack of organized groups dedicated to facilitating the participation of displaced persons in truth commissions is a serious obstacle, it is also important to recognize the obstacles that may emerge when organized groups of refugees and IDPs compete against one another for attention and assistance. For example, the success Guatemalan refugees had in collectively negotiating their return from Mexico and obtaining redress through national restitution and truth-telling processes generated resentment in the much larger IDP population, which did not benefit from equally "generous" assistance and redress policies.

Even when they are well-organized and represented by respected organizations such as Mama Maquín in Guatemala, refugee and IDP women may encounter significant obstacles to their participation in truth-telling processes. In particular, their meaningful participation has sometimes been limited by blinkered conceptions of the contributions they may make to truth-telling.[69] As Susan Harris Rimmer argues, when refugee women do participate in truth commissions, their "script" has been limited because they are simply not asked a sufficiently broad range of questions that elicit important information about their gendered experiences of displacement.[70] When interviewing female refugee witnesses, bodies such as the CAVR have tended to focus narrowly on issues such as sexual and gender-based violence, rather than exploring women's experiences of the broader range of abuses to which the displaced are often exposed or the strategies displaced women employ to adapt and survive in these circumstances.[71]

The negative effect of these obstacles on the participation of refugees and IDPs in the work of truth commissions has been exacerbated by the current ad hoc approach to involving them. Lessons learned about overcoming these hurdles and effectively incorporating displaced and diaspora communities have not been compiled or systematically shared, forcing each new commission to reinvent the wheel.

INNOVATIONS TO SUPPORT THE PARTICIPATION OF REFUGEES AND DISPLACED PERSONS

Various innovations have helped to overcome the obstacles discussed here and facilitate the participation of displaced persons and formerly displaced persons in the work of truth commissions. Even though it did not address forced migration per se, the first Chilean truth commission broke new ground in advertising internationally to seek contributions from exiles. The Chilean, Argentinean, and Ecuadorian commissions built on this kind of outreach by allowing members of the diaspora to testify at embassies and consulates worldwide. Chile's National Commission on Political Imprisonment and Torture (2003–5) accepted written submissions through more than forty Chilean consulates in different countries, discovering that many victims had never before shared their stories in detail.[72] Outreach by the Argentinean National Commission on the Disappeared (1983–84) also prompted various survivors to return to the country to testify in person.

Returning from abroad or testifying at a formal state institution, such as an embassy or consulate, may be emotionally daunting or financially prohibitive for many refugees. The creation of "remote hearings" in communities with numerous diaspora members is an apposite response to this challenge. For example, the Liberian truth commission held hearings in St Paul, Minneapolis, and in the United Kingdom, where there are large Liberian diaspora communities. Paraguay's Truth and Justice Commission (2004–8) convened public hearings in Argentina, as many Paraguayan exiles sought shelter there. Such efforts may bring risks, though. "In one hearing that took place in Argentina," Hayner writes, "the ambassador of Paraguay to Argentina was unexpectedly named as having collaborated with the Stroessner regime. As a direct result, he was quickly dismissed from his post."[73] This incident reflects the potential shortcomings of facilitating the participation of exiles through embassies and consulates, institutions that are not at arm's length from the government and that may employ individuals who have not been carefully vetted to ensure that they do not have ties to abusive regimes.

As discussed earlier, some commissions, such as the CAVR, have held special hearings on forced migration, which may increase the active participation of refugees and IDPs by demonstrating strong interest in their experiences and perspectives. Several commissions, including the bodies for Guatemala, Liberia, Timor-Leste, and Sierra Leone, actively sought out the perspectives of refugees and IDPs by dispatching investigators to interview witnesses in refugee camps and remote IDP settlements, and the final report of Sierra Leone's truth commission was informed by 175 statements from refugees in Nigeria, Guinea, Gambia, and Ghana.[74]

The Liberian truth commission, in partnership with the Georgia Institute of Technology, has been at the vanguard of efforts to use new technologies to increase the participation of poor and displaced persons and members of the diaspora in truth-telling processes. The Liberian commission boasted the "world's first truly interactive TRC web site," which could be used by members of the public to submit formal statements, upload news and memorials, and even apply for amnesty. Videos of the truth commission proceedings are also available to watch online, and a Mobile Story Exchange System that traveled around the country was used to record and share statements.[75] In the abstract, these innovations may cost-effectively facilitate the participation of refugees and IDPs. However, serious hurdles and concerns remain. First, many displaced and impoverished Liberians who could hypothetically benefit from these tools lack access to computers and Internet services. Second, the use of technology to gather statements raises important concerns about the protection of witnesses, defamation, the blurring of lines between official and unofficial truth-telling initiatives, and the "dehumanization" of truth-telling processes.[76] Indeed, Liberians and Sierra Leoneans have proved very hesitant or simply unable to use the online testimony mechanisms developed by their national truth commissions. Despite "extensive pretesting, outreach to diaspora communities and security guarantees, the [Liberian Truth and Reconciliation Commission's] online statement taking generated only a few statements. ... The Sierra Leone web-based statement process generated none," demonstrating that "even in today's tech-savvy environment personal interaction remains the most powerful tool for investigating human rights violations."[77]

Despite the limitations of these high-tech tools, the Liberian commission nonetheless stands out for its innovative efforts to develop and execute a concerted diaspora engagement strategy, in cooperation with an overseas human rights NGO, the Advocates for Human Rights (the Advocates). Although the TRC had no official mandate for diaspora engagement, this partnership was highly successful, resulting in more than 1,600 statements taken from Liberians living in the United States, the United Kingdom, and a refugee camp in Ghana, as well as in official public hearings in the United States. The diaspora project raised its own funds and published its own report, A House with Two Rooms, and also fed its findings into the official report of the Liberian TRC. The commission was motivated to engage the diaspora because Liberians living overseas were believed to have played a pivotal role in starting and financing the conflict, and because the commissioners were optimistic that the diaspora could help fund reparations for survivors. Indeed, the final report of the truth commission recommended that Liberians living overseas donate at least one dollar a month to the Reparations Truth Fund, "as the beginning of [their] contribution as citizens of Liberia to the economic and social development of their motherland."[78] This process yielded recommendations of special interest to those outside Liberia, such as formal acceptance of dual citizenship and allowing diaspora members to vote in national elections. The process also underlined the importance of truth commissions not adhering too tightly to definitions of refugees and IDPs when they set out to engage the displaced. Although refugees and IDPs should generally be defined as important categories of victims to be engaged in truth-telling processes, it is important to recognize that those who leave a war-torn country on a largely voluntary basis—for example, to pursue education or economic opportunities—may also be negatively affected by the conflict in their state of origin and may thus have a strong stake in the success of truth commissions. Since refugees and IDPs are known to have experienced human rights violations, when commissions have limited resources for engaging with uprooted or nonresident populations, it may be broadly advisable to focus first and foremost on reaching out to these groups. Nevertheless, developing a holistic strategy that could engage Liberians who migrated for a variety of reasons proved effective in this case and has already sparked the interest of Zimbabwean, Somali, and Kenyan diaspora groups who wish to build on the Liberian diaspora project's approach to advancing truth-telling processes in their own countries.[79]

Taken in total, these initiatives demonstrate that there is considerable scope for creativity and innovation with a view to facilitating the engagement of displaced persons in the work of truth commissions. Relatively modest initial outreach efforts have given way to thoughtful and sophisticated initiatives such as the Liberian diaspora project; however, further steps are needed to make truth commissions more accessible and responsive to the concerns of displaced persons. First, there is a need for more strategic assistance to facilitate forced migrants' participation, such as small grants to enable travel to truth commission sessions and more satellite hearings in refugee camps and diaspora communities. There is also a need for more tailored outreach efforts that explain the purpose of truth commissions and how displaced persons may participate. Effectively facilitating the participation of displaced persons and substantively addressing forced migration as a human rights violation requires knowledge of both the transitional justice process and the dynamics of displaced and host communities. More strategic use of intermediaries who have in-depth knowledge of both truth-telling processes and displaced communities could advance the achievement of these goals. For example, displaced communities could nominate liaisons to represent their concerns, and they could be integrated into the staff of the relevant truth commission. In nominating such liaison officers, it would be essential to ensure equitable representation of IDPs and refugees in different host states. Finally, there is room for greater innovation in facilitating exchanges between refugees and IDPs who have met with some success in participating in past truth-telling processes and those who are struggling to be heard in contemporary efforts. By sharing their experiences and strategies, refugees and IDPs who have effectively engaged in transitional justice processes may inform and inspire their counterparts in other countries, giving them a clearer sense of what they may expect and demand.[80]

PARTICIPATION OF HUMANITARIAN, DEVELOPMENT, AND PEACEBUILDING ACTORS IN TRUTH-TELLING

Many of the agents most closely involved with displaced populations, including humanitarian, development, and peacebuilding actors, have not historically been deeply involved in transitional justice processes such as truth commissions. As efforts to incorporate forced migration and displaced populations into the work of truth commissions become more systematic, these actors may have important roles to play in advising truth commissions on engaging refugees and IDPs and addressing the substantive issues associated with displacement. Because of concerns about maintaining neutrality and access to needy populations, humanitarian actors such as the International Committee of the Red Cross have often been extremely reluctant to share information from the field with national and international criminal justice efforts. However, for some humanitarian, development, and peacebuilding organizations, sharing information with truth commissions on the scope and conditions of displacement may be less problematic than cooperating with trials, as truth commissions do not typically impose penalties on individual offenders and are therefore subject to less concerted opposition from authorities who may "punish" organizations by limiting access.

Among humanitarian, development, and peacebuilding actors, the Office of the UN High Commissioner for Refugees (UNHCR) has played a particularly important role in facilitating the work of truth commissions in a variety of post-conflict contexts. In Sierra Leone, the national truth commission and UNHCR worked together to facilitate refugees' participation in the process.[81] In Timor-Leste, UNHCR and other actors such as the International Organization for Migration cooperated with the CAVR on efforts to promote return, reintegration, and reconciliation, a natural fit in light of the CAVR's mandate to support the resolution of displacement.[82] The insights UNHCR gained through these and other experiences have not yet been collected and integrated into the organization's operational handbooks for post-conflict settings, but doing so could help ensure more systematic and effective support for truth-telling processes.[83]

Beyond supporting formal truth commissions, humanitarian, peacebuilding, and development actors may help facilitate so-called coexistence activities that bring together members of different ethnic groups in divided return communities, which may open up more informal truth-telling opportunities. For example, in Burundi UNHCR has been involved in establishing a new village called Muriza, which provides a place where displaced, landless Hutus and Tutsis may settle peacefully together. The hope is that providing a concrete example of how Hutus and Tutsis may live together will help set the stage for the successful operation of the national truth commission and tribunal.[84] UNHCR also supported a range of coexistence activities in Rwanda and Bosnia designed to bring together members of opposing groups in divided return communities. These activities often involved income-generating initiatives and bringing members of different groups together to socialize or pursue education in shared spaces. Research on coexistence and income-generating projects in Bosnia suggests that these activities may have a positive effect on reintegration and peacebuilding in return communities. Although they are not truth-telling initiatives per se, such projects can create "space for dialogue" that can be used to generate deeper, shared understandings of what happened during the war and may thus be complementary to more traditional transitional justice mechanisms such as truth commissions.[85]

One of the positive potential outcomes for humanitarian, peacebuilding, and development actors of supporting truth-telling processes is the establishment of an ethos of open discussion with different stakeholders, which may helpfully inform not only truth-telling efforts but also the design and implementation of durable solution strategies and projects intended to improve conditions in post-conflict communities. This development of a culture of dialogue was evident in Timor-Leste, yet experiences there also underlined the risk that community members may gradually develop a kind of discussion or reconciliation "fatigue," resulting in a situation in which dialogue is simply a matter of form, rather than a meaningful exercise.[86] Another risk is that participation in decisionmaking and dialogue processes may be seen as a substitute for tangible accomplishments in tackling critical challenges. For example, in Guatemala the leadership of the UN peacebuilding mission (MINUGUA) reflected that the "imperative on participation and consensus-building has at times slowed the implementation process, enabling the Government and other State institutions to evade their responsibilities and substitute dialogue for action."[87] If humanitarian, peacebuilding, and development actors already juggling a range of complex demands are to be convinced to contribute to truth commissions, the proponents of these processes will need to demonstrate that such undertakings can move beyond just talk and have a significant positive effect on primary goals such as the resolution of displacement.

IMPLICATIONS OF TRUTH-TELLING FOR ENDING DISPLACEMENT

The Framework on Durable Solutions for Internally Displaced Persons makes some commonsense arguments about the role of transitional justice mechanisms such as truth commissions in resolving displacement:

> Securing effective remedies for the violations … which caused displacement, or which occurred during displacement, may have a major impact on prospects for durable solutions for IDPs. Failure to secure effective remedies for such violations may cause risks of further displacement, impede reconciliation processes, [or] create a prolonged sense of injustice or prejudice among IDPs, and thereby undermine the achievement of durable solutions.[88]

The Framework goes on to indicate:

> In some situations, it is therefore necessary in order to achieve dura-
> ble solutions to formally address past violations by holding perpetra-
> tors accountable, providing victims with reparations in a formal sense,
> (including compensation), and/or providing information on the causes
> of displacement. This would be particularly important in cases where
> IDPs became victims of war crimes or crimes against humanity, where
> they remain at risk from the perpetrators of violations or abuse, or
> where they themselves feel that formal justice must be done to enable
> them to physically, socially and emotionally overcome their displace-
> ment experience.[89]

Indeed, in addition to formal court proceedings and legal sanctions, truth
commissions may play a valuable role in enabling refugees and IDPs to "overcome their displacement experiences" and benefit from a durable solution, be
it resettlement, local integration, or voluntary return.

Further empirical research is needed to fully explain the practical links
between truth-telling processes and the resolution of different displacement
situations. As a first step toward understanding the connections between these
processes, my aim in this section is to consider the possible ways in which
truth-telling initiatives may affect efforts to resolve displacement, and to reflect
on how truth commissions may best contribute to this goal. Achieving durable
solutions to displacement has not typically been an explicit goal of most transitional justice actors, who have more often adopted goals such as recognizing and redressing injustice and building social trust. However, it is clear that
these goals may be intimately connected to the resolution of displacement, and
in particular to the long-term sustainability of return and local integration.
Realizing solutions such as return and reintegration may require that the narratives of host and displaced populations be recognized, as a first step toward
kindling social trust among the members of divided or fragmented societies.
For humanitarian, peacebuilding, and development actors, the possibility that
initiatives such as truth commissions may contribute to the resolution of displacement represents one of the most persuasive reasons to cooperate with
transitional justice processes.

TRUTH-TELLING AND DURABLE SOLUTIONS

To the limited extent that humanitarian, peacebuilding, and development
actors have considered the relationship between truth-telling and durable

solutions, they have tended to focus attention on the potential link between transitional justice and the "preferred" solution of voluntary return. This is evident in the work of UNHCR staffers[90] and in the 2004 Report of the Secretary-General on Transitional Justice and the Rule of Law.[91] The Timorese CAVR is the sole truth commission to date to explicitly support the resolution of displacement; its efforts in this regard focused predominantly on supporting return and reintegration in displaced persons' communities of origin. By facilitating a local process through which perpetrators of "less serious" violations could acknowledge their crimes, carry out reparative acts identified by the community, and then return home, the CAVR contributed to resolving the displacement of both former militia members and refugees,[92] including approximately ten thousand former militia members and low-level offenders displaced in West Timor. At the same time, the participatory nature of the process and the fact that it was rooted in traditional customs arguably strengthened governance structures at the local level, which in turn facilitated reintegration and community reconstruction processes. Unfortunately, the CAVR's focus on supporting return and reintegration, which the political leadership saw as imperative to the stability of the fledgling state, effectively deprioritized other goals, such as ensuring accountability for sexual and gender-based violence.[93] This underlines the difficulty of ensuring that no elements of truth commission mandates are sacrificed when these institutions become involved in the complex task of supporting durable solutions to displacement.

The potential links between truth-telling, resettlement, and local integration have received even less attention than the connections between truth-telling and return, though truth-telling processes may also have an important role to play in making these solutions viable and acceptable for displaced communities. Reflecting on the longstanding displacement of the Palestinian refugees, Rashid Khalidi argues that solutions for the refugees "must be grounded in the difficult process of accepting the truth. This includes both the truth about what happened in 1948 and the truth about what is attainable [sixty] years later."[94] In cases such as the Palestinian refugee situation, truth-telling processes may perhaps lead to recognition of the refugees' narratives and their claim in principle, if not in practice, to their lost lands. This type of recognition is perceived by many observers to be essential to unlocking this entrenched conflict. Such acts of truth-telling and recognition may make it more socially acceptable for the refugees to accept durable solutions other than repatriation to their original homes, such as moving to a newly independent Palestinian state or remaining in host states such as Jordan. Acknowledgment of the refugees' narrative and rights claims (again, in principle if not in practice) may also increase their willingness to accept compensation in lieu of restitution, in amounts that Israel can realistically finance.[95]

Truth-telling may also facilitate the equitable integration of refugees into host societies while durable solutions are being negotiated. For example, the Lebanese-Palestinian Dialogue Committee (LPDC) is a high-level initiative launched in 2005 with a view to reforming the country's longstanding policies of discrimination against the Palestinian refugees sheltered within its borders. While not a truth commission, the LPDC is based on the recognition that regardless of the duration of the refugees' stay in Lebanon, dialogue is needed to improve community relations. The LPDC dialogue focuses on critical forward-looking issues such as arms control, livelihoods, and conditions in the camps, but it is premised on the acknowledgment of historical and contemporary truths about the relationship between the refugees and their host state, such as the fact that

> the living conditions of the refugees within the camps are dire and unacceptable, and that the lack of opportunities available to the refugees is an impediment to their welfare and their right to live a dignified and prosperous life under the rule of law. ... By recognizing this we have turned a new leaf on a difficult and painful past full of mistakes on all sides and for which both the Lebanese and Palestinians have paid too high a price. We are looking towards a brighter future under the rule of law for all people living on Lebanese soil.[96]

These examples suggest that truth-telling processes may facilitate the realization of durable solutions to displacement in a variety of ways. First, truth-telling processes may acknowledge and affirm displaced persons' narratives and experiences. Such acknowledgment and acceptance may make it more socially and politically acceptable for refugees to choose solutions other than a return to their original homes (which in many cases have been occupied by other families for decades), and may improve relations between displaced persons and their neighbors, whether in host or return communities. This is particularly important in cases where animosity toward refugees and IDPs has developed among the nondisplaced, who may feel betrayed by those who escaped, leaving them to bear the brunt of the conflict.[97] Second, truth-telling processes may improve relations between displaced persons and their states. Formal recognition of the wrongs endured by refugees and IDPs may help reposition the displaced as full, rights-bearing members of the political community whose claims for protection and assistance must be taken seriously and treated equitably.[98] Such reform of relations between the state and its displaced citizens is essential to ensuring that solutions to displacement are truly durable. Third, by producing recommendations relevant to the pursuit of durable solutions, truth commission reports can support efforts to resolve displacement in accordance with respect for human rights. For example, by developing recommendations on issues such as housing, land distribution, and property restitution, truth commission reports can help ensure that refugees, IDPs, and returnees can access resources and services essential to rebuilding their lives. Even when truth commissions do not specifically address forced migration or engage displaced populations, recommendations on issues such as security sector reform, lustration, and equal rights for marginalized and minority citizens may be highly significant for displaced persons. Like their nondisplaced conationals, refugees and IDPs have vested interests in broad processes of state reform and accountability, and not only in targeted responses to the problem of displacement.

Truth-telling processes often fail to contribute to the pursuit of durable solutions because of a lack of equitable participation of displaced populations in truth-telling initiatives, lackluster political commitment to implementing truth commission recommendations, and poor timing. Truth commissions often do their work *after* large-scale return or resettlement has already begun, thus reducing their potential positive influence on early phases of the durable solutions process, though they may still contribute to reintegration and reconciliation processes in return communities. Indeed, the potential positive effects of truth-telling processes may have on the resolution of displacement are most likely to pertain to the long-term, sustainable (re)integration of displaced persons.[99] Nonetheless, better timing of transitional justice initiatives, including the prompt creation of truth commissions, could potentially augment their positive effects on the pursuit of durable solutions.

Truth-telling processes, traditionally focused on the nation as a whole, could arguably further increase their effectiveness by more concertedly examining the regional dynamics of conflict and displacement and engaging a wider range of actors from across the affected region. Although reforming the state and increasing citizens' ability to trust their government are vital goals that require a strong focus on the role of the state and its agents in conflict and human rights abuses, many recent and ongoing protracted displacement crises in areas such as the Balkans in Europe and the Great Lakes region of Africa have a definitively regional character, with a wide range of governments, non-state actors, and agencies involved in instigating displacement and perpetrating abuses against the displaced.[100] In many of these cases, the displaced themselves represent important regional actors who may be involved in transborder political movements, economic networks, and armed conflicts. While the barriers to effective regional transitional justice processes are formidable, expanding truth-telling processes to engage and take into account the role of actors throughout the region may be an important step toward increasing the relevance of these processes for the displaced and may be particularly important when the displaced are likely to integrate locally, rather than return to their countries of origin.[101]

As has already been discussed, truth commissions can also negatively affect efforts to resolve displacement by fostering competition between groups, particularly when the recommendations are expected to translate into tangible benefits, and by identifying the displaced as victims, which may lead them to develop unrealistic expectations of the process. Furthermore, in some contexts, public truth-telling about past injustices is not inherently valuable or meaningful. Speaking about past wrongs and grievances may be deeply disturbing for survivors and may generate anger and even violence on the part of perpetrators who oppose the truth-telling process. If the narratives produced by national truth commissions do not reflect displaced persons' own conceptions of the truth, the entire process may be alienating, resulting in greater disenfranchisement of the displaced from the political community, rather than the reestablishment of refugees and IDPs as respected, rights-bearing citizens. Similarly, if the truth-telling process is geared toward promoting a particular durable solution such as return, rather than opening up a range of choices to refugees and IDPs regarding the resolution of displacement, the process may ultimately be frustrating and disempowering, rather than helping to mend relations and restore to the displaced a stronger degree of control over their lives.

INSIGHTS FROM CASES WITHOUT FORMAL TRUTH-TELLING PROCESSES

In considering the potential impact of truth commissions on the resolution of displacement, it is also important to reflect on cases where there has been no official truth-telling process. For example, peacebuilding and the resolution of displacement in Mozambique is widely considered to have been a success, despite the fact that the egregious atrocities that characterized the war and prompted the massive uprooting of the civilian population were not tackled head on by formal national or international institutions. Edward Green and Alcinda Honwana argue that in the Mozambican cultural context, "to talk and recall the past is not necessarily seen as a prelude to healing or diminishing pain. Indeed, it is often believed to open the space for the malevolent forces to intervene."[102] In a similar vein, a detailed UNHCR study on the Mozambican

repatriation operation concluded that "despite the intensity of the Mozambican conflict, the many atrocities which took place during the war and the
enormous amount of social dislocation which it generated, there has been a
remarkable absence of revenge and recrimination since the conflict came to
an end. While War Crimes Tribunals and Truth Commissions may have an
important role to play in other war-torn societies, the Mozambican experience demonstrates that some communities may be capable of reconciliation
without such formal structures."[103] This is not to say that there was no redress
process in post-conflict Mozambique. In this instance, redress was typically
mediated at the local level, where, Carolyn Nordstrom argues, Mozambicans
fought an extraordinary "war against violence" by creatively drawing on spiritual traditions and indigenous medicine to treat, in the words of a Mozambican *curandeiro* (traditional healer), the "rash on the soul" caused by conflict.[104]
Although these traditional approaches did not necessarily involve explicitly
articulating the nature and scope of past abuses, in some cases they nonetheless had an important truth-telling function, as it was through these traditions
that community members were able to recognize and come to terms with legacies of violence and reintegrate former community members, including perpetrators and displaced survivors of egregious human rights violations such
as rape. There are, however, inevitable limitations to customary approaches to
promoting post-conflict reconciliation and dealing with the legacy of war. Religious or spiritual reconciliation rituals do not resonate universally, and many
Mozambicans cannot simply "erase" their traumatic memories, as customary
practices often require.[105] In the longer term, a lack of formal recognition of
the crimes that took place during the war may also foster denial and further
social unrest, suggesting that room may remain for formal truth-telling processes in Mozambique.[106]

In other cases such as Bosnia, where there has been no official truth-telling
process and where war crimes trials are criticized as far removed from the reality of local citizens, the negative implications for the pursuit of reconciliation
and durable solutions to displacement have been stark. Minority returnees
have been subject to attacks and rampant discrimination, as well as flagrant
denial or even celebration of the violations inflicted on them. For example, the
Serb-run concentration camp of Trnopolji has reverted to being a primary
school. However, local Serbs rescheduled the school's annual celebrations to
commemorate the day Trnopolji was transformed into a camp and invited
former Bosniak prisoners to attend the party, underscoring the persistent animosity between Serb residents and Bosniak returnees.[107] Establishing a truth
commission for Bosnia would not necessarily have avoided these cruelties,

but by challenging ethno-nationalist myths and explicitly denouncing the intercommunal violence that characterized the war, a truth commission could potentially make such malicious actions less socially acceptable. Even today, years after the large-scale return of displaced persons to Bosnia and Herzegovina, an official renunciation of the atrocities that took place at Trnopolji could embolden some of the more open-minded locals to reach out to their neighbors, thus advancing the ongoing process of reintegration.

CONCLUSION

More research is required to fully understand the links between truth-telling processes, accountability for forced migration, and the resolution of displacement. While many past truth commissions have not investigated forced migration as a human rights violation, this issue is gradually being incorporated into the work of these institutions. Furthermore, important steps have been taken to facilitate the participation of refugees and IDPs in truth commission activities at all stages of the process. Nevertheless, an ad hoc approach persists both to addressing forced migration as a substantive concern and to engaging displaced persons in truth-telling processes; significant obstacles remain to be overcome to ensure that truth commissions respond to displacement as effectively as possible.

First, there is a need to raise awareness among transitional justice actors of the importance of incorporating displacement into truth commission mandates, reports, and recommendations and the value of making truth-telling processes accessible to displaced and diaspora populations. Second, a more systematic approach is required to engaging humanitarian, peacebuilding, and development actors that are closely involved with displaced populations in the work of truth commissions; compiling and communicating the lessons that organizations such as UNHCR have learned in the course of their involvement with truth-telling processes would be an important first step toward more informed, consistent, and effective engagement of these actors. Third, more concerted, tailored efforts are needed to inform displaced populations of truth-telling processes and support their involvement. Mechanisms such as satellite hearings and the use of truth commission investigators to collect testimony in displaced persons' camps represent important steps in this direction; other potentially positive steps could include appointing liaisons from displaced communities to work directly on the staff of national truth commissions. Fourth, more information sharing is needed on a range of levels, between international transitional justice experts, national truth commission staff, civil society advocates, and displaced populations who have participated directly in truth-telling processes. Exchanges between these actors should ensure that insights gained through the work of truth commissions are incorporated into contemporary efforts, rather than leaving new initiatives to reinvent the wheel.

Fifth, where possible, truth-telling initiatives and other transitional justice processes involving displaced populations should be designed and implemented in a harmonized manner, ideally with a view toward supporting durable solutions to displacement. For example, property restitution, a matter of critical concern to refugees and IDPs, is often managed through administrative mass claims processes that do not give displaced claimants or secondary occupants the opportunity to express their perspectives or concerns. While this leads to greater efficiency in processing claims, it arguably cuts short opportunities to use the property restitution process as a vehicle for interpersonal or communal reconciliation. Addressing land claims issues through the work of truth commissions may create a valuable opportunity for stakeholders to air their grievances and generate some degree of consensus around the legitimacy of different claims and productive approaches to post-conflict land reform (although land issues tend to be complicated and highly contentious, so there is a risk of this leading not to consensus but division, depending on how the matter is handled). Similarly, high-level tribunals may be used in concert with grassroots conflict resolution techniques, such as those pioneered by the CAVR to support the resolution of displacement by permanently removing war criminals from return communities while enabling low-level offenders to make amends for their actions upon returning to their homes.[108] Truth commission recommendations should also be closely connected to lustration policies, which ensure that the architects of large-scale displacement and human rights violations cannot access positions of power from which they could repeat their crimes.

These recommendations represent only a small fraction of the ways in which truth commissions could more effectively engage with displacement. Making good on them is admittedly challenging, because of competing priorities and limited financial resources and capacity in post-conflict environments, as well as the difficulty of timing transitional justice processes so that they effectively support efforts to resolve displacement. Truth commissions are often established after large-scale return processes have already taken place and thus may not have any effect on the early and volatile stages of the reintegration process. However, pursuing accountability for forced migration, supporting reconciliation, and crafting solutions to displacement are long-term, nonlinear processes.[109] Even if their work unfolds years after governments have declared displacement crises to be resolved, truth commissions may still affect ongoing reintegration and settlement processes. Perhaps one of the thorniest unresolved questions surrounding the timing of transitional justice initiatives is how truth-telling processes may contribute to the resolution of longstanding conflicts and protracted displacement. Cases such as the Colombian IDP and Palestinian refugee situations will arguably never be resolved until the protagonists accept or at least recognize displaced persons' narratives of injustice and struggle. These cases bring the contentious, changing nature of "truth" into sharp relief and underscore the critical importance of having realistic expectations of the contributions truth commissions may make to resolving displacement: these institutions may play a pivotal role in denouncing past injustices and establishing inclusive national narratives, but they will never be able to establish universally accepted truths or tell the full stories of the suffering and resilience of refugees, IDPs, and other survivors of war and atrocity. Yet despite these challenges and limitations, it is increasingly clear that including forced migration in truth commission mandates and creating space for displaced persons to share their experiences promises to enrich the work of these institutions and may in turn enhance their contributions to peace and reconciliation.

NOTES

1   United Nations Commission on Human Rights, Report of the Independent Expert to Update the Set of Principles to Combat Impunity, Diane Orentlicher: Addendum, E/ CN.4/2005/102/Add.1, February 8, 2005; Office of the United Nations High Commissioner for Human Rights, *Rule-of-Law Tools for Post-conflict States: Truth Commissions* (Geneva: OHCHR, 2006).

2   Priscilla Hayner, *Unspeakable Truths: Transitional Justice and the Challenge of Truth Commissions* (London: Routledge, 2010), 6.

3   Ibid., 11–12.

4   Eitan Bronstein, "The *Nakba* in Hebrew: Israeli-Jewish Awareness of the Palestinian Catastrophe and Internal Refugees," in *Catastrophe Remembered: Palestine, Israel and the Internal Refugees*, ed. Nur Masalha (London: Zed Books, 2005); Laleh Khalili, "Grass-Roots

Commemorations: Remembering the Land in the Camps of Lebanon," *Journal of Palestine Studies* 34, no. 1 (Autumn 2004): 6–22; Laleh Khalili, "Commemorating Contested Lands," in *Exile and Return: Predicaments of Palestinians and Jews*, ed. Ian Lustick and Ann Lesch (Philadelphia: University of Pennsylvania Press, 2005).

5   Craig Evan Pollack, "Returning to a Safe Area? The Importance of Burial for Return to Srebrenica," *Journal of Refugee Studies* 16, no. 2 (June 2003): 186–201.

6   Elie Podeh, "The Right of Return versus the Law of Return: Contrasting Historical Narratives in Israeli and Palestinian School Textbooks," in Lustick and Lesch, *Exile and Return*.

7   Monika Nalepa, "Reconciliation, Refugee Returns, and the Impact of International Criminal Justice: The Case of Bosnia and Herzegovina," in *Nomos LI: Transitional Justice*, ed. Melissa Williams, Rosemary Nagy, and Jon Elster (New York: New York University Press, 2012).

8   International refugee law does not specifically address the right of refugees to participate in institutions such as truth commissions. *The Handbook on Voluntary Repatriation* put out by the Office of the UN High Commissioner for Refugees (UNHCR) does not address the potential connections between truth-telling processes and the resolution of displacement through return, while UNHCR's *Handbook for Repatriation and Reintegration Activities* makes only passing reference to truth-telling, directing field officers to consider whether women have the opportunity to participate in truth and reconciliation processes, while overlooking the broader issues of whether displaced populations in general are involved in truth-telling activities, and whether these initiatives are relevant to the concerns of the displaced. UNHCR, *Handbook on Voluntary Repatriation: International Protection* (Geneva: UNHCR, 1996); and *Handbook for Repatriation and Reintegration Activities* (Geneva: UNHCR, 2004).

9   United Nations Security Council, "The Rule of Law and Transitional Justice in Conflict and Post-conflict Societies," Report of the Secretary-General, S/2004/616, August 23, 2004.

10   United Nations Commission on Human Rights, "Human Rights, Mass Exoduses and Displaced Persons: Addendum–Guiding Principles on Internal Displacement," Report of the Representative of the Secretary-General, Mr. Francis M. Deng, E/CN.4/1998/53/Add.2, February 11, 1998 ("Guiding Principles").

11   Megan Bradley, "Back to Basics: The Conditions of Just Refugee Returns," *Journal of Refugee Studies* 21, no. 3 (2008): 285–304.

12   Brookings-Bern Project on Internal Displacement, *IASC Framework on Durable Solutions for Displaced Persons* (Washington, DC: Brookings Institution / University of Bern, April 2010), 25.

13   Ibid., 26.

14   Ibid., 42.

15   Pablo de Greiff, "Repairing the Past: Compensation for Victims of Human Rights Violations," in *The Handbook of Reparations*, ed. Pablo de Greiff (Oxford: Oxford University

Press, 2006); and "Justice and Reparations," in *Reparations: Interdisciplinary Inquiries*, ed. Jon Miller and Rahul Kumar (Oxford: Oxford University Press, 2007).

16 De Greiff, "Justice and Reparations," 154–67.

17 De Greiff, "Repairing the Past," 6–13. While de Greiff is particularly interested in financial reparations, his framework is applicable to a wider range of remedial activities, including truth commissions.

18 Redressing displacement in a comprehensive way may require a range of measures including truth-telling, criminal justice, compensation, and land restitution processes. In particular, concerted pressure and support from international actors may play a critical role in ensuring that displacement is tackled as a crime, and that all those with similar claims can access redress on an equitable basis.

19 Many Mizrahi Jews who migrated to Israel from Arab countries—often under duress— reject attempts to label them "refugees" and negotiate reparations on their behalf from Arab governments, seeing these efforts as a derisive reinterpretation of their history, in which they are cast as hapless refugees who came to Israel under duress, rather than as active supporters of Zionism. For example, former Knesset speaker Yisrael Yeshayahu has insisted, "We are not refugees. [Some of us] came to this country before the state was born. We had messianic aspirations." At a Knesset meeting on the issue, Israeli Mizrahi Ran Cohen declared, "I have this to say: I am not a refugee ... I came at the behest of Zionism, due to the pull that this land exerts, and due to the idea of redemption. Nobody is going to define me as a refugee." Yehouda Shenhav, "Hitching a Ride on the Magic Carpet: Any Analogy between Palestinian Refugees and Jewish Immigrants from Arab Lands Is Folly in Historical and Political Terms," *Haaretz*, August 8, 2003. For more on this issue, see Yehouda Shenhav, "The Jews of Iraq, Zionist Ideology, and the Property of the Palestinian Refugees of 1948: An Anomaly of National Accounting," *International Journal of Middle East Studies* 31, no. 4 (November 1999): 605–30; "Ethnicity and National Memory: The World Organization of Jews from Arab Countries (WOJAC) in the Context of the Palestinian National Struggle," *British Journal of Middle Eastern Studies* 29, no. 1 (May 2002): 27–56; and "Arab Jews, Population Exchange, and the Palestinian Right of Return," in *Exile and Return: Predicaments of Palestinians and Jews*, ed. Ian Lustick and Ann Lesch (Philadelphia: University of Pennsylvania Press, 2005). See also Michael Fischbach, "Palestinian and Mizrahi Jewish Property Claims in Discourse and Diplomacy," in Lustick and Lesch, *Exile and Return*; *Jewish Property Claims against Arab Countries* (New York: Columbia University Press, 2008); and "Palestinian Refugee Compensation and Israeli Counterclaims for Jewish Property in Arab Countries," *Journal of Palestine Studies* 31, no. 1 (Autumn 2008): 6.

20 While forced migration may in some cases be legally permissible, for example, to enable the construction of critical infrastructure projects or to remove populations from areas at extreme risk of natural disaster, arbitrary displacement is prohibited in agreements including the Fourth Geneva Convention of 1949 (article 49) and the African Union

Convention on the Protection and Assistance of Internally Displaced Persons in Africa (article 3.1.a).

21   Hayner, *Unspeakable Truths*, 76–77.

22   Mahmoud Mamdani, "Reconciliation without Justice," *Southern African Review of Books*, no. 46 (December 1996): 3–6; Hayner, *Unspeakable Truths*, 76–77. The South African Truth and Reconciliation Commission did address the broad history of forced removals in the introduction to its final report. Truth and Reconciliation Commission of South Africa, *Truth and Reconciliation Commission of South Africa Report*, 5 vols. (Cape Town: TRC of South Africa, October 29, 1998), http://www.justice.gov.za/trc/report/index.htm.

23   Laura A. Young and Rosalyn Park, "Engaging Diasporas in Truth Commissions: Lessons from the Liberia Truth and Reconciliation Commission Diaspora Project," *International Journal of Transitional Justice* 3, no. 3 (November 2009): 341–61.

24   Hayner, *Unspeakable Truths*, 76.

25   Susan Harris Rimmer, "Reconceiving Refugees and Internally Displaced Persons as Transitional Justice Actors" (New Issues in Refugee Research Papers, Research Paper no. 187, UNHCR, April 2010), 1.

26   Hayner, *Unspeakable Truths*, 267.

27   Solomon Islands, Truth and Reconciliation Commission Act, 8th National Parliament, August 28, 2008, art. 5.b.

28   Susan Harris Rimmer, "Women Cut in Half: Refugee Women and the Commission for Reception, Truth-Seeking and Reconciliation in Timor-Leste," *Refugee Survey Quarterly* 29, no. 2 (March 2010): 102–3.

29   Hayner, *Unspeakable Truths*, 85; Harris Rimmer, "Women Cut in Half," 85. For a more detailed discussion of gender, displacement, and transitional justice, see Lucy Hovil, in this volume.

30   This includes the truth commission reports for Liberia, Timor-Leste, Indonesia and Timor-Leste, Morocco, Ghana, Sierra Leone, Peru, Guatemala, and South Africa (which has a brief discussion of forced removals). This list of publicly released truth commission reports is drawn from Hayner, *Unspeakable Truths*.

31   Liberia Truth and Reconciliation Commission, *Liberian Truth and Reconciliation Commission Consolidated Final Report* (Monrovia: Liberia TRC, 2009), www.trcofliberia.org/reports/final-report; Sierra Leone Truth and Reconciliation Commission, *Witness to Truth: Report of the Sierra Leone Truth and Reconciliation Commissions*, 5 vols. (Accra: GPL Press, 2004), www.sierra-leone.org/TRCDocuments.html.

32   Commission for Reception, Truth and Reconciliation in Timor-Leste, *Chega! Final Report of the Commission for Reception, Truth and Reconciliation in East Timor* (Dili: CAVR, 2005), www.cavr-timorleste.org/en/chegaReport.htm.

33   Guatemalan Commission for Historical Clarification, *Guatemala: Memory of Silence* (Guatemala City: CEH, 1999), http://shr.aaas.org/guatemala/ceh/report/english/toc.html;

Paula Worby, *Lessons Learned from UNHCR's Involvement in the Guatemalan Refugee Repatriation and Reintegration Programme (1987–1999)* (Geneva: UNHCR, 1999), http://www.crid.or.cr/digitalizacion/pdf/eng/doc13135/doc13135.pdf.

34   Hayner, *Unspeakable Truths*, 166.

35   Ghana National Reconciliation Commission, *National Reconciliation Commission Report* (Accra: NRC, 2004), http://www.ghana.gov.gh/index.php?option=com_content&view =category&layout=blog&id=59&Itemid=208.

36   Guatemalan CEH, "Recommendations," *Guatemala: Memory of Silence*, sec. 3, para. 9.a.

37   Guatemalan CEH, *Guatemala: Memory of Silence*, 6.

38   Martín Arévalo (director, National Reparations Program), in discussion with Cristian Correa of the International Center for Transitional Justice, June 2010.

39   Carlos Martín Beristain, "The Legacy of Genocide in Guatemala: Memory and Psychosocial Recovery in Affected Communities," in *Dealing with the Past in Post-conflict Societies: Ten Years after the Peace Accords in Guatemala and Bosnia-Herzegovina*, ed. Jonathan Sisson (Bern: Swisspeace, 2007), 41; Internal Displacement Monitoring Center, "Guatemala: Ten Years after Peace Accords, Key Provisions Benefiting the Displaced Remain Unimplemented," (Internal Displacement Profile, IDMC, Geneva, June 9, 2006), http://www.internal-displacement.org/8025708F004BE3B1/(httpInfoFiles)/097D0D136EE4FD7BC12 571860046E2A6/$file/Guatemala%20-June%202006.pdf.

40   Guatemalan CEH, *Guatemala: Memory of Silence*, 6.

41   While researchers such as Vicky Tennant suggest that efforts to support return and reintegration are most effective when they support the displaced and nondisplaced alike, thereby promoting reconciliation, the Guatemalan government's strategy was contentious. Arguably, the government's goal was to conflate the displaced and nondisplaced populations, allowing it to claim in relatively short order that the country no longer had an IDP population with specific rights and concerns. Vicky Tennant, "Return and Reintegration," in *Post-conflict Peacebuilding: A Lexicon*, ed. Vincent Chetail (Oxford: Oxford University Press, 2009).

42   Yodit Fitigu, "Forgotten People: Internally Displaced Persons in Guatemala," (RI Bulletin, Refugees International, Washington, DC, July 12, 2005), 3, http://www.internal-displacement.org.

43   For a detailed discussion of the challenges associated with collective redress programs and attempts to link development and transitional justice, see Pablo de Greiff and Roger Duthie, eds., *Transitional Justice and Development: Making Connections* (New York: Social Science Research Council, 2009).

44   UN Commission on Human Rights, Principles to Combat Impunity.

45   As with provisions underpinning the view that truth commissions should address displacement as a substantive issue, the majority of frameworks that support the direct engagement of displaced persons in truth-telling processes pertain to IDPs, rather than

to refugees. However, as mentioned earlier, the logic supporting the participation of IDPs in truth-telling processes also applies to the involvement of refugees, although there may be additional complications with the latter.

46   United Nations General Assembly, Resolution 60/147, "Basic Principles and Guidelines on the Right to a Remedy and Reparation for Victims of Gross Violations of International Human Rights Law and Serious Violations of International Humanitarian Law," A/RES/60/147, March 21, 2006, principle xi.

47   UN Commission on Human Rights, "Guiding Principles," principle 22.

48   Ibid., principle 28.2.

49   Brookings-Bern Project on Internal Displacement, *Framework on Durable Solutions*, 45.

50   Ibid., 46; Bradley, "Back to Basics."

51   UN Security Council, "Rule of Law and Transitional Justice," para. 64.f; emphasis added.

52   Young and Park, "Engaging Diasporas," 349.

53   Ibid., 348; Hayner, *Unspeakable Truths*, 54.

54   Arafat Jamal, *Refugee Repatriation and Reintegration in Guatemala: Lessons from UNHCR's Experience* (Geneva: UNHCR Evaluation and Policy Analysis Unit, 2000); Young and Park, "Engaging Diasporas."

55   See the following section entitled "Truth-Telling and Durable Solutions" for a more detailed discussion of the CAVR's reception function. See also Luiz Vieira, "The CAVR and the 2006 Displacement Crisis in East Timor: Reflections on Truth-Telling, Dialogue and Durable Solutions" (paper prepared for ICTJ / Brookings Project on Transitional Justice and Displacement, 2012).

56   Paul Seils, "Reconciliation in Guatemala: The Role of Intelligent Justice," *Race and Class* 44, no. 1 (July 2002): 36.

57   However, in many cases IDPs who had spent years hiding in the Guatemalan highlands were simply too frightened to emerge and participate in the work of the CEH, fearing retaliation from a state that had provided ample evidence of its hostility toward those who dared to speak up about human rights violations.

58   Craig Evan Pollack, "Returning to a Safe Area? The Importance of Burial for Return to Srebrenica," *Journal of Refugee Studies* 16, no. 2 (June 2003): 186–201.

59   Dilek Kurban, "Reparations and Displacement in Turkey: Lessons Learned from the Compensation Law" (paper prepared for ICTJ / Brookings Project on Transitional Justice and Displacement, 2012).

60   Finn Stepputat, "Repatriation and the Politics of Space: The Case of the Mayan Diaspora and Return Movement," *Journal of Refugee Studies* 7, no. 2–3 (1994): 178; Beate Thoresen, "The Return of Guatemalan Refugees: Two Years After," *Migration World* 23, no. 5 (1995).

61   Eitan Bronstein, "The *Nakba* in Hebrew: Israeli-Jewish Awareness of the Palestinian Catastrophe and Internal Refugees," in *Catastrophe Remembered: Palestine, Israel and the Internal Refugees*, ed. Nur Masalha (London: Zed Books, 2005); Yolande Knell, "Legal

Battle over an Abandoned Palestinian Village," BBC News, May 29, 2011, http://www.bbc.co.uk/news/world-middle-east-13373719.

62 See the District Six Museum website at http://www.districtsix.co.za/frames.htm. Other examples of commemorative activities related to displacement include the creation of the Africville Museum in Nova Scotia, Canada, to acknowledge the expulsion of four hundred black Nova Scotians from their community between 1964 and 1967 to make way for a bridge to service the predominantly white city of Halifax. See "Halifax Council Ratifies Africville Apology," CBC News, February 23, 2010, http://www.cbc.ca/news/canada/nova-scotia/story/2010/02/23/ns-africville-halifax-council.html. In the same city, a new memorial marks the refusal of the Canadian government to provide shelter to the Jewish refugees aboard the MS St Louis. Having been refused entry to Canada, the United States, and Cuba, the ship returned to Europe, where more than 250 of its passengers were murdered in concentration camps. See "Halifax's Pier 21 Designated National Museum," CBC News, February 7, 2011, http://www.cbc.ca/news/canada/nova-scotia/story/2011/02/07/ns-pier-21-immigration-museum.html.

63 Rhodri C. Williams, "The Contemporary Right to Property Restitution in the Context of Transitional Justice," (ICTJ Occasional Paper Series, International Center for Transitional Justice, New York, 2007); de Greiff, "Justice and Reparations."

64 Harris Rimmer, "Reconceiving Refugees," 2–3.

65 Clara Ramírez-Barat, *Making an Impact: Guidelines on Designing and Implementing Outreach Programs for Transitional Justice* (New York: ICTJ, 2011), 26.

66 Rafael Barrantes Segura, "Reparations and Displacement in Peru" (paper prepared for ICTJ / Brookings Project on Transitional Justice and Displacement, 2012).

67 Roberto Vidal-López, "Truth-Telling and Internal Displacement: The Case of Colombia" (paper prepared for ICTJ / Brookings Project on Transitional Justice and Displacement, 2012).

68 Awa Dabo, "In the Presence of Absence: Transitional Justice and Displacement in Liberia" (paper prepared for ICTJ / Brookings Project on Transitional Justice and Displacement, 2012). The conditions that may facilitate the effective organization of displaced persons vary according to political, cultural, and historical contexts. In countries such as Colombia, governmental recognition of displaced persons as victims entitled to different forms of redress has had a catalytic effect on organization within the displaced community, as IDPs have mobilized themselves to maximize the potential benefits of this status. See Roger Duthie, in this volume; and Donny Meertens, "Forced Displacement and Gender Justice in Colombia: Between Disproportional Effects of Violence and Historical Injustice" (paper prepared for ICTJ / Brookings Project on Transitional Justice and Displacement, 2012). Cases such as Guatemala that involved high levels of strategic mobilization and participation of displaced populations in the pursuit of both durable solutions and transitional justice underscore that the active organization and engage-

ment of forced migrants may develop over the course of a protracted displacement situation, and may benefit from the support of international backers. Initially, many displaced persons may be preoccupied with basic survival, unaware of their rights, and afraid to raise their voices in opposition to violent political actors. Donors and civil society organizations can support the gradual emergence of displaced persons' organizations by providing early and strategic support to fledgling refugee and IDP leaders. In Guatemala, human rights training for the displaced proved a critical contribution, as this prepared the displaced to express their concerns in a discourse understood by the international community and equipped them with clear standards to use in lobbying their government. The Guatemalan case further suggests that displaced persons' organizing flourishes when UN agencies, NGOs, and other actors involved in protection and assistance efforts do not merely consult with the displaced on program design and delivery but provide a platform from which the displaced may advance overtly political goals. Reclaiming this approach would not recreate the high levels of mobilization and participation that characterized the Guatemalan case but could help the international community encourage the emergence of well-organized refugee and IDP groups that might then actively contribute to peace processes, the negotiation of durable solutions, and transitional justice.

69　Hovil, in this volume.

70　Harris Rimmer, "Reconceiving Refugees," 8.

71　Susan Harris Rimmer, *Gender and Transitional Justice: The Women of East Timor* (London: Routledge, 2010); "Reconceiving Refugees"; and "Women Cut in Half."

72　Hayner, *Unspeakable Truths*, 46, 61.

73　Ibid., 63.

74　Young and Park, "Engaging Diasporas," 348–49.

75　Shawn Pelsinger, "Liberia's Long Tail: How Web 2.0 Is Changing and Challenging Truth Commissions," *Human Rights Law Review* 10, no. 4 (December 2010): 736–37.

76　Ibid., 736–42.

77　Young and Park, "Engaging Diasporas," 355.

78　Liberia Truth and Reconciliation Commission, *Consolidated Final Report*, vol. 2 (unedited version), 238, para. 19.4; Young and Park, "Engaging Diasporas," 344.

79　Young and Park, "Engaging Diasporas"; Hayner, *Unspeakable Truths*, 67. For a valuable critique of the Liberian diaspora's involvement in the truth-telling process, see Jonny Steinberg, "A Truth Commission Goes Abroad: Liberian Transitional Justice in New York," *African Affairs* 110, no. 438 (2010): 35–53.

80　For an example of an exchange project linking Guatemalan and Burmese refugee women, see Inter Pares, "Building the Road Home," *Inter Pares Bulletin* 25, no. 4 (September 2003).

81　Young and Park, "Engaging Diasporas."

82 Jayne Huckerby, "Transitional Justice and Treatment of Refugee Returnees Suspected of Criminal Offences: East Timor and Beyond" (Center for Human Rights and Global Justice Working Paper, Transitional Justice Series no. 9, NYU School of Law, 2004).

83 Harris Rimmer, "Women Cut in Half," 95–96.

84 Thijs Bouwknegt, "Muriza Seeks Reconciliation between Hutu and Tutsi in Burundi: Truth and Justice in the Long-Term?" Radio Netherlands Worldwide, October 6, 2008, http://www.rnw.nl/international-justice/article/muriza-seeks-reconciliation-between-hutu-and-tutsi-burundi-truth-and-j. For a discussion of the significant flaws associated with this endeavor, see Hovil, in this volume.

85 Huma Haider, "(Re)Imagining Coexistence: Striving for Sustainable Return, Reintegration and Reconciliation in Bosnia and Herzegovina," *International Journal of Transitional Justice* 3, no. 1 (March 2009): 110.

86 Vieira, "The CAVR and the 2006 Displacement Crisis."

87 United Nations General Assembly, "United Nations Verification Mission in Guatemala," Report of the Secretary-General, A/59/307, August 30, 2004.

88 Brookings-Bern Project on Internal Displacement, *Framework on Durable Solutions*, 43.

89 Ibid., 43.

90 See for example, Steven Wolfson, "Refugees and Transitional Justice," *Refugee Survey Quarterly* 24, no. 4 (2005): 55–59.

91 UN Security Council, "Rule of Law and Transitional Justice."

92 Naomi Roht-Arriaza, "Reparations in the Aftermath of Repression and Mass Violence," in *My Neighbor, My Enemy: Justice and Community in the Aftermath of Mass Atrocity*, ed. Eric Stover and Harvey M. Weinstein (Cambridge: Cambridge University Press, 2004), 133–34; Harris Rimmer, "Reconceiving Refugees," 85–103.

93 Harris Rimmer, "Reconceiving Refugees," 4–6; and "Women Cut in Half," 85.

94 Rashid Khalidi, "Attainable Justice: Elements of a Solution to the Palestinian Refugee Issue," *International Journal* 53, no. 2 (Spring 1998): 252.

95 Rex Brynen, "Financing Palestinian Refugee Compensation" (paper presented at the Workshop on Compensation for Palestinian Refugees, International Development Research Centre, Ottawa, July 14–15, 1999).

96 See Lebanese-Palestine Dialogue Committee, "Background," About LPDC, http://www.lpdc.gov.lb/About-Lpdc/BackGround.aspx.

97 Duthie, in this volume; Haider, "(Re)Imagining Coexistence," 99.

98 Peru's national Truth and Reconciliation Commission (Comisión de la Verdad y Reconciliación—CVR) played an important role in acknowledging the rights of the displaced and destigmatizing the IDP population, who were often assumed to sympathize with Shining Path "terrorists." Barrantes Segura, "Reparations and Displacement in Peru." Colombia does not yet have a comprehensive national truth commission, though various truth-telling initiatives launched by the government and by civil society actors

have examined the country's internal displacement crisis, drawn attention to the pervasive human rights violations inflicted on Colombian IDPs, and backstopped calls for enhanced protection for this population. Truth-telling initiatives such as the Historical Memory Group, launched in accordance with the 2005 Peace and Justice Act, challenge discrimination against IDPs and underscore that the displaced are citizens entitled to full respect for their rights under Colombian and international law. The conclusions these truth-telling initiatives reached when peace was achieved about the development, scope, and characteristics of Colombia's displacement crisis may feed into the work of a formal truth commission and may serve as the foundation for a rights-based approach to enabling durable solutions, including the repossession of lost lands and the provision of compensation for past abuses. Vidal-López, "Truth-Telling and Internal Displacement."

99   For a discussion of the links between transitional justice and reintegration processes, see Duthie, in this volume.

100 James Milner, "Refugees and the Regional Dynamics of Peacebuilding," *Refugee Survey Quarterly* 28, no. 1 (2009): 13–30.

101 For a discussion of the proposed regional truth-seeking commission for the Western Balkans (RECOM), see Iavor Rangelov, "A Regional Approach to Justice? Rethinking EU Justice Policies in Conflict and Transition" (Policy Brief, European Policy Centre, May 2011), http://www.epc.eu/documents/uploads/pub_1272_a_regional_approach_to_justice.pdf.

102 Edward Green and Alcinda Honwana, "Indigenous Healing of War Affected Children in Africa," *IK Notes* 10 (July 1999).

103 Jeff Crisp et al., "Rebuilding a War-Torn Society: A Review of the UNHCR Reintegration Programme for Mozambican Returnees," *Refugee Survey Quarterly* 16, no. 2 (1997): 28.

104 Carolyn Nordstrom, *A Different Kind of War Story* (Philadelphia: University of Pennsylvania Press, 1997), 144.

105 Alcinda Honwana, "Sealing the Past, Facing the Future: Trauma and Healing in Rural Mozambique," in *The Mozambican Peace Process in Perspective*, ed. Jeremy Armon, Dylan Hendrickson, and Alex Vines (London: Conciliation Resources, 1998).

106 Victor Igreja, "Memories as Weapons: The Politics of Peace and Silence in Post-conflict Mozambique," *Journal of Southern African Studies* 34, no. 3 (September 2008): 539–56; Victor Igreja, Beatrice Dias-Lambranca, and Annemiek Richters, "Gamba Spirits, Gender Relations, and Healing in Post-Civil War Gorongosa, Mozambique," *Journal of the Royal Anthropological Institute* 14, no. 2 (2008): 353–71.

107 International Crisis Group, *The Continuing Challenge of Refugee Returns in Bosnia and Herzegovina*, Europe Report no. 137 (Brussels: ICG, 2002): 25.

108 For a discussion of the links between criminal prosecutions and displacement, see Federico Andreu-Guzmán, in this volume.

109　Elizabeth Ferris, "Internal Displacement, Transitional Justice, and Peacebuilding: Lessons Learned" (paper presented at the Seminar on Internal Displacement and the Construction of Peace, Bogotá, 2008).

CHAPTER 6

Criminal Justice and Forced Displacement: International and National Perspectives

Federico Andreu-Guzmán

The crime of forced displacement is a notion that comes from international law. Indeed, an international legal framework has developed with the instruments and jurisprudence to criminally prosecute forced displacement as a war crime or a crime against humanity, irrespective of whether the displacement in question is internal or across international borders. When it constitutes a serious crime under international law, forced displacement should be prosecuted for the same reasons that other serious crimes are. Failure to prosecute this crime invites impunity, which in contexts of mass displacement undermines the goals of transitional justice, including ensuring accountability for perpetrators and recognition of victims, fostering civic trust, and strengthening the rule of law.[1] However, in contrast to "classic" crimes such as murder and torture, legal traditions do not exist in national systems around the world to tackle the crime of forced displacement.

The nature of this particular crime and its emergence entirely from international law create challenges that must be addressed by lawyers, judges, and investigators. These include legal challenges stemming from inaccurate definitions of forced displacement at the national level, as well as difficulties in assessing the unlawfulness of acts of displacement, and political challenges, such as resistance from the wide array of powerful actors that may be implicated in these crimes. At this juncture, there is sufficient international jurisprudence to prosecute the crime of forced displacement, but it is not as strong as it is for other serious crimes. National criminal justice systems, on the other hand, are generally not familiar with the crime of forced displacement. Often, their focus is on the crimes connected to displacement rather than displacement itself, which is frequently seen as a "natural" consequence of other crimes or as an inherent effect of armed conflict, and so the criminal responsibility of the actors involved in these crimes is not investigated.

Other chapters in this volume explore the consequences of large-scale displacement, from the suffering of individuals to the fragmentation of communities to distorted patterns of economic activity. From a justice perspective, the chapters show that displacement is very often linked to human rights abuses in a number of ways. When harms of this sort take place, criminal justice measures represent one of the ways in which transitional justice can respond. As has been argued by others, however, transitional justice measures are more likely to achieve their aims if they are designed and implemented in a coherent fashion.[2]

Furthermore, in contexts of mass displacement, which often overlap with post-conflict or ongoing conflict contexts, some level of coherence is required not just between justice measures but between them and other types of policy interventions, including those of humanitarian, peacebuilding, and development actors. From the perspective of criminal justice efforts, at one level there may be opportunities for direct cooperation with humanitarian organizations, whose members are likely in some cases to have information about crimes that may be useful for investigators and prosecutors. Humanitarian organizations may, for good reason, resist associating with such processes out of concern for their access to displaced populations and the safety of their staff, but the possibility of cooperation exists.[3]

At another level, criminal justice measures may, depending on the context, reinforce or be in tension with efforts to achieve durable solutions to displacement. On the one hand, prosecuting those responsible for crimes of forced displacement or other abuses (or removing them from security institutions) may facilitate return and sustainable reintegration processes by improving returnees' sense of safety and reducing the likelihood that displacement will recur.[4] On the other hand, though, the threat of criminal prosecution may hinder return processes by creating a disincentive for those who think they may be implicated, perhaps falsely, in past crimes. This may be most likely when criminal justice processes are perceived to be one sided or to lack adequate due process.[5] In any event, it is important from a broader perspective to consider the ways in which criminal justice and other transitional justice processes may interact, directly or indirectly, with other types of interventions addressing displacement.

That being said, in this chapter I take a narrower look at the available legal avenues for pursuing criminal accountability for crimes of forced displacement. The expectation is not that criminal justice efforts should substitute for other interventions, but that, in addition to being legally justified and deserved in their own right, they will in the long run be complementary to other interventions, including those that are not justice related. The precise links between such activities need to be determined in specific contexts, but convincing arguments have been made concerning the broader relation-ship between justice, security, and development,[6] which are all relevant to displacement.

I examine criminal justice and forced displacement from both international and national perspectives. The first section reviews the international legal framework for the crime of forced displacement. This includes the numerous international legal instruments—in particular those of international humani-tarian and criminal law—that provide the framework for prosecuting forced displacement as either a war crime or a crime against humanity. I also consider how crimes of forced displacement can be committed as part of other interna-tional crimes, such as genocide, apartheid, and collective punishment. I then discuss some of the important legal aspects of the crime of forced displace-ment within the international framework, including the non-applicability of statutory limitations, amnesty laws, and pardons and the issues of criminal liability and personal criminal responsibility. The second section moves to an analysis of national criminal jurisdictions and the crime of forced displace-ment. I begin by looking at how definitions of forced displacement vary among national legal systems; then I consider the temporal application of criminal law to this crime and the relevance of the principle of non-retroactivity, the com-petence of national criminal jurisdictions to deal with the crime, and, again, the non-applicability of statutes of limitations.

THE INTERNATIONAL LEGAL FRAMEWORK FOR THE CRIME OF FORCED DISPLACEMENT

Forced displacement is recognized as a crime under international custom-ary law. The International Committee of the Red Cross (ICRC) has concluded that the prohibition of the deportation, forcible transfer, and forced displace-ment of civilian populations—unless the security of the civilians involved or imperative military reasons so demand—is a rule of customary international humanitarian law, applicable to both international and internal armed con-flicts.[7] UN political bodies have reaffirmed this: the UN General Assembly[8] and the Security Council[9] have condemned in several resolutions the practice of forced displacement—internal and across borders—and called for the alleged perpetrators to be brought to justice. The former UN Commission on Human Rights also reiteratively declared that "acts of deportation or forcible transfer of populations which, *inter alia*, lead to or result from mass exoduses and dis-placements, are included as crimes against humanity in the Rome Statute of the International Criminal Court," and emphasized "the importance of ending impunity for perpetrators of such crimes."[10]

The crime of forced displacement emerged closely linked with the crimes of deportation and transfer of populations. Indeed, the first contemporary legal precedents criminalizing the unlawful moving of a civilian population referred to "deportation" and "transfer." In both the Nuremberg Charter[11] and the IMTFE Charter (or Tokyo Charter),[12] immediately following World War II, deportation was considered a crime against humanity. A few years later, the 1949 Fourth Geneva Convention stated that individual or mass forcible transfers, as well as deportations of protected persons from occupied territory to other territories, whether occupied or not, were prohibited regardless of motive,[13] and that the "unlawful deportation or transfer or unlawful confinement of a protected person"[14] constituted a grave breach—that is, a war crime. Following that, the 1977 Additional Protocol I to the Geneva Conventions regarded the following as grave breaches: "the transfer by the occupying Power of parts of its own civilian population into the territory it occupies, or the deportation or transfer of all or parts of the population of the occupied territory within or outside this territory, in violation of Article 49 of the Fourth Convention."[15] However, the crime of forced displacement was initially limited to international armed conflict. Indeed, the Additional Protocol II to the Geneva Conventions bans illegal forced internal displacement[16] but does not qualify it as a crime or a grave breach.

INTERNATIONAL INSTRUMENTS FOR THE CRIME OF FORCED DISPLACEMENT

Several international instruments, in particular those of international humanitarian law and criminal law, provide a legal framework to deal with the crime of forced displacement of civilian populations. These include the Nuremberg Charter,[17] the IMTFE Charter,[18] the Fourth Geneva Convention,[19] Additional Protocol I,[20] Additional Protocol II,[21] the Statute of the International Criminal Tribunal for the Former Yugoslavia (ICTY),[22] the Statute of the International Criminal Tribunal for Rwanda (ICTR),[23] the Rome Statute of the International Criminal Court[24] and the Elements of Crimes of the Rome Statute (ECRS),[25] the Statute of the Special Court for Sierra Leone,[26] the UN Transitional Administration in East Timor's Regulation no. 2000/15, On the Establishment of Panels with Exclusive Jurisdiction over Serious Criminal Offences,[27] the Agreement between the United Nations and the Royal Government of Cambodia Extraordinary Chambers of Cambodia,[28] and the Draft Code of Crimes against the Peace and Security of Mankind[29] of the UN International Law Commission (see appendix to this chapter).

It is important to recognize that the treatment of forced displacement as a crime—especially internal displacement—is the result of a long process in which the jurisprudence of international tribunals has played an essential role. The ICTR, the tribunal set up to prosecute those responsible for the 1994 Rwandan genocide, despite the absence of the crime of forced displacement from its statute, has addressed displacement through the crime against humanity of "inhuman acts." Particularly important, however, has been the ICTY, which deals with serious crimes committed in the former Yugoslavia in the 1990s. Although forced displacement is also absent from the list of crimes under its jurisdiction, the tribunal's statute incorporates deportation and transfer of civilians as war crimes and deportation as a crime against humanity.[30]

In a case referring to the displacement of the civilian Serb population in the southern Krajina region of Croatia by the Croatian military, the ICTY determined that "forcible transfer" can amount to a crime against humanity or other inhumane acts, under article 5.i of its statute:

Deportation and forcible transfer both entail the forcible displacement of persons from the area in which they are lawfully present, without grounds permitted under international law. The crime of deportation requires that the victims be displaced across a *de jure* state border, or, in certain circumstances, a *de facto* border. Forcible transfer involves displacement of persons within national boundaries. ... Forcible displacement means that people are moved against their will or without a genuine choice. Fear of violence, duress, detention, psychological oppression, and other such circumstances may create an environment where there is no choice but to leave, thus amounting to the forcible displacement of people. Displacement of persons carried out pursuant to an agreement among political or military leaders, or under the auspices of the ICRC or another neutral organization, does not necessarily make it voluntary.[31]

The ICTY has also stated that while a perpetrator of deportation or forcible transfer must intend to forcibly displace people, the intent does not need to be to permanently displace them.[32]

The jurisprudence of the ICTY, ICTR, and the Special Court for Sierra Leone, the work of the International Law Commission on the Draft Code of Crimes against the Peace and Security of Mankind, the *travaux préparatoires* of the Rome Statute, and the ICRC commentaries on the Fourth Convention and its protocols all constitute relevant legal sources for the interpretation and understanding of the scope of the crime of forced displacement. However, the development of international jurisprudence on this particular issue is not as rich as it is for other crimes. To date, the ICC has had only a few cases—at early stages of proceedings—referring to the crime of forced displacement, in Sudan[33] and Kenya.[34]

Nevertheless, three approaches for criminalizing the forced displacement of civilian populations have been retained under international law (see appendix). They entail treating displacement as

- a crime against humanity, when displacement is part of a widespread, massive, or systematic attack against a civilian population;
- a war crime in the context of an international armed conflict; and
- a war crime in the context of a noninternational armed conflict.

The ECRS is particularly relevant with regard to these approaches. In the ECRS, "deported or forcibly transferred" is used interchangeable with "forcibly displaced," and the term *forcibly* is not restricted to physical force but may include the threat of force or coercion, such as that caused by fear of violence, duress, detention, psychological oppression, or abuse of power against such person or persons or by taking advantage of a coercive environment.[35]

Depending on the context, then, the forced displacement of civilians can constitute a war crime or a crime against humanity, or both.[36] In the case of a war crime, the displacement has to take place in the context of and be associated with an international armed conflict or an internal armed conflict. In the case of a crime against humanity, the forced displacement has to be committed as part of a widespread or systematic attack directed against a civilian population, regardless of the existence of or any connection with an armed conflict. In line with the work done by the UN International Law Commission, the ECRS clarifies that

[An] attack directed against a civilian population in these context elements is understood to mean a course of conduct involving the multiple commission of acts ... against any civilian population, pursuant to or in furtherance of a State or organizational policy to commit such attack. The acts need not constitute a military attack. It is understood that 'policy to commit such attack' requires that the State or organization actively promote or encourage such an attack against a civilian population.[37]

An attack could constitute a crime against humanity if it is either "widespread" or "systematic."[38] It is also the case that a single criminal act could constitute a crime against humanity if it is part of a systematic attack against civilians. The UN International Law Commission has established that "systematic" means "pursuant to a preconceived plan or policy. The implementation of this plan or policy could result in the repeated or continuous commission of inhumane acts. The thrust of this requirement is to exclude a random act which was not committed as part of a broader plan or policy."[39] On this issue, the Inter-American Court of Human Rights has declared that "crimes against humanity include the commission of inhuman acts, such as murder, committed in a context of generalized or systematic attacks against civilians. A single illegal act as those mentioned above, committed within the described background, would suffice for a crime against humanity to arise."[40] Along the same lines, the ICTY, in its judgment of *Prosecutor v. Dusko Tadic*, considered that "a single act committed by a perpetrator within a context of a generalized or systematic attack against the civilian population brings about individual criminal liability and it is not necessary for the perpetrator to commit numerous offenses in order to be considered responsible."[41] Forced displacement as a crime against humanity requires that "the perpetrator knew that the conduct was part of or intended the conduct to be part of a widespread or systematic attack directed against a civilian population." However, the ECRS points out that this "should not be interpreted as requiring proof that the perpetrator had knowledge of all characteristics of the attack or the precise details of the plan or policy of the State or organization."[42]

ASSESSING THE UNLAWFULNESS OF FORCED DISPLACEMENT

Forced displacement is not *necessarily* a crime under international law. According to the ICRC, in both international and noninternational armed conflicts, an exception to the prohibition on displacement exists "where the security of the civilians involved or imperative military reasons (such as clearing a combat zone) require the evacuation for as long as the conditions warranting it exist."[43] The question of whether forced displacement amounts to a crime— a crime against humanity or a war crime in the context of armed conflicts— then, raises the question of how to assess its unlawfulness.[44] Indeed, for forced displacement to be considered a crime at all, it has to be "arbitrary displacement"—that is, it has to have been ordered or committed without grounds permitted under international law.[45]

In the case of forced displacement as a war crime, international humanitarian law and criminal law provide a legal framework to assess the lawfulness of the action.[46] Indeed, article 17 of Additional Protocol II and the Rome Statute and the ECRS refer to the notions of the "security of the civilians involved" and "imperative military reasons." Regarding the former, the ICRC considers it to be "self-evident that a displacement designed to prevent the population from being exposed to grave danger cannot be expressly prohibited."[47] Regarding "imperative military reasons," it has stated that these require

> the most meticulous assessment of the circumstances. ... The situation should be scrutinized most carefully as the adjective "imperative" reduces to a minimum cases in which displacement may be ordered. ... Clearly, imperative military reasons cannot be justified by political motives. For example, it would be prohibited to move a population in order to exercise more effective control over a dissident ethnic group.[48]

The ICRC has also stated that "imperative military reasons" do not include the "removal of the civilian population in order to persecute it."[49] As explained by Human Rights Watch,

> The term "imperative military reasons" usually refers to evacuation because of imminent military operations. Such evacuation assumes proper procedures for notification and evacuation, and proper means of transport to a safe place. It does not allow for a military attack on a civilian population or civilian property to force the displacement, as civilians are not legitimate military objectives under international humanitarian law. ... Displacement or detention of civilians solely to deny a support base to the enemy cannot be considered to promote the security of the civilians.[50]

The "meticulous assessment of the circumstances" of forced displacement, in view of establishing its unlawfulness, is a critical issue for judges, prosecutors, and judicial investigators. This assessment frequently requires expertise in military matters to determine whether "imperative military reasons" existed—expertise that judicial officers generally lack, though expert witness could fill this gap.

In the case of forced displacement as crime against humanity, international criminal law requires assessment of the unlawfulness of the displacement. For example, the Rome Statute and the ECRS refer to "forced displacement of the persons concerned by expulsion or other coercive acts from the area in which they are lawfully present, without grounds permitted under international law."[51] In describing the elements of the crime against humanity of deportation or forcible transfer of population, the ECRS refers to the same notion of displacement "without grounds permitted under international law." With crimes against humanity, the notions of "security of the civilians involved" and "imperative military reasons," which come from international humanitarian law, are not sufficient—as crimes against humanity may be committed during both peace and war.[52] These notions imply a context of ongoing hostilities and therefore cannot be used to make an assessment of whether a forced displacement was committed "without grounds permitted under international law" when the action took place outside the context of an armed conflict.

International jurisprudence is relevant here, as it provides legal and objective criteria to make this assessment. In the context of the postelection violence of 2007 and 2008 in Kenya, for example, the ICC determined that internal displacement did not take place on a voluntary basis, but that it was forced as a result of violence or as a consequence of threats of violence (made through leaflets, eviction notices, and radio programs, spread by word of mouth, or supported by the actual destruction of property) and therefore amounted to a crime against humanity.[53] The ICC underlined that "in most cases, IDPs were forcefully evicted through direct physical violence against them, the burning of their houses and the destruction of their property. Most IDPs left their homes in panic, under emergency conditions, often under direct attack from gangs of armed youth. Sexual violence was another means to forcibly evict women and their families from particular communities."[54] The ICTY also held that even if a deportation or forced transfer of a civilian population were carried out according to the provisions of international humanitarian law, it could still be unlawful in a particular context and on discriminatory grounds could amount to a crime against humanity.[55]

THE CRIME OF FORCED DISPLACEMENT AS PART OF OTHER CRIMES

The crime of forced displacement is frequently associated with the commission of other crimes under international law, such as massacres, murders, torture, and enforced disappearances. In certain contexts, however, crimes of forced displacement have been committed as part of the commission of other crimes, such as genocide, apartheid, and collective punishment—which means that they can be criminalized under these other crimes. Here it is useful to point out that the UN Guiding Principles on Internal Displacement,[56] which are "without prejudice to individual criminal responsibility under international law, in particular relating to genocide, crimes against humanity and war crimes," prohibit arbitrary displacement, including when it is "based on policies of apartheid, 'ethnic cleansing' or similar practices aimed at/or resulting in altering the ethnic, religious or racial composition of the affected population" and when "used as a collective punishment." The principles also state that internally displaced persons shall be protected in particular against genocide, murder, summary or arbitrary execution, and enforced disappearance.[57]

FORCED DISPLACEMENT AND THE CRIME OF GENOCIDE

The definition of the crime of genocide[58] does not explicitly include the forced displacement of civilians in its list of acts committed with the intent to destroy, in whole or in part, a national, ethnic, racial, or religious group. However, experience shows that displacement has in fact been used as a method of destroying these groups. It is relevant to note here that during the drafting process of the Draft Code of Crimes against the Peace and Security of Mankind, the UN International Law Commission considered whether the transfer of a population (including internal displacement) could, in certain circumstances, be a modality of genocide. The commission in the end determined that the existing definition of the crime of genocide, according to the Convention on the Prevention and Punishment of the Crime of Genocide, covered deportation when carried out with the intent to destroy the target group in whole or in part.[59] Thus, when forced displacement is carried out with this intent, such criminal behavior should be among the prohibited acts of genocide and should be criminalized as such. However, few national criminal law systems have incorporated the forced displacement of populations in their lists of prohibited acts of genocide.[60]

FORCED DISPLACEMENT AND THE CRIME OF APARTHEID

History shows that forced displacement has frequently been part of racial segregationist policies and has been committed as part of the crime of apartheid, as in South Africa. Although the UN General Assembly suspended the International Convention on the Suppression and Punishment of the Crime of Apartheid after the end of South Africa's apartheid regime, apartheid remains a crime under international customary law.[61] Additional Protocol I of the Geneva Conventions recognizes apartheid as a "grave breach" without any geographical limitation,[62] and the 1991 version of the Draft Code of Crimes against the Peace and Security of Mankind incorporated the crime.[63] In particular, the UN International Law Commission listed the following acts of apartheid in its draft code: the "deliberate imposition on a racial group of living conditions calculated to cause its physical destruction in whole or in part" and "any measures, including legislative measures, designed to divide the population along racial lines, in particular by the creation of separate reserves and ghettos for the members of a racial group ... or the expropriation of landed property belonging to a racial group or to members thereof."[64] The commission pointed out that the definition of the crime of apartheid is applicable without any restrictions.[65]

The crime of apartheid is implicitly incorporated into various legal instruments, such as the Rome Statute (art. 7.1.h), through the crime against humanity of persecution. The UN Transitional Administration in East Timor's Regulation no. 2000/15, On the Establishment of Panels with Exclusive Jurisdiction over Serious Offences[66] also incorporates apartheid as a crime against humanity (section 5). However, few countries list apartheid in their national criminal law codes as an autonomous crime, a crime against humanity, or a war crime.[67]

COLLECTIVE PUNISHMENT AND FORCED DISPLACEMENT

In certain contexts, such as armed conflict, forced displacement has been used, generally in connection with other crimes under international law, to punish a civilian population that is considered part of the "enemy" or the social base of the enemy. In such situations, displacement is part of a strategy to collectively punish a civilian population and could amount to the crime of collective punishment, which is prohibited in any kind of armed conflict,[68] international or noninternational, and constitutes a war crime.[69] If initially the concept of collective punishment was limited to the issue of judicial sanctions imposed in violation of the principle of individual criminal responsibility, the contemporary notion of this crime also covers "sanctions and harassment of any sort, administrative, by police action or otherwise."[70] The 2009 African Union Convention for the Protection and Assistance of Internally Displaced Persons in Africa cites this modality of internal "displacement used as a collective punishment."[71]

OTHER LEGAL ASPECTS OF THE CRIME OF FORCED DISPLACEMENT

Because forced displacement is a crime under international law, the qualification, incrimination, criminal liability, and legal regime (including prescription and statutory limitations, aggravating and mitigating circumstances, and causes of extinction or exoneration of criminal responsibility, extradition, refuge, and asylum) that are applicable to treatment of the crime are established by international law, regardless of what can be established in the domestic laws of states.[72] As the Supreme Court of Argentina has pointed out, for example, "The qualification of crimes against humanity does not depend on the wishes of the requesting or the requested States in the process of extradition but rather on the principles of *jus cogens* in international law."[73] Although all of these issues could merit a comment, in this section I address only questions and legal problems that judges, examining magistrates, public prosecutors, and lawyers will more frequently confront in practice when dealing with crimes of forced displacement.

THE NON-APPLICABILITY OF STATUTORY LIMITATIONS

The crime of forced displacement, when it constitutes a crime against humanity or a war crime, is not extinguishable, and statutory limitations do not apply, meaning that in such cases there is no time limit on prosecuting the crime, because of its nature. Indeed, international customary law prohibits statutes of limitation for war crimes and crimes against humanity.[74] The ICRC, in its Study on International Customary Law, has concluded that the non-applicability of statutory limitations to war crimes is a rule applicable to both international and noninternational armed conflicts.[75] The special rapporteur on the Draft Code of Crimes against the Peace and Security of Mankind, Doudou Thiam, has stated that the Convention on the Non-applicability of Statutory Limitations to War Crimes and Crimes against Humanity "is simply declaratory in character. Because the offences involved are crimes by their very nature, statutory limitations are not applicable to them, regardless of when they were committed."[76] In the same vein, the Inter-American Court of Human Rights has determined that, concerning crimes against humanity, "the State may not invoke the statute of limitations, the non-retroactivity of criminal law or the ne bis in idem principle to decline its duty to investigate and punish those responsible. ... The non-applicability of statutes of limitations to crimes against humanity is a norm of General International Law (ius cogens), which is not created by said Convention [on the Non-applicability of Statutory Limitations to War Crimes and Crimes Against Humanity]."[77]

AMNESTY LAWS, PARDONS, AND OTHER LEGAL MECHANISMS

The obligation to investigate crimes against international law such as forced displacement and to bring to trial and punish perpetrators is explicitly enshrined in numerous human rights treaties and several declaratory instruments. The UN Human Rights Committee has pointed out that states party to the International Covenant on Civil and Political Rights have a duty to investigate alleged violations of human rights and to criminally prosecute, try, and punish those held responsible.[78] The Inter-American Court of Human Rights has also ruled that, in light of their obligations under the American Convention on Human Rights, state parties have the obligation to prevent and investigate violations of human rights committed within the scope of their jurisdictions, "in order to identify those responsible, impose appropriate sanctions on them and ensure the victim an adequate reparation."[79] The court has also argued that "impunity fosters chronic recidivism of human rights violations, and total defenselessness of victims and their relatives,"[80] and has ruled that states have a duty "to avoid and combat impunity."[81]

The nonfulfillment of these obligations amounts in practice to a denial of justice and thus to impunity,[82] which can manifest itself in a number of ways. Impunity de jure results directly from legal norms such as amnesties, procedural immunity, and the improper application of due obedience. There is unanimous consensus in the international human rights jurisprudence that amnesties and other similar measures that impede the perpetrators of gross human rights violations—including forced displacement—from being brought to trial, judged, and punished are incompatible with the obligations imposed on states by international human rights law.[83] From the perspective of international criminal law, some international instruments[84] and jurisprudence have expressly excluded crimes against humanity and war crimes from the scope of application of amnesties. International tribunals have considered this to be a rule of international customary law.[85] As emphasized by the Inter-American Court of Human Rights, "Since the individual and the whole [of] mankind are the victims of all crimes against humanity, the General Assembly of the United Nations has held since 1946[86] that those responsible for the commission of such crimes must be punished. In that respect, they point out Resolutions 2583 (XXIV) of 1969 and 3074 (XXVIII) of 1973."[87]

The argument that in transitional contexts, whether they involve ending an armed conflict or a return to democracy, amnesties or similar measures are needed to ensure stability has been rejected by human rights bodies and courts, international tribunals, and UN political bodies such as the General Assembly[88] and the Security Council.[89] The UN secretary-general has pointed out that in view of the rules and principles of the United Nations, peace agreements approved by the organization can never promise amnesty for crimes against humanity and war crimes.[90] The majority of peace agreements adopted in the past two decades have reaffirmed this principle.[91] When forced displacement qualifies as a crime against humanity or a war crime, then, there is an established obligation to prosecute those responsible.

CRIMINAL LIABILITY AND LEGAL FIGURES OF PERSONAL
CRIMINAL RESPONSIBILITY

The rules of criminal liability of hierarchical superiors are applicable to—but inadequate for—the crime of forced displacement under international law. For both war crimes and crimes against humanity, the well-recognized principle of the responsibility of negligent commanders is recognized in numerous international instruments[92] and by international jurisprudence.[93] The ICRC has considered it to be a rule of international customary law.[94] Other kinds of criminal responsibility have been established by international criminal law, including joint criminal enterprise and individual responsibility through another person (*autoría mediata*[95]), although the notion of "*autoría mediata* through control of an organized apparatus of power" comes from national criminal law. International law criminalizes the conduct of all those who participated, in varying degrees, in the commission of crimes but did not necessarily perform the same acts.[96] Regarding this issue, the UN secretary-general has pointed out that "it would be illogical and inconsistent only to punish the person who is at the end of the chain, the man who pulls the trigger."[97] The ICTY has also declared that "if the agreed crime is committed by one or other of the participants in the joint criminal enterprise, all of the participants in that enterprise are guilty of the crime regardless of the part played by each in its commission."[98]

These kinds of criminal responsibility should be particularly relevant in cases where forced displacement is part of a practice or strategy to dispossess people of land, which often involves the criminal liability of legal and economic actors (such as agribusiness and mining companies, both domestic and international, and politicians). The classical rules of criminal liability—that is, the responsibility of the hierarchical superior—are inadequate for capturing all participants involved in crimes of forced displacement, particularly those who are not part of the armed structures but are still responsible for the crime. For that reason, in Darfur the UN International Commission of Inquiry on Darfur emphasized the application of the doctrine of joint criminal enterprise to forced displacement.[99] The ICTY has also frequently referred to the doctrine of joint criminal enterprise in cases involving the displacement of Kosovo Albanian civilians, both within and outside Kosovo, by forces of the Federal Republic of Yugoslavia and Serbia,[100] as well as in cases involving the displacement of civilian Serbs in the southern Krajina region of Croatia by Croatian military troops.[101]

The defense of due obedience cannot be invoked as grounds for exonerating criminal responsibility or as justification for the crime of forced displacement. This long-established principle was reiterated, with regard to crimes against humanity and war crimes, by the charters and judgments of the Nuremberg and Tokyo Tribunals as well as by numerous judgments of Allied courts after World War II. UN General Assembly Resolution 95 (I) in 1946 confirmed the principles of international law recognized by the Charter of the Nuremberg Tribunal and in the tribunal's judgments. The UN International Law Commission, in codifying these principles, stipulated that in the case of an act constituting a crime under international law, "the fact that a person acted pursuant to an order of his Government or of a superior does not relieve him from responsibility under international law, provided a moral choice was in fact possible to him" (principle 4). This principle has been reiterated by various international instruments with regard to war crimes and crimes against humanity as well as to gross violations of human rights.[102] It has likewise been reiterated in the jurisprudence of the ICTY,[103] and the ICRC has considered it to be a rule of international customary law.[104] Even in the field of military criminal law, as Sahir Erman has pointed out, "the duty of obedience is not absolute."[105]

NATIONAL CRIMINAL JURISDICTION AND THE CRIME OF FORCED DISPLACEMENT

The crime of forced displacement raises significant issues for national criminal justice systems. Indeed, given the fact that this crime is historically a construct of international law, there is no legal tradition within individual countries to tackle it. When judges, examining magistrates, public prosecutors, lawyers, and judicial investigators try to integrate into their judicial practices notions and rules of international law, especially when those notions and rules are not fully incorporated into national law, they face major legal challenges. International law—and in particular its humanitarian, criminal, and human rights branches—provides a legal framework within which national criminal systems can address the crime of forced displacement. However, those systems— whether common law or civil law—and their constitutional rules present specific legal obstacles to the application of international law in criminal cases of forced displacement. That said, national judicial systems around the world are increasingly likely to use international law in domestic criminal cases, a trend seen most clearly in Latin America.[106]

Although many national laws have introduced the crime of forced displacement, the reality is that, in general, national judges, prosecutors, and judicial investigators are not very experienced in dealing with the crime, particularly in terms of criminal investigations. As explained earlier, forced displacement is generally committed jointly or in connection with other crimes, such as massacres, extrajudicial executions, and enforced disappearances. Too frequently, I would argue, examining magistrates, public prosecutors, and judicial investigators focus their attention on these connected crimes and do not develop methodologies to investigate the crime of forced displacement in particular. In such situations, displacement is seen by investigating authorities and judges as a "natural" consequence of those other crimes or as an inherent effect of the armed conflict. Investigating authorities and judges therefore do not investigate the crime of forced displacement itself or its rationale and purpose (for example, whether it was part of a military strategy, a strategy to dispossess people of land, or a political strategy to control an electorate). The criminal responsibility of actors involved in these crimes is ignored, opening an avenue for impunity. Such investigative gaps have been highlighted in Colombia by the Supreme Court of Justice[107] and the Constitutional Court[108] as well as by the field office of the UN High Commissioner for Human Rights.[109] The Colombian Constitutional Court has repeatedly called for investigating authorities and the Office of the Attorney General to design and adopt a methodology of investigation for the crime of forced displacement independent of the crimes it may have been committed in connection with.[110]

Beyond cases of war crimes and crimes against humanity, international law does not provide a legal framework to address forced displacement, but some national systems have addressed it outside of this context—that is, as an autonomous crime. In Colombia, for example, forced displacement has been used for several decades as a military strategy or tactic of war in the internal armed conflict, but it has also been part of a strategy of land dispossession by economic actors, mainly through paramilitary groups or "private armies." The Colombian Criminal Code establishes that the crime of "forced displacement" (*desplazamiento forzado*)[111] does not require "widespread or systematic attack against civilians" (a crime against humanity), and that it is different from the crime of "deportation, expulsion, transfer or displacement of civilians" (a war crime) established by article 159 of the code.

NATIONAL DEFINITIONS OF THE CRIME OF FORCED DISPLACEMENT

A large number of states have incorporated into their criminal legislation the crime of forced displacement.[112] Most of these national definitions reflect the provisions of the Rome Statute but do not necessarily accurately capture the criminal phenomenon of forced displacement. Certain legal problems therefore remain:

1. Several states have incorporated in their national criminal legislation definitions of the crime of forced displacement restricted to situations of armed conflict and, in certain cases, to international armed conflicts. In certain countries, the definition is limited to situations of occupation.

2. In various states, the domestic definition of the crime of forced displacement includes additional elements that are not contained in the contemporary international definition. For example, certain national definitions of displacement require that its purpose be to submit the civilian population to slave labor.

3. Some domestic definitions of the war crime of forced displacement include an additional element: its widespread or systematic commission.

4. In others states, the definitions of crimes against humanity or war crimes have not incorporated in a legally accurate way the crime of forced displacement.[113]

5. A few states have not incorporated forced displacement as a crime against humanity or a war crime but as a crime of inhuman treatment.[114]

In all these cases, judges, examining magistrates, public prosecutors, lawyers, and judicial investigators face a number of legal challenges, and the gaps in national definitions open the door to impunity. Indeed, inaccurate national legal definitions of the crime can prevent the judiciary from prosecuting forced displacement—in certain cases because only deportation and not internal displacement is criminalized in national law, in others because forced displacement is only a crime when committed during and in connection with an armed conflict, and in others because national law requires the existence of additional elements that are not part of the crime of forced displacement. To overcome such obstacles, national judicial officers and legal practitioners have used legal arguments from international law and the definitions of crimes under international law.

THE TEMPORAL DIMENSIONS OF THE APPLICATION OF CRIMINAL LAW AND THE PRINCIPLE OF NON-RETROACTIVITY

If a large number of states have incorporated into their criminal legislation the crime of forced displacement, the great majority of those have done so over the past thirteen years, following and as a consequence of the adoption of the Rome Statute. In several countries, forced displacement had occurred before this type of criminal behavior was incorporated into national criminal law. For example, in Colombia, where forced displacement has been a widespread practice for several decades during the internal armed conflict, the crime was only incorporated into national criminal law in 2000. For judges, prosecutors, and judicial investigators, this raises serious problems related to the application—and particularly the retroactive application—of criminal law to the issue.

The non-retroactivity of criminal law is a fundamental principle of contemporary criminal law and a key safeguard of international law, one closely linked to the principle of the legality of criminal offences (*nullum crimen sine lege*). The non-retroactive application of criminal law has been considered, under international law, absolute and applicable in all circumstances and at all times, including during states of emergency and in time of war.[115]

However, nothing in the principle of non-retroactivity shall prejudice the trial and punishment of any person for any act or omission that, at the time it was committed, was criminal according to an international treaty or international customary law.[116] Indeed, the principle of legality of criminal offences is not limited to national criminal legislation and includes crimes under international law, both treaty and customary law. International law, then, can authorize the retroactive application of domestic criminal law, a notion that has been reiterated by the UN Human Rights Committee, the European Court of Human Rights, and the Inter-American Court of Human Rights.[117] In 2003, for example, two individuals were tried and convicted by the Estonian courts of deporting a civilian population in 1949, when the Criminal Code of 1946 applicable in Estonia did not contemplate crimes against humanity. The European Court of Human Rights agreed with the Estonian courts that even though the acts committed by those persons might have been legal pursuant to the domestic legislation then in force, they were crimes against humanity under international law at the moment of their commission.[118] The European Court noted that

> the deportation of the civilian population was expressly recognized by the Charter of the Nuremberg Tribunal of 1945 as a crime against humanity (article 6 (c)). Even when the Nuremberg Tribunal was established to prosecute the principal war criminals of the European Axis countries for the crimes committed before or during the Second World War ... the universal validity of the principles regarding crimes against humanity was subsequently confirmed by ... the General Assembly of

the United Nations ... and afterwards, by the International Law Commission. Therefore, the responsibility for crimes against humanity cannot be restricted to nationals of some countries and only to those acts that were committed during the Second World War. ... Furthermore, there is no statutory limitation that may be applicable to the crimes against humanity, irrespective of the date on which they were committed. ... The Court does not find any reason whatsoever to challenge the interpretation and application of the domestic law that the Estonian courts made in the light of the applicable international law provisions."[119]

National courts have decided that the absence of national legislation on war crimes or crimes against humanity at the moment of the commission of these actions is not a legal obstacle to retroactively applying domestic criminal law.[120] In Colombia, for example, in a case regarding forced displacement, among other crimes, the Chamber of Justice and Peace of the Superior Tribunal of the Judicial District of Bogotá adopted this line, making reference to Additional Protocol II and the Rome Statute.[121]

NATIONAL CRIMINAL JURISDICTIONAL COMPETENCE TO DEAL WITH THE CRIME OF FORCED DISPLACEMENT

The forced displacement of civilian populations, whether it constitutes a war crime or a crime against humanity, is a gross human rights violation—a violation of ordinary juridical rights and interests, not the legally protected interests of military order. International jurisprudence has consistently determined that in cases of human rights violations committed against civilians, the alleged perpetrators shall be tried only by the competent ordinary courts and not by military tribunals.[122] The UN Human Rights Committee, the African Commission on Human and Peoples' Rights, the European Court of Human Rights, the Inter-American Court of Human Rights, and the Inter-American Commission of Human Rights have all found that, as a general principle, military tribunals should not be competent to try civilians or to try military or police personnel for cases of human rights violations committed against civilians.

This principle has been codified in the Draft Principles Governing the Administration of Justice through Military Tribunals, adopted by the former UN Sub-commission on the Promotion and Protection of Human Rights.[123] Even though these are draft principles, the European Court of Human Rights has stated that they reflect the evolution of international human rights law in the field of military tribunals and has used them as a source of law.[124] In addition, the Principles and Guidelines on the Right to a Fair Trial and Legal Assistance in Africa[125] and the UN Updated Principles for the Protection and Promotion of Human Rights through Action to Combat Impunity[126] have reiterated the limited scope of competence of military jurisdictions to offences of a purely military nature committed by military personnel.

Nevertheless, according to international human rights jurisprudence, in exceptional circumstances, military tribunals could be competent to deal with human rights violations: when they are allowed under international humanitarian law,[127] when no civilian court exists, when trial by such courts is materially impossible, or when such courts are unable to undertake the trials.[128] However, in various countries, military jurisdictions have competence to deal with the crime of forced displacement, particularly when it is a war crime.[129]

THE NON-APPLICABILITY OF STATUTORY LIMITATIONS TO THE CRIME OF FORCED DISPLACEMENT

As has been discussed, under international law the crime of forced displacement, either as a crime against humanity or as a war crime, is not subject to statutory limitations. At the national level, several countries have reflected this rule in their constitutions[130] or legislation.[131] The non-applicability of statutory limitations for forced displacement has been confirmed by national tribunals—criminal or constitutional—in various countries.[132] However, a number of countries, often common law countries, are silent about statutes of limitation because they do not use this legal concept.[133] Other countries have constitutional rules or legislation[134] that provides in a general way the prescription of statutory limitations to crimes, independent of their nature or gravity. In some countries, this legal obstacle has been overcome by national tribunals invoking the international obligations of the state or international customary law.[135]

CONCLUSION

An international legal framework exists for the prosecution of forced displacement as a war crime or a crime against humanity. When it constitutes a serious crime under international law, forced displacement should be prosecuted for much the same reasons that other serious crimes are. Furthermore, impunity for crimes of forced displacement undermines the goals of transitional justice. The nature of this crime and its emergence from international law, however, create particular political and legal challenges that must be addressed. Although international jurisprudence exists for prosecuting forced displacement, it is not as rich as it is for other serious crimes. At the national level, most legal systems are not familiar with the crime of forced displacement, and the focus in these contexts is usually on the crimes that may be connected to displacement rather than displacement itself. Displacement is often seen as a natural consequence of other crimes or as an inherent product of armed conflict, and so despite existing frameworks, perpetrators continue to commit this crime with impunity.

APPENDIX: INTERNATIONAL LEGAL INSTRUMENTS AND THE CRIME OF FORCED DISPLACEMENT

INSTRUMENT	CRIME AGAINST HUMANITY	WAR CRIME	OTHERS
Nuremberg Charter	Article 6.c, "deportation"	Article 6.b, "deportation to slave labour or for any other purpose of civilian population of or in occupied territory"	
IMTFE Charter	Article 5.c, "deportation, and other inhumane acts committed against any civilian population"	Article 5.c, "deportation, and other inhumane acts committed against any civilian population"	
Control Council Law No. 10 of December 20, 1945	Article II.c, "deportation"	Article II.b, "Ill-treatment or deportation to slave-labour or for any other purpose of civilian population, of civilian population from occupied territory"	
Principles of International Law Recognized in the Charter of the Nuremberg Tribunal and in the Judgment of the Tribunal, 1950	Principle VI.c, "deportation and other inhuman acts done against any civilian population"	Principle VI.b, "ill-treatment or deportation to slave-labour or for any other purpose of civilian population of or in occupied territory"	
Draft Code of Crimes against the Peace and Security of Mankind (1996)	Article 18.g, "arbitrary deportation or forcible transfer of population"	Article 20.a.vii, "unlawful deportation or transfer or unlawful confinement of protected persons," and 20.c.i, "the transfer by the Occupying Power of parts of its own civilian population into the territory it occupies"	

Fourth Geneva Convention	Article 49, "Individual or mass forcible transfers, as well as deportations of protected persons from occupied territory to the territory of the Occupying Power or to that of any other country, occupied or not, are prohibited, regardless of their motive." Article 147, "Grave Breaches," "unlawful deportation or transfer or unlawful confinement of a protected person"
Additional Protocol I of the Geneva Conventions	Article 85.4.a, "In addition to the grave breaches defined in the preceding paragraphs and in the Conventions, the following shall be regarded as grave breaches of this Protocol, when committed wilfully and in violation of the Conventions or the Protocol: (a) the transfer by the occupying Power of parts of its own civilian population into the territory it occupies, or the deportation or transfer of all or parts of the population of the occupied territory within or outside this territory, in violation of Article 49 of the Fourth Convention."
Additional Protocol II of the Geneva Conventions	Article 17, "1. The displacement of the civilian population shall not be ordered for reasons related to the conflict unless the security of the civilians involved or imperative military reasons so demand. Should such displacements have to be carried out, all possible measures shall be taken in order that the civilian population may be received under satisfactory conditions of shelter, hygiene, health, safety and nutrition. 2. Civilians shall not be compelled to leave their own territory for reasons connected with the conflict."

INSTRUMENT	CRIME AGAINST HUMANITY	WAR CRIME	OTHERS
Statute of the ICTY	Article 5, "Crimes against humanity," 5.d, "deportation"	Article 2, "Grave breaches of the Geneva Conventions of 1949," 2.g, "unlawful deportation or transfer or unlawful confinement of a civilian"	
Statute of the ICTR	Article 3, "Crimes against Humanity," 3.d, "Deportation"	Article 4, "Violations of Article 3 common to the Geneva Conventions and of Additional Protocol II," 4.b, "Collective punishments"	
Rome Statute of the ICC	Article 7, "Crimes against humanity," 7.1.d, "Deportation or forcible transfer of population," and 7.2.d: "Deportation or forcible transfer of population means forced displacement of the persons concerned by expulsion or other coercive acts from the area in which they are lawfully present, without grounds permitted under international law."	Article 8, "War Crimes" (International Armed Conflict), 8.2.a.vii, "Unlawful deportation or transfer or unlawful confinement," and 8.2.b.viii, "The transfer, directly or indirectly, by the Occupying Power of parts of its own civilian population into the territory it occupies, or the deportation or transfer of all or parts of the population of the occupied territory within or outside this territory"; article 8, "War Crimes" (noninternational armed conflict), 8.e.viii, "Ordering the displacement of the civilian population for reasons related to the conflict, unless the security of the civilians involved or imperative military reasons so demand"	
Statute of the Special Court for Sierra Leone	Article 2, "Crimes against humanity" (deportation)	Article 3, "violations of article 3 common to the Geneva Conventions of 12 August 1949 for the Protection of War Victims, and of Additional Protocol II thereto of 8 June 1977," b, "collective punishment"	

UN Transitional Administration in East Timor, Regulation no. 2000/15	Section 5, "Crimes against Humanity," 5.1.d, "Deportation or forcible transfer of population," and 5.2.c: "Deportation or forcible transfer of population means forced displacement of the persons concerned by expulsion or other coercive acts from the area in which they are lawfully present, without grounds permitted under international law."	Section 6, "War Crimes," 6.1.a.vii, "Unlawful deportation or transfer or unlawful confinement"; 6.1.b.viii, "The transfer, directly or indirectly, by the Occupying Power of parts of its own civilian population into the territory it occupies, or the deportation or transfer of all or parts of the population of the occupied territory within or outside this territory"; and 6.1.e.viii, "Ordering the displacement of the civilian population for reasons related to the conflict, unless the security of the civilians involved or imperative military reasons so demand"
UN Guiding Principles on Internal Displacement		Principle 6, "1. Every human being shall have the right to be protected against being arbitrarily displaced from his or her home or place of habitual residence. 2. The prohibition of arbitrary displacement includes displacement: (a) When it is based on policies of apartheid, 'ethnic cleansing' or similar practices aimed at/ or resulting in altering the ethnic, religious or racial composition of the affected population; … and (e) When it is used as a collective punishment." Additionally, principle 10.1 states that "internally displaced persons shall be protected in particular against: (a) Genocide."

INSTRUMENT	CRIME AGAINST HUMANITY	WAR CRIME	OTHERS
African Union Convention for the Protection and Assistance of Internally Displaced Persons in Africa			Article 4.4. "All persons have a right to be protected against arbitrary displacement. The prohibited categories of arbitrary displacement include but are not limited to: a) Displacement based on policies of racial discrimination or other similar practices aimed at/or resulting in altering the ethnic, religious or racial composition of the population; b) Individual or mass displacement of civilians in situations of armed conflict, unless the security of the civilians involved or imperative military reasons so demand, in accordance with international humanitarian law; c) Displacement intentionally used as a method of warfare or due to other violations of international humanitarian law in situations of armed conflict; d) Displacement caused by generalized violence or violations of human rights; e) Displacement as a result of harmful practices; ... g) Displacement used as a collective punishment; h) Displacement caused by any act, event, factor, or phenomenon of comparable gravity to all of the above and which is not justified under international law, including human rights and international humanitarian law."

NOTES

1   Pablo de Greiff, "Theorizing Transitional Justice," in *NOMOS LI: Transitional Justice*, ed. Melissa Williams, Rosemary Nagy, and Jon Elster (New York: New York University Press, 2012).

2   Ibid.

3   See Bryce Campbell, in this volume.

4   See Marina Caparini, in this volume.

5   See Roger Duthie, in this volume.

6   See, for example, Pablo de Greiff, "Transitional Justice, Security, and Development," Background Paper, *World Development Report 2011* (Washington, DC: World Bank, October 2010); and Ana Cutter Patel, Pablo de Greiff, and Lars Waldorf, eds., *Disarming the Past: Transitional Justice and Ex-combatants* (New York: Social Science Research Council, 2010).

7   Rules 129 and 130 in Louise Doswald-Beck and Jean-Marie Henckaerts, *Customary International Humanitarian Law*, vol. 1, *Rules* (Cambridge: Cambridge University Press / ICRC, 2005). See also Jean-Marie Henckaerts, "Study on Customary International Humanitarian Law: A Contribution to the Understanding and Respect for the Rule of Law in Armed Conflict," *International Review of the Red Cross* 87, no. 857 (March 2005): 175–212.

8   See, among others, United Nations General Assembly, Resolution 3318 (XXIX), "Declaration on the Protection of Women and Children in Emergency and Armed Conflict," A/RES/3318 (XXIX), December 14, 1974, art. 5; Resolution 2675 (XXV), "Basic Principles for the Protection of Civilian Populations in Armed Conflict," A/RES/2675 (XXV), December 9, 1970; and Resolution 55/116, "Situation of Human Rights in the Sudan," A/RES/55/116, March 12, 2001.

9   See, among others, United Nations Security Council, Resolution 1952, "The Situation Concerning the Democratic Republic of the Congo," S/RES/1952, November 29, 2010; Resolution 1894, "Protection of Civilians in Armed Conflict," S/RES/1894, November 11, 2009; and Resolution 1674, "Protection of Civilians in Armed Conflict," S/RES/1674, April 28, 2006.

10 United Nations Commission on Human Rights, Resolution 2003/52, "Human Rights and Mass Exoduses," E/CN.4/RES/2003/52, April 24, 2003. See also United Nations Commission on Human Rights, Resolution 2002/20, "Situation of Human Rights in Sierra Leone," E/CN.4/RES/2002/20, April 22, 2002; Resolution 2003/78, "Assistance to Somalia in the Field of Human Rights," E/CN.4/RES/2003/78, April 25, 2003; Resolution 2002/88, "Assistance to Somalia in the Field of Human Rights," E/CN.4/RES/2002/88, April 26, 2002; Resolution 1998/67, "Situation of Human Rights in the Sudan," E/CN.4/RES/1998/67, April 21, 1998; Resolution 2000/26, "Situation of Human Rights in the Federal Republic of Yugoslavia (Serbia and Montenegro), the Republic of Croatia and Bosnia and Herzegovina," E/CN.4/RES/2000/26, April 18, 2000; and

Resolution 1999/18, "The Situation of Human Rights in the Federal Republic of Yugoslavia (Serbia and Montenegro), the Republic of Croatia and Bosnia and Herzegovina," E/CN.4/RES/1999/18, April 23, 1999.

11   Charter of the International Military Tribunal, August 8, 1945, art. 6.c, http://avalon.law.yale.edu/imt/imtconst.asp ("Nuremberg Charter").

12   International Military Tribunal for the Far East Charter, January 19, 1946, art. 5.c, http://www.uni-marburg.de/icwc/dateien/ ("IMTFE Charter").

13   Geneva Convention Relative to the Protection of Civilian Persons in Time of War (Fourth Geneva Convention), August 12, 1949, 75 U.N.T.S. 287 art. 49, http://www.icrc.org/ihl.nsf/full/380.

14   Fourth Geneva Convention, art. 147.

15   Protocol Additional to the Geneva Conventions of 12 August 1949, and Relating to the Protection of Victims of International Armed Conflicts, June 8, 1977, art. 85.4.a, http://www.icrc.org/eng/war-and-law/treaties-customary-law/geneva-conventions/index.jsp ("Additional Protocol I").

16   Protocol Additional to the Geneva Conventions of 12 August 1949, and Relating to the Protection of Victims of Non-international Armed Conflicts, June 8, 1977, art. 17, http://www.icrc.org/ihl.nsf/full/475?opendocument ("Additional Protocol II").

17   Nuremberg Charter, art. 6.c.

18   IMTFE Charter, art. 5.c.

19   Fourth Geneva Convention, arts. 49 and 147.

20   Additional Protocol I, art. 85.4.a.

21   Additional Protocol II, art. 17.

22   United Nations Security Council, Resolution 827, "Statute of the International Criminal Tribunal for the Prosecution of Persons Responsible for Serious Violations of International Humanitarian Law Committed in the Territory of the Former Yugoslavia since 1991," S/RES/827, May 25, 1993, arts. 2 and 5 ("Statute of the ICTY").

23   United Nations Security Council, Resolution 955, "Statute of the International Criminal Tribunal for the Prosecution of Persons Responsible for Genocide and Other Serious Violations of International Humanitarian Law Committed in the Territory of Rwanda and Rwandan Citizens Responsible for Genocide and Other Such Violations Committed in the Territory of Neighbouring States, between 1 January 1994 and 31 December 1994," S/RES/955, November 8, 1994, arts. 3 and 4 ("Statute of the ICTR").

24   United Nations General Assembly, Rome Statute of the International Criminal Court, A/CONF.183/9, July 17, 1998, arts. 7.1.d, 7.2.d, 8.2.a.vii, 8.2.b.viii, and 8.2.e.viii ("Rome Statute").

25   International Criminal Court, Elements of Crimes, ICC-ASP/1/3, part II.B, September 9, 2002, http://www.icc-cpi.int/Menus/ICC/Legal+Texts+and+Tools/Official+Journal/Elements+of+Crimes.htm.

26   United Nations Security Council, Resolution 1315, "Statute of the Special Court for Sierra Leone," S/RES/1315, January 16, 2002, arts. 2, 3.

27   United Nations Transitional Administration in East Timor, Regulation no. 2000/15, "On the Establishment of Panels with Exclusive Jurisdiction over Serious Criminal Offences," UNTAET/REG/2000/15, June 6, 2000, secs. 5.1.d, 5.2.c, 6.1.a.vii, 6.1.b.viii, and 6.1.e.viii.

28   United Nations, Agreement between the United Nations and the Royal Government of Cambodia Concerning the Prosecution under Cambodian Law of Crimes Committed during the Period of Democratic Kampuchea, June 6, 2003, art. 9. Article 9 states that the "subject-matter jurisdiction of the Extraordinary Chambers shall be the crime of genocide as defined in the 1948 Convention on the Prevention and Punishment of the Crime of Genocide, crimes against humanity as defined in the 1998 Rome Statute of the International Criminal Court and grave breaches of the 1949 Geneva Conventions."

29   United Nations International Law Commission, "Draft Code of Crimes against the Peace and Security of Mankind with Commentaries, 1996," *Yearbook of the International Law Commission, 1996* (Geneva: United Nations Publications, 1996), vol. 2, part 2; see also http://untreaty.un.org/ilc/texts/7_4.htm.

30   Historically, transfer and deportation have been considered two separate crimes. In practice, the nature of the evidence dictates which of the two crimes is prosecuted. See Joanna Korner, "Criminal Justice and Forced Displacement in the Former Yugoslavia" (paper prepared for ICTJ / Brookings Project on Transitional Justice and Displacement, 2012); Prosecutor v. Milomir Stakic, judgment, IT-97-24-T, Trial Chamber, ICTY, July 31, 2003, para. 680; Prosecutor v. Milomir Stakic, judgment, IT-97-24-A, Appeals Chamber, ICTY, March 22, 2006; Prosecutor v. Radislav Krstic, judgment, IT-98-33-T, Trial Chamber, ICTY, August 2, 2001, paras. 521–22.

31   Prosecutor v. Ante Govovina et al., judgment, IT-06-90-T, Trial Chamber, ICTY, April 15, 2011, paras. 1738 and 1739.

32   Ibid., paras. 1740 and 1741. In the same line, see *Prosecutor v. Stakic,* appeal judgment, IT-97-24-A, para. 307; and Prosecutor v. Radoslav Brđanin, judgment, IT-99-36-A, Appeals Chamber, ICTY, April 3, 2007, para. 167.

33   Prosecutor v. Ahmad Muhammad Harun ("Ahmad Harun") and Ali Muhammad Ali Abd-Al-Rahman ("Ali Kushayb"), Warrant of Arrest for Ahmed Harun, ICC-02/05-01/07-2, April 27, 2007; and Prosecutor v. Ahmad Muhammad Harun ("Ahmad Harun") and Ali Muhammad Ali Abd-Al-Rahman ("Ali Kushayb"), Warrant of Arrest for Ali Kushayb, ICC-02/05-01/07-3, April 27, 2007.

34   Situation in the Republic of Kenya, Decision Pursuant to Article 15 of the Rome Statute on the Authorization of an Investigation into the Situation in the Republic of Kenya, ICC-01/09-19, March 31, 2010.

35   International Criminal Court, Elements of Crimes.

36 See Fourth Geneva Convention, art. 147; and Additional Protocol I, art. 85.4.a. See also UN General Assembly, Rome Statute, arts. 7.1.d and 8.2.e.viii.

37 International Criminal Court, Elements of Crimes, art. 7 (introduction), para. 3.

38 United Nations International Law Commission, Report of the International Law Commission on the Work of Its Forty-Eighth Session, 6 May–26 July 1996, A/51/10, art. 18 (commentary).

39 Ibid., art. 18.3 (commentary).

40 Almonacid Arellano et al. v. Chile, judgment, series C, no. 154, Inter-American Court of Human Rights, September 26, 2006, para. 96.

41 Prosecutor v. Dusko Tadic, opinion and judgment, IT-94-1-T, Trial Chamber, ICTY, May 7, 1997, para. 649. This was subsequently confirmed by the same court in Prosecutor v. Kupreskic et al., judgment, IT-95-16-T, Trial Chamber, ICTY, January 14, 2000, para. 550; and Prosecutor v. Kordic and Cerkez, judgment, IT-95-14/2-T, Trial Chamber, ICTY, February 26, 2001, para. 178.

42 International Criminal Court, Elements of Crimes, art. 7 (introduction), para. 2.

43 This exception is contained in the Fourth Geneva Convention and Additional Protocol II. The possibility of evacuation is also provided for in numerous military manuals, as well as in the legislation of many states. International Committee of the Red Cross, "Commentary: Rule 129: The Act of Displacement," in Customary International Humanitarian Law (Cambridge: Cambridge University Press, 2005), http://www.icrc.org/customary-ihl/eng/docs/v1_rul_rule129#Fn26.

44 The only exception could be the "War Crime of transfer of population" by the occupying power, which does not raise the issue of assessing the unlawfulness of forced displacement. See International Criminal Court, Elements of Crimes.

45 See, among others, UN General Assembly, Rome Statute, arts. 7.1.d, 7.2.d, 8.2.a.vii, 8.2.b.viii, and 8.2.e.viii; and International Criminal Court, Elements of Crimes.

46 See, among others, Additional Protocol II, art. 17.

47 International Committee of the Red Cross, "Commentary: Article 17, Protocol II," International Humanitarian Law: Treaties and Documents, http://www.icrc.org/ihl.nsf/COM/475-760023?OpenDocument.

48 Ibid.

49 International Committee of the Red Cross, "Commentary: Rule 129."

50 Human Rights Watch, Ethiopia: Collective Punishment—War Crimes and Crimes against Humanity in the Ogaden Area of Ethiopia's Somali Region, (New York: HRW, June 2008), 108.

51 UN General Assembly, Rome Statute, art. 7.2.d.

52 See, among others, United States v. Ohlendorf (Einsatzgruppen Case), 1948, 4 T.W.C. 1 (US Military Tribunal at Nuremberg, case no. 9); United States v. Alstotter et al (Justice Case), 1947, 3 T.W.C. 1 (US Military Tribunal at Nuremburg, case no. 3); United Nations War Crimes Commission, History of the UN War Crimes Commission and the Development of

the *Laws of War* (London: HMSO, 1948); United Nations International Law Commission, "Principles of International Law Recognized in the Charter of the Nuremberg Tribunal and the Judgment of the Tribunal, 1950," A/1316 (1950), part 3, para. 123; and United Nations, Convention on the Non-applicability of Statutory Limitations to War Crimes and Crimes against Humanity, November 26, 1968, 754 U.N.T.S. 73, art. 1.b.

53   Situation in the Republic of Kenya, para. 162.

54   Ibid., para. 164.

55   *Prosecutor v. Brđanin*, judgment, IT-99-36-A, para. 167.

56   United Nations Commission on Human Rights, "Human Rights, Mass Exoduses and Displaced Persons: Addendum–Guiding Principles on Internal Displacement," Report of the Representative of the Secretary-General, Mr. Francis M. Deng, E/CN.4/1998/53/Add.2, February 11, 1998.

57   Ibid., principle 1.2, principle 6, and principle 10.1.

58   See, for example, United Nations, Convention on the Prevention and Punishment of the Crime of Genocide, December 9, 1948, 78 U.N.T.S. 1021; UN Security Council, Resolution 827, Statute of the ICTY, art. 4; UN Security Council, Resolution 955, Statute of the ICTR, art. 2; UN General Assembly, Rome Statute, art. 6; and UN Transitional Administration in East Timor, Regulation no. 2000/15, "On the Establishment of Panels," sec. 4.

59   UN International Law Commission, "Draft Code of Crimes."

60   See, among others, Côte d'Ivoire, Penal Code, art. 137; El Salvador, Penal Code, art. 361; Nicaragua, Penal Code (Law no. 641 of 2008), art. 484; Panama, Penal Code (Law no. 14 of 2007), art. 341.7; and Paraguay, Penal Code (1997), art. 319 (Genocide).

61   See, among others, Steven R. Ratner and Jason S. Abrams, *Accountability for Human Rights Atrocities in International Law*, 2nd ed. (Oxford: Oxford University Press, 2001), 122; and John Dugard, "L'apartheid," in *Droit international pénal*, ed. Hervé Ascensio, Emmanuel Decaux, and Alain Pellet (Paris: A. Pedone, 2000), 349.

62   Additional Protocol I, art. 85.4.c.

63   United Nations International Law Commission, Report of the International Law Commission on the Work of Its Forty-Third Session, 29 April–19 July 1991, A/46/10, supplement no. 10.

64   UN International Law Commission, "Draft Code of Crimes," art. 20.

65   UN International Law Commission, Report on the Forty-Third Session, supplement no. 10, 103.

66   UN Transitional Administration in East Timor, Regulation no. 2000/15, "On the Establishment of Panels."

67   See, among others, Azerbaijan, Criminal Code, art. 111 ("Racial discrimination (apartheid)"); Bulgaria, Penal Code, art. 416; Hungary, Criminal Code (1978), sec. 157; Malta, Criminal Code (2005), art. 54.c ("Crimes against Humanity"); Nicaragua, Penal Code (Law no. 641 of 2008), art. 487; Philippines, act no. 9851 (2009), Crimes against Interna-

tional Humanitarian Law, Genocide and Other Crimes against Humanity; Philippines, Law no. 33 bis/2003, Repressing the Crime of Genocide, Crimes against Humanity and War Crimes, arts. 5 and 8; Senegal, Penal Code, arts. 431–32 ("crimes against humanity").

68 Doswald-Beck and Henckaerts, *Customary International Humanitarian Law*, rule 103; and Henckaerts, "Study on Customary International Humanitarian Law," 207. See, among others, Fourth Geneva Convention, art. 33; Additional Protocol II, art. 4.2.b; UN General Assembly, Resolution 3318 (XXIX), "Declaration on the Protection of Women and Children," art. 5; Resolution 2675, "Basic Principles for the Protection of Civilian Populations"; Resolution 55/116, "Situation of Human Rights in the Sudan"; UN Commission on Human Rights, Guiding Principles; Human Rights Committee, General Comment No. 29, States of Emergency, CCPR/C/21/Rev.1/Add.11, August 31, 2001, art. 4.

69 See, among others, UN Security Council, Resolution 955, Statute of the ICTR, art. 4; United Nations Security Council, Resolution 1315 (2000), "On Establishment of a Special Court for Sierra Leone," S/RES/1315, August 14, 2000, art. 3 ("Statute of the SCSL"); and Prosecutor v. Alex Tamba Brima, Brima Bazzy Kamara, and Santigie Borbor Kanu, judgment, SCSL-2004-16-T, Trial Chamber 2, Special Court for Sierra Leone, June 20, 2007, paras. 672–73. See also Shane Darcy, "Prosecuting the War Crime of Collective Punishment," *Journal of International Criminal Justice* 8, no. 1 (March 2010).

70 Yves Sandoz, Christophe Swinarski, Bruno Zimmermann, eds., *Commentary on the Additional Protocols* (Geneva: ICRC, 1987), para. 3055; see also para. 4536.

71 African Union Convention for the Protection and Assistance of Internally Displaced Persons, Kampala, Uganda, October 23, 2009, art. 4.4.g, http://www.unhcr.org/refworld/docid/4ae572d82.html.

72 See, among others, UN International Law Commission, "Principles Recognized in the Charter of the Nuremberg Tribunal."

73 Priebke, Erich s/ solicitud de extradición, judgment, Rol No.16.063/94, Supreme Court of Argentina, November 2, 1995.

74 See, among others, Control Council Law No. 10, Punishment of Persons Guilty of War Crimes, Crimes Against Peace and Against Humanity, December 20, 1945, 3 Official Gazette of the Control Council for Germany, 50–55 (1946), art. II.5; United Nations, Convention on the Non-applicability of Statutory Limitations to War Crimes; United Nations General Assembly, Resolution 3074 (XVIII), "Principles of International Cooperation in the Detection, Arrest, Extradition and Punishment of Persons Guilty of War Crimes and Crimes against Humanity," A/RES/3074 (XVIII), December 3, 1973, principle 1; UN General Assembly, Rome Statute, art. 29; European Convention on the Non-applicability of Statutory Limitation to Crimes against Humanity and War Crimes, Strasbourg, January 25, 1974, CETS No. 082; UN Transitional Administration in East Timor, Regulation no. 2000/15, "On the Establishment of Panels," sec. 17; Cambodia, Law on the Establishment of Extraordinary Chambers in the Courts of Cambodia for

the Prosecution of Crimes Committed during the Period of Democratic Kampuchea, NS/RKM/0801/12, January 2, 2001, arts. 4, 5; United Nations General Assembly, Resolution 60/147, "Basic Principles and Guidelines on the Right to a Remedy and Reparation for Victims of Gross Violations of International Human Rights Law and Serious Violations of International Humanitarian Law," A/RES/60/147, March 21, 2006, principle 6; and United Nations Commission on Human Rights, "Promotion and Protection of Human Rights—Addendum: Updated Set of Principles for the Protection and Promotion of Human Rights through Action to Combat Impunity," Report of Diane Orentlicher, Independent Expert to Update the Set of Principles to Combat Impunity, E/CN.4/2005/102/Add.1, February 8, 2005, principle 23.

75   Doswald-Beck and Henckaerts, *Customary International Humanitarian Law,* rule 169.

76   United Nations International Law Commission, Fourth Report on the Draft Code of Offences against the Peace and Security of Mankind, by Mr. Doudou Thiam, Special Rapporteur, A/CN.4/398 and Corr. 1-3, March 11, 1986.

77   *Almonacid Arellano*, Inter-American Court of Human Rights, series C, no. 154, paras. 151 and 153.

78   Bautista de Arellana v. Colombia, Communication no. 563/1993, CCPR/C/55/D/563/1993 (1995), Human Rights Committee, October 27, 1995, para. 8.6. See also the decision in the case of José Vicente and Amado Villafañe Chaparro, Luis Napoleón Torres Crespo, Angel María Torres Arroyo and Antonio Hugues Chaparro Torres v. Colombia, Communication no. 612/1995 (June 14, 1994), CCPR/C/60/D/612/1995, Human Rights Committee, July 29, 1997, para. 8.8.

79   Velásquez Rodríguez v. Honduras, judgment, series C, no. 4, Inter-American Court of Human Rights, July 1988, para. 174; and Godínez Cruz v. Honduras, judgment, series C, no. 5, Inter-American Court of Human Rights, January 20, 1989, para. 184 (author's translation).

80   Paniagua Morales et al. v. Guatemala, judgment, series C, no. 37, Inter-American Court of Human Rights, March 8, 1998, para. 173.

81   Caso Blake v. Guatemala, judgment, series C, no. 48, Inter-American Court of Human Rights, January 22, 1999, para. 64 (author's translation).

82   *Paniagua Morales*, Inter-American Court of Human Rights, series C, no. 37, para. 173.

83   The Inter-American Court of Human Rights has determined that amnesty provisions, provisions on prescription, and the establishment of measures meant to eliminate responsibility are inadmissible "because they are intended to prevent the investigation and punishment of those responsible for serious human rights violations." Barrios Altos v. Peru, judgment (merits), series C, no. 75, Inter-American Court of Human Rights, March 14, 2001, para. 41. See also La Cantuta v. Peru, judgment, series C, no. 162, Inter-American Court of Human Rights, November 29, 2006, para. 174ff; *Almonacid Arellano*, Inter-American Court of Human Rights, series C, no. 154, paras. 128–29. This

rule was codified by the UN Commission on Human Rights, "Addendum: Updated Set of Principles for the Protection and Promotion of Human Rights through Action to Combat Impunity," principle 24. See, among others, Human Rights Committee, "Concluding Observations of the Human Rights Committee: Chile, 03/30/1999," CCPR/C/79/Add.104, March 30, 1999, para. 7; Human Rights Committee, "Comments on Argentina," CCPR/C/79/Add.46, April 5, 1995; Human Rights Committee, Report of the Human Rights Committee, A/50/40, October 3, 1995, para. 144 (Argentina); Human Rights Committee, "Concluding Observations of the Human Rights Committee: Argentina, 11/03/2000," CCPR/CO/70/ARG, November 3, 2000, para. 9; Human Rights Committee, "Concluding Observations of the Human Rights Committee: Peru, 11/15/2000," CCPR/CO/70/PER, November 15, 2000, para. 9; Human Rights Committee, "Concluding Observations of the Human Rights Committee: France, 08/04/1997," CCPR/C/79/Add.80, August 4, 1997, para. 13; Human Rights Committee, "Concluding Observations of the Human Rights Committee: El Salvador, 04/18/1994," CCPR/C/79/Add.34, April 18, 1994, para. 7; Human Rights Committee, Report of the Human Rights Committee, A/50/40, October 3, 1995, paras. 224–41 (Haiti); Human Rights Committee, "Comments on Uruguay," CCPR/C/79/Add.19, May 5, 1993, paras. 7 and 11; Human Rights Committee, "Concluding Observations of the Human Rights Committee: Uruguay, 04/08/1998," CCPR/C/79/Add.90, April 8, 1998, part C ("Principal Subjects of Concern and Recommendations"); Hugo Rodriguez v. Uruguay, Communication no. 322/1988, CCPR/C/51/D/322/1988, Human Rights Committee, August 9, 1994, para. 12.4; Garay Hermosa v. Chile, Case 10.843, Inter-American Court of Human Rights, Report no. 36/96, OEA/Ser.L/V/II.97, doc. 7 rev. (1996), para. 50. See also Meneses Reyes, Lagos Salinas, Alsina Hurtos and Vegara Inostroza v. Chile, Cases 11.228, 11.229, 11.231, and 11282, Inter-American Court of Human Rights, Report no. 34/96, OEA/Ser.L/V/II.95, doc. 7 rev. (1997), para. 50; Alfonso René Chanfeau Orayce et al. v. Chile, Cases 11.505, 11.532, 11.541, 11.546, 11.549, 11.569, 11.572, 11.573, 11.583, 11.585, 11.595, 11.652, 11.657, 11.675, and 11.705, Inter-American Court of Human Rights, Report no. 25/98, OEA/Ser.L/V/II.98, doc. 6 rev. (1998), para. 42; Ignacio Ellacuría, S.J. et al. v. El Salvador, Case 10.488, Inter-American Court of Human Rights, Report no. 136/99, OEA/Ser.L/V/II.106, doc. 6 rev. (1999), para. 200; Lucio Parada Cea et al. v. El Salvador, Case 10.480, Inter-American Court of Human Rights, Report no. 1/99, OEA Ser.L/C/II.102, Doc. 6 rev. (1999), para. 107; Masacre Las Hojas v. El Salvador, Case 10.287, Inter-American Court of Human Rights, Report no. 26/92, OEA/Ser.L/V/II.83, doc. 14 (1993), para. 6; Consuelo et al. v. Argentina, Case 10.147, 10.181, 10.240, 10.262, 10.309, and 10.311, Inter-American Court of Human Rights, Report no. 28/92, OEA/Ser.L/V/II.83, doc. 14 (1993); and Mendoza et al. v. Uruguay, Case 10.029, 10.036, 10.145, 10.305, 10.372, 10.373, 10.374, and 10.375, Inter-American Court of Human Rights, Report no. 29/92, OEA/Ser.L/V/II.83, doc. 14 (1993).

84   See Control Council Law No. 10, art. II.5; and United Nations Security Council, Resolution 1315 (2000), Statute of the SCSL, art. 10.

85   Prosecutor v. Morris Kallon and Brima Bazzy Kamara, Case no. SCSL-2004-15-AR72(E),
Appeals Chamber, Special Court for Sierra Leone, Decision on Challenge to Jurisdiction:
Lomé Accord Amnesty, March 13, 2004, para. 88; Prosecutor v. Moinina Fofana, Case
no. SCSL-2004-14-AR72(e), Appeals Chamber, Special Court for Sierra Leone, Decision
on Preliminary Motions on Lack of Jurisdiction, May 25, 2004; and Prosecutor v. Anto
Furundžija, judgment, IT-95-17/1-T, Trial Chamber, ICTY, December 10, 1998, paras. 151–57.

86   Cf. United Nations General Assembly, Resolution 3 (I), "Extradition and Punishment
of War Criminals," A/RES/3, February 13, 1946; Resolution 95 (I), "Affirmation of the
Principles of International Law Recognized by the Charter of the Nuremberg Tribunal," A/RES/95(I), December 11, 1946; Resolution 170 (II), "Surrender of War Criminals
and Traitors," A/RES/170(II), October 31, 1947; Resolution 2338 (XXII), "Question of the
Punishment of War Criminals and of Persons Who Have Committed Crimes against
Humanity," A/RES/2338(XXII), December 18, 1967; United Nations, Convention on
the Non-applicability of Statutory Limitations to War Crimes; United Nations General Assembly, Resolution 2712 (XXV), "Question of the Punishment of War Criminals
and of Persons Who Have Committed Crimes against Humanity, A/RES/2712, December 14, 1970; Resolution 2840 (XXVI), "Question of the Punishment of War Criminals
and of Persons Who Have Committed Crimes against Humanity," A/RES/2840(XXVI),
December 18, 1971; and Resolution 3021 (XXVII), "Crime Prevention and Control," A/
RES/3021(XXVII), December 18, 1972.

87   *Almonacid Arellano*, Inter-American Court of Human Rights, series C, no. 154, para. 106. It
is relevant here to highlight the ICRC's interpretation of the scope of application of article 6.5 of the Additional Protocol II of the Geneva Conventions. This provision allows
amnesties to be granted to members of the parties to the conflict for taking part in the
hostilities; however, according to the ICRC, it does not apply to those who commit serious violations of human rights and humanitarian law. Doswald-Beck and Henckaerts,
Customary International Humanitarian Law, rule 159 and its commentaries.

88   United Nations General Assembly, Resolution 57/228, "Khmer Rouge Trials," A/
RES/57/228A, December 18, 2002; and Resolution 57/190, "Rights of the Child," A/
RES/57/190, December 18, 2002.

89   See, among others, United Nations Security Council, Resolution 1479 (2003), "The Situation in Côte d'Ivoire," S/RES/1479 (2003), May 13, 2003; Resolution 1120 (1997), "The Situation in Croatia," S/RES/1120 (1997), July 14, 1997; and Resolution 1315 (2000), "On the
Situation in Sierra Leone," S/RES/1315 (2000), August 14, 2000.

90   United Nations Security Council, "The Rule of Law and Transitional Justice in Conflict
and Post-conflict Societies," Report of the Secretary-General, S/2004/616, August 23,
2004, para. 10.

91 See UN Secretary-General, Agreement on the Basis for the Legal Integration of the Unidad Revolucionaria Guatemalteca, Annex II, A/51/776, S/1997/51, January 20, 1997, paras. 17 et seq; Guatemala, Decreto número 145-1996, Ley de reconciliación nacional [National reconciliation law], December 27, 1996, art. 8; Law on the Establishment of Extraordinary Chambers in the Courts of Cambodia, art. 40; Linas-Marcoussis Agreement, Annex I to the Letter Dated 27 January 2003 from the Permanent Representative of France to the United Nations Addressed to the President of the Security Council, S/2003/99, January 27, 2003.

92 See, among others, Additional Protocol I, art. 86, para. 2; UN Security Council, Resolution 827, Statute of the ICTY, art. 7.3; UN General Assembly, Rome Statute, art. 28; United Nations Economic and Social Council, Resolution 1989/65, "Principles on the Effective Prevention and Investigation of Extralegal, Arbitrary and Summary Executions," E/RES/1989/65, May 24, 1989, principle 19; United Nations General Assembly, Resolution 61/177, "International Convention for the Protection of All Persons from Enforced Disappearance," A/RES/61/177, December 20, 2006, art. 6; and Resolution 34/169, "Code of Conduct for Law Enforcement Officials," A/RES/34/169, February 5, 1980, art. 5.

93 This principle has been recognized by jurisprudence since the Second World War. The Nuremberg Tribunal did so in its sentence of October 11, 1946, in the case of Wilhelm Frick, concerning euthanasia practiced in hospitals and other centers under his control. Nuremberg Tribunal, *Trial of the Major War Criminals before the International Military Tribunal, November 14, 1945–October 1, 1946* (Nuremberg: Nuremburg Tribunal, 1948). The principle was broadly developed by the IMTFE Tribunal in its sentence of November 12, 1948, especially with regard to the responsibility of superior officers for crimes committed against prisoners of war. The principle was also applied in the sentences relating to the following cases: In re Yamashita, 327 U.S. 1 (1946); Application of Homma, 327 U.S. 759 (1946); United States v. Von Leeb et al. (German High Command Trial), 1948, 12 L.R.T.W.C. 1 (US Military Tribunal at Nuremberg, case no. 72); United States v. Pohl et al., 1947, 5 T.W.C. 200 (US Military Tribunal at Nuremberg, case no. 4); and Wilhelm List et al. ("Hostages Trial"), 1948, 11 T.W.C. 1230–1319 (United States Military Tribunal at Nuremberg, case no. 47). Likewise, the ICTY has reiterated this principle in Prosecutor v. Mucic et al., judgment, IT-96-21-T, Trial Chamber, ICTY, November 16, 1998, para. 734; Prosecutor v. Blaskic, judgment, IT-95-14-T, Trial Chamber, ICTY, March 3, 2000, paras. 289ff.; *Prosecutor v. Kordic and Cerkez*, judgment, IT-95-14/2-T, paras. 366–71, 401ff. See also United Nations International Law Commission, "Draft Code of Crimes against the Peace and Security of Mankind," Report of the International Law Commission on the Work of Its Forty-Eighth Session, supplement no. 10, 22–30.

94 Doswald-Beck and Henckaerts, *Customary International Humanitarian Law*, rule 153 and its commentaries.

95 The concept of *autoría mediata*, which refers to criminal responsibility for those who commit a crime through an intermediary, has a well-recognized history in national criminal law, especially in legal systems from German-Romanic tradition or continental law. See also UN General Assembly, Rome Statute, art. 25.

96 United Nations International Commission of Inquiry on Darfur, Report to the United Nations Secretary-General, January 25, 2005, para. 538.

97 Ibid.

98 Prosecutor v. Milorad Krnojelac, judgment, IT-97-25-T, Trial Chamber, ICTY, March 15, 2002, para. 82.

99 UN International Commission of Inquiry on Darfur, Report, paras. 534, 542, 543, 544.

100 See, among others, Prosecutor v. Milan Milutinovi et al., judgment, IT-05-87-T, Trial Chamber, ICTY, February 26, 2009.

101 See, among others, Prosecutor v. Ante Gotovina et al., judgment, IT-06-90-T, Trial Chamber, ICTY, April 15, 2011.

102 Convention against Torture and Other Cruel, Inhuman or Degrading Treatment or Punishment, New York, December 10, 1984, 1465 U.N.T.S. 85, art. 2.3; General Assembly, Resolution 34/169, "Code of Conduct for Law Enforcement Officials," art. 5; and UN Economic and Social Council, Resolution 1989/65, "Principles on the Effective Prevention and Investigation of Extralegal, Arbitrary and Summary Executions," principle 19. See also UN Security Council, Resolution 827, Statute of the ICTY, art. 7.4; UN Security Council, Resolution 955, Statute of the ICTR, art. 6.4; and UN General Assembly, Rome Statute, art. 33.

103 In the national sphere, legislation in various countries has expressly incorporated this prohibition, and various courts have rejected due obedience as grounds for exoneration of responsibility. See, for example, United States v. William L. Calley Jr. ("My Lai case"), 22 U.S.C.M.A. 534, December 21, 1973.

104 Doswald-Beck and Henckaerts, *Customary International Humanitarian Law*, rule 155 and its commentaries.

105 Sahir Erman, "Rapport général: L'obéisance militaire au regard des droits pénaux internes et du droit de la guerre," in *Recueils de la Société international de droit pénal militaire et de droit de la guerre: V - Cinquième Congrès international, Dublin, 25–30 mai 1970*, vol. 1, *L'obéisance militaire au regard des droits pénaux internes et du droit de la guerre*, (Strasbourg: La Société, 1971), 357 (author's translation).

106 On national jurisprudence from Latin-American tribunals using international law in their judgments, see the excellent compilation of the Due Process of Law Foundation, *Digest of Latin-American Jurisprudence on International Crimes* (Washington, DC: DPLF, 2010).

107 See, among others, Supreme Court of Justice of Colombia, case no. 30120, Decision of July 23, 2008, Magistrate Rapporteur Alfredo Gómez Quintero.

108 See, for example, Constitutional Court of Colombia, Auto no. 008 of 2009, Magistrate Rapporteur Manuel José Cepeda Espinosa.

109 "Cases of forced displacement ... have not been properly investigated, and very few perpetrators have been convicted and reparation has been granted in very few cases." United Nations High Commissioner for Human Rights, Report of the United Nations High Commissioner for Human Rights on the Situation of Human Rights in Colombia, A/HRC/7/39, February 29, 2008, para. 54.

110 See, for example, Constitutional Court of Colombia, Auto no. 008 of 2009, Magistrate Rapporteur Manuel José Cepeda Espinosa.

111 Colombia, Criminal Code, art. 180 (Law 599), which defines the crime in the following terms: "Any arbitrary act that, either through violence or by any other coercive means directed against a segment of the population, thereby causing one or more of its members to change their place of residence, shall be punishable. ... In accordance with international law, displacement caused by public forces, when its object is the safety of the population, or during the course of a military operation executed under pressing circumstances, is not to be considered an instance of forced migration."

112 See, among others, Argentina, Law no. 26.200, On the Implementation of the Rome Statute, 2007; Australia, War Crimes Act, 1945 (Cth); Australia, International Criminal Court of Act 2002 (Cth); Armenia, Criminal Code, art. 390, "Serious breach of international humanitarian law during armed conflicts" and art. 392, "Crimes against human security"; Azerbaijan, Criminal Code, art. 107, "Deportation or forcible transfer of population"; Austria, Federal Law on Cooperation with the International Tribunals, 1996; Bangladesh, Act no. 19, International Crimes (Tribunals) Act, 1973; Barbados, Geneva Conventions Act, 1980; Belarus, Criminal Code, art. 136, "War crimes"; Belgium, Law on the Repression of Serious Violations of International Humanitarian Law, 1993 (as amended in 2003); Belgium, Criminal Code, art. 136, "Crimes against humanity"; Bosnia and Herzegovina, Law on Implementation of the Rome Statute of the ICC and Cooperation with the ICC, 2009; Bulgaria, Penal Code, art. 412, "War Crimes"; Burkina Faso, Penal Code, art. 314, "Crimes against Humanity"; Burkina Faso, Law 52-2009/AN, Law Regarding the Competences and Procedures Required for the Implementation of the Rome Statute of the International Criminal Court by Local Courts, 2009, arts. 17, 19; Burundi, Law no. 1/004, On the Repression of the Crimes of Genocide, Crimes against Humanity and War Crimes, May 8, 2003, arts. 3, 4; Canada, Crimes against Humanity and War Crimes Act, S.C. 2000, c. 24, 2000; Canada, Criminal Code sec. 469, Genocide, and War Crimes, 2009; Colombia, Law no. 589, "Crime of Forced Displacement," 2000; Colombia, Penal Code, Law no. 599, 2000, arts. 180, "Forced Displacement," and 159, "Deportation, Expulsion, Transfer or Displacement of Civilians"; Congo, Law no. 8-98, On the Definition and the Repression of Genocide, War Crimes and Crimes against Humanity, October 31, 1998, art. 4; Costa Rica, Criminal Code (as amended by Law no. 8272, On Penal Repression as a Sanction for War Crimes, 2002) arts. 7, 378, and 379; Côte d'Ivoire, Penal Code, Law no. 81-640, 1982, art. 138; Czech Republic, Criminal Code,

sec. 263a, "Persecution of a Population" (specifically, 263.a.2.c prohibits "resettle[ing] the civilians of an occupied territory without grounds"); Denmark, Act no. 1099, Act on Criminal Proceedings before the International Tribunal for the Prosecution of Persons Responsible for War Crimes Committed in the Territory of Former Yugoslavia, 1994; Ecuador, Law no. 196, Law Amending the Penal Code for the Penalisation of Offenses Committed during Military and Police Service, 2010; El Salvador, Penal Code, 1998, art. 362, "War crimes"; Estonia, Penal Code, 2002 and 2008, sec. 89, "Crimes against Humanity," and secs. 94–109, "War Crimes"; Ethiopia, proclamation no. 414 of 2004, Criminal Code of the Federal Democratic Republic of Ethiopia, arts. 270, "War Crimes against the Civilian Population," and 281, "Genocide and Crime against humanity"; Fiji, decree no. 44, Crimes Decree, 2009, division 3, "Crimes against Humanity"; Finland, Penal Code, 212/2008, chapter 11 sec. 3, "Crimes against Humanity," and sec. 5, "War Crimes"; France, Law no. 2010-930 of 2010, On Adapting Criminal Law to the Establishment of the International Criminal Court; France, Penal Code, art. 212-1; Georgia, Criminal Code, arts. 408, "Crimes against Humanity," and 411, "Willful Breach of Norms of International Humanitarian Law Committed in Armed Conflict"; Germany, Act to Introduce the Code of Crimes against International Law, 2002, sec. 7, "Crimes against Humanity," and sec. 8, "War Crimes"; Hungary, Criminal Code, 1978, sec. 158, "Violence against the Civilian Population"; India, Geneva Conventions Act, 1960, sec. 3, "Punishment of Grave Breaches of Conventions"; Ireland, International Criminal Court Act, 2006; Italy, Criminal Military Code of War, art. 185 bis; Kenya, International Crimes Act, 2008; Latvia, Criminal Code (as amended in 2009), sec. 74, "War Crimes"; Luxembourg, Law Concerning the Punishment of Grave Breaches of the Geneva Conventions of 12 August 1949, 1985, art. 1; Malaysia, Act 512, Geneva Convention Act, 1962, part 2, "Punishment of Offenders against Conventions"; Mali, Penal Code (as amended by Law no. 01-079 of August 20, 2001), arts. 29, "Crimes against Humanity," and 31, "War Crimes"; Malta, Criminal Code (as amended in 2005), arts. 54.C, "Crimes against Humanity," and 54.D, "War Crimes"; Mauritius, Geneva Conventions Act, 1970 (as amended in 2003); Netherlands, Act of 19 June 2003 Containing Rules Concerning Serious Violations of International Humanitarian Law (International Crimes Act), 2003, sec. 4 (on crimes against humanity) and secs. 5–7 (on war crimes); Moldova, Criminal Code, arts. 137.2, "Crimes against Humanity," and 138, "Violation of International Humanitarian Laws"; New Zealand, Geneva Conventions Act, 1958, sec. 3, "Punishment for Grave Breaches of Conventions or First Protocol"; New Zealand, International Crimes and International Criminal Court Act, 2000, secs. 10, "Crimes against Humanity," and 11, "War Crimes"; Nicaragua, Penal Code (as amended by Law no. 641 of 2008), art. 503, "Deportation or Illegal Transfer"; Nigeria, Geneva Conventions Act, 1960; Norway, Penal Code (as amended in 2008), chapter 16, secs. 102, "Crimes against Humanity," and 103, "War Crimes against Persons"; Panama, Penal Code (as amended by Law no. 14 of 2007), sec. 15, "Crimes against

Humanity"; Paraguay, Penal Code (as amended by Law no. 1.160/97 of 1997), arts. 319, "Genocide," and 320, "War Crimes"; Peru, Code of Military Justice, art. 88, "War Crimes"; Philippines, Act no. 9851, Act on Crimes against International Humanitarian Law, Genocide and Other Crimes against Humanity, 2009; Poland, Penal Code, chapter 16, "Crimes against Peace, Humanity, and War Crimes"; Portugal, Criminal Code, art. 241, "War Crimes against Civilians"; Portugal, Law no. 31/2004, Adapting Portuguese Criminal Legislation to the Statute of the International Criminal Court Specifying Conduct Constituting Crimes against International Humanitarian Law—17th Amendment to the Criminal Code, 2004; Romania, Criminal Code, arts. 173, "Inhuman Treatment," 174, "Crimes against Humankind Committed in Wartime," and 175, "Other Crimes against Humankind"; Republic of Korea, Act no. 8719, Act on the Punishment of Crimes within the Jurisdiction of the International Criminal Court, 2007; Russian Federation, Criminal Code, art. 356, "Use of Prohibited Means and Methods of Warfare"; Rwanda, Law no. 33 bis/2003, Repressing the Crime of Genocide, Crimes against Humanity and War Crimes, arts. 5 (on crimes against humanity) and 8 (on war crimes); Samoa, International Criminal Court Act, 2007; Senegal, Penal Code (as amended by Law no. 2007-02, Modifying the Penal Code, 2007), arts. 431-2, "Crimes against Humanity," and 431-3, "War Crimes"; Serbia, Criminal Code, arts. 371, "Crimes against Humanity," and 372, "War Crimes against Civilian Population"; Serbia, Law on Organization and Competence of Government Authorities in War Crimes Proceedings, 2003; Slovenia, Penal Code, art. 374, "War Crimes against the Civilian Population"; South Africa, Implementation of the Rome Statute of the International Criminal Court Act, 27 of 2002, schedule 1, parts 2, "Crimes against Humanity," and 3, "War Crimes"; Spain, Penal Code (as amended by Organic Law no. 15/2003, modifying the Penal Code of 1995), arts. 607 bis, "Crimes against Humanity," and 611 (on war crimes); Sudan, Armed Forces Act, 2007, arts. 153.2 (on offences against civilians during military operations) and 159, "Threatening and Displacement of the Population"; Sweden, Penal Code, chapter 22, sec. 6 (on crimes against international law); Switzerland, Military Penal Code, art. 109, "War crimes"; Tajikistan, Criminal Code, art. 403, "Willful Breaches of Norms of International Humanitarian Law Committed in Armed Conflict"; Former Yugoslav Republic of Macedonia, Criminal Code, arts. 403-a, "Crimes against Humanity," and 404, "War Crimes against the Civilian Population"; Trinidad and Tobago, International Criminal Court Act, 2006; Uganda, International Criminal Court Act, 2010; Ukraine, Criminal Code, 2001, art. 438, "Violation of the Rules of Warfare"; Great Britain, Geneva Conventions Act, 1957, War Crimes Act, 1991, and International Criminal Court Act, 2001 (part 5, "Offences under Domestic Law"); United States, War Crimes, 18 U.S.C. chapter 118, "War Crimes," sec. 2441; Uruguay, Law 18.026, Implementing the ICC Statute and Amending the Penal Code, 2006, arts. 19, "Crimes against Humanity," and 26, "War Crimes"; Venezuela, Penal Code, 1964, art. 156, "Violations of the Principles of the Law of War"; Venezuela, Code of Military Justice; and Zimbabwe, Geneva Conventions Act, 1981 (as amended by the Geneva Conventions Amendment Act, 1996), sec. 3, "Grave Breaches of Scheduled Conventions."

113　See, among others, Bangladesh, act no. 19, International Crimes (Tribunals) Act, 1973, arts. 3.2.a, 3.2.d, "Deportation"; Bulgaria, Penal Code, art. 412, "Illegal deportation"; Czech Republic, Criminal Code, sec. 263a, "Persecution of a Population," (specifically, subsection 2.c, "resettles the civilians of an occupied territory without grounds"); Hungary, Criminal Code, 1978, sec. 158, "Violence against the Civilian Population"); India, Geneva Conventions Act, 1960, sec. 3, "Punishment of Grave Breaches of Conventions"; and Luxembourg, Law Concerning the Punishment of Grave Breaches of the Geneva Conventions of 12 August 1949, 1985.

114　See, for example, Moldova, Criminal Code, arts. 137.2, "Crimes Against Humanity," and 138, "Violation of International Humanitarian Laws"; and Romania, Criminal Code, art. 173, "Inhuman Treatment."

115　The right not to be convicted for acts or omissions that were not crimes at the time they were committed is a non-derogable right. See, among others, International Covenant on Civil and Political Rights, New York, December 16, 1966, 993 U.N.T.S. 171, art. 4; European Convention on Human Rights, Rome, November 4, 1950, 312 E.T.S. 5, art. 15; American Convention on Human Rights, San José, Costa Rica, November 22, 1969, 9 I.L.M. 673 (1970), art. 27; African Charter on Human and Peoples' Rights, Nairobi, June 27, 1981, 21 I.L.M. 59, art. 7; and Arab Charter on Human Rights, Tunis, May 22, 2004, art. 15. See also David Michael Nicholas v. Australia, Communication no. 1080/2002, CCPR/C/80/D/1080/2002 (2004), Human Rights Committee, paras. 7.2 et seq; De la Cruz-Flores v. Peru, judgment, series C, no. 115, Inter-American Court of Human Rights, November 18, 2004, paras. 104 et seq; Ricardo Canese v. Paraguay, judgment, series C, no. 111, Inter-American Court of Human Rights, August 31, 2004, para. 175; García Asto and Ramírez Rojas v. Peru, judgment, series C, no. 137, Inter-American Court of Human Rights, November 25, 2005, para. 206; and Fermín Ramírez v. Guatemala, judgment, series C, no. 126, Inter-American Court of Human Rights, June 20, 2005, para. 90. See also Geneva Convention Relative to the Treatment of Prisoners in War (Third Geneva Convention), August 12, 1949, 75 U.N.T.S. 135, art. 99; Fourth Geneva Convention, art. 67; Additional Protocol I, art. 75.4.c; and Additional Protocol II, art. 6.2.c.

116　International Covenant on Civil and Political Rights, art. 15.2; European Convention on Human Rights, art. 7.2; American Convention on Human Rights, art. 9; UN International Law Commission, "Principles Recognized in the Charter of the Nuremberg Tribunal," principle 1. See also International Commission of Jurists, *Impunidad y graves violaciones de derechos humanos—Practitioners' Guide No. 3* (Geneva: International Commission of Jurists, 2008), 129–33.

117　Klaus Dieter Baumgarten v. Germany, Communication no. 960/2000, CCPR/C/78/D/960/2000 (2003), Human Rights Committee; Kononov v. Latvia (just satisfaction), no. 36376/04, European Court of Human Rights, July 28, 2008; Kolk and Kislyiy v. Estonia (dec.), nos. 23052/04 and 24018/04, European Court of Human Rights, January 17, 2006; and *Almonacid Arellano*, Inter-American Court of Human Rights, series C, no. 154, para. 151.

118 *Kolk and Kislyiy*, nos. 23052/04 and 24018/04, European Court of Human Rights. In the same line, see also Jorgic v. Germany, no. 74613/01, European Court of Human Rights, July 12, 2007; Korbely v. Hungary (GC), no. 9174/02, European Court of Human Rights, September 19, 2008; and Streletz et al. v. Germany (GC), nos. 34044/96 and 44801/98, European Court of Human Rights, March 22, 2001.

119 *Kolk and Kislyiy*, nos. 23052/04 and 24018/04, European Court of Human Rights.

120 See, among others, Supreme Court of Justice of Colombia, judgment, case no. 32022, Criminal Cassation Chamber, September 21, 2009, Magistrate Rapporteur Sigifredo Espinosa Pérez; Supreme Court of Justice of Colombia, case no. 33.118, Criminal Cassation Chamber, May 13, 2010 (decision against Cesar Pérez García); and Supreme Court of Justice of Colombia, case no. 28476, Criminal Cassation Chamber (decision against Cesar Emilio Camargo Cuchía and others); State of Israel v. Adolf Eichmann, Criminal Case 40/61, District Court of Jerusalem and Supreme Court of Israel; Ekanayake v. the Attorney General, judgment, 87 I.L.R., Court of Appeal of Sri Lanka, May 28, 1986, 298; Constitutional Court of Peru, judgment, case no. 2798-04-HC/TC, December 9, 2004; and José Nino Gavazzo Pereira et al. (case "Condor Plan"), sentence no. 036, case no. 98-247/2006, Criminal Judge no. 19, Uruguay Supreme Court of Justice, March 26, 2009.

121 Jorge Iván Laverde Zapata, alias "El Iguano," judgment, case no. 2006 80201, Superior Tribunal of the Judicial District of Bogotá, Chamber of Justice and Peace, Colombia, December 2, 2010, Magistrate Rapporteur Uldi Teresa Jiménez López.

122 For a compilation of the international human rights jurisprudence, see International Commission of Jurists, *Military Jurisdiction and International Law: Military Courts and Gross Human Rights Violations*, vol. 1 (Geneva: International Commission of Jurists, 2005), http://www.icj.org/dwn/database/ElecDist-BB-MilitaryTribunals.pdf.

123 Commission on Human Rights, "Draft Principles Governing the Administration of Justice through Military Tribunals," Report by the Special Rapporteur of the Subcommission on the Promotion and Protection of Human Rights, Emmanuel Decaux, CN.4/2006/58, January 13, 2006.

124 Ergin v. Turkey (no. 6) (just satisfaction), no. 47533/99, European Court of Human Rights, May 4, 2006; and Maszni v. Romania (just satisfaction), no. 59892/00, European Court of Human Rights, September 21, 2006.

125 African Commission on Human and Peoples' Rights, Principles and Guidelines on the Right to a Fair Trial and Legal Assistance in Africa, DOC/OS(XXX)247, 2001, principle L, http://www.afrimap.org/standards.php

126 UN Commission on Human Rights, "Addendum: Updated Set of Principles for the Protection and Promotion of Human Rights through Action to Combat Impunity," principle 29.

127 See, for example, Fourth Geneva Convention, arts. 64 and 66.

128 Human Rights Committee, General Comment no. 32, art. 14, Right to Equality Before Courts and Tribunals and to a Fair Trial, CCPR/C/GC/32, August 23, 2007, para. 22; Inter-American Commission on Human Rights, Resolution on "Terrorism and Human Rights," December 12, 2001; and Inter-American Commission on Human Rights, Report on Terrorism and Human Rights, OEA/Ser.L/V/ll.116, Doc. 5 rev. 1 corr., October 22, 2002.

129 See, for example, Italy, Peru, Mexico, Switzerland, and Venezuela.

130 See, among others, the constitutions of Venezuela, 1999, art. 29; Bulgaria, 1991, art. 31; Ecuador, 1998, art. 23; Ethiopia, 1994, art. 28; Honduras, 1982; Paraguay, 1992, art. 5; Poland, 1997, art. 43; and Rwanda, 2003, art. 13.

131 See, among others, Azerbaijan, Criminal Code; Armenia, Criminal Code; Belgium, Law on the Repression of Serious Violations of International Humanitarian Law, 1993 (as amended in 2003); Bosnia and Herzegovina, Criminal Code; Croatia, Criminal Code; Burkina Faso, Penal Code; Congo, Law no. 8-98, On the Definition and the Repression of Genocide, War Crimes and Crimes against Humanity, October 31, 1998; Czech Republic, Criminal Code; El Salvador, Criminal Code; Estonia, Criminal Code; France, Penal Code; Germany, Code of Crimes against International Law; Hungary, Criminal Code; Kyrgyz- stan, Penal Code; Mali, Penal Code; Poland, Criminal Code; Russian Federation, Crimi- nal Code; Republic of Moldova, Criminal Code; Slovenia, Penal Code; Slovakia, Penal Code; Spain, Penal Code; Switzerland, Penal Code; Tajikistan, Criminal Code.

132 See, among others *State of Israel*, judgment, Criminal Case 40/61, District Court of Jerusalem, December 12, 1961; Prosecutor v. Klaus Barbie, judgment, Cour de Cassa- tion, Criminal Chamber, France, December 20, 1985; Haas and Priebke, judgment, Rome Military Court of Appeal, Italy, July 22, 1997; Haas and Priebke, judgment, Supreme Court of Cassation, Italy, November 16, 1998; Erich Priebke v. Argentina, judgment no. 16.063/94, Argentina, November 2, 1995; Constitutional Court, Decision nos. 53/1993 (X. 13.) AB and 36/1996 (IX.4.) AB, Hungary; Constitutional Court, judg- ment no. 578/02, Colombia, July 30, 2002; and Supreme Court of Justice, judgment no. 585, Paraguay, December 31, 1996.

133 See, among others, Australia, International Criminal Court Act, 2002 (Cth); Ireland, International Criminal Court Act, 2003; Great Britain, International Criminal Court Act, 2001; and Canada, Crimes against Humanity and War Crimes Act.

134 See, for example, Colombia, Criminal Code.

135 See, among others, "Massacre of Riofrío," judgment, no. 17550, Supreme Court of Justice of Colombia, March 6, 2003, Magistrate Rapporteur Yesid Ramírez Bastidas; Colombia,

Constitutional Court, judgment C-176/94 of 1994; "Episode Carlos Prats," judgment, no. 2.182-98, Chile, July 29, 2008; and Supreme Court of Justice, judgment, no. 585/96, Paraguay, December 31, 1996 ("Capitán de Caballería Modesto Napoleón Ortigoza s/ supuesto homicidio del cadete Alberto Anastasio Benítez").

CHAPTER 7

Ensuring Long-Term Protection: Justice-Sensitive Security Sector Reform and Displacement

Marina Caparini

This chapter explores the intersection between displacement and one particular mechanism of transitional justice—justice-sensitive security sector reform (JSSR). It aims to identify various ways in which JSSR can contribute to protection of refugees and internally displaced persons (IDPs), and how applying the principles of JSSR can improve the prospects of developing durable solutions to displacement—that is, meeting the long-term safety, security, and justice needs of the displaced. The chapter focuses first on key concepts and developments within the fields of displacement and JSSR, and it examines why the relevant communities of theory and practice have evolved separately but are now witnessing a growing convergence. It then considers two temporal periods in which displaced populations have distinct security and justice needs: the phase when they require protection from imminent harm and the phase when durable solutions that provide long-term security and justice are sought. I examine specific efforts to respond to the security and justice needs of displaced populations in each phase to understand what worked and what did not and how JSSR was relevant to those efforts. The chapter then draws out insights and directions for further research.

Although the findings in this chapter are preliminary and more empirical research on this underexamined topic is required, the cases here suggest that the principles of JSSR are relevant to developing effective means of serving the security and justice needs of the displaced in both temporal phases, and that they contribute to sounder and more effective and sustainable responses. First, in settings where it is imperative to provide protection from immediate harm, initiatives that ignored the holistic perspective—consisting of a system-wide approach and addressing issues of accountability, integrity, legitimacy, and empowerment through inclusion—tended to be ineffective, flawed, or unsustainable. In some IDP camps in Darfur, peacekeeper patrols and escorts to protect vulnerable inhabitants could not be maintained over the longer term, while the establishment of community safety initiatives by the peacekeeping force that explicitly sought to include and empower marginalized and vulnerable subgroups, such as women and youth, offered more lasting contributions to the protection of camp inhabitants. In eastern Chad, peacekeepers training a special Chadian unit set up specifically to police the IDP camps successfully included women in an effort to better respond to the rampant problems of sexual violence. However, despite more effective policing of the camps, justice processes—formal and traditional—remained very weak or biased, and this failure to adopt a more holistic approach to strengthening the rule of law undermined the effectiveness of the overall effort to combat sexual violence against displaced women. In the Democratic Republic of Congo (DRC), the peacekeeping force devised important innovations to improve communication and build trust with local communities, but the failure to enforce accountability through vetting of the armed forces and the removal of human rights abusers has been a key factor in the continuing predations against civilians, including the displaced.

Second, in settings where durable solutions to the long-term security and justice needs of the displaced are sought, the principles of JSSR appear even more relevant. However, the need to understand the interrelation of security and justice initiatives and address the complex mix of factors required to arrive at durable solutions also becomes more apparent in these examples. Efforts of the Kosovo Police Service to recruit ethnic minorities and women in order to create a more representative service were important to rebuilding legitimacy and public confidence in the police. Nevertheless, continuing problems in addressing corruption and dysfunction in the justice system as well as in the police have limited the extent to which IDPs have returned to their places of origin. In Bosnia and Herzegovina, the judicial reselection, or vetting, process to remove from the judiciary those who had committed abuses, were political appointments, or were not professionally competent not only improved trust and confidence in the judiciary but also empowered citizens to lodge public complaints about an array of problems and helped target other judicial reform efforts. Judicial reselection contributed to efforts to erode the embedded systems of ethnocratic and corrupt governance that obstructed returns.

In Liberia, unresolved land and property disputes have sustained intra- and intercommunal conflict and displacement and have constituted one of the main causes of insecurity for those who had been displaced and returned to find their land taken. Justice-sensitive approaches to resolving these disputes have focused on inclusion and legitimacy, empowering displaced individuals and educating and building the capacity of both customary authorities and state officials. In Colombia, the Constitutional Court is strengthening the integrity and accountability of the response to internal displacement by holding the government to its constitutional and legal obligations; through specific decisions it has also legally empowered displaced persons. Perhaps the least conclusive findings are in post-conflict urban settings where the displaced often constitute the most vulnerable section of the population, subject to the predations of criminal gangs in the absence of state policing authority. Informal policing and governance authorities that hold some measure of public legitimacy in such places should be considered valid interlocutors in efforts to develop security and justice arrangements, but the presence of criminal gangs and the failure to hold perpetrators accountable for past human rights abuses, as was the case in Timor-Leste, pose serious obstacles to applying JSSR principles in these environments.

CONCEPTS OF JUSTICE-SENSITIVE SECURITY SECTOR REFORM AND DISPLACEMENT

This chapter focuses on the intersection of three distinct communities of knowledge and practice that have emerged or undergone rapid development over the past twenty years: forced migration, transitional justice, and security sector reform (SSR). The end of the Cold War system of bipolarity opened up space for domestic transformation in many former client states, frequently resulting in intrastate conflicts driven largely by ethnic, communal, or religious strife. The end of bipolarity also stimulated more diverse international responses to armed conflict and its consequences. The fields of forced migration, transitional justice, and SSR have sought to mitigate the effects of instability, armed conflict, and human rights abuses. The field of forced migration contends with the displacement of large numbers of people from their homes, usually as a result of instability or conflict, but increasingly also as a result of natural disasters and development projects; transitional justice addresses the legacies of serious crimes and atrocities committed during conflict or under authoritarian rule; and SSR attempts to transform dysfunctional or abusive security institutions and in so doing address the failure of states to provide their citizens with even basic levels of safety, security, and access to justice. Despite the shared impetus and broadly common interest in dealing with the consequences of internal disorder, instability, political oppression, human rights abuses, and armed conflict, these three fields have remained broadly separate, with distinct academic literatures, policy communities, modes of practical intervention, and pools of practitioners.

SECURITY SECTOR REFORM

SSR emerged in 1999 from the UK development community as a framework for donor action to support the building of effective, well-governed, accountable, and transparent security and justice institutions.[1] One of the main challenges faced by countries emerging from conflict or authoritarian rule is in transforming their security institutions—the police and other law enforcement bodies, intelligence and security agencies, and armed forces—and related governance and oversight structures. Similarly, reform is frequently necessary in the justice sector—the prosecutors, courts, judiciary, and penal system. Security and justice institutions in states emerging from conflict or authoritarian rule are often bloated, politicized, abusive, unaccountable, and corrupt. They frequently serve primarily to protect the members of the former political regime rather than as core providers of the essential public services of safety, security, and justice. The personnel of such security institutions may have committed serious human rights violations, been the cause of displacement and other abuses, and continue to be deeply mistrusted by the public they are supposed to serve. When states are in transition toward more democratic systems, an essential aspect of reforming the security sector involves changing how these core institutions are governed—in particular developing effective means of holding them accountable for their actions, while making them operationally effective and financially sustainable. However, these institutions must also be made responsive to the needs of all citizens, not merely those who control political or economic power.

While institutional capacity building, training, and mentoring have long constituted elements of bilateral assistance, SSR is distinguished from earlier efforts to provide technical support for reform in two key respects. The first is its focus on *governance*—that is, ensuring that security institutions are not only operationally effective (the primary purpose of security assistance during the Cold War) but also accountable, democratically controlled, financially sustainable, appropriately sized and budgeted for the country, and responsive to the needs of citizens. The governance aspect underscores that SSR is not merely technical but fundamentally a political undertaking. The second characteristic of SSR is its emphasis on a *holistic perspective*—that is, viewing the security and justice sectors as components within an integrated system, with corresponding attention given to the interrelated nature of how safety, security, and justice are provided and experienced. The linkages between the police, criminal courts, and the prison system illustrate the need to maintain awareness of how the functioning of one institution affects that of another and to coordinate approaches in security and justice reform.[2]

JUSTICE-SENSITIVE SECURITY SECTOR REFORM

Justice in transitional settings means holding key individuals responsible for grave human rights abuses, establishing the truth about past abuses, and acknowledging victims by providing reparations and other forms of compensation. These measures often directly affect the victims of mass crimes and their families. SSR, on the other hand, is arguably the most indirectly experienced and least understood of transitional justice mechanisms, though the reform of abusive, unaccountable, and corrupt security and justice institutions is essential to achieving the transitional justice goal of preventing the recurrence of abuses. At an abstract and systemic level, justice results when individuals who were denied protection of their human rights and fair treatment under the law can reclaim those rights from the state and its agents through the provision of justice and security in an equitable, fair, and responsive manner. Transitional justice can help SSR achieve its future objectives by drawing attention to the importance of the past. Specifically, justice measures such as truth commissions and criminal prosecutions can help SSR understand and address the systemic causes of an abusive past, to acknowledge the victims of past abuses as among those in most need of security reform, and to take steps to effectively address the legacy of those abuses.[3]

With this in mind, a justice-sensitive approach to SSR has been explicitly advanced by members of the transitional justice community. What distinguishes JSSR is its emphasis on four principles: integrity, accountability, legitimacy, and inclusion.[4] Integrity means that security and justice institutions and actors are firmly grounded in the rule of law and respect for human rights. Accountability for human rights abuses is pursued through the establishment of effective mechanisms within institutions of security and justice as well as sound oversight systems—thus encompassing both decisionmakers and agents. Critically, the conception of accountability articulated by JSSR is a holistic one. Standard SSR approaches focus primarily on establishing effective accountability mechanisms for present and future abuses; JSSR, on the other hand, also seeks accountability for *past* abuses and includes measures such as vetting that exclude human rights abusers from public institutions. Legitimacy means that security and justice institutions enjoy public trust and confidence. Legitimacy derives in part from the recognition that security and justice actors are responsive not only to the political or economic elite but to the needs of all groups within society, including those who are most vulnerable—victims of human rights abuses (including displacement), the poor, and marginalized groups. Inclusion means enabling the participation of all citizens, including members of vulnerable and marginalized groups, in SSR processes and ultimately in the governance of their safety, security, and access to justice. Inclusion in such processes and governance is empowering.

Thus, transitional justice intersects with SSR through their shared interest in building accountable, legitimate, and inclusive security and justice systems that respect and uphold human rights. While it could be argued that these principles of JSSR also conform to the definition of regular SSR as it has emerged over the past decade, in practice there tends to be more emphasis in SSR on security forces becoming more effective, modern, and professional. JSSR is not only or even primarily about modernizing security forces and improving their operational capabilities, although that is often an important objective. JSSR does not implicitly subordinate the goals of inclusion, responsiveness, and public trust but pushes them out front as the sine qua non of reform of abusive and dysfunctional systems. Both transitional justice and SSR share the goal of preventing the recurrence of human rights abuses and armed conflict. But considering SSR through a transitional justice lens can lead to a specific justice-sensitive approach, one that emphasizes the importance of the past and the value of the principles explained here in achieving that prevention.

DISPLACEMENT

The contemporary international refugee regime emerged as a result of World War II and persecution by the fascist and Nazi regimes, which displaced millions of people in Europe alone.[5] A new agency, the United Nations High Commissioner for Refugees, emerged in 1951, and the fundamental elements of the refugee regime were codified in the 1951 UN Convention Relating to the Status of Refugees and its 1967 protocol.[6] During the Cold War, the issue of refugees was framed largely in ideological terms, and those fleeing communist states especially were welcomed in Western countries through generous resettlement arrangements.[7] The nature of displacement; the response of states, especially of developed Western states to refugees; and forced migration as a focus of international assistance began to change in the 1970s and especially from the late 1980s with the end of the stable bipolar world order. Socioeconomic problems and the eruption of internal interethnic conflicts in newly independent states generated dramatically higher numbers of IDPs and refugees from the developing world, while attitudes toward accepting refugees in receiving states became more hostile and acceptance policies more restrictive.[8]

HUMANITARIAN PROTECTION

The international humanitarian community has been the primary actor responding to the immediate needs of displaced populations that flee conflict and seek refuge. Physical safety and the human rights of the displaced were traditionally not a prominent focus of humanitarian efforts, even though physical security was recognized as often being as important as food to many IDPs.[9] Rather, humanitarian agencies sought to preserve life and alleviate suffering through the provision of material relief. Humanitarian aid has traditionally been concerned with providing people who have been affected by the fighting with food, clean water, shelter, and health care.

With the growth of internal armed conflicts through the 1990s, protection emerged as a key concern of those seeking to assist displaced persons. Protection was originally addressed by only two institutional actors having a specific mandate to do so under international law: the International Committee of the Red Cross (ICRC) and the Office of the UN High Commissioner for Refugees (UNHCR), which emphasized legal and diplomatic engagement with state and non-state actors to persuade them to respect the Geneva Conventions and human rights law. The definition of protection that is currently the most widely used in the humanitarian community reflects a discussion between international humanitarian law and human rights proponents and focuses on the legal entitlements of civilians. In the humanitarian community, protection has come to mean "all activities aimed at obtaining full respect for the rights of the individual in accordance with the letter and spirit of the relevant bodies of law, namely human rights law, international humanitarian law and refugee law."[10] Furthermore, "protection is not limited to survival and physical security, but covers the full range of rights, including civil and political rights, such as the right to freedom of movement, the right to political participation, and economic, social and cultural rights, including the rights to education and health."[11] It is vital to understand that the idea of protection, when invoked today by many humanitarian actors, has this specific, rights-based focus. Within this framework, displacement is understood as a consequence of the breakdown of the state's willingness or ability to protect the fundamental rights of its citizens. Displacement is often caused directly by widespread human rights violations. The displaced also tend to become vulnerable to other abuses and human rights violations, including forced military recruitment, forced labor, sexual and gender-based violence, and trafficking. Women and children are especially vulnerable to such abuses.[12]

The humanitarian community views the protection of rights as consisting of three types of action: (1) *responsive* action taken to prevent or stop violations of rights; (2) *remedial* action taken to ensure a remedy when rights have been violated, including the rights to security, property, housing, education, health care, and livelihoods, which may entail restoring rights through access to truth, justice, and reparations; and (3) *environment-building* action, with a more developmental and peacebuilding perspective, taken to promote respect for rights and the rule of law.[13] Humanitarian actors tend to focus on remedial action, although increasingly some are engaging in responsive and environment-building activities as well. The end result is that today protection is no longer an issue addressed in the humanitarian community solely by the ICRC and UNHCR or only in terms of diplomatic-legal dialogue with state and non-state actors. Rather, many new actors have emerged to advance the protection of civilians in many different ways, primarily within a rights-based framework. These include UN agencies such as the Office of the UN High Commissioner for Human Rights, intergovernmental organizations such as the International Organization for Migration, and a number of international nongovernmental organizations such as the Norwegian Refugee Council, Save the Children, and the International Rescue Committee. And in contrast to the earlier focus on working primarily with state-level actors, many tend to focus on the substate level, working directly with affected local communities and groups and with intergovernmental organizations.[14]

The rights-based concept of protection outlined earlier has significantly broadened the potential scope of action for humanitarian agencies beyond meeting the essential material needs of those affected by conflict. The move toward a rights-based emphasis has not been uncontroversial within the humanitarian community, which is reflected in the differing approaches of humanitarian agencies. Some have adopted a minimalist approach in which they "mainstream" or incorporate protection principles into relief assistance—essentially seeking to minimize safety risks to recipient populations in meeting their essential needs. At the other end of the spectrum, some agencies devise dedicated protection programming aimed at enabling civilians to reclaim their rights—for example, by helping to build the rule of law, by monitoring and reporting on compliance with international humanitarian law, or by helping IDPs and refugees acquire personal documentation. A middle ground between these two approaches employs some combination of assistance and protection objectives.[15]

The increasing engagement of humanitarian actors in civilian protection is criticized by those in the community who believe that humanitarian agencies can do little to protect civilians and that other actors are better equipped to fulfill that function. According to this view, humanitarians have enthusiastically adopted the terminology of protection without being able to provide protection in the basic sense that most people would understand it—that is, through activities designed to stop violence against people and ensure their basic physical integrity and safety. Rather, the humanitarian meaning of protection is specialized—referring to activities designed to promote the respect of the legal rights framework—and does not involve military or police defending people's lives but a civilian bureaucracy defending rights through activities such as training, raising awareness, monitoring, documenting, and advocacy. Critics claim that, rather than focusing on providing relief, humanitarians are replicating the work of human rights organizations and, in so doing, turning their back on neutrality and risking their access to populations of concern. Humanitarian access is already seen as being risked by human rights–focused organizations that investigate and document the crimes of individuals to support the work of the International Criminal Court.[16]

Humanitarian protection has nevertheless become one of the eleven core areas of humanitarian action coordinated under the "cluster approach," a new international mechanism for humanitarian coordination that has sought to reduce confusion about roles and response gaps in humanitarian emergencies, especially in situations of mass internal displacement, by assigning formal responsibility for leadership and coordination of each core area to specific international agencies. The humanitarian protection cluster is generally assigned to UNHCR on the global level, though other agencies may act as focal points on specific issues or areas within the cluster, such as gender and responses to sexual or gender-based violence, as well as children and the rule of law.[17] In specific cases, organizations may lead the protection cluster jointly. For example, the protection cluster for the DRC for the first time implemented coleadership between a politically neutral humanitarian agency, UNHCR, and a UN peacekeeping mission with a political-military mandate, the UN Mission in the DRC (MONUC).[18]

The emphasis on coordination and integration of efforts by multiple international actors in the cluster approach is mirrored by the development of the concept of integrated multidimensional UN missions. With the growing complexity of international peacekeeping operations—involving a diversity of actors, including humanitarian agencies, human rights actors, military and police components, and development actors, and a more diverse range of mandates that may include responsibilities as varied as implementation of peace agreements, protection of civilians, post-conflict reconstruction, and peace enforcement—there has been an acknowledged need to improve strategic coherence and effectiveness through greater clarification of roles and coordination of all UN actors and main partners. Humanitarian actors have tended to be skeptical toward integrated missions, seeing them as reducing "humanitarian space," in part because of the blurring of distinctions between humanitarian and political and military actors, especially when the nonhumanitarian ones carry out activities that are designed to win hearts and minds but that also compromise basic humanitarian principles of impartiality and neutrality.

The debate among humanitarians over humanitarian protection has been portrayed as the needs-versus-rights or the assistance-versus-protection dilemma. Those advocating *needs* maintain that assistance should be provided regardless of political factors. This is the classic humanitarian position, perhaps most clearly embodied by the ICRC, which maintains that humanitarianism is best served through neutrality and impartiality, thus remaining insulated from political factors. Those advocating a *rights*-based approach to humanitarianism tend to argue for politically informed decisions and efforts that would better enable humanitarian actors to engage protection issues from a strategic position.[19] This ongoing debate is relevant to JSSR's potential contributions to durable solutions, as it derives from fundamental disagreement about appropriate roles, division of responsibility, and extent of cooperation or interaction between the various actors involved in responding to the critical needs of the displaced and other vulnerable groups.[20]

DURABLE SOLUTIONS

The framework for assisting displaced persons is centered on the notion of durable solutions, which entail the *return* of the displaced to their places of origin (for refugees, this means the countries of origin), their local *integration* in the places where they have sought refuge, or their *resettlement*, whether elsewhere in countries of origin or in other countries.[21] Durable solutions are achieved when IDPs and refugees enjoy the restoration of rights vis-à-vis the state and enjoy those rights to the same extent as their nondisplaced neighbors. The Framework on Durable Solutions for Internally Displaced Persons identifies eight criteria for determining the extent to which durable solutions have been achieved: long-term safety and security; adequate standard of living; access to livelihoods; restoration of housing, land, and property; access to documentation; family reunification; participation in public affairs; and access to effective remedies and justice. All of these criteria are underpinned by the principle of nondiscrimination.[22]

Because the focus here is on the intersection between JSSR and displacement, the most relevant criterion is the provision of long-term safety and security. This clearly depends on the willingness and capacity of both national and local authorities to provide effective protection to IDPs—protection that is not "less effective" than that provided to the nondisplaced populations.[23] The Framework notes that while "absolute safety and security" may not be possible, IDPs must not be subject to attack, harassment, intimidation, persecution, or other forms of punitive action on their return home or settlement elsewhere in the country.[24] The Framework asserts that IDPs who have achieved a durable solution should have

> full and non-discriminatory access to national and local protection mechanisms, including police, courts, national human rights institutions and national disaster management services. The state, namely national and local authorities, bear primary responsibility for ensuring that IDPs do not face dangers to their physical safety and security. Consequently, the establishment of effective courts and police in areas of return, settlement or local integration should be a priority.[25]

Furthermore, it notes that where the international community has been brought in to establish safety and security following conflict or natural disaster, durable solutions are promoted by the gradual handover of responsibility for protection to national and local authorities[26]

The long-term safety and security criteria for durable solutions clearly reflect some core concerns of SSR. However, the nondiscriminatory element most closely links it to JSSR, specifically, the principle that security and justice systems must enjoy integrity insofar as they function as public services, treat all citizens fairly, and do not engage in human rights abuses. This nondiscriminatory provision of safety and security is also linked to JSSR's notion of legitimacy insofar as it requires that security and justice institutions enjoy the confidence of all groups in society, particularly those who are most vulnerable, including IDPs. A discriminatory police or judicial system would have neither integrity nor legitimacy in the eyes of those it discriminates against. Armed forces, police, and militia and other paramilitary forces as well as nonstate armed groups whose members have committed abuses that resulted in displacement must therefore be held accountable for past discrimination affecting the human rights of displaced populations. More than merely ensuring that police and court systems are restored and effective, then, durable solutions emphasize that the qualitative factor of nondiscrimination must be present and thus that returnees and IDPs must not be excluded from the services such systems offer. A justice-sensitive approach extends nondiscrimination through its insistence on accountability for past abuses, including the removal of those who have committed abuses.

Two other criteria for durable solutions are also relevant to JSSR: the restoration of housing, land, and property[27] and access to remedies and justice. First, according to the Framework on Durable Solutions, a durable solution is achieved when IDPs have effective and accessible mechanisms for timely restitution of their housing, land, or property.[28] While the restitution process may be long and complex, it requires that IDPs have access to an effective justice and compensation mechanism, and that they can live safely and securely in the meantime.[29] The Framework also notes that special attention is needed to help women and children gain ownership or access to property, especially when they face legal barriers to inheriting property.[30] With regard to restitution, the core principles of JSSR apply equally to the informal justice system. While SSR has focused primarily on formal justice mechanisms, there has been growing awareness that informal or customary justice mechanisms constitute the avenue of choice or necessity for the majority of people, and certainly those in marginalized or vulnerable groups, in many post-conflict and developing contexts. SSR, especially justice-sensitive efforts, must take into account these dual systems when seeking to ensure the restoration of land or property.[31] Although not reflected in the Framework, some interventions on the ground to help IDPs gain access to justice and resolve property and housing disputes have involved working with customary justice (as will be discussed later).

Effective remedies and justice for IDPs who have been victims of human rights violations require access to "transitional-justice mechanisms, reparations and information on the causes of violations."[32] Securing effective remedies and justice for IDPs is considered an essential component of long-term peace and stability.[33] JSSR is concerned with access to justice, since it is often denied to the poorest, most vulnerable groups in a society. Much mainstream SSR tends to be focused on reforming institutions and processes, and access to justice has thus been advanced within the SSR field mostly by development actors such as the UK Department for International Development. JSSR has said little thus far about access to justice or securing effective legal remedies, but these clearly fall within its scope, based on the normative principles underlying it. Access to effective remedies facilitates accountability for rights violations—not just present and future but past violations as well. The ability of IDPs and other vulnerable or marginalized individuals to access effective justice mechanisms demonstrates the integrity and legitimacy of a justice system that treats all claimants equally and empowers those who were denied justice and suffered violations, including displacement.

Displacement and SSR as fields of study emerged at different times, with different areas of focus, and with different communities of research and practice. The primary international actors responding to displaced populations were originally humanitarian agencies, which observed the principles of neutrality, independence, and impartiality in the provision of relief. Over time, the work of forced migration agencies and experts, primarily in the humanitarian community, has become increasingly situated within a rights-based framework. Although contested, the notion of humanitarian protection has moved the field closer to developing responses to a range of rights violations beyond the traditional focus on emergency material relief, and to encompassing a greater emphasis on ensuring that the displaced can reclaim all of their essential rights. On the other hand, SSR emerged as donors became increasingly involved in supporting the reform or reconstitution of state institutions to provide safety, security, and justice, often in the aftermath of armed conflict or authoritarian rule. Emerging originally from a development framework, SSR drew on a growing community of rule-of-law, governance, and security specialists. The enunciation of JSSR reasserts the importance of key principles underlying SSR, including integrity, accountability, legitimacy, and citizen inclusion and empowerment, and could be argued to thus have a more explicit focus on the rights of those populations than the original formulation of SSR. Certainly, the identification of JSSR as one mechanism of transitional justice underlines that the citizens of any state are rights-bearing individuals and that the state bears obligations under international law to provide for their basic needs and rights, including physical safety and the rights to justice and truth.

THE GROWING CONVERGENCE BETWEEN ASSISTING THE DISPLACED AND JSSR

Despite having distinct origins and disparate communities of practice, forced migration and JSSR have increasingly converged on the conceptual level through their intensifying focus on rights. At a more specific level, it is long-term safety and security—which are essential for durable solutions and have come to feature in thinking about the kinds of assistance and interventions that are needed—that most evidently provide the link between displacement and JSSR. Transitional justice's goals include recognizing victims as citizens and equal rights bearers, restoring the civic relationship between state and citizen and thus civic trust, and achieving reconciliation and ultimately democracy.[34] Since displacement indicates a fundamental failure of the state to provide for the physical safety and protection of the rights of its citizens, the achievement of justice in the aftermath of conflict and displacement represents the potential restoration of the political contract between the displaced and the state, rebuilding the bonds of citizenship and civic trust.[35] Critical to the restoration of that bond is the renewed responsibility of the state to protect the fundamental rights of its citizens, including by providing essential levels of safety, security, and justice. A justice-sensitive approach aims for the provision of these in an equitable, legitimate, inclusive, and accountable way.

People displaced by conflict or repression are often already marginalized in social, economic, or political terms. As the former representative of the UN secretary-general on the human rights of IDPs has noted, "All IDPs are vulnerable in ways that non-displaced persons are not. However, certain groups of IDPs require particular attention. These include women (especially women heading households), children, the elderly, persons with disabilities or chronic illnesses, and those belonging to ethnic and religious minorities and indigenous peoples."[36] Such groups are often subject to discrimination and abuse because of their membership in more than one identity group, also known as intersectionality, or the overlapping of multiple forms of discrimination. For example, indigenous women may be subject to discrimination as women, as members of a minority group, and as members of a particular social class. A justice-sensitive approach, therefore, recognizes the need to address the specific security and justice concerns of vulnerable groups, acknowledges that needs may vary within groups, and seeks to promote the participation of the marginalized and vulnerable in finding solutions at multiple levels to address those needs.

Accountability requires dealing with impunity, which means, most immediately, seeking to ensure that those directly responsible for past abuses are held accountable and ensuring that systems of accountability are developed in tandem with any restructuring, downsizing, modernization, or capacity building of security forces. Since 2010 the UN Security Council has increasingly supported durable solutions for IDPs while recognizing that these should be coordinated with SSR and the disarmament, demobilization, and reintegration (DDR) of ex-combatants in wider post-conflict peacebuilding strategies.[37] A justice-sensitive approach to SSR similarly recognizes that concerns for justice, equity, and legitimacy may need to be figured into reforms at the earliest stages, not left until later, because they may directly impact the effectiveness of other reforms. For example, this is important both for encouraging returns and for rebuilding the bonds of community after return, when former combatants and the formerly displaced live next to one another, which has significant ramifications for DDR processes. Where former combatants have received retraining and resettlement, and in some instances payments to start new small businesses, former fighters may be perceived by returned and local communities as being unfairly rewarded for their roles in the conflict without any acknowledgment of abuses they may have inflicted on the civilian victims of war.[38] Consequently, if the broader goal of reintegration is to be achieved, it is vital that an appropriate balance govern the provision of assistance to different parties, civilian and ex-combatant, who were affected by the conflict. DDR programs should be coordinated with and if possible directly integrate reconciliation dimensions.[39]

Similarly, returns of refugees and IDPs to their places of origin hinges on their assurance of some measure of physical security and, at the very least, that state security forces will not engage in the types of human rights abuses that may have caused people to flee their homes and communities. Effective vetting of the worst perpetrators of crimes from police, military, and paramilitary forces is essential for applying some measure of accountability and rebuilding trust in and the legitimacy of the state. In some contexts, when documentary records are missing or have been destroyed, the involvement of communities through public appeals for information about proposed recruits, as happened in Liberia, is not only necessary for identifying perpetrators but also further gives people a sense that they are participating in the rebuilding of the state.

Displacement has largely been seen as a focus of humanitarian efforts. But as Roger Duthie notes, "humanitarian actors seek primarily to assist and protect the displaced, not to pursue accountability and redress for past human rights violations. The goals and the approach are different."[40] Using a transitional justice approach helps to broaden the frame in which we see displaced persons, from a classic humanitarian one to a rights-based one in which victims are seen as having rights to truth, justice, and reconciliation, as well as to humanitarian assistance and protection of basic physical needs including food, water, medicine, and shelter. JSSR, which focuses attention on measures that build integrity, accountability, legitimacy, and public participation in security and justice systems, clearly aligns with the concept of durable solutions, which has a long-term perspective regarding displaced persons' claims to security and justice. Solutions are inherently more durable for the wider community as well if they are inclusive, integrated, and holistic.

The convergence between the conceptual frameworks for addressing displacement and JSSR has been mirrored on the practical and operational levels of institutions involved in both fields, as a better understanding of the complexities of post-conflict peacebuilding and reconstruction has highlighted the need to address key elements of concern as early as possible—in peace negotiations or during stabilization missions, for example—and to transcend institutional and disciplinary boundaries. Thus, as sequences or phases of international assistance efforts have become progressively more blurred, the links between the traditionally humanitarian concerns of protection and finding durable solutions for displaced populations and the transitional justice concern of transforming security and justice systems in ways that offer legitimacy, accountability, integrity, and inclusion have strengthened.

JSSR ENGAGEMENT WITH DISPLACEMENT IN PRACTICE

When considering how, in practice, JSSR has met the security and justice needs of the displaced, it is useful to think in terms of the three temporal periods suggested by Robert Muggah.[41] The first of these, the prevention period, concerns the types of measures that can be implemented with the aim of preventing displacement from occurring in the first place. This category may be extremely broad, and its measures can include those aimed at general conflict prevention, though it also includes JSSR measures that could prevent secondary or multiple displacements. While recognizing the difficulty of proving a preventive or deterrent effect, one could argue that measures that do not succeed in preventing secondary displacement self-evidently fail to meet the criteria for durable solutions. Often the main cause of secondary displacement, as with displacement in the first instance, is threats to one's physical safety.[42] The rest of this chapter will therefore concentrate on the two other periods in which measures to address displacement can be applied: the immediate protection and durable solutions periods. To the extent that JSSR can prevent the recurrence of future abuses that lead to and are associated with displacement, it will primarily do so through its contribution in these two periods.

Interventions in the protection period address the immediate physical safety and security needs of the displaced while they are fleeing and once they have taken refuge from conflict or violence. As noted earlier, protection is a slippery concept because of its contested definition and different uses. I prefer to use the phrase *immediate protection from harm*, which more clearly focuses on the imminent risk of physical harm or violence. In this context, the international community has viewed civilian protection as a means of creating a safe environment for displaced persons and for humanitarian action, possibly through the mandating of international military or police in peacekeeping missions. These peacekeeping missions now emphasize division of roles, information sharing, and coordination among the many different international agencies and actors that take part. This section considers several examples of measures implemented during the protection phase and whether they have contained elements of JSSR. The focus here is on how specific efforts to meet the physical safety needs of the displaced have incorporated the values of legitimacy, accountability, integrity, and inclusion, which can contribute to wider efforts or longer-range processes of security or justice reform.

Activities in the durable solutions phase undertake to encourage returns or resettlement and serve the needs of the formerly displaced for long-term security and justice and political, economic, and social reintegration. As mentioned earlier, the requirement that durable solutions address the long-term safety and security of the displaced clearly reflects core concerns of JSSR in establishing or reestablishing security and justice institutions that are effective, nondiscriminatory, and sensitive to an abusive past. After examining the phase of meeting the immediate physical safety needs of displaced persons, this section looks at durable solutions for long-term security.

PROTECTION FROM HARM: MEETING THE IMMEDIATE SAFETY, SECURITY, AND JUSTICE NEEDS OF THE DISPLACED

The phase of immediate protection from harm covers the period when displaced persons flee their homes and seek refuge from the imminent threat or occurrence of violence, intimidation, or conflict. This subsection focuses on two settings: IDP and refugee camps, where many humanitarian efforts have focused to date, and unstable or post-conflict areas where displacement has occurred and where international peacekeeping missions are operating. Refugee and IDP camps are not commonly thought of as settings for SSR, but those responsible for refugee and IDP camps must contend with meeting the immediate safety needs of their inhabitants. As demonstrated in camps in Darfur and Chad, the effectiveness of immediate physical protection efforts in camp settings tends to be linked to the application of a holistic perspective linking security and justice efforts, efforts to tackle impunity and find means to hold perpetrators accountable, and the inclusiveness of processes in which the safety needs of various camp groups are considered.

In conflict and post-conflict environments, multidimensional integrated missions often work to ensure the physical safety of civilians, and particularly of displaced persons who are not housed in camps. Efforts by peacekeepers in the DRC to implement protection of civilians have included several innovations that have strengthened mission legitimacy in the eyes of local communities by improving communication between locals and peacekeepers. The missions have also achieved better inclusion of the views of populations at risk in the development of protection strategies. However, experience in the DRC also illustrates the failure to achieve accountability and end impunity for the myriad abuses committed against civilians, which has contributed to continued abuse.

REFUGEE AND IDP CAMPS: DARFUR AND CHAD

Forced migration camps are meant to serve as humanitarian spaces within which the displaced can receive relief and, ostensibly, protection from the international community. In reality, refugee and IDP camps, especially those located in fragile states, often are places of acute insecurity for the displaced who live in them and for humanitarian workers who seek to assist the camp populations. The physical threats encountered in these camps may include direct attacks by government or rebel forces because of the presence of combatants in the camps, and threats that result from the politicization and militarization of the camps, which turn them into sources of recruitment, funding, and support for combatant forces. Threats may also include armed raids by, for example, rebel groups to capture resources or hostages or to forcibly conscript fighters, including children. Other threats to the safety of displaced persons may involve intergroup violence and intimidation from elements inside the camps, including camp guards and vigilante groups that have formed in the absence of law and order. Refugee and IDP camps are often characterized by very weak rule of law and may have a negative economic, environmental, and social impact on local communities by placing added pressure on already limited resources or exacerbating already existing tensions, particularly if the displaced are viewed as lacking a shared group identity or affinity with the host population.[43] Physical threats may also arise from local actors in areas surrounding the camps and may include attacks on camp inhabitants when they venture out, such as when women collect firewood or walk to fields or markets. Without a means of enforcing basic law and order, crimes are carried out with impunity. These camps often feature high levels of sexual harassment, exploitation, and physical violence. Women, children, the elderly, and the disabled are especially vulnerable.[44] Even where there has been an international mandate to protect people in refugee and IDP camps, severe abuses have occurred, as recounted, for example, by Cambodian refugees living in camps in Thailand during the Cambodian civil war.[45] JSSR mechanisms have been introduced in camps in Darfur and Chad to protect the displaced from violence and other human rights violations with mixed results, and I will now examine these two cases in detail.

Sudan has been a site of massive displacement, with the largest number of internally displaced persons in the world. At the end of 2010, there were an estimated 4.5 to 5.2 million displaced persons in the country.[46] By 2008 the Darfur region alone contained 2.5 million IDPs, of which about one-third lived in large camps while the rest lived in smaller camps, in gatherings near villages, and in towns and villages among the local population.[47] The UN–African Union Mission in Darfur (UNAMID), the joint peace support mission that replaced the African Union Mission in Sudan (AMIS) at the beginning of 2008, is mandated to "contribute to the protection of civilian populations under imminent threat of physical violence and prevent attacks against civilians, within its capability and areas of deployment."[48] UNAMID responded to an acute need for protection of civilians, particularly of IDPs in Darfur, who had suffered through five years of conflict and acute insecurity because of continuing aerial and ground attacks by rebel groups and government forces, intertribal conflict, and increasing rates of criminality and banditry.

Some of these camps became zones of acute insecurity rather than refuge. Kalma IDP camp in Darfur, established in 2004, became heavily politicized and rife with criminal activity, rival armed elements, and violence against minorities. Government raids on Kalma and other camps also made IDPs vulnerable to forced relocation or being prevented from returning to the camps after fleeing the raids.[49] This insecurity prompted UNAMID to maintain a constant twenty-four-hour presence in the camp and attempt to depoliticize it. The mission also launched a community policing program, complemented by workshops and roundtable meetings with camp sheikhs (leaders elected by the camp inhabitants), the general camp population, and members of groups often excluded from camp decisionmaking—women, youth representatives, teachers—to foster in them a sense of collective responsibility for security and to discourage tolerance for criminality, arms, and political violence within the camp.[50] UNAMID further set out to create specific "gender desks" at the community policing centers in IDP camps, supported by female police advisers who were to be trained and deployed as gender officers. Gender advisers meet regularly with women in IDP camps on gender-based violence (GBV) and to encourage them to report GBV cases to police, both local and international. Police gender advisers follow up cases reported to local police and assist them with the appropriate procedures.[51] Another UNAMID initiative to increase protection in IDP camps in Darfur was the introduction of "firewood escorts," or less frequently, "harvest patrols," to dissuade banditry, attacks, and abductions of camp inhabitants who venture from the camp to collect firewood for their stoves and walk to the fields to tend their crops. Women are particularly vulnerable to sexual attacks when they leave the camps.

The initiatives undertaken by UNAMID to improve the physical safety of IDPs appeared to have some positive effect. Once UNAMID increased its presence and activities in Kalma camp, reported criminal activity declined sharply.[52] Empirical evidence from other studies also indicates that through the deployment of additional troops in 2009, UNAMID was able to provide increased physical protection by expanding the territory in which it was present, conducting night patrols, and maintaining a police presence in more than fifteen IDP camps.[53] However, impact was also linked to the sustainability of the initiatives. Introduction of patrols accompanying women from Kalma camp to collect firewood decreased attacks and increased the women's feelings of physical safety. But IDPs also noted that the patrols were too short and sporadic in nature, and the women were again vulnerable to attack when unescorted.[54] Similarly, in camps where there was no twenty-four-hour presence, which relied on the use of international contingents of formed police units (FPUs), violence and intimidation were commonly experienced after dark.[55] Such initiatives failed when they were inconsistent, not well communicated, or rejected by residents. Moreover, the firewood and harvest patrols did not address underlying causes of the attacks on inhabitants who left the camps, which often involved conflict between the camps and pastoralist groups in the surrounding areas over access to resources.[56] Without mediation efforts, or improved efforts to apprehend, arrest, and try perpetrators of attacks outside of camps, patrols or escorts were merely a stopgap measure, with inconsistent and temporary effects on physical safety.

Measures to address immediate physical safety needs of the displaced, then, need to be built into broader strategies for addressing underlying drivers of conflict. Involving camp residents in discussions about their safety and how they can cooperate with community policing is potentially empowering for residents—such discussions informed UNAMID patrols and other security measures in Darfur. UNAMID's police also supported "Police Reform and Restructuring" seminars aimed at reforming and building the capacity and professionalism of local police so that they could effectively fulfill policing functions in accordance with international human rights standards, especially for vulnerable groups, including women and children. UNAMID sought to monitor all cases reported to the local police as well.[57] However, it is unclear whether the police reform seminars were focused on the need to address the day-to-day threats to physical safety faced by IDPs in the camps, and whether the seminars were effective in influencing local police behavior. More research is needed to establish the extent to which police reform initiatives have affected the safety of camp inhabitants.

One of the most notable examples of improved efforts to create a safe environment for refugees and IDPs, particularly in the context of international peacekeeping operations, has been underway in Chad since 2007. William O'Neill describes the development of the Détachement Intégré de Sécurité (DIS), a special national police unit with members selected from the Chadian police and gendarmerie who were then trained and mentored by international peacekeepers in the UN Mission in the Central African Republic and Chad (MINURCAT) to provide security in refugee and IDP camps, as well as for UN employees and humanitarian workers in eastern Chad.[58] The DIS was professional, well trained, and responsive to the needs of camp inhabitants in implementing community policing programs in the camps. It also was mandated to provide escorts to humanitarian workers, and there are some indications that those duties may have absorbed much of the unit's attention at the expense of IDP safety. Nevertheless, the DIS has generally been considered a successful innovation that improved security for refugees and IDPs housed in camps. The deliberate inclusion of female officers proved to be vital for connecting with women in the camps on sexual and gender-based violence (SGBV) issues. The international community directly influenced the selection, training, and monitoring of the DIS, a likely factor in its success.[59]

While the DIS may serve as a model for future UN peacekeeping operations, there are nevertheless several grounds for caution regarding its experience. First, in response to the increased security provided to the camps and humanitarian actors by the DIS, bandits adapted by moving further west and focusing more on local populations living beyond the unit's operating zone. Bandits did make fewer attempts to rob and carjack humanitarians within that zone, but those attacks were carried out with higher levels of violence than before.[60] The DIS increased safety and security for the camp inhabitants, but without corresponding measures for public security beyond its area of responsibility, attacks by armed bands were merely pushed further out into those communities lacking such protection.

The second reason to be cautious regarding the DIS model is that focusing narrowly on the unit's successful role in preventing and responding to crimes within the camp and the surrounding area misses the broader picture of a dysfunctional and discriminatory criminal justice system. The courts and formal justice system do not reach all areas in eastern Chad, and prisons, where they exist, are insecure. MINURCAT sought to strengthen Chad's formal justice system through its Judicial Advisory Unit (JAU) by supporting DIS training on proper investigation techniques and reporting procedures, as well as by training nonprofessional and auxiliary judges and building and refurbishing courthouses. Nevertheless, the DIS's effectiveness in upholding law and order was broadly impeded by the weakness of the formal justice system, which translated into a continuing problem with impunity. Furthermore, local authorities and justice structures tend to "discriminate against lower-class Chadians, while granting amnesty to certain ethnic groups as well as high-ranking army officials."[61]

The fear of discrimination in the formal justice system led refugee women to seek recourse in traditional justice mechanisms, such as family- or community-based arbitration arrangements. However, the traditional justice system, which typically handles most cases of domestic violence, was viewed by international observers as problematic and the "weak link" in the judicial response to SGBV. In an attempt to improve the neutrality of processes and improve access to justice for victims of SGBV, MINURCAT implemented a mobile court system. But the mobile courts, which required the training of judicial personnel, were perceived as threatening the authority of provincial officials, who traditionally enjoyed absolute power throughout the areas under their control.[62]

Additionally, problems existed in the relationship between the DIS and the regular Chadian police and gendarmerie. O'Neill notes the confusion over the DIS's jurisdiction and chain of command, as the organization was popularly associated with the UN because of its close relationship with the mission, though it was formally under government control. The DIS also aroused resentment in the Chadian police and gendarmerie forces because it was a privileged unit. At the time of MINURCAT's withdrawal from Chad, there were concerns that, despite the commitment of the Chadian government to take over support of the DIS, this effective and well-trained unit would collapse and its well-equipped, unemployed former members could resort to banditry.[63] These concerns have been allayed to some extent by the development of a joint program run by the United Nations Development Program (UNDP) and UNHCR to continue providing funding, training, and equipment to the DIS.[64]

The example of the DIS in Chad illustrates the interrelated nature of security and justice problems and that solutions cannot focus only on one institutional element of either sector but must be developed and coordinated within the broader context of interlinked security and justice processes. This is particularly true of the policing and justice systems, as the Chad example and others have repeatedly shown that reforms in one sector may be limited or even undermined by failure to introduce corresponding reforms in the other.

MINURCAT's mandate focused on protecting civilians, with three main components: (1) the use of a military force mandated to improve security and contribute to protecting civilians in danger, especially refugees and IDPs, (2) the establishment of the DIS to ensure security in and around IDP and refugee camp sites, and (3) the development of the justice system's capacity through deployment of a MINURCAT civilian component. Thus, long-term reform of state institutions, specifically in the justice sector, was part of the mission's mandate. The DIS proved a partial solution to some of the security problems faced by a segment of the population, and it had the potential for spreading good practices to other parts of the police and gendarmerie. But although MINURCAT addressed some aspects of capacity building in the formal justice sector, training lower-level judicial officials and building courthouses, the impunity gap remained throughout much of eastern Chad while the DIS was operating. A justice-sensitive approach to SSR in this context includes ensuring accountability for SGBV abuses through the formal or traditional justice system. The creation of mobile courts, while responsive especially to the needs of female victims of sexual violence, also demonstrated the relevance of the political context in which security and justice reforms take place and the capacity of political actors to undermine reforms. At the same time, judicial reform is notoriously slow to achieve and invariably proceeds more slowly than police reform,[65] highlighting an inherent challenge in any holistic approach to reforming both police and justice institutions.

DISPLACEMENT, PROTECTION OF CIVILIANS, AND INTEGRATED MISSIONS

Complex, integrated peacekeeping missions present one of the most promising contexts for developing multidimensional (military, police, civilian) mechanisms to protect civilians facing the threat of imminent violence, a category that often includes displaced populations or those at risk of being displaced. While protection of civilians has been a component of virtually all peacekeeping mandates since 1999, in reality, lack of political agreement among UN member states on how to define civilian protection, the absence of concrete guidance for the implementation of protection of civilians mandates, and inadequate training and resourcing for protection roles has resulted in a situation where there is still more high-level rhetoric than action.[66] Despite these problems, certain peacekeeping missions, such as the one in the DRC, have made various attempts to improve their approach to the protection of civilians mandate.

The DRC, particularly in its eastern provinces, remains a place of extreme violence and insecurity, with some 1.7 million IDPs in the North and South Kivu provinces as of July 2011.[67] In the past, despite having as part of its Chapter 7 mandate the authorization to take necessary action to "protect civilians under imminent threat of physical violence,"[68] the UN peacekeeping mission in the DRC has often failed to do so. This situation is not unique to the DRC; there is a now well-documented gap between the objective of protecting civilians from imminent harm, present in most UN peacekeeping mandates, and its operationalization on the ground.[69]

Nevertheless, some important innovations have recently improved the prospects for effective UN action with regard to civilian protection in the DRC. These include the creation of Joint Protection Teams (JPT), made up of representatives from the civilian agencies and departments (political affairs, civil affairs, DDR, human rights, and child protection) in addition to police and military components of the mission, which are deployed to an area where civilians are threatened and produce a joint assessment of the threat that is then used for military planning by MONUC (subsequently MONUSCO). In addition to improving situational awareness and contributing to security plans more tailored to local conditions, the JPTs are considered to have created a better working relationship between the peacekeeping troops and the local population, and to have significantly improved implementation of the protection-of-civilians mandate.[70] Another innovation is the establishment of Community Liaison Interpreters, subsequently renamed Community Liaison Assistants (CLAs)—locally recruited UN staff who function as the link between local communities and the UN mission. In addition to acting as the eyes and ears of the mission, reporting on crimes and abuses that take place in local communities, CLAs provide an insider's understanding of local politics to the mission commander. The CLAs are considered a highly effective means of engaging with the local community, which tends to trust them and find them more accessible than international mission personnel.[71]

Holistic team approaches to needs assessment and liaison mechanisms with local communities are admittedly modest advances. At the same time, though, events in the DRC also demonstrate how a flawed SSR process can perpetuate and even compound abuses of vulnerable populations. One example is provided by the integration of former combatant forces into the Armed Forces of the DRC (FARDC). According to the process of "brassage," or military integration, former members of rebel militias should join and be retrained with FARDC soldiers to form integrated brigades. Linked to the DDR process of civilian reintegration of former combatants, brassage was developed as a key component of overall military reform and SSR in the DRC. However, it has faced continuing difficulties, including the failure to apply vetting and retraining to former combatants as well as a process that has become known as "mixage," which was initiated by dissident general Laurent Nkunda in late 2006 when he agreed to mix his battalions with those of the FARDC while leaving existing command and control structures in place, thereby undermining integration into the FARDC and enabling his forces to remain in control in North Kivu.[72] Mixage enabled Nkunda's forces to remain in control of key mining, farming, and cattle areas and to pose severe risks to the civilian population in the area. Nkunda's political organization, the National Congress for the Defence of the People (CNDP), further exacerbated land disputes in the region by applying civil land laws that conflicted with traditional land allocation practices. The CNDP split in 2009 and one faction was integrated into the FARDC, again without adequate vetting to identify and remove human rights abusers.[73]

The prospect of protracted internal displacement and political pressures on states to demonstrate progress has in various contexts resulted in forced returns of IDPs even when conditions do not provide for voluntary, safe, or dignified return. In settings like the eastern DRC, where civilians have been subjected to armed attacks, rapes, forced labor, and looting by all sides in the conflict, resulting in recurrent mass displacement, forced returns of IDPs have been driven by pressures, threats, and intimidation from both rebel forces and Congolese authorities. CNDP forces have intimidated and continued to commit abuses against IDPs in order to force their apparent return, in an effort to demonstrate to national and international audiences that territory under its control can now be considered to offer safe conditions for return. The use of threats and the destruction of IDP camps in North Kivu by CNDP combatants or local residents forced many of the area's displaced to leave (before the arrival of CNDP, there were twenty-seven thousand people living in camps and unofficial sites and more than twenty-five thousand living with host families in the area), including some twelve thousand displaced persons surrounding a MONUC base, who were intimidated into leaving but shortly thereafter returned, having nowhere else to go and having received no assistance.[74]

Similarly, in 2009 the Congolese army launched the second phase of a military operation, supported by the UN peacekeeping mission MONUC, aimed at defeating the mainly Hutu militia, the Forces Démocratiques de Libération du Rwanda (FDLR). In September 2009, in Goma, eastern Congo, Congolese authorities claimed that the areas it had taken from the FDLR were safe for people displaced by the conflict to return to. The authorities consequently closed five of the seven official IDP camps around Goma. The inhabitants of those camps, numbering some sixty thousand people, were pressured by the authorities to leave immediately—a process facilitated by raids of the camps conducted by armed police and youth gangs, which looted, destroyed camp structures, and wounded IDPs who had not yet left. According to Human Rights Watch, the camps had important symbolic value, as they "had become an almost obligatory stop on diplomatic or other high-level visits to eastern Congo and a continuous embarrassment for President Joseph Kabila, eager to show that his government had brought peace to the east."[75] Closing the camps supported the claim of some Western diplomats that the UN-backed Congolese army operation Kimia 2 had produced sufficiently safe and secure conditions to enable IDPs in the camps and Congolese refugees in Rwanda to spontaneously return home.[76] In reality, little was known about where camp residents went once they left the camps or how many returned to their villages of origin, and in retrospect, humanitarian workers acknowledge that government pressure along with other factors such as reduced humanitarian assistance for IDP camp residents and assistance incentives in return areas combined to empty the camps.[77]

These examples from the DRC demonstrate how the displaced can be intimidated and the process of return manipulated, forced, and falsely portrayed as voluntary by parties with their own agendas. Furthermore, the rapprochement between CNDP and the Congolese government resulted in an incomplete integration of the rebel group into the FARDC, which lacked both a vetting mechanism aimed at removing those linked to human rights abuses and a retraining process. Human Rights Watch found many IDPs fearful of returning to areas ostensibly controlled by the government but in practice under the control of CNDP forces that had "integrated" with the army: "they retain their positions, continue to pursue their political agendas, and perpetuate abusive practices—only now under the cover of the name of the state."[78]

DURABLE SOLUTIONS: MEETING THE LONG-TERM SAFETY, SECURITY, AND JUSTICE NEEDS OF THE DISPLACED

This section examines measures intended to achieve durable solutions that would enable displaced persons to return to their places of origin, integrate locally, or resettle elsewhere, including in another country. It specifically considers contexts in which durable solutions have resulted in part from security sector reforms that have been justice-sensitive. In Kosovo, attempts to secure adequate representation of minorities in the police helped to reestablish legitimacy and trust but were not sufficient to encourage returns of many IDPs. In

Bosnia, a reselection process in the judiciary did contribute to return in areas that had been ethnically cleansed during the war. In Liberia and Afghanistan, justice-sensitive approaches have sought to ensure that property restitution and dispute resolution are sustainable, inclusive, and legitimate. In Colombia, the Constitutional Court has demonstrated the potential role of judicial oversight—and governance more broadly—in establishing access to effective remedies and justice for the displaced. The section also examines displacement in urban environments, which tends to be neglected by the humanitarian and SSR communities but is nevertheless where the majority of the displaced tend to flee and settle.

ADEQUATE REPRESENTATION OF MINORITIES IN POLICE ORGANIZATIONS

Durable solutions to displacement cannot be achieved without a basic level of security in the place of return, integration, or settlement, and basic security cannot exist without institutions capable of providing for the safety of the community and enforcing the rule of law in a nondiscriminatory and accountable manner. As Madeline England describes, the Organization for Security and Cooperation in Europe (OSCE) applied a justice-sensitive approach to SSR in creating a new police force in Kosovo that would be representative of the diversity of Kosovar society and, being more inclusive, would also enjoy greater public trust and legitimacy.[79] A police service that contains more representation of minority groups is more likely to be responsive to the needs of all Kosovars, not merely those of the ethnic majority.

Representation in and legitimacy of the police were of particular urgency for the reconstruction and democratization of post-conflict Kosovo. When Serbian president Slobodan Milosevic revoked Kosovo's status as an autonomous province in the Federal Republic of Yugoslavia in 1989, most ethnic Albanian police officers were either expelled from the police force or resigned from it. The police force was then abolished, and responsibility for law enforcement was transferred to the Serbian Ministry of Interior. Severe human rights abuses were subsequently committed by the Serbian police, military, and paramilitary forces against the ethnic Albanian population, leading to NATO's military intervention in 1999.

The OSCE, in coordination with the UN Interim Administration Mission in Kosovo, recognized in the aftermath of the intervention that the development of a representative and legitimate local police force was a top priority. The target for recruitment of women and minorities was set at 15 percent. Furthermore, a significant number of former police who had been expelled or resigned in 1989 were brought back as police officers, after receiving training in democratic policing and human rights. While the Kosovo Liberation Army originally demanded that its members constitute the entire police organization, agreement was eventually reached that they would be allocated 50 percent of all positions. Applicants had to have a high-school education, reside in Kosovo, be physically and mentally fit, and have no criminal history. A vetting procedure was implemented to exclude anyone with extremist views, with screening carried out by the OSCE through interviews, written examinations, medical exams, psychological tests, and background investigations.[80] The Kosovo Police Service (KPS) made consistent and focused efforts to recruit Kosovo Serbs and members of other ethnic minorities, and the 15 percent target was reached in mid-2001. Kosovo Serbs now comprise about 10 percent, other ethnic minorities about 6 percent, and women 13.8 percent (there were none before 1999) of the KPS (renamed following the unilateral declaration of independence by Kosovo in February 2008).[81] The Kosovo Police has consistently enjoyed one of the highest rates of public confidence and trust among all of Kosovo's state institutions.

Nevertheless, a 2006 poll indicated that while there was general satisfaction with the KPS, Kosovo Serbs still distrusted the police force and believed it did not meet the needs of their community.[82] This is a problem linked not only to the police but more broadly to the justice system, as there is widespread lack of trust and confidence in the judiciary resulting from a large number of backlogged cases, perceptions of endemic corruption, ethnic bias displayed by court officials, and weak representation of minorities in the judiciary.[83] As England notes, a population migration along ethnic lines has taken place within Kosovo, with members of minority communities generally settling in areas where they represent the majority. Kosovo Serbs have mostly settled in the northern municipalities, while Kosovo Albanians have concentrated and settled in the south. There are also indications that composition of the KPS in these localities has tended to mirror the divided concentration of ethnic groups in Kosovo.[84]

While a representative police force may encourage a greater sense of personal safety, the KPS has been unable to overcome perceptions that the broader justice system is dysfunctional, corrupt, and biased. The KPS generally enjoys public confidence in Kosovo, though to a lesser extent among Kosovo Serbs. A broader and longer-term perspective may be required in order to see the full results of the minority-representation emphasis in the police; reconciliation between ethnic communities may require much longer than the ten to fifteen years examined here. The broader systemic problems that continue to afflict the rule-of-law sector in Kosovo, however, including politicization and abuse of office in both the police and justice systems, constitute convincing explanations for the migration and de facto segregation of ethnic Serb and ethnic Albanian communities in Kosovo and the failure of many IDPs to return to their places of origin.[85]

JUDICIAL VETTING AND RESELECTION

Integrity vetting of personnel is applicable to different security and justice sector actors. Vetting the judiciary is less common and more complex than vetting the police or military, yet the establishment of a neutral, professional judiciary can be essential to convincing returnees that they will enjoy rights and justice to the same degree as their neighbors, and more generally to restoring confidence in the core institutions of a post-conflict state.

As a result of ethnic cleansing during the 1992–95 conflict in Bosnia, about one-half of the population was displaced and not encouraged to return. Following the war, international institutions sought to promote substantial minority returns as a fundamental means of consolidating stability, peace, and reconciliation in Bosnia. However, local authorities posed a significant obstruction to minority returns through the frequently sectarian control they exercised over policing and public security, the legal system and judiciary, and public authorities that enforced property rights and laws, access to public services such as health care and pensions, and the provision of essential public utilities.[86]

Among the displaced were many judges and prosecutors. In particular, many non-Serbs were required to leave the territory of what became the Republika Srpska and either did not return or were discouraged from returning after the war. Appointments to the judiciary across Bosnia and Herzegovina had been made often on the basis of ethnicity or political considerations. The judiciary therefore lacked independence and was not ethnically representative of the society—instead, it was overwhelmingly constituted of members of the ethnic majority, raising concerns about access to justice of minority citizens and returnees. Physical intimidation of minority returnees was often ignored by monoethnic local police, prosecutors, and courts.[87] The Dayton Agreement only partially addressed judicial reform, leaving a problematic judiciary in place. Efforts to monitor the courts and identify and remove incompetent judges or those with ethnic biases and other disciplinary issues proved ineffective. Thus, the composition of the judiciary in Bosnia and Herzegovina, with its ramifications for the institution's integrity and legitimacy, was of direct concern to returnees.

Following two failed attempts to reform the judiciary, a third and more aggressive effort involved reselection. The Office of the High Representative (OHR) commissioned an expert review that determined that a restructuring of the judiciary would be necessary to bring the number of judges in line with European standards. High judicial councils, based on the continental model, would be created to prevent political interference in the justice system. High judicial councils are self-governing bodies entrusted with the appointment, training, promotion, transfer, and removal of judges and prosecutors. The model is based on the principle that judicial independence is better served by entrusting governance of the judiciary to a body composed mostly of judges and prosecutors, rather than to the ministry of justice. Although specific models vary in the degree of influence exercised by the ministry of justice, all countries that have undergone democratic transition and consolidation have introduced such a body to ensure the independence of the judiciary. Thus, in Bosnia's reselection process, all current judges and prosecutors were required to reapply for their positions and undergo a comprehensive valuation—by the new High Judicial and Prosecutorial Councils (HJPCs) created in 2002.

Reselection can be understood as a fairly robust subset of screening or vetting to exclude from public service individuals who do not meet basic employment criteria. These criteria in the Bosnian example were clear and transparent, with appointments for judicial and prosecutorial posts based on merit alone. The reselection procedure turned sitting judges and prosecutors into applicants in an open competition with external applicants for a limited number of new positions. The burden fell to these applicants to demonstrate why they should be selected for their own or any other job in the judiciary.

According to Christopher Harland, the reselection system had at least four positive outcomes. First, judges who were suspected of the most serious types of misconduct were not retained or decided not to reapply. Second, 20 percent of those appointed were not incumbents. Overall, some four hundred judges and prosecutors lost their positions, while some two hundred new candidates were appointed. Moreover, about 80 percent of those appointed to leadership positions (chief prosecutors, court presidents) did not hold those positions prior to reselection. Third, the ethnicity of judges and prosecutors changed significantly, especially in the Republika Srpska, where Serbs represented 56 percent of judges and prosecutors prior to the war, 91 percent of judges and prosecutors after the war and ethnic cleansing and ethnicity-based appointments, and finally, 66 percent after the reappointment system. And fourth, the procedure generated a large number of public complaints (regarding incompetence, errors, bias, and misconduct) about the preexisting judiciary, helping to better fine-tune the reselection procedures and other judicial reform efforts more broadly.[88]

Although there were some problems with the reselection procedure, it can nevertheless be credited with increasing the independence of the judiciary (judges are now accountable to other judges, not politicians), bringing Bosnia and Herzegovina closer to the European Union, creating a more competent judiciary that enjoys higher levels of public trust, and establishing in the HJPCs a now fully locally owned judicial appointment, promotion, and removal body (involving only Bosnia and Herzegovina nationals as judges and prosecutors). By seeking to remove ethnic bias, politicized appointments, and incompetence in the judiciary, the reselection procedure contributed to rebuilding public confidence in the integrity and inclusive (nonethnically biased) character of the Bosnian state justice system. By improving access to justice for all Bosnians through a more neutral, representative, and professional judiciary, reselection also contributed to a durable solution for formerly displaced persons who returned to areas that had been ethnically cleansed during the war.

LAND AND PROPERTY RESTITUTION AND DISPUTE RESOLUTION

Restoring land and property rights is a major challenge for displaced persons, and resolution of land disputes is an essential component of durable solutions. Disputes over housing and land ownership are a major source of conflict between returnees and those who in their absence have occupied their land, sometimes including relatives who stayed behind. Land disputes are common within and between families, communities, tribes, ethnic groups, armed groups, and the government. Without access to land and the ability to sustain themselves and their families, returnees are likely to become secondarily displaced. While restitution of housing, property, and land is the subject of a separate chapter in this volume,[89] it can also have underaddressed but important links to JSSR. Settling land and property disputes and providing access to justice for violations of land and property rights through formal justice, traditional/customary justice, or alternative dispute-resolution mechanisms is often necessary. How such settlements and access are sought can be affected by SSR. Whether facilitating access to existing mechanisms, improving existing mechanisms, or developing new ones, a justice-sensitive approach seeks to ensure that dispute resolution is sustainable, inclusive, and legitimate.

The situation in Liberia offers one example, where more than one million people were displaced during the 1989–2003 civil war, and access to land was a key factor underpinning the conflict. Although all IDPs have now returned, many land conflicts remain unresolved, with people who returned to villages finding that others have occupied their land. These disputes exist across Liberia and are sustaining tensions and frequently violence within and between communities. Judicial remedies are difficult to access and enforce, are costly and slow, and tend to inflame tensions rather than calm them. Informal remedies are often biased by elite interests and therefore do not enjoy widespread trust. Formal SSR processes have done little if anything to resolve land disputes. As noted by England, the formulation of Liberia's National Security Strategy (NSS) in 2008 failed to integrate durable solutions for returnees and the displaced. And while the NSS was framed within the National Poverty Reduction Strategy, this too failed to address the needs of the most vulnerable in Liberian society, including the displaced.[90] Thus, unresolved land disputes, one of the biggest sources of insecurity to returned and displaced Liberians and one the most predictable drivers of internal conflict, were ignored in two major initiatives seeking to strengthen the security of the Liberian people.

A traditional approach to SSR would focus on strengthening the laws, policies, and institutions relating to the regulation and administration of land in Liberia—that is, reforming land governance. However, one NGO, the Norwegian Refugee Council (NRC), has implemented an approach that is more focused on inclusiveness and empowerment of the displaced. NRC seeks to build the capacity of individuals, communities, and institutions involved in land disputes. It teaches not only displaced individuals but also local customary leaders as well as local and state authorities involved in land administration about mediation in resolution of land disputes.[91] Facilitating access to justice in this way involves helping individuals articulate their legal rights and interests during the settlement process and increasing the capacity of local authorities, formal and customary, to mediate and resolve disputes effectively.

Similarly, in Afghanistan, where refugees and IDPs have often been absent from their land and property for years or even decades, returnees face major obstacles in reclaiming land that has been occupied or sold, sometimes repeatedly by different parties and sometimes to local warlords and other powerful elites. In this largely agrarian country, where land is the key to one's ability to maintain a livelihood, land ownership is closely linked to both economic and political power. Afghanistan's high population growth rate and massive returns of refugees and IDPs have increased pressure on land and fuelled conflicts surrounding its ownership and use.[92] Attempting to resolve land disputes through the formal justice system is extremely challenging, in part because of confusing land laws and regulations—some of which are contradictory, introduced by different regimes over several decades—and a contentious system of land ownership, the result of past seizures of land by some regimes and its redistribution to political and military elites. Because the formal justice system in Afghanistan remains extremely weak and distrusted, especially in rural areas, about 80 percent of legal cases end up before traditional dispute resolution mechanisms (*jirgas* and *shuras*). These customary justice mechanisms tend to discriminate against women, among other problems. Returnees and the displaced are disproportionately affected by these systemic problems in accessing justice, whether formal or customary, for resolution of land disputes.[93]

Again, NRC's pragmatic approach seeks to address the immediate need of the displaced and returnees to resolve land disputes while simultaneously working to strengthen formal justice mechanisms and promote settlements that are equitable and fair for both men and women. NRC offers free legal assistance to returnees and the displaced to facilitate access to justice, working with cases in both the formal and customary justice systems. Furthermore, recognizing that improving the formal justice system will be a long-term process, NRC provides training to both legal professionals (judges and lawyers) and community elders on resolution of land and property disputes, with the objective of achieving fair outcomes through the appropriate application of Afghanistan's codified laws and Shari'a, rather than through the traditional informal system that often discriminates against female owners and claimants.[94] In facilitating fair resolution of land disputes for male and female IDPs, NRC's approach is inclusive and empowering and therefore justice sensitive.

NON-STATE AUTHORITY IN URBAN ENVIRONMENTS

The majority of displaced persons do not live in camps. They live outside camps with host families or dispersed in large urban environments. Often relocating clandestinely from official refugee and IDP camps, the displaced in urban environments are not formally separated from the local community and may therefore be invisible to the international community. Living invisibly alongside economic migrants and other residents of poor communities, squatter slums, and shantytowns, the displaced tend to receive little assistance and are believed to be among the poorest and most vulnerable in post-conflict urban settings. When they lack documentation, refugees and IDPs are particularly vulnerable, often suffering discrimination, unemployment, and lack of access to basic services.[95] Some cities, such as Khartoum (with an estimated 1 to 1.2 million IDPs), have no system for IDP registration, nor any means of tracking the displaced, many of whom live in dire circumstances. Urban refugees and IDPs frequently lack the strong social networks on which they would normally draw for information, material, and psychological support. Impoverishment further isolates the displaced in urban settings. When host municipalities lack the resources to meet the basic needs of displaced populations, as in Colombia, criminal gangs may emerge—or may be perceived to emerge—from among them, creating fear and resentment among the host population and resulting in harassment of the displaced by authorities and local security forces.[96] Refugees and IDPs may also be subjected to harassment by the civilian population and "are more likely to be the victims of looting, intimidation and extortion by militia and criminal groups in the urban area."[97]

Providing for basic safety and justice needs of the displaced in urban settings poses distinct challenges in terms of involving local authorities. Local "authorities," meaning those who exercise de facto control in a community, may or may not be state actors. In post-conflict and fragile states, state police and security forces may be inadequate or even absent from large urban slums. Refugees and IDPs may encounter the same broad levels of insecurity as their nondisplaced neighbors in terms of the absence of state security and justice systems or the presence of abusive and corrupt police and courts. Self-policing arrangements, or non-state community-level security initiatives, typically emerge in large urban slums. These may range from neighborhood watch-type arrangements to community patrols to vigilante groups and criminal gangs. In settings where central state authority has collapsed, local communities may respond to the absence of state systems and services with informal arrangements for local safety and justice. For example, after the collapse of the central governmental authority in Somalia, policing-type functions were provided by "a variety of overlapping and fluid local authorities—ranging from militia to clan elders, Mafia-like rackets, and fundamentalist mosques."[98]

Informal or self-policing arrangements are recognized as shaping the physical safety and security of many post-conflict environments but have not been well studied to date. Ordinary citizens, seeking to defend themselves against violent and criminal behavior in an environment where the state is unable or unwilling to protect them, may create private self-defense units, vigilante groups, or local civil militia groups.[99] There is a need to look at the specific informal structures that have emerged to provide some measure of security or justice in these areas. Such informal, non-state structures may be community based or may emerge less palatably from criminal gangs or as private commercial initiatives. Non-state providers of physical protection or justice may be perceived as legitimate by the local community but may not uphold human rights principles. Community leaders may constitute the ruling authorities but may not dispense justice neutrally. In the absence of state capacity, how should non-state actors—whether customary leaders or leaders of armed groups—be engaged to better meet the security and justice needs of the displaced and returnees? Each situation must be assessed, and some displacement researchers maintain that popular non-state formations such as vigilante groups and civil militias should be monitored to ensure they are not committing abuses against those whom they ostensibly are protecting in the absence of state security institutions.[100]

Displaced persons are often new arrivals in communities and become more vulnerable when the host community experiences tensions and conflict, commonly over increased pressure on existing resources. In some contexts, displaced persons and returnees add further pressures to existing intercommunal tensions. In Dili, the capital of Timor-Leste, massive unregulated population growth, in part because of people returning after previous periods of conflict, has intensified communal tensions resulting from unequal access to resources, competition over land and markets, and unemployment. In this complex and fluid situation, security—though also insecurity—is provided informally by groups of remobilized veterans and youths, martial arts groups, and numerous gangs. In urban Dili, a recent survey found that residents often were least likely to turn to police for security and safety, and that traditional authorities were the preferred means of resolving local disputes. However, resorting to traditional authorities is not a clear-cut means of accessing security or justice, given the transient nature of the communities in which traditional leaders live.[101] Some efforts to defuse future violence, which have met with some success, have used mediation involving traditional ceremonies and authorities such as village chiefs. But martial arts groups and gangs have not been involved in these initiatives.[102] Furthermore, given a history of periodic outbreaks of collective violence, the continuing, almost complete impunity of the perpetrators of past violence is considered an important factor in predicting future urban violence.[103]

One approach to bridging divisions and mediating tensions has focused on strengthening the relationship between the displaced and host communities through the development of community safety processes, which bring both groups together and seek to encourage dialogue and strengthen the capacities of the community as a whole to resolve disputes and conflicts peacefully. This approach has been applied even where non-state armed groups constitute the de facto local governing authority. In Somalia, a failed state whose population has been subjected to years of civil war, poverty, and famine, the security of large IDP populations is frequently in the hands of non-state armed groups who control large areas of state territory. In this context, where the

Transitional Federal Government in Mogadishu has been unable to establish its authority over the entire country in the face of resistance from Al Shabaab, some international actors supporting SSR have moved beyond the state-centric paradigm to engage with non-state armed groups. Where such a group is perceived locally as the legitimate governing authority, these actors have engaged with it to help it more effectively serve the security and justice needs of the local population, including the displaced.

An example from Somalia is provided by a Danish NGO, Danish Demining Group (DDG), which works with the non-state armed group Ahlu-Sunna Wal-Jamaa (ASWJ), the governing authority in South Galkayo, the capital of Galmudug State. Galmudug State is a self-declared administration established by clan elders and ASWJ following the 2006 defeat of Mogadishu warlords. ASWJ provides security in the area administered by Galmudug State. South Galkayo contains many IDPs, and although past relations with the host community were good because of clan loyalties, the growing number of displaced persons threatens to increase both pressure on local resources and tensions with the host community. DDG operates in several ways to improve community safety. For example, it works with two communities in South Galkayo to develop safety plans through participatory processes that give voice to IDPs and other members of each community in meeting inhabitants' safety and justice needs. DDG has also provided training in conflict management and helped to establish community-based policing committees that serve as a link between formal security institutions (police officers trained and employed by the ASWJ-run Galmudug State) and informal security institutions (the clan leaders, to whom many in the community still turn in the event of a crime).[104] This case demonstrates that ensuring the physical safety of displaced persons in complex environments where there is no discernible formal state presence may require working with what does exist—informal and customary authorities—and that even in such challenging environments, inclusive and participatory approaches can be used to give voice to the concerns of the displaced and contribute to intracommunal dialogue.

ACCESS TO EFFECTIVE REMEDIES AND JUSTICE

One of the key criteria for a durable solution is that displaced persons, as victims of human rights violations, have full and nondiscriminatory access to effective remedies. The case of Colombia stands as a leading example of the role of law and the courts in seeking effective remedies and justice for displaced persons. Colombia's Constitutional Court has in effect conducted continuous oversight of the government's response to internal displacement. The court's judgments have relied specifically on the Guiding Principles on Internal Displacement to determine the scope of IDP rights and the extent of state obligations to promote those rights and have been key influences on policies regarding internal displacement.

By the end of 2010, Colombia was vying with Sudan as the country with the most internally displaced persons in the world, numbering between 3.6 and 5.2 million.[105] Because of the country's long history of internal conflict, there has been a constant flow of displaced persons, usually from rural to urban areas. Displacement has disproportionately affected women, indigenous people, and the Afro-Colombian minority. Arbitrary displacement is included as a crime in the Colombian Penal Code. The relevant provision goes beyond the minimum standard of defining arbitrary displacement as a crime against humanity or a war crime. It criminalizes acts that through violence or other coercive measures arbitrarily cause one or several members of the population to change their residency and imposes a prison sentence of fifteen to thirty years, a fine, and a ban from public office for five to ten years.[106] In 1997 Law 387 was passed, establishing the processes by which IDPs could register with the government in order to achieve displaced status and become eligible for emergency humanitarian assistance. Law 387 was passed before the articulation of the Guiding Principles on Internal Displacement and constituted a major achievement in establishing IPD rights; however, successive governments have failed to implement the law effectively, particularly by failing to allocate sufficient funds to the agencies it established to provide support to IDPs.

Between 1997 and 2008, Colombia's Constitutional Court ruled seventeen times that the state had violated the fundamental rights of IDPs.[107] In January 2004, it handed down a landmark ruling that deemed the inhumane conditions in which IDPs lived "unconstitutional" and required the relevant national and local authorities to take action. The court declared in sentence T-25/04 that as a result of the failure of the authorities to provide the displaced population with effective protection, thousands of IDPs experienced "multiple and continuous violations of their human rights."[108] It ordered that budgetary resources and institutional (administrative) resources be increased and established minimum mandatory levels of protection of IDP rights to be provided in an effective and timely manner. The court further required the government to establish outcome indicators regarding the enjoyment of rights of the displaced—in other words, mechanisms to monitor the effectiveness of the government's own policies—and to provide regular updates on its progress in protecting those rights. Faced with government inaction, the court then set out guidelines for the indicators.

The Constitutional Court decision resulted in increased funding for IDP programs and permanent evaluation mechanisms, including indicators for measuring progress in the realization of IDP rights.[109] Nevertheless, many problems continue to afflict IDPs in Colombia. IDP leaders and representatives continue to be subject to persecution, often by illegal armed groups. Subsequent rulings by the court have upheld and given further legal force to the protection of IDP rights. In decision Auto no. 200 of August 13, 2007, the court noted that urgent action by the Colombian authorities was required to protect the right to life and personal security of leaders and representatives of IDPs in special risk situations.[110] A 2008 ruling, recognizing that women were particularly affected by conflict and displacement, required the government to create thirteen programs specifically targeted at IDP women.[111] More recently, in 2009, the court required the government to address underregistration of IDPs in the government registry, the Unified Registry of Displaced Population (RUPD), which is the only way IDPs can access special assistance. The government was also ordered to conduct information campaigns, register applicants rejected previously, share information between the RUPD and other government databases, and register children born to IDPs after they had registered.[112]

Although severe problems persist for many of Colombia's internally displaced, the role of the Constitutional Court has been significant in narrowing the gap between legislation and policy, on the one hand, and the reality of how government agencies treat IDPs, on the other. The court has made more than one hundred rulings on IDPs since its landmark decision in 2004, and these have forced the development of government policies helping IDPs to reclaim some of their fundamental rights.[113] However, while important progress has been made, significant challenges remain regarding the institutional capacity and will to apply existing laws and implement government policies to arrive at durable solutions for Colombia's IDPs.

In the view of one legal analysis, even more important than the Constitutional Court's enforcement of the Colombian government's obligations under Law 387 was its affirmation through sentence T-25/04 that *tutela* actions could be brought by third parties on behalf of IDPs. This has provided an important measure of political empowerment for IDPs.[114] A tutela action allows any individual whose rights are being violated or are in threat of violation to informally bring a case without an attorney before any judge. The judge must prioritize tutela actions and must render a decision within ten days.[115] The tutela in effect gave IDPs, whom the Constitutional Court recognized as often being vulnerable, greater access to the Colombian court system. Instead of having to bring a claim personally, T-25/04 established that organizations created to help IDPs defend their rights could file collective tutela actions.[116] In practice, this enabled more claims to be brought before the courts and gave IDPs a stronger political voice in Colombia.[117] This decision was in effect a justice-sensitive reform; by allowing collective tutela actions, it increased access to justice for IDPs who would most likely be unable to undertake such actions individually, and by widening the scope of the measure to include more IDPs in the legal process of tutela, it legally empowered them to take greater control of their own lives.

The role of the Colombian Constitutional Court highlights an aspect of JSSR that has been largely unexplored. In defending the constitutional rights of IDPs and holding the government to its commitments, the court has been an important governance actor. In its judicial oversight role, it functions as an independent check on government. Through specific decisions, such as that on tutela actions, it helps to achieve fair outcomes for those who are among the most vulnerable in Colombian society. Consideration of its role regarding the displaced shifts the focus away from the typical SSR concerns about dysfunctional security and justice institutions and toward the political, economic, and social problems of this disadvantaged group. In this sense, the court's engagement with IDP issues highlights that, above all, a justice-sensitive approach should not lose sight of the human problems that need to be addressed, and that while reforming aspects of security and justice institutions may be part of the solution, other parts may require different or broader initiatives.

CONCLUSION

This chapter has argued that JSSR shares with those working to achieve durable solutions an interest in finding means of ensuring the longer-term safety, security, and justice needs of IDPs and refugees. Efforts to improve the accountability, legitimacy, integrity, and inclusiveness of security and justice arrangements are fundamental to meeting these needs.

One of the lessons that emerges is that the failure to adopt a holistic approach to reform will likely limit if not undermine the effectiveness of initiatives to mitigate harm at all stages of displacement, including the protection-from-immediate-harm phase. State policing is closely linked to the formal justice sector, and attempts to improve law enforcement responses will fail if concomitant efforts to improve prosecution and penal responses are not also made. As demonstrated by both the Darfur and Chad cases, policing measures that were not accompanied by efforts to address impunity and prosecute perpetrators of crimes and violence against displaced persons were at best Band-Aid solutions that were not sustainable over the long term without broader reform, and as such could only be considered partially successful. More broadly, a justice-sensitive approach to SSR that responds to the needs of the displaced must focus not only on safety and security arrangements but also on access to justice. Moreover, security and justice needs should be analyzed together, with the objective of formulating integrated, coordinated solutions. This interrelationship between security and justice is vividly demonstrated by the issues surrounding land ownership and the inability to address long-term insecurity or find durable solutions for displaced persons who are unable to resolve disputes to reclaim seized or occupied land or property.

In the case of Chad, efforts to improve security for IDPs through the DIS were not coordinated or integrated with efforts (which were high risk and poorly crafted) to address justice deficits, nor were they linked with continuing and profound governance deficits. The DIS made arrests and was relatively successful in terms of increasing protection for IDPs and humanitarian workers, but suspects were released because of dysfunction in the justice sector. A JSSR focus shows that it is important to coordinate humanitarian assistance for returnees with development efforts and not persist in treating them as consecutive endeavors. However, justice sector reforms almost uniformly take longer to implement than police reforms, and finding ways to reconcile the differing paces of successful reform requires more research.

Furthermore, since displacement commonly takes place in conflict-affected environments, usually in fragile states, both formal and traditional justice systems must be considered as a locus for JSSR. While much attention in transitional justice has rightly focused on countering impunity for the worst abuses of human rights, including forced migration, the justice needs of refugees and IDPs and other vulnerable and marginalized communities cannot be ignored. It is clear that efforts must focus not only on central state justice structures but also on justice at the grassroots level, which is often poorly served or not served at all by the formal justice system in post-conflict environments. The overriding majority of people in fragile states turn to informal, traditional, or alternative justice mechanisms to resolve interpersonal and intracommunal disputes.

This chapter has argued for a shift in how we think about and respond to the immediate physical protection needs of the displaced. Humanitarian efforts that focus only on meeting basic needs have sometimes been ad hoc and often ineffective because of the failure to address the broader context in which conflict, predation, and impunity thrive. Wherever possible and appropriate, the international community should ground protection responses in a wider understanding of the systemic security- and justice-system deficits and provide and encourage protection in a way that promotes the transformation of dysfunctional security and justice sectors.

One added value of approaching displacement from a JSSR perspective is the increased likelihood of reforms being sustainable. JSSR's emphasis on efforts that build legitimacy, accountability, integrity, and citizen empowerment is qualitatively distinct from quick-fix efforts, as seen sometimes with purely capacity-building efforts. The emphasis on building a relationship of trust and accountability between the population and the providers of security and justice, whether the provider is a state or a non-state or traditional actor, is inherently holistic and more likely to result in durable solutions for the displaced.

One of the major challenges in developing more effective responses to displacement is overcoming the compartmentalization of approaches by the justice, humanitarian, peacekeeping, and development communities. While there has been some progress in the development of physical protection instruments in the context of integrated missions, there remains a long way to go, particularly at the level of strategic reform. The history of the UN mission in the DRC underscores the necessity for SSR to address issues of integrity, accountability, and legitimacy. In the absence of these justice-sensitive elements, military reforms that have merely blended former combatants with the Congolese military, without human rights vetting, retraining, or an integrated command, not only continue to fail to meet the essential security needs of civilians but are also likely to result in further abuses.

The efforts of the international community to enable minority returns as a central mechanism of peacebuilding in post-war Bosnia similarly demonstrate the links between returns; security; property reclamation; unbiased laws; fair enforcement by police, prosecutors, and courts; and other elements such as access to local services and employment opportunities. Improving the accountability and legitimacy of the courts and empowering citizens seeking to reclaim their property has been essential to developing the durable solution of minority returns in Bosnia, but it is only one of several necessary interrelated reforms in local and national governance.

Finally, what emerges from this overview of security and justice initiatives toward the displaced is the value of a justice-sensitive approach to SSR in maintaining a focus on the broader objective of attaining fair outcomes for IDPs and refugees, who are often among the most vulnerable victims of conflict. Reforming security and justice systems is a challenging undertaking and requires complex multidimensional efforts, political insight, and technical expertise across a diverse range of disciplines. These efforts accordingly tend to concentrate attention at the level of laws, institutions, and procedures. Without challenging the importance of such efforts, the justice-sensitive approach helps to shift attention from a narrow focus on institutions back to the security and justice problems and needs of people.

NOTES

1   See Clare Short, "Security Sector Reform and the Elimination of Poverty" (speech delivered to the Centre for Defence Studies, King's College London, March 9, 1999), www.clareshort.co.uk/speeches/DFID/9%20March%201999.pdf.

2   See Mark Sedra, "Introduction: The Future of Security Sector Reform," in *The Future of Security Sector Reform*, ed. Mark Sedra (Waterloo, Ontario: Centre for International Governance Innovation, 2010), 16.

3   See Alexander Mayer-Rieckh and Roger Duthie, "Enhancing Justice and Development through Justice-Sensitive Security Sector Reform," in *Transitional Justice and Development: Making Connections*, ed. Pablo de Greiff and Roger Duthie (New York: Social Science Research Council, 2009), 229–34.

4   See Alexander Mayer-Rieckh and Serge Rumin, *Confronting an Abusive Past in Security Sector Reform after Conflict: Guidelines for Practitioners* (Brussels: Initiative for Peacebuilding / ICTJ, 2010).

5   Tony Kushner and Katharine Knox, *Refugees in an Age of Genocide* (London: Frank Cass, 1999), 172.

6   Laura Barnett, "Global Governance and the Evolution of the International Refugee Regime," *International Journal of Refugee Law* 14, no. 2/3 (2002): 243–46.

7   Ibid., 249.

8   Erika Feller, "The Evolution of the International Refugee Protection Regime," *Journal of Law and Policy* 5 (2001): 129–38.

9   Roberta Cohen and Frances Deng, *Masses in Flight: The Global Crisis of Internal Displacement* (Washington, DC: Brookings Institution, 1998), 10.

10 This is the standard definition that was arrived at during a series of workshops held by the ICRC in the late 1990s and subsequently adopted by the Inter-Agency Standing Committee.

11 Inter-Agency Standing Committee, *Handbook for the Protection of Internally Displaced Persons* (Geneva: IASC, June 2010), 7, http://www.unhcr.org/refworld/docid/4790cbc02.html.

See also Brookings-Bern Project on Internal Displacement, *IASC Framework on Durable Solutions for Internally Displaced Persons* (Washington, DC: Brookings Institution / University of Bern Project on Internal Displacement, April 2010), 7.

12   Roger Duthie, "Transitional Justice and Displacement," *International Journal of Transitional Justice* 5, no. 2 (2011): 241–61.

13   Inter-Agency Standing Committee, *Handbook for the Protection of Internally Displaced Persons*, 7.

14   Sorcha O'Callaghan and Sara Pantuliano, "Protective Action: Incorporating Civilian Protection into Humanitarian Response" (HPG Policy Brief 29, Humanitarian Policy Group, Overseas Development Institute, December 2007), 9–13.

15   Ibid., 3.

16   See, for example, Marc Dubois, "Protection: The New Humanitarian Fig-Leaf," *Dialogues* 4 (2007): 2–5; and "Protection: Fig-Leaves and Other Delusions," *Humanitarian Exchange Magazine*, no. 46 (March 2010): 2–4. See also Bryce Campbell, in this volume.

17   Inter-Agency Standing Committee, "The International Institutional Framework," part 1-3 of *Handbook for the Protection of Internally Displaced Persons*, 44–47.

18   Under the renewed follow-up mission, renamed the UN Organization Stabilization Mission in the Democratic Republic of Congo (MONUSCO), the cluster is being led solely by UNHCR.

19   Edward Benson, Bhavani Fonseka, and Ambika Satkunanathan, "Civilian Protection in Sri Lanka under Threat" (Working Paper Series no. 58, Refugee Studies Centre, Oxford University, January 2010), 39.

20   A degree of ambiguity surrounds the use of the term *protection* because of the different meanings accorded by different actors, so the meaning developed by humanitarian actors described here will be referred to in this chapter as "humanitarian protection."

21   Brookings-Bern Project on Internal Displacement, *Framework on Durable Solutions*, 5.

22   Ibid., 27.

23   Ibid.

24   Ibid., 29.

25   "Protection that depends on the continued presence of international actors, namely peacekeeping forces, without a hand over strategy is generally not durable." Ibid., 30.

26   Ibid., 30.

27   See Rhodri Williams, in this volume.

28   Brookings-Bern Project on Internal Displacement, *Framework for Durable Solutions*, 35.

29   Ibid., 36.

30   Ibid., 37.

31   UK Department for International Development, "Non-state Justice and Security Systems" (DFID Briefing, Policy Division, May 2004), http://www.gsdrc.org/docs/open/SSAJ101.pdf.

32   Brookings-Bern Project on Internal Displacement, *Framework on Durable Solutions*, 42.

33 Ibid., 43.

34 Pablo de Greiff, "Theorizing Transitional Justice," in *NOMOS LI: Transitional Justice*, ed. Melissa Williams, Rosemary Nagy, and Jon Elster (New York: New York University Press, 2012).

35 See Lucy Hovil, in this volume.

36 Walter Kälin, "Walter Kälin on the Outlook for IDPs," *Forced Migration Review*, no. 37 (March 2011): 44.

37 Internal Displacement Monitoring Centre and Norwegian Refugee Council, *Internal Displacement: Global Overview of Trends and Developments in 2010* (Geneva: IDMC / NRC, 2010), 35.

38 This was the case in Liberia. See Erika Feller, "Giving Peace a Chance: Displacement and Rule of Law During Peacebuilding," *Refugee Survey Quarterly* 28, no. 1 (2009): 86.

39 See Ana Cutter Patel, Pablo de Greiff, and Lars Waldorf, eds., *Disarming the Past: Transitional Justice and Ex-combatants* (New York: Social Science Research Council, 2010).

40 Duthie, "Transitional Justice and Displacement," 261.

41 See Robert Muggah, "Preventing, Protecting, and Promoting Durable Solutions for Refugees and IDPs through Security Sector Reform" (paper prepared for ICTJ / Brookings Project on Transitional Justice and Displacement, 2012).

42 Internal Displacement Monitoring Centre, *Internal Displacement*, 3.

43 Gil Loescher and James Milner, "Protracted Refugee Situations and State and Regional Security," *Conflict, Security and Development* 4, no. 1 (2004): 15.

44 Michel Agier, *Managing the Undesirables: Refugee Camps and Humanitarian Government*, trans. David Fernbach (Cambridge: Polity, 2011), 81–82. See also Hovil, in this volume.

45 Dayna Brown and Kathryn Mansfield, "Listening to the Experiences of the Long-Term Displaced," *Forced Migration Review*, no. 33 (September 2009): 17.

46 Internal Displacement Monitoring Centre, *Internal Displacement*.

47 Clea Kahn, "Conflict, Arms, and Militarization: The Dynamics of Darfur's IDP Camps" (Human Security Baseline Assessment Working Paper 15, Small Arms Survey, Geneva, 2008), 11.

48 See United Nations Security Council, Report of the Secretary-General and the Chairperson of the African Union Commission on the Hybrid Operation in Darfur, S/2007/307/Rev.1, June 5, 2007, paras. 54 and 55.

49 Kahn, "Conflict, Arms, and Militarization," 26–27.

50 Katherine Reyes, "Rights and Responsibilities in Darfur," *Forced Migration Review*, no. 33 (September 2009): 67.

51 "Interview with Officer in Charge of UNAMID Police Gender Unit," *UN Police Chronicle*, no. 3 (June 2008): 2.

52 Reyes, "Rights and Responsibilities in Darfur."

53 Alex de Waal, Chad Hazlett, Christian Davenport, and Joshua Kennedy, "Evidence-Based Peacekeeping: Exploring the Epidemiology of Lethal Violence in Darfur" (Harvard Humanitarian Initiative, Cambridge, MA, March 2010), 13, http://www.hhi.harvard.edu.

54 Darfur Consortium, "Putting People First: The Protection Challenge Facing UNAMID in Darfur" (Kampala, Uganda, 2008), 6, http://www.darfurconsortium.org/darfur_consortium_actions/reports/2008/Putting_People_First_UNAMID_report.pdf.

55 Ibid.

56 Kahn, "Conflict, Arms, and Militarization," 54.

57 "UNAMID Police to Implement Security Committees in Camps—Says Sector North Commander," UN Police Chronicle, no. 5 (August 2008): 2.

58 William G. O'Neill, "Police Reform in Situations of Forced Displacement" (paper prepared for ICTJ / Brookings Project on Transitional Justice and Displacement, 2012).

59 Unlike the (unrealized) plans to establish some means of improving security in the huge refugee camps in Zaire along the border with Rwanda in 1994–95, which O'Neill also describes. Ibid.

60 Maxime Godefroy, L'espace humanitaire au Tchad: Analyse du "pilier sécurité" à l'est du Tchad, mission report (Groupe Urgence-Réhabilitation-Développement, March 2011), 15.

61 Randi Soljhell, John Karlsrud, and Jon Harald Sande Lie, "Protecting Civilians against Sexual and Gender-Based Violence in Eastern Chad," Security in Practice 7 (Norwegian Institute of International Affairs Report, July 2010), 21–22.

62 Randi Solhjell, Benjamin de Carvalho, and Jon Harald Sande Lie, "Somewhere to Turn? MINURCAT and the Protection of Civilians in Eastern Chad and Darfur" (Working Paper 788, Norwegian Institute of International Affairs, May 2011), 17.

63 John Karlsrud and Randi Solhjell, "An Honourable Exit for MINURCAT?" (Policy Brief, Norwegian Institute of International Affairs, March 2010), 2.

64 However, at the time of writing, no details had yet emerged on the nature of international support planned for the DIS. "The Détachement Intégré de Sécurité in Chad," Coginta, http://www.coginta.org/DIS.html.

65 William O'Neill, communication with author, New York, April 2011.

66 Nicki Bennett, "International Peacekeeping Missions and Civilian Protection Mandates: Oxfam's Experiences," Humanitarian Practice Network, no. 46 (March 2010): 22–24.

67 Internal Displacement Monitoring Centre and Norwegian Refugee Council, "Democratic Republic of Congo: IDPs Need Further Assistance in Context of Continued Attacks and Insecurity," September 14, 2011.

68 UN Security Council, Resolution 1291 (2000), "On the Situation in the Democratic Republic of Congo," S/RES/1291, February 24, 2000, para. 8.

69 Victoria K. Holt and Glyn Taylor, Protecting Civilians in the Context of UN Peacekeeping Operations: Successes, Setbacks and Remaining Challenges (New York: United Nations, 2009).

70 Stian Kjeksrud and Jacob Aasland Ravndal, "Protection of Civilians in Practice—Emerging Lessons from the UN Mission in the DR Congo" (Report 02378, Norwegian Defence Research Establishment, 2010), 23, http://www.ffi.no/no/Rapporter/10-02378.pdf.

71 Refugees International, "DR Congo: Support Community-Based Tools for MONUSCO" (Refugees International Field Report, Washington, DC, May 2, 2011).

72 "Military Integration ('Brassage') in the DRC," US diplomatic cable, *Wikileaks*, 08KIN-SHASA283, April 3, 2008.

73 Remarks by Mary Robinson, high commissioner for human rights, Kigali, Rwanda, March 15, 2009. See "Rwanda Defence Forces Top Leadership on Eastern Congo," US diplomatic cable, *Wikileaks*, 09KIGALI172, March 20, 2009.

74 Human Rights Watch, *Always on the Run: The Vicious Cycle of Displacement in Eastern Congo* (New York: Human Rights Watch, 2010), 50–52.

75 Ibid., 52.

76 Ibid.

77 Ibid.

78 Ibid., 64.

79 Madeline England, "Linkages between Justice-Sensitive Security Sector Reform and Displacement: Examples of Police and Justice Reform from Liberia and Kosovo" (paper prepared for ICTJ / Brookings Project on Transitional Justice and Displacement, 2012).

80 Katy Crossley-Frolick and Oya Dursun–Ozkanca, "Transitional Justice and Security Sector Reform: The Role of the EU and Other Multilateral Institutions in Building Kosovo's Police Force" (paper delivered at the 2011 European Union Studies Association biennial meeting, March 3–5, 2011, Boston, MA), 13.

81 Ibid., 33.

82 Internal Security Sector Review and UN Development Programme, *Kosovo Internal Security Sector Review 2006* (Pristina: ISSR, 2006), 21.

83 Council of Europe Commissioner for Human Rights, Report of the Council of Europe Commissioner for Human Rights' Special Mission to Kosovo 23–27 March 2009, CommDH(2009)23, July 2, 2009, paras. 46–48.

84 England, "Linkages between Justice-Sensitive Security Sector Reform and Displacement."

85 International Crisis Group, "The Rule of Law in Independent Kosovo" (Europe Report no. 204, ICG, May 19, 2010).

86 For a fine-grained account of international efforts to facilitate minority returns in Bosnia, see Gerard Toal and Carl T. Dahlman, *Bosnia Remade: Ethnic Cleansing and Its Reversal* (Oxford: Oxford University Press, 2011).

87 International Crisis Group, "The Continuing Challenge of Refugee Return in Bosnia and Herzegovina" (Balkans Report no. 137, ICG, December 13, 2002), ii, 16.

88 Christopher Harland, "The Screening of Judges and Prosecutors by the High Judicial and Prosecutorial Councils through the 2002–4 'Re-selection' Procedure: Lessons from Bosnia and Herzegovina for Other Contexts" (unpublished manuscript, ICTJ, December 2008), 10.

89 See Williams, in this volume.

90 England, "Linkages between Justice-Sensitive Security Sector Reform and Displacement."

91 Norwegian Refugee Council, "Project Factsheet: Information, Counseling and Legal

Assistance (ICLA)" in Liberia, http://www.nrc.no/arch/_img/9429411.pdf.

92 Ingrid Macdonald, "Landlessness and Insecurity: Obstacles to Reintegration in Afghanistan" (Middle East Institute / Fondation pour la Recherche Stratégique, February 9, 2011), 3.

93 Ibid., 4.

94 Ibid., 4.

95 Loescher and Milner, "Protracted Refugee Situations," 10.

96 Ruben Dario Guevara Corral and Diego Andres Guevara Fletcher, "The Journey towards Social Exclusion in Colombia," *Forced Migration Review*, no. 34 (February 2010): 19.

97 Anne Davies and Karen Jacobsen, "Profiling Urban IDPs," *Forced Migration Review*, no. 34 (February 2010): 14.

98 Alice Hills, *Policing Africa: Internal Security and the Limits of Liberalization* (Boulder: Lynne Rienner, 2000), 149.

99 Comfort Ero, "Vigilantes, Civil Defence Forces and Militia Groups," *Conflict Trends* (2000): 25–29.

100 Rebecca Jones, "State Failure and Extra-legal Justice: Vigilante Groups, Civil Militias and the Rule of Law in West Africa" (Research Paper no. 166, New Issues in Refugee Research Series, UNHCR, October 2008), 9.

101 Robert Muggah (ed.), Oliver Jütersonke, Ryan Murray, Edward Rees, and James Scambary, "Urban Violence in an Urban Village: A Case Study of Dili, Timor-Leste" (Working Paper, Geneva Declaration on Armed Violence and Development, 2010), 42.

102 Ibid., 63.

103 Ibid., 20.

104 Siris Hartkorn, "Community-Led Stabilisation in Somalia," *Forced Migration Review*, no. 37 (March 2011): 25–26.

105 Internal Displacement Monitoring Centre, *Internal Displacement*.

106 Colombia, Penal Code (as amended July 6, 2000), article 284.A, cited in Brookings-Bern Project on Internal Displacement, *Framework on Durable Solutions*, 44.

107 Jacob Rothing and Marco Romero, "Measuring the Enjoyment of Rights in Colombia," *Forced Migration Review*, no. 30 (April 2008): 64.

108 Cited in Manuel José Cepeda-Espinosa, "How Far May Colombia's Constitutional Court Go to Protect IDP Rights?," *Forced Migration Review*, special issue (December 2006): 22.

109 Ibid., 22.

110 Juan Pablo Serrano Frattali, "The Importance of IDP Organisations in Colombia," *Insight on Conflict*, August 2010, http://www.insightonconflict.org/2010/07/the-importance-of-idp-organisations-in-colombia/.

111 Alice Taylor, "Protecting Internally Displaced Women in Colombia: From Policy to Practice," *Oxford Monitor of Forced Migration* 1, no. 1 (February 2011): 20–25.

112 Internal Displacement Monitoring Centre, "Colombia," in *Internal Displacement*, 72.

113 Taylor, "Protecting Internally Displaced Women in Colombia."
114 Jennifer Easterday, "Litigation or Legislation: Protecting the Rights of Internally Displaced Persons in Colombia" (unpublished paper, January 2008), 26, http://works.
bepress.com/jennifer_easterday/1/.
115 Ibid., 33.
116 Ibid., 40.
117 Ibid., 41.

CHAPTER 8

The Nexus between Displacement and Transitional Justice: A Gender-Justice Dimension

Lucy Hovil

Although transitional justice processes are intended to help heal and restore society following conflict or authoritarian rule or both, marginalized groups often struggle to make their voices heard during such processes.[1] These groups include those who have been displaced and, within that category, those who have specifically faced gender-based violence and injustice. In this chapter, I explore the relationship between transitional justice and forced migration from a gendered perspective. I argue that a gendered perspective on justice in the aftermath of conflict and displacement is important for those who have suffered gender-based abuses and for ensuring that transitional justice mechanisms are more fully engaged with their contexts. Furthermore, from an advocacy perspective, the struggle to open up space for displaced groups to be heard might be facilitated by collaboration between the two "fields" of displacement and transitional justice, and along these lines, I argue that gendered understandings of displacement need to be embedded in the discussions, processes, and goals of transitional justice from which they are currently sidelined.

I begin the chapter with an outline of the lack of convergence between the fields of displacement and transitional justice and how such a convergence is necessary to restore the bond of citizenship between the displaced and their state. I then view the interaction of the two fields through a specific gender lens, exploring the many areas of gender injustice that characterize all stages of the trajectory of displacement, thereby showing the need for issues of gender justice to be embedded in any transitional justice mechanisms that deal with the fallout from displacement. I outline three approaches to the possible convergence of displacement and transitional justice from a gender perspective: (1) ensuring that displaced groups have a voice in transitional justice processes so that those processes develop displacement-sensitive approaches to understanding and responding to crimes, particularly those that lead to additional gender-based marginalization, (2) incorporating transitional justice approaches into discussions about and the implementation of durable solutions, and (3) highlighting the transformative potential of transitional justice for gender-based crimes committed before, during, and in the aftermath of displacement. I conclude the chapter by discussing ways of mending the broken bond of citizenship and by considering some of its gender-specific dimensions.

DISPLACEMENT AND TRANSITIONAL JUSTICE: A NEED FOR CONVERGENCE?

To date, the fields of displacement and transitional justice have, in practice, remained largely disconnected.[2] The lack of convergence is curious given that both fields focus on the fallout from armed conflict, repression, and human rights abuses on a scale that too often prizes people out of their homes and forces them to live in exile, sometimes for decades, and that it is the very causes and consequences of this violence that transitional justice seeks to address. Furthermore, both are concerned with addressing the political implications of conflict, at least at a theoretical level.

While curious, however, this disconnect is also somewhat predictable. Practical considerations of context and sequencing are partly responsible. In terms of context, displacement takes place either physically outside of the country, in the case of refugees, or in spaces that are often neglected and marginalized within the national setting, in the case of internally displaced persons (IDPs), and displacement actors may therefore be forced to work far afield from their transitional justice counterparts, making coordination difficult. In terms of sequencing, transitional justice mechanisms tend to be an "after-the-event" engagement (the event, in this case, being displacement), which can further complicate efforts to bring actors in both fields together.

Yet the divergence between the fields is not simply about a lack of coordination. In many respects, it is a product of the ways in which the goals of refugee protection (which, in practice, are defined primarily in humanitarian terms) and those of transitional justice are constructed.[3] The former have evolved from their more political roots into an overtly humanitarian enterprise, leading to a strong assumption that refugees and internally displaced persons are a humanitarian problem that can be fixed with adequate international aid money, particularly in situations of mass exodus.[4] This depoliticizing of the humanitarian space has disconnected displaced people from the wider political context and violence that led to their exile and, by extension, leaves them marginalized in peace processes, political transitions, and other mechanisms that are designed to allow them to return home and genuinely reintegrate (at a social, economic, cultural, *and* political level). Indeed, return is constructed as a simple process of stepping over the border with the promise of a few months' supply of food,[5] rather than as the basis for a restoration of the political contract broken by exile.[6]

While a broader array of actors come into play at the point of return as returnees are absorbed into wider development and peacebuilding strategies (where those strategies exist), specific issues of displacement often get lost among the overwhelming number of demands that characterize any post-conflict or post-authoritarian context. Therefore, the political dimension to forced migration remains somewhat implicit.

On the other hand, transitional justice—defined as "the full range of processes and mechanisms associated with a society's attempts to come to terms with a legacy of large-scale past abuses, in order to ensure accountability, serve justice and achieve reconciliation"[7]—arguably has a strong level of political engagement, whether implicitly or explicitly, and as such is often discussed in different spaces from the more humanitarian-dominated forced-migration discussions.[8] For instance, Pablo de Greiff provides a formulation for the goals of transitional justice that clearly incorporates the broader political and security context:

> Transitional justice refers to the set of measures that can be implemented to redress the legacies of massive human rights abuses, where "redressing the legacies" means, primarily, giving force to human rights norms that were systematically violated. A non-exhaustive list of these measures includes criminal prosecutions, truth-telling, reparations, and institutional reform. Far from being elements of a random list, these measures are a part of transitional justice in virtue of sharing two mediate goals (providing recognition to victims and fostering civic trust) and two final goals (contributing to reconciliation and to democratization).[9]

As these goals demonstrate, transitional justice, with its imperative to right wrongs, is a significant tool, which could potentially be used to address what is often a massive deficit in justice in the aftermath of displacement and to work toward the breaking of vicious cycles of conflict that generate displacement, thereby ensuring that solutions become genuinely durable. I therefore argue in this chapter that the transitional justice discourse has the potential to reconnect forced-migration discussions to their political roots—to move them away from being predominantly livelihood or humanitarian assessments and toward more social and political engagement, not least through the recognition of displaced persons as rights-bearers.

In particular, transitional justice mechanisms can play a key role in ensuring that rhetoric about the protection of forced migrants reaches the ground. In as much as displacement represents a violation, or a series of violations, of the rights of those who have been displaced, transitional justice processes present an opportunity to address some of the injustices associated with forced migration and to ensure that displaced persons are genuinely treated as rights-bearers. The turmoil of violence that uproots people from their homes; the chaos of flight; the experience of exile, which is often characterized by continued insecurity and a lack of protection; and the fraught process of return (as the most favored of the three so-called durable solutions[10]) all represent a litany of human rights abuses that need to be acknowledged and addressed if displacement is to be truly resolved.

The national and political focus of transitional justice—which can be seen as a restricting factor in the context of displacement, where people have often physically removed themselves from the polity—actually makes distinct sense in any discussion on the resolution of displacement. By definition, displacement represents a rupture between the individual and his or her homeland; it is a clear demonstration of a government's failure to protect—or, worse still, of its role as the perpetrator of abuses against its citizens. Displacement represents a failure on the part of a government to ensure the safety of its citizens, whether they are refugees who have fled over an international border or IDPs who have remained within their state. And if displacement and conflict are representative of a break in the bond between citizens and the state, appropriate and meaningful forms of justice in the aftermath of conflict represent the potential restoration of that bond—the foundation on which the future stability of the country lies—and a reinstatement of "the right to have rights."[11] In other words, the very fact that those who have been displaced have been physically removed from the national arena or discourse makes their engagement in transitional justice processes all the more crucial.

Yet despite the many areas of overlap, in practice, synergy between the two fields is lacking. On the one hand, there has been a general failure to place issues of justice and the broader political implications of displacement within the parameters of so-called refugee or IDP protection—both during displacement and in the implementation of durable solutions. On the other hand, despite both the scale and implications of displacement, the field of transitional justice has remained relatively silent on the issue, and until now, there has been no study of refugees or IDPs and their relation to transitional justice.[12] As a result, displaced populations rarely participate in the negotiation of transitional justice mechanisms, and those mechanisms rarely address the concerns of displaced persons as substantively as they could.

That said, there are signs that the discourse is beginning to shift. In Colombia, as Donny Meertens puts it, "formerly in a *'humanitarian category'*, recent debates on victimhood place [displaced persons] in a *'rights category'*—that is, as victims of conflict with a right not only to humanitarian assistance and economic recovery, but also to truth, justice and reparations."[13] Likewise, in Kenya IDP-related issues have been placed firmly on the transitional justice agenda: the Truth and Justice Reconciliation Commission (TJRC) developed procedures and recruited people to specifically target IDPs for recorded statements and took statements from refugees living in camps in neighboring Uganda.[14] Similarly, there has been considerable discussion about the need to engage with the thousands of Sudanese IDPs displaced by conflict in any potential post-conflict reconstruction process, including the need to somehow fill the chronic deficit of justice in Darfur. Furthermore, the argument is being made that any repatriation process that includes the recovery of land and other property is, in and of itself, an enactment of transitional justice.[15]

In sum, dealing with the fallout from forced migration is critical to the future reconstruction of the state in the aftermath of conflict and to the reforging of the essential bond of citizenship. While those who have been displaced are not the only ones who have had this bond broken, their ability to return home and reactivate their citizenship is a crucial indicator that peace has been restored and that some degree of justice has been provided. The restoration of this bond therefore lies at the heart of the relationship between transitional justice and displacement and forms the basis for genuinely durable solutions to displacement. Conversely, the failure to address the injustices that generated and were created by displacement threatens to derail, or certainly calls into question, the integrity of any transitional justice process and the potential durability of peace.

THE GENDER DIMENSION

So where does gender fit within this discussion? Given that no group of displaced people is homogeneous, it is vital to have an understanding of the individuals or communities that make up such populations, which in turn may lead to the formulation of appropriate responses to the injustices they have suffered. In pushing for connectivity between displacement and transitional justice, therefore, I assert that any relationship will be meaningless if it is not somehow disaggregated in order to ensure that responses are contextually appropriate; it is all too easy to pay lip service to the need for transitional justice and far harder to define what that justice might and should look like in practice.[16] Equally, it is important to recognize not only where the points of convergence might lie but also where, realistically, they do not.

One approach to addressing this challenge is to view displacement and transitional justice responses through a gender lens—to look at some of the specific gender injustices related to any given context of forced migration. A gender lens reveals the need to ensure contextually relevant and timely responses. As Laurel Fletcher and Harvey Weinstein have argued, "We suggest that the appropriate sequencing is to first gain a comprehensive understanding of the local context and then to ask what, whether, and when transitional justice interventions should be initiated."[17] Such issues of context and sequencing, important in any transitional justice process, are only highlighted when dealing with displacement, which by definition incorporates geographical dispersal and therefore calls for different experiences, timescales, and processes to be taken into consideration.

Deploying a gender lens provides one possible framework for promoting a nuanced and contextually relevant approach to considering the relationship between displacement and transitional justice. Specifically, it is argued here, a gender lens brings a measure of social analysis into the discussion, helping us identify and describe social patterns of exclusion and providing a means for exploring ways of addressing structural inequities. It gives substance to any discussion that focuses on assessing and responding to violations experienced by the displaced.

It is important to stress that the notion of gender refers broadly to injustices that can be suffered by men, women, boys, and girls. Human rights violations are often gendered, in the sense that some violations are more often inflicted on persons of a given gender. Also, those of different genders are likely to experience and respond to violations differently. A gender lens helps us to understand patterns of violations and responses that are not necessarily limited to women and girls and reflects an increasing recognition of the need for a more nuanced understanding of masculinities and their relationship to transitional justice mechanisms.[18]

To a certain extent, discourses surrounding both displacement and transitional justice have increasingly recognized—in theory if not in practice—the need to ensure gender sensitivity at some level, though this is especially true of displacement.[19] While gender is not included in the international definition

of a refugee as a person with a "well-founded fear of being persecuted for reasons of race, religion, nationality, membership of a particular social group,
or political opinion,"[20] in 2002 the Office of the UN High Commissioner for
Refugees (UNHCR) issued guidelines for state parties and those conducting
refugee status determinations on the need for gender-sensitive assessments
of cases, which noted that although gender is not specifically referenced in
the refugee definition, "it is widely accepted that it can influence, or dictate,
the type of persecution or harm suffered and the reasons for this treatment.
The refugee definition, properly interpreted, therefore covers gender-related
claims. As such, there is no need to add an additional ground to the 1951 Convention definition."[21]

At the same time, there has been increasing recognition that transitional
justice processes have tended to overlook the issue of who is included in and
excluded from transitional justice decisions, especially—but not limited to—
women and displaced persons.[22] With a growing awareness that the concept
of "untold numbers," or the lack of agency attributed to groups of exiles, is
not good enough,[23] a push for transitional justice processes to be far more
cognizant of categories of exclusion, including gender, is gaining momen-
tum.[24] There is a need, for instance, to better understand and respond to
women's experiences of violations as well as those of other categories of people who suffer gender-based violence. Indeed, the failure to include these specific experiences—as with the failure to incorporate the explicit concerns of
the displaced—ultimately undermines the ability to respond to the true social
cost of violence.

Furthermore, there has been a growing understanding of the *transformative*
potential of transitional justice processes when discussing gender-specific
injustices—the opportunity to address not only the specific gender violations
of conflict or authoritarian rule but also the deeper structural disparities that
provide the context for, if not the direct causes of, conflict and human rights
violations. This is in part because the provision of legal responses to rights
violations offers a chance to assess the gender sensitivity of those responses—
"an unusual laboratory," as Fionnuala Ni Aolain puts it.[25] Transitions, therefore, "provide opportunities to further gender justice, in particular through the
implementation of a gender-sensitive transitional justice agenda. Transitional
justice processes can be leveraged not simply to secure justice for individual
human rights violations, but also to address the context of inequality and
injustice that gives rise to conflict, transforming the structures of inequality
that underpin this violence."[26] Moreover, one could suggest that applying such
logic to displacement contexts might help to identify and begin to address

structural inequalities that might make certain segments of the population more vulnerable to displacement.

However, in reality, international law—and as a result, transitional justice—often fails to "capture" women's experiences of conflict and violation.[27] Where the law does recognize the gendered dimension to violations, implementation does not. For instance, UN Security Council Resolution 1820, passed in 2008, provides important guidance for both states and civil society on issues related to sexual violence during conflict. It recognizes sexual violence as an impediment to international peace and security and demands that all parties to armed conflict "take appropriate measures to protect civilians ... from all forms of sexual violence," including training and other preventive measures.[28] It also references the importance of ending the culture of impunity in many countries emerging from conflict.[29] Importantly, the resolution also allows the Security Council to consider sexual violence in establishing and maintaining sanctions regimes.[30] Yet in practice, little has been done to implement this and subsequent resolutions.

This chapter, then, contributes to a growing body of literature that pushes for transitional justice mechanisms to become more gender nuanced in policy *and* practice, by considering what this might look like for those individuals and communities that have suffered displacement. It is a preliminary exploration of some of the issues surrounding this topic that is by no means intended to be an exhaustive examination of the relationship between transitional justice and displacement from a gender perspective.

GENDER DYNAMICS WITHIN A DISPLACEMENT CONTEXT

While the majority of conflicts today take a heavy toll on the civilian population in general, such conflicts, which can lead to displacement, often have a strongly gendered dimension to them. Although it is hard to generalize, the prevalence of sexual violence is perhaps the most tangible example: while sexual violence is often nondiscriminatory in its reach (all are potential victims),[31] it is common for certain groups to be at particular risk. Mayan women, for instance, were specifically targeted in *la violencia* in Guatemala, which in turn was a factor in their displacement.[32] Notoriously high levels of sexual violence are increasingly coming to light in the eastern Democratic Republic of Congo, where vast numbers of people have been internally displaced. In addition to sexual violence, other gender dynamics can play a role in displacement. For instance, young men might be specifically in danger of forced recruitment within a context of ongoing conflict or under an authoritarian regime that sees young men as a threat to national security, or women might flee their homes because their husbands or other men within their households have been killed and they feel particularly vulnerable as a result.

In exile, the violence of war is often replaced by other injustices, some of which have a clear gender dimension. Once again, sexual violence, including exploitation and abuse, is a well-known and high-risk problem.[33] It is often linked to the economic hardships associated with displacement: within both camp and noncamp/urban environments, poor access to basic services can force men and women to resort to harmful measures to survive—working as commercial sex workers, trading sex for food or shelter, or illegally hawking goods on unsafe streets.[34] Likewise, those living in camps are often vulnerable to sexual violence from rebel groups operating in the area as well as from government forces;[35] the notion of camps being places of sanctuary and protection is too often far from reality. For instance, extensive documentation shows that girls and women collecting firewood continue to be vulnerable to attack as they leave the central areas of camps in Uganda.[36] As Binaifer Nowrojee explains, "Refugee and displaced women, uprooted from their homes and countries by war, internal strife, or natural catastrophe are vulnerable to violence both as a result of the surrounding problem and because of their dependency on outsiders for relief provisions. The internally displaced are further at risk because the abuses they seek to escape are often being committed by the very government that should afford them protection."[37]

In addition to problems of sexual violence, displacement can have a profound effect on gender relations, with regard to both the role of women in households and communities[38] and the role of men in providing for their families. While many of these tensions are likely to have predated displacement, it is particularly true that in a context of restrictions on freedom of movement and limited access to livelihoods, men's traditional roles are effectively taken over by agencies such as UNHCR and the UN World Food Programme, which provide their families tents to sleep in and food to eat. As a result, women often find UNHCR to be a "better husband."[39] Outside the camp environment, other problems exist. Ruth Judge writes about the precarious situation many young refugee men find themselves in as a result of stereotypes and assumptions made about them. In particular, advocacy efforts too often exclude these men in a context in which the vulnerability of women and children is strongly emphasized.[40]

While one could interpret such challenges to rigidly defined "traditional" roles in a positive light in as much as they are a potential driver of social transformation, too often the consequences are overwhelmingly negative. The anger and helplessness felt by many refugee men as a result of this construction of gender relations are often channeled against women, leading to violent behavior toward women as men try to assert their traditional dominant roles.[41] This is only exacerbated by a context in which the ability of people to absorb additional change is likely to be limited. Social and cultural norms and networks that men and women would normally rely on to help them address problems such as domestic violence seldom exist in a camp environment or abroad, leaving victims of such abuse particularly vulnerable.[42] Men in the camps often leave to seek work in urban areas in order to support their families. Their legal status then becomes ambiguous, and they must confront a plethora of problems, including assumed associations with rebel, criminal, or political elements, and suffer an array of abuses, including arbitrary arrest and, at times, rape.[43]

At the point of return, gender dynamics can play an important role in the ability of groups and individuals to safely reintegrate. In particular, security concerns can (re)emerge as people return, not least for those who have suffered gender-related crimes and in instances where perpetrators remain in return communities—which is often the norm rather than the exception.[44] However, once again, humanitarian norms tend to dictate the return process, and specific protection concerns are often overlooked or ignored as a result. And large repatriation exercises can leave little room for refugees who have suffered specific injustices—such as those that relate to gender-based violence—to voice fears over their safety at the point of return.

THE GENDER DISCONNECT

Despite these realities, in practice gendered understandings and responses to forced migration are often seriously lacking. Gender "mainstreaming," while recognized as critical in many areas—including both the development and humanitarian spheres—still lags chronically behind in terms of implementation.[45] The international relief community, which is often the main presence within displaced-person camps, has been slow to respond with any effectiveness to these issues. Although guidelines on the protection of women in camps have been developed, ongoing empirical research suggests that their implementation is still hugely inadequate,[46] as specific gender needs continue to be responded to in token ways by UNHCR and its implementing partners.[47]

Furthermore, although development goals might converge with the goals of transitional justice more generally, especially in the area of redress, in practice, development organizations can be reluctant to engage with wider issues of justice.[48] In particular, they rarely engage with the more politically sensitive areas of compensation or redress or with legal issues relating to land rights, citizenship documentation, marriage status, and other factors that are critically important for reintegration and that often relate directly to gender-specific issues.

Thus, much of what passes for gender mainstreaming remains relatively palliative: while the provision of assistance can deal with certain economic disparities, ideological underpinnings that feed discrimination are far harder to address.[49] For instance, too often humanitarian actors believe that they have ticked the gender-sensitive "protection" box by locating a borehole or a toilet in an accessible location. This important, but nevertheless superficial, adherence to gender-specific dynamics in a displaced context does little to address the deep-rooted systemic injustice that lies behind gender divisions.[50]

Tackling the problems of sexual violence prior to, during, and after displacement is a particularly significant area of neglect. For instance, women who have had experiences that are painful and difficult to describe often face specific problems when making their cases for asylum, even more so when the interviewers are male.[51] Furthermore, one of the characteristics of sexual violence is underreporting of the crimes committed because of fear of reprisals, mistrust of authorities, and the stigma associated with such crimes, and victims are at risk of long-lasting and severe health problems—both mental and physical—as a result.[52] In a context of displacement, underreporting only increases. The stigma of rape within a settlement environment—where privacy is often compromised—cannot be overemphasized. UNHCR officials report situations in which refugee families have begged them to relocate their daughters to another camp after they have been raped because of the stigma on the family.[53]

Lack of access to justice within camps is compounded by the fact that refugee or IDP camps and settlements are often perceived and run as if they were isolated islands outside national jurisdiction, particularly in cases where UNHCR or other international actors effectively run the camps in a context of limited national capacity. Linked to this is the somewhat xenophobic notion that what takes place inside the camp is irrelevant to wider national processes unless it has a direct bearing on the "outside."[54] As a result, the response to sexual violence and other gender-related injustices is often hugely inadequate or inappropriate, with minimal coordination taking place with other bodies or organizations that might have the capacity and expertise to help. Susan Harris Rimmer, for instance, points out the failure of UNHCR to gather information about the gendered experiences and needs of displaced women that could have been used by the Commission for Reception, Truth and Reconciliation in Timor-Leste (Comissão de Acolhimento, Verdade e Reconciliação de Timor-Leste—CAVR). In this way, "the truth-telling goals of the CAVR project were compromised by the failure of refugee protection and the limited script offered to returnees."[55]

This isolation of camps is compounded by the fact that community leaders often act in cases that, under their country's national law, should be heard by state courts, and these cases are therefore more vulnerable to preexisting cultural conditioning and discrimination. For example, all community leaders in camps are typically men. Guglielmo Verdirame and Barbara Harrell-Bond found in Kenya's Kakuma camp that most people who had been imprisoned were being held for adultery and that often the woman was the one imprisoned while the man was given a fine.[56] Furthermore, because gender discrimination is generally considered to be a "cultural" issue, UNHCR and other humanitarian actors seldom get involved.[57] In this way, institutions can too easily reinforce and perpetuate gender discrimination.[58]

In addition, the way in which humanitarian-assistance structures construct the notion of vulnerability can further that discrimination: women and children are typically classified as "vulnerable" to the exclusion of men. As Liisa Malkki puts it, women are viewed as being more "true" refugees, as the victims of war rather than the perpetrators.[59] Thus, the oft-used cliché in humanitarian circles that "the majority of refugees are women and children" (which could likely be said of any cross section of the population around the world, displaced or not) has become a somewhat unhelpful truism—and in some cases is simply inaccurate.[60] All too frequently, male refugees and IDPs are left to cope not only with the violations that led to their displacement but also with the layers of injustice that are added by their experience of exile.

In addition, although humanitarian groups are aware of "vulnerable groups" within the return process—including women-headed households—in practice this often amounts to little more than their providing of some extra supplies. Indeed, in many cases, it does not even translate into such minimal support: in Burundi, women were left sleeping under trees with their children at the point of return, unable to access land, reconstruct their homes, or provide for their families despite having been identified as "vulnerable."[61] Humanitarian engagement, therefore, even at its most effective, is not an intervention that seriously addresses gender-based injustice.

Another example of such a lack of awareness can be seen in efforts that were made to resolve displacement in Timor-Leste in 2006, where money that was given to returnee families was wrongly appropriated and as a result enforced rather than challenged discriminatory practice. Violence in and around Dili that year led to significant internal displacement, which at its peak saw close to one hundred thousand people living in IDP camps. When the camps eventually began to close, kiosk owners called in debts for payment. Although it was largely female IDPs who had relied on credit for the small necessities of life, often accumulating considerable debt during their time in the camps, they were not the ones selected to receive returnee payments from the government; instead, payment was made to the male heads of households. The numbers of men simply disappearing with this money rose in the face of polygamy and family breakdowns, and women were left unable to pay off their debts.[62]

As discussed earlier, to date, transitional justice mechanisms have remained relatively disengaged from issues relating to the fallout from displacement. And with gender-specific dynamics lagging behind in broader transitional justice debates, gender issues are in danger of being doubly marginalized when connected directly with displacement. As Harris Rimmer says, with reference to the CAVR in Timor-Leste, "The narrative of refugee and internally displaced women, as well as women generally, is often silent or marginalised in the new national narrative that emerges from transitional justice processes. This is so even with those mechanisms traditionally considered more inclusive of victims' voices, such as truth commissions."[63]

GENDER JUSTICE AND DISPLACEMENT

So where can, and should, the points of convergence lie? Clearly, the causes of displacement—which generally occur within the geographical space of the country in which the transition is taking place—are a key area to be addressed and could be potentially absorbed into wider national discussions on root causes of violations. Such issues can, in theory, be addressed throughout the stages of displacement—prior to, as part of, and after any repatriation process. In particular, the emphasis on nonrepetition that lies at the heart of transitional justice is crucial to addressing causes of violence and displacement. However, with transitional justice mechanisms continuing to lag behind with regard to issues of gender-based violence, including sexual violence, the problem here is about not only a lack of convergence between the two discussions but also, and more importantly, the lack of gender justice generally—which only makes the need for increased awareness and coordination more pressing.

Transitional justice and displacement should also overlap during the process of return. Restitution, for example, with its links to reparations and the process of return, should be fundamental to both fields—and it is certainly foundational to ensuring gender justice.[64] Restitution has the unique potential to not only redress singular violations committed prior to or during displacement but also address some of the underlying gender inequalities.[65] In practice, however, return continues to be conceived of primarily as a one-off event rather than a slow process of reintegration that can take months or even years. By contrast, restitution can create a longer-term engagement with communities and individuals who are struggling to reconstruct their lives in the months and years after returning to their homes.

What is less clear is the extent to which injustices suffered *during* displacement—which are often committed under the watch of actors outside the normal jurisdiction of national transitional justice processes—can fall under the purview of those processes. In reality, the broader experience of injustice in exile often represents a continuation of injustices that occurred prior to displacement and that are likely to reignite at the point of return. As a result, while perpetrators might be located in different environments (for instance, government soldiers in the country of exile might be the main perpetrators of sexual violence in certain instances), from the perspective of those who have been displaced, the impact is cumulative and needs to be addressed in an inclusive way. Realistically (and somewhat less than optimally), while it might go beyond the capability of transitional justice mechanisms in a neighboring country to hold perpetrators accountable in situations of exile, broader engagement with issues of injustice associated with displacement still remains firmly within reach.

In order to begin to unravel some of these dynamics, I now suggest three areas where the aspirations of transitional justice and the need to resolve the injustice of displacement overlap from a gender-specific perspective: promoting empowerment of the displaced by ensuring they have a voice in transitional justice processes, engaging with discussions on durable solutions, and encouraging a transformative agenda. As stated previously, in discussing these areas this chapter is not prescriptive: I do not offer solutions so much as point to potential convergences between the goals of transitional justice and a rediscovered understanding of refugee-IDP protection and resolution.

EMPOWERMENT THROUGH PARTICIPATION IN TRANSITIONAL JUSTICE PROCESSES

By definition, displaced people are geographically marginalized. This physical marginalization often reflects wider exclusion from the social, economic, cultural, and political processes of their countries. In particular, emphasis on institutional reform and the overtly national nature of peace processes, political transitions, and post-conflict discussions can, by their very focus, exclude those physically not present. As a result, displacement renders people particularly voiceless—all too often, refugees and IDPs are consulted neither in peace negotiation processes nor in discussions regarding the viability of durable solutions. That is not to suggest that refugees and IDPs are passive victims: displaced people listen to the radio; they unofficially travel over borders and move in and out of their home areas to assess the security situation, check on their homes, and bury their dead; and there is a steady exchange of information through transborder networks. However, for the most part this interaction exists outside the broader discourse, and engagement at an official level is minimal.

With increasing awareness of the need for transitional justice to more closely incorporate displacement, it is important to ensure that those who are displaced are more deliberately consulted in any discussions about the resolution of problems associated with displacement. For instance, it is vital that the concerns of those displaced are represented at any peace negotiations, and by extension, that they adequately participate in discussions on the design of any proposed transitional justice mechanisms. Indeed, it is possible that the former will make the latter more likely. Furthermore, it is important that this engagement be fully inclusive. Lack of consultation generally with groups of displaced people should not be replaced with partial or exclusive engagement; gender discrimination is one area of concern in this regard, particularly in situations where women and girls typically do not have a voice (and certainly not a political voice).

Yet a number of factors can prevent this inclusive engagement from happening, many of which appear logistical but reflect deeper structural inequalities. First, within a camp environment, discussions with anyone coming in from outside are often controlled by a few key individuals, or gatekeepers. These gatekeepers are typically male and have often reached their positions of prominence by currying favor with the camp authorities rather than as a result of democratic elections. Second, in a context in which women have been constructed primarily as the recipients of aid, their political views are unlikely to be heard, let alone seen as significant. And third, structures of inequality that existed prior to displacement are often transplanted into a displacement context.

As Harris Rimmer explains, "When displaced or refugee women are considered in a post-conflict context, it is often as beneficiaries in a welfare paradigm, rather than as potential political actors in a post-conflict State."[66] Likewise, Judy El-Bushra states:

> The notion of vulnerability has figured highly in humanitarian discourse for years. It has particular implications for displaced women, children and the disabled, who are often categorised as "vulnerable groups." "Victim" may well be an appropriate word for those women and men who have suffered rape, for example, and the attendant multiple crises of physical and psychological injury, and rejection by families, communities and legal systems. Yet the use of the word, denying as it does the resilience and determination of those who have undergone such experiences, predisposes assistance programs towards offering palliative care rather than confronting underlying systemic injustices.[67]

As a result, women are particularly in danger of being excluded from any discussions that might take place, especially where they are viewed primarily as passive victims and thereby robbed of agency. On the other hand, as Meertens points out, "being a victim" can be empowering for displaced persons if it means being considered a rights-claimant. In Colombia, being a victim has "acquired a new political and practical meaning" for displaced women, who now demand more from the government than just humanitarian assistance.[68]

By ensuring adequate engagement of women and other marginalized groups with mechanisms that might render peace and justice more attainable, the perception of refugees and IDPs as passive victims and recipients of aid can be subverted. Instead, they are empowered to act. Post-conflict Guatemala, for example, presents a context in which displaced women were specifically consulted and deliberately accorded agency during both displacement and the return process.[69] Elsewhere, in Uganda's West Nile region, women who had suffered under years of conflict were consulted about how best to end a rebellion by the West Nile Bank Front rebel group, which was comprised of their own sons, brothers, and husbands. In discussions with the head of the Ugandan army unit posted to the area, who instituted an informal amnesty process, the women decided they could contribute to ending the conflict by putting pressure on their husbands to renounce rebellion, including refusing to have sex with them until they handed in their guns.[70] These women were not just victims of war but also actors in resolving it by helping create the conditions for durable peace and the return home of the displaced.

Likewise, in Liberia the Women in Peacebuilding Network (WIPNET) mobilized women in the early days of the country's first civil war. They staged public marches in 1991 to advocate for peace and security and started to attend peace talks in 1993. When war resumed in 2000, WIPNET intensified its efforts to mobilize women to call for peace. A defining moment for the group was when Charles Taylor challenged WIPNET to find the rebel leaders. The women funded a small delegation to Sierra Leone, where some of the rebel leaders were staying, and arranged meetings between them and Taylor. In 2003 WIPNET spearheaded the Women of Liberia Mass Action for Peace campaign to confront and engage the rebels directly, traveling all over the country and region.[71] A coalition of Christian and Muslim women under the leadership of Nobel Peace Prize winner Leymah Gbowee, the campaign forced a meeting with Taylor, extracting a promise from him to attend peace talks in Ghana. Gbowee then led a delegation of women to Ghana to apply pressure on the warring factions during the peace process.[72] As these examples show, women are not passive victims either during war or in negotiations to end war and need to be adequately recognized as such, whether in contexts of displacement or otherwise.

Deliberately ensuring that displaced people, including women, are consulted in designing transitional processes in an inclusive way provides an opportunity to ensure that voices that are often marginalized in such discussions are given adequate hearing. As Ruth Rubio-Marín asserts with regard to reparations programs—though it could equally be applied to the incorporation of displaced women in discussions on peace and justice issues more generally, under certain conditions—the very involvement of women can be, in and of itself, a form of reparation.[73] Likewise, as Valérie Couillard states, "participative reparations programs ensure the direct and full involvement of women at all stages of reparation, because their role in peacebuilding is recognised as essential and their voice as under-represented."[74] Participation, in this context, is an objective in itself,[75] but it can also be instrumental in helping to ensure that transitional justice measures specifically respond to the needs of victims of gender injustice and displacement.

In particular, the symbolic and actual significance of governments reaching out to those in exile (whether internal or external) in order to include them in transitional justice processes cannot be underestimated for groups of people who have been displaced through inadequate government protection, as when the Liberian Truth and Reconciliation Commission held meetings with refugees and the diaspora to solicit their views. The commission also made special efforts to reach out to women. However, from a gendered justice and displacement perspective, the process could have been improved, as the commission did not explicitly consider the vulnerabilities and needs of women *that resulted from* their displacement.[76]

The opportunity to engage with transitional justice measures can also help mobilize groups to come together to discuss these issues. In Colombia, for example, a ruling by the Constitutional Court (Auto no. 092), which called for the government to enact a series of measures to ensure, among other things, the right of displaced women to truth, justice, and reparations, has "fueled displaced women's mobilization and carried far-reaching implications both for the way in which a gender-sensitive approach has to be conceived and for the way in which humanitarian action may be linked to transitional justice and development measures."[77]

Such engagement also represents a strong point of convergence between the eventual political goal of repatriation (namely, restoring the link between citizens and the state) and the goals of transitional justice, not least the promotion of civic trust.

DURABLE SOLUTIONS

Another key area of displacement in which transitional justice can play a role from a gender perspective is in the implementation of durable solutions. The argument here is that in the absence of transitional justice, levels of physical and economic insecurity can make long-term return and reintegration not viable for certain groups. Different justice measures may in some cases make important contributions to raising the level of these types of security by addressing specific gender-based injustices. Throughout the return and reintegration process (which takes place over years rather than weeks), transitional justice can potentially play a role in ensuring the timeliness and the viability of return and improving the longer-term prospects for formerly displaced populations. In addition, justice measures may also highlight the importance of considering solutions other than return.

Durable solutions are the end game of displacement, which is generally understood to be resolved when displaced persons achieve local integration, return or repatriation, or resettlement to a third country or location. Of the three, return/repatriation has typically been viewed as the optimal outcome by host governments, the international community, and in many cases, the region or country from which the displaced persons fled. As such, many situations of displacement are configured around the assumption that refugees and IDPs are living in temporary circumstances until such time as they can return home. As soon as a peace deal has been signed or a new dispensation established, it is often assumed that the conditions are now ripe for return.

Yet an end to hostilities does not necessarily mean that it is either safe or timely to return home. When the displaced are not consulted in discussions about the viability and timing of different durable solutions—as is typically the case—the process becomes highly fraught. While in theory return is supposed to be voluntary, in practice it is often a highly coerced process. Alternatives to repatriation are rarely given adequate consideration, and the needs of individuals within groups of displaced persons are often overlooked. For example, for those who have suffered specific crimes—in particular sexual violence—returning to an area in which perpetrators are still living is likely to be both painful and dangerous. It might be necessary for offenders to be removed before those who have suffered can return home. In many contexts, however, there is little prospect of perpetrators being physically removed—as a result of either amnesties and ex-combatant reintegration programs or a broader deficit of justice that has created a culture of impunity or both.

In the case of the latter, impunity can generate enormous fear, as the silence that surrounds unacknowledged crimes can be utterly devastating for their victims, particularly when they are implicitly or explicitly blamed for what has happened to them. For instance, as Evelyne Josse discusses, victims of sexual violence are often blamed for their fate: "Victims of sexual violence are also discriminated against, in that they may be shunned, stripped of their rights (whether legal or traditional), and deprived of access to goods and services. ... In some cases, whether in war or peace, they are 'buried alive' by society."[78] The point of return can thus underscore the marginalization that victims of sexual violence often suffer, making them increasingly vulnerable as a result. Yet in situations where alternative durable solutions are not offered, victims are left with little choice but to return. In this context, incorporating the broader goals associated with transitional justice into a discussion of repatriation can ensure that issues of accountability and redress are put on the agenda from the beginning.[79]

Other gender-defined groups might be prohibited from returning. Research I did recently among Rwandan refugees living in Uganda highlights some of the issues relating to the negative association of men with armed conflict. In particular, men who are considered old enough to have participated in the Rwandan genocide in 1994 and are currently displaced are having considerable problems returning to Rwanda. For this group, particularly those who are of Hutu ethnicity, there is an assumption that those who have not returned to Rwanda must be *génocidaires*. Ironically, mechanisms of transitional justice that have been implemented since the genocide—in particular the *gacaca* courts—have become part of the problem, not least as a result of being state-controlled and delivering partial, victor's justice.[80]

In addition to specific protection concerns, the point of return can be a moment of extreme economic vulnerability—a vulnerability that affects groups differently and therefore demands a context-specific response. Lack of infrastructure, a wrecked economy, the presence of land mines, and numerous other factors all make the return process fraught. And specific groups face particular economic challenges. For instance, return can be especially challenging for women who are trying to support themselves and their families alone. Recovering property lost through displacement can be highly problematic for these women, particularly with regard to land reclamation, which is often dependent on proof of ownership, complicated by the fact that in patriarchal societies, women are often excluded from owning land. In Colombia, for example, "many women do not have the means to prove their possession of land before displacement. This is related to historical discriminations, as displaced women report having had less formal land ownership than men."[81] Gender discrimination can present this challenge both in countries with customary rules for administering land and in those with formal land-tenure systems.[82]

While humanitarian and development organizations typically try to address some of the key economic implications of return, the response is often inadequate, misdirected, and short term. In order to ensure that return is both viable and durable, there must be adequate recognition of both the short-term and longer-term needs of returnees and of the specific needs that are represented within any returnee context. Realistically, in most cases transitional justice mechanisms are unlikely to be in place at the point of return. But the longer-term emphasis associated with transitional justice is important in the aftermath of displacement—for instance, redress mechanisms are likely to be crucial in a context of limited aid and development resources, where people are left trying to patch up livelihoods that have been decimated by displacement. For women who lack the patronage of a husband or other male relatives, vulnerability is significantly enhanced.

Restitution is likely to be the optimal measure in this regard: returning to the specific house or piece of land from which people fled holds huge significance, both materially and psychologically. Yet for many, this is unrealistic, particularly for women in situations where they are unable to inherit land. In instances where recovering property is not possible, compensation is vital. Reparations in the form of material compensation are also likely to play a key role. While material compensation does not necessarily satisfy all the demands of justice, it can certainly play a strong role in protecting those who are most vulnerable.[83]

Furthermore, and as previously stated, incorporating mechanisms of transitional justice into the repatriation process ensures that repatriation is viewed not just as a humanitarian process but also as a political reinstatement of the bond of citizenship. Whether through reparations or restitution mechanisms that are seen to have been implemented by the government or through truth processes that show that their experiences are important, ensuring that returnees feel genuinely reconnected to the polity is a critical component of any repatriation process. Ensuring equal citizenship in this context is vital: if women are treated as second-class citizens, it undermines the inclusive agenda of any post-conflict or post-authoritarian reconstruction.

Transitional justice processes, such as truth commissions and criminal trials, may also raise awareness of the need for the enactment of alternative durable solutions, in cases where return is not possible, by incorporating the views and concerns of those who have suffered specific gender-based injustice. Resettlement and local integration, the other two durable solutions, are characteristically less popular than repatriation—host countries are generally reluctant to allow refugees to naturalize, and resettlement countries have limited quotas. In such cases, alternatives must be sought for those who cannot return home. Proof that return is not safe is vital in this regard—and that proof depends on the broader task of ascertaining the nature of the crimes that took place.

THE TRANSFORMATIVE POTENTIAL OF TRANSITIONAL JUSTICE

Ensuring that those who are displaced can voice their concerns in discussions on durable solutions is important but ultimately only palliative unless the structural injustices that underpin the causes of displacement are addressed— including those that have a gender dimension. Therefore, the most meaningful overlap between ending displacement and the goals of transitional justice lies in the compulsion to transform injustice—past and present—and prevent repetition. Work in both fields may have transformative aims in that they both seek "to address not just the consequences of violations committed during conflict but the social relationships that enabled these violations in the first place, and this includes the correction of unequal gendered power relations in society."[84] As Meertens puts it as well, for displaced women, dealing with the past "means not only truth-telling and historical memory about the impact of conflict, but also recognition of structural (gender) injustices that should be addressed by transitional justice measures."[85] Neither transitional justice measures nor interventions to resolve displacement by themselves are likely to transform these structural injustices, but in addressing such issues they can (a) avoid reinforcing them, (b) contribute to long-term change, and (c) draw attention to the need for broader reform efforts.

While the need for transformation is clear outside any discussion on forced migration, the resolution of displacement, particularly through return, offers both challenges and opportunities: challenges in as much as many of the preexisting problems (for instance, access to land for women) are highlighted, but also opportunities in as much as the situation is one of substantial change. Just as displacement can be an opportunity for renegotiating gender relations,[86] return presents an opportunity for transforming society. As Rubio-Marín and de Greiff state with regard to the issue of reparations, "One of the problems of conceptualising reparations primarily as actions to restore the *status quo ante* is that prior to the violence or abuse, the victim often suffered all sorts of disadvantages, such as in the holding and exercise of rights. Even if the measures do not simply try to restore that status but attempt to compensate for losses, the very evaluation of the losses is affected by the unequal starting point."[87] Add the impact of displacement to this, and the specific category of gender injustice in relation to displacement as a further subcategory, and the starting point becomes even more unequal—and even more in need of transformation.

Economic empowerment is one key area in which a transformative agenda can be pushed. As this chapter has described, women are often forced to become heads of households in exile. While this leads to numerous problems, it also serves to alter gender dynamics. Although this makes women potentially more vulnerable as they return on their own with limited support, it also provides opportunities for the redistribution of resources. This process needs to be led from the ground up, with adequate coordination between humanitarian and development programs and broader justice initiatives. Ensuring that beneficiaries lead and define the process is an essential element of this.

Land restitution is another area in which a transitional justice framework might facilitate a far more gender-aware and transformative approach to reintegration. Donny Meertens and Margarita Zambrano, for instance, in their case study of land restitution for women in Colombia, argue that "special protection measures, land deeds for women and better access to justice must be included in transitional justice processes as a means of fostering gender-equitable development."[88] Specifically ensuring that practical measures that assist women in reclaiming their land are embedded within the broader transitional justice endeavor increases their profile. Ultimately, transformation is only likely to be achieved through multiple and complementary interventions. It is unlikely that humanitarian, development, or justice programs, on their own, are going to achieve these ends.

Burundi provides an example of a highly misguided approach to trying to transform structural economic injustice from within an exclusively humanitarian paradigm. In dealing with the return of over half a million people in a context of huge land shortages, UNHCR instituted a system of "peace villages" that were supposed to represent a vision of an ethnically reconciled Burundi. Under this system, those who either did not know where their original land was or who were unable to secure their land for various reasons, some of whom were widows, were relocated to pieces of land allocated by the government. However, discussions with these returnees revealed how profoundly unpopular the villages were and how far this system strayed from reaching its goal of compensation; not only were the allocated plots of land seen as hugely inadequate for returnees' needs, they were also generally located in isolated places, far from markets and infrastructure. They were also, in practice, monoethnic. Women who already felt excluded felt even more so in these villages and saw their situation as a new form of exile. These artificially created villages therefore neither functioned as compensation for land that had been lost nor provided much-needed assistance to those who were unable to locate or reclaim their land. Most important, they were not seen to offer the potential for returnees to genuinely reintegrate within Burundi and to feel included within the wider processes of their country.[89]

This example of a no doubt well-meaning, but misguided, intervention on the part of UNHCR illustrates the extent to which the promotion of "reconciliation" as an ideal can be extremely harmful—particularly when it is equated with an exclusively humanitarian gift of a small, infertile piece of land. At the very least, there needed to have been adequate recognition of the limitations of what was taking place and an acknowledgment of the acute need for complementary transitional justice mechanisms. In other words, humanitarian intervention, when divorced from the wider political, social, cultural, and judicial context, can be profoundly unhelpful. It should not be conflated with justice being done.

In addition to (and strongly linked to) economic injustice, the problem of sexual violence needs to be addressed. As described earlier, vulnerability to sexual violence is part of a continuum that often begins with the causes of flight, continues throughout exile (whether external or internal), and remains a threat at the point of return. Not only must the immediate physical and psychological needs of the victims be considered in this context, but the structures that allow sexual violence to take place—such as security forces that regularly abuse their positions of authority or courts of law that mishandle sensitive cases of sexual violence—must also be reformed. Recommendations made by truth commissions that lead to legal and institutional reforms that address such structural inequalities are a potential means for promoting trans- formation. Security-sector and judicial reforms are crucial components in this regard. According to Emily Rosser, "Activists have worked for decades to gain public and institutional recognition that sexual violence results not from men's 'natural' urges or the supposed chaos of war but from structures of power and domination that are often linked to gendered notions of nationalism."[90]

The transformative potential of transitional justice is a central area for overlap with efforts to resolve displacement—not just through the promotion of prosecutions for main offenders or reparations for victims but also through the reformation of power structures within a society. How this reform actually takes place, of course, is the challenge. But the reality of displacement, as yet another tangible manifestation of the causes and consequences of sexual vio- lence, needs to be incorporated into this wider process of transformation.

CONCLUSION

Transitional justice, despite its many limitations in practice, has a clear role to play in ensuring that discussions about the future of displaced populations are infused with a broader understanding of the need to turn objects of humanitar- ian aid into politically engaged citizens of the state. Specific categories of exclu- sion need to be acknowledged and addressed, of which gender-based injustice is one area that needs deliberate attention. A gender-justice lens makes pos- sible a framework for ensuring that any transitional justice mechanisms are more fully engaged with gender-specific contexts. Ultimately, the discourse of transitional justice, when applied to situations of ongoing or resolved displace- ment, can help protection regain its edge, and conversely, transitional justice mechanisms can be strongly legitimized by their engagement with the injus- tices of displacement.

Transitional justice has established itself at "the strategic forefront of trans- national democratic state building, rule-of-law promotion and postconflict peacebuilding."[91] It now has the responsibility to ensure that it delivers. One key area with regard to its capacity is its grass-roots salience. Too often, mech- anisms are implemented, or ideas are mooted, without adequate reflection on the priorities and wishes of those who are its anticipated beneficiaries, or they are simply unrealistic and unworkable on the ground. The lack of convergence between transitional justice and the overly humanitarian approach to refugee and IDP protection presents a significant challenge in this regard, and the problems that result can be seen particularly clearly with regard to its impact on vulnerable groups.

As this chapter has described, a critical convergence between the goals of transitional justice and the need to resolve displacement, particularly in the context of gender-specific injustices, is a restoration of the bond of citizenship that was broken by displacement. As a country deals with the legacy of violence by past governments and politicians, which has effectively severed the connection between the government and its people, the ability of those who have been living in exile to genuinely reintegrate into their former homeland is an indicator of the potential to restore this broken bond or social contract— and may be in part the result of steps taken by the government to recreate the citizenship bond. These steps can act as signals to displaced or formerly displaced persons that their reintegration is of concern to their state. It is precisely the restoration of such broken bonds that is the heartbeat of transitional justice. But in order to be effective, the restoration of these bonds needs to be inclusive rather than exclusive. If sections of the population continue to be left on the margins, then little is achieved by the inclusion of a few.

Therefore, this process of genuine repatriation has to be done in an inclusive way. For instance, if women continue to be treated as second-class citizens at the point of return (or, perhaps worse, as no more than passive victims), then the process has effectively failed, whereas the genuine reintegration of women can help ensure that they are seen not simply as apolitical victims but as political actors. The success of such a process depends, though, on the meaningful participation of refugees and IDPs—both men and women. As a recent report by the UN secretary-general states, in the context of seeking to understand why some countries descend into spirals of conflict, "States that handle their internal diversity well, foster respect among disparate groups, and have effective mechanisms for handling domestic disputes and protecting the rights of women, youth and minorities are unlikely to follow such a destructive path."[92] Ensuring that gender-specific injustices related to displacement are put on the agenda for any transitional process, therefore, helps to reinstate "the right to have rights"[93] in an equal and inclusive way.

NOTES

1   The author would like to thank a number of people who commented on earlier drafts of this chapter, including Roger Duthie, Kelli Muddell, Marcie Mersky, Nahla Valji, and Deirdre Clancy.

2   The application of the word *field* to transitional justice is much debated, in contrast to displacement, which is more established as a field. Christine Bell, for instance, explains that transitional justice is not a "field" but a "label or cloak that aims to rationalise the diverse set of bargains in relation to the past in an integrated endeavour, so as to obscure the quite different normative, moral and political implications of the bargains." Christine Bell, "Transitional Justice, Interdisciplinarity and the State of the 'Field' or 'Non-Field,'" *International Journal of Transitional Justice* 3, no. 1 (March 2009): 5–27. Paige Arthur, on the other hand, defines the field of transitional justice as "an international web of individuals and institutions whose internal coherence is held together by common concepts, practical aims, and distinctive claims for legitimacy." Paige Arthur, "How 'Transitions' Reshaped Human Rights: A Conceptual History of Transitional Justice," *Human Rights Quarterly* 31, no. 2 (May 2009): 324. The term is used here in its loosest sense.

3   Susan Harris Rimmer makes this point eloquently in relation to the Commission for Reception, Truth-seeking and Reconciliation in Timor-Leste (Comissão de Acolhimento, Verdade e Reconciliação de Timor-Leste—CAVR) in "Women Cut in Half: Refugee Women and the Commission for Reception, Truth-Seeking and Reconciliation in Timor-Leste," *Refugee Survey Quarterly* 29, no. 2 (March 2010): 85–103.

4   For more on this assumption, see Guglielmo Verdirame and Barbara Harrell-Bond, *Rights in Exile: Janus-Faced Humanitarianism* (New York: Berghahn Books, 2005).

5   Lucy Hovil, "'Two People Can't Share the Same Pair of Shoes': Citizenship, Land and the Return of Refugees to Burundi" (Working Paper no. 2, Citizenship and Displacement in the Great Lakes Region, International Refugee Rights Initiative and Rema Ministries, November 2009).

6   See, for example, Katy Long, *Home Alone? A Review of the Relationship between Repatriation, Mobility and Durable Solutions for Refugees* (Geneva: UNHCR, Policy Development and Evaluation Service, March 2010).

7   United Nations Security Council, "The Rule of Law and Transitional Justice in Conflict and Post-conflict Societies," Report of the Secretary-General, S/2004/616, August 23, 2004. While there is no single definition of transitional justice, this statement both defines its scope and puts it within the broader context in which the idea of transitional justice is recognized.

8   Of course, there is also a strong tension within transitional justice in this regard: on the one hand, it seeks to address political problems, but on the other, particularly in the area of international justice, many mechanisms would claim to be outside the political

sphere. For the purposes of this chapter, however, I assert that the political cannot be separated from the legal in a context of transitional justice.

9   Pablo de Greiff, "Theorising Transitional Justice," in *Nomos LI: Transitional Justice*, ed. Melissa Williams, Rosemary Nagy, and Jon Elster (New York: New York University Press, 2012).

10   In refugee situations, durable solutions are defined as repatriation to the country of origin, local integration in the country of refuge, or resettlement in a third country. In situations of internal displacement, they are defined as return and reintegration into the place of origin, local integration in the area of refuge, or resettlement and integration into another part of the country.

11   Hannah Arendt, *The Origins of Totalitarianism* (London: Andre Deutsch, 1986), 295–96; as cited in Open Society Justice Initiative, "More Primitive than Torture: Statelessness and Arbitrary Denial of Citizenship in Africa—A Call to Action" (background briefing for Africa Programming Advisory Committee meeting, Kampala, Uganda, February 2007).

12   Harris Rimmer, "Women Cut in Half."

13   Donny Meertens, "Forced Displacement and Gender Justice in Colombia: Between Disproportional Effects of Violence and Historical Injustice" (paper prepared for ICTJ / Brookings Project on Transitional Justice and Displacement, 2012).

14   See, for example, Bernadette Iyodu, "Kenyan Refugees Heard Away from Home: The Inclusion of Refugees in Transitional Justice Processes," *Fahamu Refugee Legal Aid Newsletter* (May 2011).

15   See Rhodri Williams, in this volume.

16   The recent special issue of the *International Journal of Transitional Justice*, "Transitional Justice on Trial—Evaluating Its Impact," explicitly addresses this: *International Journal of Transitional Justice* 4, no. 2 (November 2010).

17   Laurel E. Fletcher and Harvey M. Weinstein, with Jamie Rowen, "Context, Timing and the Dynamics of Transitional Justice: A Historical Perspective," *Human Rights Quarterly* 31, no. 1 (February 2009): 163–220.

18   Brandon Hamber, "Masculinity and Transitional Justice: An Exploratory Essay," *International Journal of Transitional Justice* 1, no. 3 (December 2007): 375–90.

19   Susan Martin, "Justice, Women's Rights, and Forced Migration," in *Refugee Rights: Ethics, Advocacy and Africa*, ed. David Hollenbach (Washington, DC: Georgetown University Press, 2008), 137–60.

20   Convention and Protocol Relating to the Status of Refugees, July 28, 1951, U.N.T.S. 189, http://www.unhcr.org/3b66c2aa10.html.

21   Office of the United Nations High Commissioner for Refugees, Guidelines on International Protection: Gender-Related Persecution within the Context of Article 1A(2) of the 1951 Convention and/or Its 1967 Protocol Relating to the Status of Refugees, HCR/GIP/02/01, May 7, 2002.

22 Harris Rimmer, "Women Cut in Half."

23 Ibid.

24 See, for example, Ruth Rubio-Marín, ed., *The Gender of Reparations: Unsettling Sexual Hierarchies While Redressing Human Rights Violations* (Cambridge: Cambridge University Press, 2009).

25 Fionnuala Ni Aolain, "Exploring a Feminist Theory of Harm in the Context of Conflicted and Post-conflict Societies" (Research Paper no. 09-45, University of Minnesota Law School, November 17, 2009).

26 Nahla Valji, *A Window of Opportunity? Making Transitional Justice Work for Women* (New York: UNIFEM, 2010), http://www.unifem.org/materials/item_detail.php?ProductID=186.

27 Ni Aolain, "Exploring a Feminist Theory of Harm."

28 United Nations Security Council, Resolution 1820, "Women and Peace and Security," S/Res/1820, June 19, 2008, para. 3.

29 UN Security Council, Resolution 1820, para. 4.

30 Ibid., para. 5.

31 As one of endless examples that could be pointed to, in a notorious attack that took place over four days in the Walikale region of North Kivu province in the eastern Democratic Republic of Congo in July and August 2010, over three hundred men, women, and children were raped by around two hundred men from a number of armed groups operating in the area. "Preliminary UN Report Confirms over 300 Rapes by Rebels in Eastern DR Congo," *UN News Centre*, September 24, 2010, http://www.un.org/apps/news/story.asp?NewsID=36129&Cr=democratic&Cr1=congo.

32 Emily Rosser, "Depoliticised Speech and Sexed Visibility: Women, Gender and Sexual Violence in the 1999 Guatemalan *Comisión para el Esclarecimiento Histórico* Report," *International Journal of Transitional Justice* 1, no. 3 (December 2007): 410.

33 Inter-Agency Standing Committee, *Guidelines for Gender-Based Violence Interventions in Humanitarian Settings, Focusing on Prevention of and Response to Sexual Violence in Emergencies* (Geneva: IASC, September 2005).

34 See Women's Refugee Commission, *The Living Ain't Easy: Urban Refugees in Kampala* (New York: Women's Refugee Commission, March 2011).

35 Moses Chrispus Okello and Lucy Hovil, "Confronting the Reality of Gender-Based Violence in Northern Uganda," *International Journal of Transitional Justice* 1, no. 3 (December 2007): 438.

36 Ibid.

37 Binaifer Nowrojee, "Sexual Violence, Gender Roles, and Displacement," in *Refugee Rights: Ethics, Advocacy, and Africa*, ed. David Hollenbach (Washington, DC: Georgetown University Press, 2008), 125.

38 Martin, "Justice, Women's Rights, and Forced Migration."

39   Simon Turner, "Vindicating Masculinity: The Fate of Promoting Gender Equality," *Forced Migration Review* 9 (December 2000): 8–10. Likewise, cultural practices are undermined, for instance, when young men are unable to raise dowries. Cathrine Brun, "Making Young Displaced Men Visible," *Forced Migration Review* 9 (December 2000): 10. Of course, the dilemma of determining to what extent "traditional" gender roles can and should be challenged within any context in which a more gendered understanding of forced migration is emerging is much debated. See, for example, Martin, "Justice, Women's Rights, and Forced Migration."

40   Ruth Judge, "Refugee Advocacy and the Biopolitics of Asylum in Britain: The Precarious Position of Young Male Asylum Seekers and Refugees" (Working Paper 60, Refugee Studies Centre, Oxford Department of International Development, University of Oxford, May 2010).

41   Okello and Hovil, "Confronting the Reality."

42   Nowrojee, "Sexual Violence, Gender Roles, and Displacement."

43   See the Refugee Law Project documentary *Gender Against Men* (2008), http://www.forcedmigration.org/podcasts-videos-photos/video/gender-against-men.

44   See Marina Caparini, in this volume.

45   Judy El-Bushra, "Gender and Forced Migration: Editorial," *Forced Migration Review* 9 (December 2000): 4–8.

46   Office of the United Nations High Commissioner for Refugees, *Sexual Violence against Refugees: Guidelines on Prevention and Response* (Geneva: UNHCR, March 1998); previous versions were produced in 1991 and 1995.

47   Verdirame and Harrell-Bond, *Rights in Exile*, 124.

48   See Pablo de Greiff and Roger Duthie, eds., *Transitional Justice and Development: Making Connections* (New York: Social Science Research Council, 2009).

49   El-Bushra, "Gender and Forced Migration."

50   For a more general discussion on understandings of protection in humanitarian contexts, with a case study on northern Uganda's IDP camps, see Chris Dolan and Lucy Hovil, "Humanitarian Protection in Uganda: A Trojan Horse?" (HPG Background Paper, Humanitarian Policy Group, Overseas Development Institute, December 2006).

51   Martin, "Justice, Women's Rights, and Forced Migration."

52   Inter-Agency Standing Committee, *Guidelines for Gender-Based Violence Interventions.*

53   Nowrojee, "Sexual Violence, Gender Roles, and Displacement."

54   See, for example, Jennifer Hyndman, "Refugee Camps as Conflict Zones: The Politics of Gender," in *Sites of Violence: Women and Conflict Zones*, ed. Wenona Giles and Jennifer Hyndman (Berkley: University of California Press, 2004): 193–211.

55   Harris Rimmer, "Women Cut in Half," 96–97.

56   Verdirame and Harrell-Bond, *Rights in Exile.*

57 Ibid.

58 El-Bushra, "Gender and Forced Migration."

59 Liisa Malkki, *Purity and Exile: Violence, Memory, and National Cosmology among Hutu Refugees in Tanzania* (Chicago: Chicago University Press, 1995).

60 This was found to be the case in Kenya's Kakuma camp, where there were more men than women. Verdirame and Harrell-Bond, *Rights in Exile*, 123.

61 Lucy Hovil, "'Two People Can't Share the Same Pair of Shoes.'"

62 Phyllis Ferguson, "IDP Camp Closure and Gender Inequality in Timor-Leste," *Forced Migration Review* 34 (February 2010): 67–69, http://www.fmreview.org/urban-displacement/FMR34/67-69.pdf. See also Peter Van der Auweraert, "Dealing with the 2006 Internal Displacement Crisis in Timor-Leste: Between Reparations and Humanitarian Policy-Making" (paper prepared for ICTJ / Brookings Project on Transitional Justice and Displacement, 2012).

63 Harris Rimmer, "Women Cut in Half."

64 See, for example, UN Women and United Nations Development Programme, "Reparations, Development and Gender" (report of the Kampala Workshop, December 1–2, 2010).

65 See Williams, in this volume.

66 Harris Rimmer, "Women Cut in Half."

67 El-Bushra, "Gender and Forced Migration."

68 Meertens, "Forced Displacement and Gender Justice in Colombia."

69 Paula Worby, *Lessons Learned from UNHCR's Involvement in the Guatemala Refugee Repatriation and Reintegration Programme (1987–1999)* (Geneva: UNHCR, 1999), http://www.crid.or.cr/digitalizacion/pdf/eng/doc13135/doc13135.pdf.

70 These stories were told to the author during research conducted in West Nile in 2003 and 2004. See Lucy Hovil and Zachary Lomo, "Negotiating Peace: Resolution of Conflict in Uganda's West Nile District" (Working Paper no. 12, Refugee Law Project, June 2004).

71 United States Institute of Peace, "Women's Role in Liberia's Reconstruction," (USIPeace Briefing, May 2007), http://www.usip.org/publications/women-s-role-liberia-s-reconstruction.

72 Center for American Progress, "Leymah Gbowee," http://www.americanprogress.org/events/2008/11/inf/GboweeLeymah.html.

73 Ruth Rubio-Marín, "The Gender of Reparations: Setting the Agenda," in *What Happened to the Women? Gender and Reparations for Human Rights Violations*, ed. Ruth Rubio-Marín (New York: Social Science Research Council, 2006).

74 Valérie Couillard, "The Nairobi Declaration: Redefining Reparations for Women Victims of Sexual Violence," *International Journal of Transitional Justice* 1, no. 3 (December 2007): 450.

75 Ibid.

76 See Awa Dabo, "In the Presence of Absence: Transitional Justice and Displacement in Liberia" (paper prepared for ICTJ / Brookings Project on Transitional Justice and Displacement, 2012).

77 See Meertens, "Forced Displacement and Gender Justice in Colombia."

78 Evelyne Josse, "'They Came with Two Guns': The Consequences of Sexual Violence for the Mental Health of Women in Armed Conflicts," *International Review of the Red Cross* 92, no. 877 (March 2010): 3.

79 On criminal justice and displacement, see Federico Andreu-Guzmán, in this volume.

80 Lucy Hovil, "A Dangerous Impasse: Rwandan Refugees in Uganda" (Working Paper no. 4, Citizenship and Displacement in the Great Lakes Region, International Refugee Rights Initiative and Refugee Law Project, June 2010).

81 See Meertens, "Forced Displacement and Gender Justice in Colombia"; and Donny Meertens and Margarita Zambrano, "Citizenship Deferred: The Politics of Victimhood, Land Restitution and Gender Justice in the Colombian (Post?) Conflict," *International Journal of Transitional Justice* 4, no. 2 (July 2010): 189–206.

82 See Williams, in this volume; and Barbara McCallin, "Transitional Justice, Restitution, and Legal Pluralism" (paper prepared for ICTJ / Brookings Project on Transitional Justice and Displacement, 2012).

83 See Williams on restitution and Peter Van der Auweraert on reparations and displacement, both in this volume.

84 Valji, *Window of Opportunity?*

85 Meertens, "Forced Displacement and Gender Justice in Colombia."

86 El-Bushra, "Gender and Forced Migration."

87 Ruth Rubio-Marín and Pablo de Greiff, "Women and Reparations," *International Journal of Transitional Justice* 1, no. 3 (December 2007): 325.

88 Meertens and Zambrano, "Citizenship Deferred."

89 Hovil, "'Two People Can't Share the Same Pair of Shoes.'"

90 Emily Rosser, "Depoliticised Speech and Sexed Visibility," 38. She cites two texts to support this assertion: Floya Anthias and Nira Yuval Davis, eds., *Woman-Nation-State* (Basingstoke, UK: MacMillan, 1989); and Norma Alarcón et al., *Between Woman and Nation: Nationalisms, Transnational Feminisms, and the State* (Durham, NC: Duke University Press, 1999). Also, on SSR and displacement, see Caparini, in this volume.

91 Geoff Dancy, "Impact Assessment, Not Evaluation: Defining a Limited Role for Positivism in the Study of Transitional Justice," *International Journal of Transitional Justice* 4, no. 3 (November 2010): 355–76.

92 United Nations General Assembly, "Implementing the Responsibility to Protect," Report of the Secretary-General, A/63/677, January 12, 2009.

93 Arendt, *Origins of Totalitarianism.*

Contributors

Federico Andreu-Guzmán is deputy director of litigation and legal protection at the Colombian Commission of Jurists. His previous positions have included general counsel of the International Commission of Jurists (2000–2009), legal adviser for the Americas and Asian Regions Programs of the International Secretariat of Amnesty International (1997–2000), and deputy secretary-general for Latin America of the Federation of International Human Rights. He has been, on several occasions, a consultant for the UN High Commissioner for Human Rights and a member of the UN Human Rights Mission in Rwanda and the International Civilian Mission in Haiti.

Megan Bradley is a fellow in the Foreign Policy Program at the Brookings Institution, where she is part of the Brookings-LSE Project on Internal Displacement. From 2009 to 2012, she worked as an assistant professor in the Conflict Studies Program at Saint Paul University in Ottawa. She holds a doctorate in international relations from St Antony's College, University of Oxford, and has worked with a number of organizations concerned with human rights, humanitarian affairs, and development, including the Canadian Department of Foreign Affairs and International Trade, the International Development Research Centre, and the Office of the UN High Commissioner for Refugees. Her first monograph, *Refugee Repatriation: Justice, Responsibility and Redress*, is forthcoming from Cambridge University Press.

Bryce Campbell is the assistant director of the Brookings-LSE Project on Internal Displacement, where he is responsible for overseeing a range of training and research initiatives, most recently on internally displaced persons and host communities. He previously managed research and consulting projects focused on the developing world for the firm Ergo. He received his master's degree in security studies from University College London and is a graduate of the School of Foreign Service at Georgetown University.

Marina Caparini is senior research fellow in the Department of Security and Conflict Management at the Norwegian Institute of International Affairs, where she conducts policy analysis and research on issues relating to security sector reform (SSR). She was previously deputy head of SSR at the International Center for Transitional Justice, and senior fellow at the Geneva Centre for the Democratic Control of Armed Forces. Her current areas of interest include UN and donor approaches to SSR, human rights vetting and lustration in security and justice systems, and the security and justice challenges faced by displaced populations and migrants. Recent publications include *A Stocktaking of Norwegian Engagement with Security Sector Reform*, with Kari Marie Kjellstad and Trine Nikolaisen (Oslo: NUPI, 2011), and "The Future of Civil Society in SSR," in *The Future of SSR*, ed. Mark Sedra (CIGI, 2010). She holds a PhD in war studies from King's College London.

Roger Duthie is a senior associate in the research unit at the International Center for Transitional Justice. Since joining the unit in 2004, he has managed multi-year research projects examining how transitional justice relates to displacement and to socioeconomic development. He has also contributed to projects on the reintegration of ex-combatants and vetting measures. His publications include *Transitional Justice and Development: Making Connections*, coedited with Pablo de Greiff (SSRC, 2009), and "Transitional Justice and Displacement," *International Journal of Transitional Justice* (2011). He previously worked at KMPG, the Carnegie Council on Ethics and International Affairs, and Oxford University Press. He has an MA in international relations from Yale University and a BA in history from Cornell University.

Lucy Hovil is senior researcher at the International Refugee Rights Initiative and coordinates a project entitled Citizenship and Displacement in the Great Lakes Region, a policy-oriented research initiative carried out in conjunction with the Social Science Research Council. To date, she has carried out studies in Tanzania, Burundi, Uganda, Democratic Republic of Congo, and South Sudan. She is also the managing editor of the *International Journal of Transitional Justice*. Previously, she spent eight years at the Refugee Law Project, Makerere University, Uganda, where she founded and developed the organization's research and advocacy department. In the course of her time at RLP she wrote and edited twenty-one working papers on displacement, conflict, and post-conflict reconstruction in Uganda. Before that, she wrote her doctoral thesis at the School of Oriental and African Studies, London University, on the relationship between violence and identity, using a case study of the conflict prior to South Africa's first democratic election.

Peter Van der Auweraert is head of the Land, Property and Reparations Division at the International Organization for Migration (IOM) in Geneva. He has worked on post-crisis land and reparations issues in, among other countries, Burundi, Colombia, Haiti, Iraq, Lebanon, Timor-Leste, Turkey, and Zimbabwe and was part of the IOM team that implemented the German Forced Labour Compensation Program. Van der Auweraert was previously executive director of Avocats sans Frontières and is currently a member of their board of directors. From 1999 to 2006, he held a visiting lectureship in international criminal and public law at the University of Turku in Finland. He earned an LLM in International Law from the University of London and a first degree in law from the University of Antwerp. He has published widely on reparations, forced migration, and post-crisis land and property issues and is currently finalizing a handbook on integrating and managing land issues in peace negotiations for the US Institute of Peace.

Rhodri C. Williams is a consultant and researcher on human rights, humanitarian, and forced migration issues. He has lectured, published, and provided technical advice on issues related to the return of displaced persons, reparations for human rights violations, and property restitution in a number of post-conflict settings. Williams also authors *TerraNullius*, a blog that explores these issues from the perspective of international law and practice. From 2000 to 2004, he worked in Bosnia for the Organization for Security and Cooperation in Europe, coordinating legal policy and field monitoring of the postwar restitution process that helped two hundred thousand displaced families repossess their prewar homes. Williams received an MA in geography from Syracuse University in 1996 and a JD from New York University in 2000 and is a member of the New York State Bar.